D0897961

The Divine Covenants

A. W. Pink

BAKER BOOK HOUSE
Grand Rapids, Michigan

Contents

Introduction

The covenants occupy no subordinate place on the pages of divine revelation, as even a superficial perusal of Scripture will show. The word *covenant* is found no fewer than twenty-five times in the very first book of the Bible; and occurs again scores of times in the remaining books of the Pentateuch, in the Psalms and in the Prophets. Nor is the word inconspicuous in the New Testament. When instituting the great memorial of His death, the Savior said, "This cup is *the new covenant* in my blood" (Luke 22:20). When enumerating the special blessings which God had conferred on the Israelites, Paul declared that to them belonged "the covenants" (Rom. 9:4). To the Galatians he expounded "the two covenants" (4:24-31). The Ephesian saints were reminded that in their unregenerate days they were "strangers to the covenants of promise" (2:12). The entire Epistle to the Hebrews is an exposition of "the better covenant" of which Christ is mediator (8:6).

Salvation through Jesus Christ is according to "the determinate counsel and foreknowledge of God" (Acts 2:23), and He was pleased to make known His eternal purpose of mercy, unto the fathers, in the form of a series of *covenants,* which were of different characters and revealed at various times. These covenants enter into the very nature, and pervade with their peculiar qualities, the whole system of divine truth. They have an intimate connection with each other and a common relation to a single purpose, being, in fact, so many successive stages in the unfolding of the scheme of divine grace. They treat the *divine* side of things, disclosing the source from which all blessings come to men, and making known the channel (Christ) through which they flow to them. Each one reveals some new and fundamental aspect of truth, and in considering them in their Scriptural order we may clearly perceive the progress of revelation which they respectively indicated. They set forth the great design of God which was to be accomplished by the redeemer of His people.

It has been well pointed out that "it is very obvious that because God is an intelligence He must have a plan. If He be an absolutely perfect intelligence, desiring and designing nothing but good; if He be an eternal and immutable intelligence, His plan must be one, eternal, all-comprehensive, immutable; that is, all things from His point of view must constitute one system and sustain a perfect logical relation in all its parts. Nevertheless, like all other comprehensive systems, it must itself be composed of an infinite number of subordinate systems. In this respect it is like these heavens which He has made, and which He has hung before our eyes, as a type and pattern of His mode of thinking and planning in all providence.

"We know that in the solar system our earth is a satellite of one of the great suns, and of this particular system we have a knowledge because of our position, but we know that this system is only one of myriads, with variations, that have been launched in the great abyss of space. So we know that this great, all-comprehensive plan of God, considered as one system, must contain a great many subordinate systems which might be studied profitably if we were in the position to do so, as self-contained whole, separate from the rest" (Lectures by A. A. Hodge). That "one system" or the eternal "plan" of God was comprised in "the everlasting covenant"; the many "subordinate systems" are the various covenants God made with different ones from time.

The everlasting covenant, with its shadowings forth in His temporal covenants, forms the basis of all His dealings with His people. Many proofs of this are to be met with in Holy Writ. For example, when God heard the groanings of the Hebrews in Egypt, we are told that He *"remembered his covenant* with Abraham, with Isaac and with Jacob" (Exod. 2:24; cf. 6:2-8). When Israel was oppressed by the Syrians in the days of Jehoahaz, we read, "And the Lord was gracious unto them, and had compassion on them, and had respect unto them, *because of his covenant* with Abraham, Isaac, and Jacob" (II Kings 13:23; cf. Ps. 106:43-45). At a later period, when God determined to show mercy unto Israel, after He had sorely afflicted them for their sins, He expressed it thus, "Nevertheless I will *remember my covenant with thee* in the days of thy youth" (Ezek. 16:60). As the psalmist declared, "He hath given meat unto them that fear him: he will ever be *mindful of his covenant"* (111:5).

The same blessed truth is set forth in the New Testament that the covenant is the foundation from which proceed all the gracious works of God. This is rendered as the reason *for sending Christ* into the world: "To perform the mercy promised to our fathers, and to *remember his holy covenant"* (Luke 1:72). Remarkable too is that word in Hebrews 13:20: "Now the God of peace, that *brought again from the dead* our Lord Jesus, that great Shepherd of the sheep, *through the blood of the everlasting covenant."* Another illustration of the same principle is found in Hebrews 10:15, 16: "Whereof the Holy Spirit also is a witness to us: *for after that he had said before,* This is the covenant that I will make with them after those days, saith the Lord, I will put my laws into their hearts, and in their minds will I write them"—the words we have placed in italics supply proof that the good which God does unto His people is grounded on His covenant Anything which in Scripture is said to be done unto us "for Christ's sake" signifies it is done by virtue of that covenant which God made with Christ as the head of His mystical body.

In like manner, when God is said to bind Himself by oath to the heirs of promise—"Wherein God, willing more abundantly to show unto the heirs of promise the immutability of his counsel, confirmed it by an oath" (Heb. 6:17)—it is upon the ground of His covenant engagement that He does so. In fact the one merges into the other, for in Scripture covenanting is often called by the name of swearing, and a covenant is called an oath. "That thou shouldest enter into *covenant* with the Lord thy God, and into his *oath,* which the Lord thy God maketh with thee this day. . . . Neither with you only do I make this covenant and this oath" (Deut. 29:12, 14). "Be ye mindful always of his covenant, the word which he commanded to a thousand generations: even of the covenant which he made with Abraham, and of his *oath* unto Isaac" (I Chron. 16:15, 16). "And they entered into *a covenant* to seek the Lord God of their fathers with all their heart and with all their soul. . . . And they *sware* unto the Lord with a loud voice. . . . And all Judah rejoiced at *the oath"* (II Chron. 15:12, 14, 15).

Sufficient should have already been said to impress us with the weightiness of our present theme, and the great importance of arriving at a right understanding of the divine covenants. A true knowledge of the covenants is indispensable to a correct presentation of the gospel, for he who is ignorant of the fundamental difference which obtains between the covenant of works and the covenant of grace is utterly incompetent for evangelism. But by whom among us are the different covenants clearly understood? Refer unto them to the average preacher, and you at once perceive you are speaking to him in an unknown tongue. Few today discern what the covenants are in themselves, their relations to each other, and their consequent bearings upon the design of God in the Redeemer. Since the covenants pertain unto the very "rudiments of the doctrine of Christ," ignorance of them must cause obscurity to rest upon the whole gospel system.

During the palmy days of the Puritans considerable attention was given to the subject of the covenants, as their writings evince, particularly the works of Usher, Witsius, Blake, and Boston. But alas, with the exception of a few high Calvinists, their massive volumes fell into general neglect, until a generation arose who had no light thereon. This made it easier for certain men to impose upon them their crudities and vagaries, and make their poor dupes believe a wonderful discovery had been made in the "rightly dividing of the word of truth." These men shuffled Scripture until they arranged the passages treating of the "covenants" to arbitrarily divide time into "seven dispensations" and partitioned off the Bible accordingly. How dreadfully superficial and faulty their "findings" are appear from the popular (far too popular to be of much value—Luke 16:15!) Scofield Bible, where no less than eight covenants are noticed, and yet *nothing* is said about the "everlasting covenant"!

If some think we have exaggerated the ignorance which now obtains upon this subject, let them put the following questions to their best-informed Christian friends, and see how many can give satisfactory answers. What did David mean when he said, "Although my house be not so with God; yet he hath made with me an everlasting covenant, ordered in all things, and sure: *for this is all my salvation"* (II Sam. 23:5)? What is meant by "The secret of the Lord is with them that fear him, and he will *show them his covenant"* (Ps. 25:14)? What does the Lord mean when He speaks of those who *"take hold of my covenant"* (Isa. 56:6)? What does God intend when He says to the Mediator: "As for thee also, by the blood of thy covenant, I have sent forth thy prisoners out of the pit wherein is no water" (Zech. 9:11)? To what does the apostle refer when he says, "That the covenant, that was confirmed before *of God is* [or "to"] *Christ"* (Gal. 3:17).

Before attempting to furnish any answers to these questions, let us point out the *nature* of a covenant: in what it consists. "An absolute complete covenant is a voluntary convention, pact, or agreement between distinct persons, about the ordering and dispensing of things in their power, unto their mutual concern and advantage" (John Owen). Blackstone, the great commentator upon English law, speaking of the parts of a deed, says, "After warrants, usually follow *covenants,* or conventions, which are clauses of agreement contained in a deed, whereby either party may stipulate for the truth of certain facts, or may bind himself to perform, or give something to the other" (Vol. 2, p. 20). So he includes three things: the parties, the terms, the binding agreement. Reducing it to still simpler language, we may say that a covenant is the entering into of a mutual agreement, a benefit being assured on the fulfillment of certain conditions.

We read of Jonathan and David making a covenant (I Sam. 18:3), which, in view of I Samuel 20:11-17, 42 evidently signified that they entered into a solemn compact (ratified by an oath: I Sam. 20:17) that in return for Jonathan's kindness in informing him of his father's plans—making possible his escape—David, when he ascended the throne, would show mercy to his descendants: cf. II Samuel 9:1. Again, in I Chronicles 11:3 we are told that all the elders of Israel (who had previously been opposed to him) came to David and he "made a covenant with them," which, in the light of II Samuel 5:1-3 evidently means that, on the consideration of his captaining their armies against the common foe, they were willing to submit unto him as their king. Once more, in II Chronicles 23:16 we read of Jehoiada the priest making a covenant with the people and the king that they should be the Lord's people, which, in the light of what immediately follows obviously denotes that he agreed to grant them certain religious privileges in return for their undertaking to destroy the system of Baal worship. A careful consideration of these *human* examples will enable us to understand better the covenants which *God* has been pleased to enter into.

Now as we pointed out in previous paragraphs, God's dealings with men are all based upon His covenant engagements with them—He promising certain blessings upon their fulfillment of certain conditions. This being so, as G. S. Bishop pointed out, "It is clear that there can be but two and only two covenants possible between God and men—a covenant founded upon what *man shall do* for salvation, a covenant founded upon what *God shall do for him* to save him: in other words, a Covenant of Works and a Covenant of Grace" *(Grace in Galatians,* p. 72). Just as all the divine promises in the Old Testament are summed up in two chief ones—the sending of Christ and the pouring out of the Spirit—so all the divine covenants may be reduced unto two, the other subordinate ones being only confirmations or adumbrations of them, or having to do with their economical administration.

We shall then take up in the chapters which follow, first, the everlasting covenant or covenant of grace, which God made with His elect in the person of their head, and show how that is the sure foundation from which proceed all blessings unto them. Next we shall consider the covenant of works, that compact into which the Creator entered with the whole race in the person of their human and federal head, and show how that had to be broken before the blessings agreed upon in the covenant of grace could be bestowed. Then we shall look briefly at the covenant God made with Noah, and more fully at the one with Abraham, in which the everlasting covenant was shadowed forth. Then we shall ponder the more difficult Sinaitic covenant, viewing it as a confirmation of the covenant of works and also in its peculiar relation to the national polity of Israel. Some consideration will also have to be given to the Davidic covenant, concerning which we feel greatly in need of more light. Finally, we shall point out how the everlasting covenant has been *administered* under the "old" and "new" covenants or economies. May the Holy Spirit graciously preserve us from all serious error, and enable us to write that which shall be to the glory of our covenant God and the blessing of His covenant people.

PART ONE

The Everlasting Covenant

I

The Word of God opens with a brief account of creation, the making of man, and his fall. From later Scripture we have no difficulty in ascertaining that the issue of the trial to which man was subjected in Eden had been divinely foreseen. "The Lamb slain [in the purpose of God] from the foundation of the world" (Rev. 13:8) makes it clear that, in view of the Fall, provision had been made by God for the recovery of His people who had apostatized in Adam, and that the means whereby their recovery would be effected were consistent with the claims of the divine holiness and justice. All the details and results of the plan of mercy had been arranged and settled from the beginning by divine wisdom.

That provision of grace which God made for His people before the foundation of the world embraced the appointment of His own Son to become the mediator, and of the work which, in that capacity, He should perform. This involved His assumption of human nature, the offering of Himself as a sacrifice for sin, His exaltation in the nature He had assumed to the right hand of God in the heavenlies, His supremacy over His church and over all things for His church, the blessings which He should be empowered to dispense, and the extent to which His work should be made effectual unto the salvation of souls. These were all matters of definite and certain arrangement, agreed upon between God and His Son in the terms of the everlasting covenant.

The first germinal publication of the everlasting covenant is found in Genesis 3:15: "I will put enmity between thee and the woman, and between thy seed and her seed; it shall bruise thy head, and thou shalt bruise his heel." Thus, immediately after the Fall, God announced to the serpent his ultimate doom through the work of the Mediator, and

15

revealed unto sinners the channel through whom alone salvation could flow to them. The continual additions which God subsequently made to the revelation He gave in Genesis 3:15 were, for a considerable time, largely through *covenants* He made with the fathers, covenants which were both *the fruit of* His eternal plan of mercy and the gradual *revealing of* the same unto the faithful. Only as those two facts are clearly recognized and held fast by us are we in any position to appreciate and perceive the force of those subordinate covenants.

God made covenants with Noah, Abraham, David; but were *they,* as fallen creatures, able to enter into covenant with their august and holy Maker? Were they able to stand for themselves, or be sureties for others? The very question answers itself. What, for instance, could Noah possibly do which would insure that the earth should never again be destroyed by a flood? Those subordinate covenants were nothing more or less than the Lord's making manifest, in an especial and public manner, the grand covenant: making known something of its glorious contents, confirming their own personal interest in it, and assuring them that Christ, the great covenant head, should be of themselves and spring from their seed.

This is what accounts for that singular expression which occurs so frequently in Scripture: "Behold, I establish my covenant with you and your seed after you" (Gen. 9:9). Yet there follows no mention of any conditions, or work to be done by them: only a promise of unconditional blessings. And why? Because the "conditions" were to be fulfilled and the "work" was to be done by Christ, and nothing remained but to bestow the blessings on His people. So when David says, "He hath made with me an everlasting covenant" (II Sam. 23:5) he simply means, God had admitted him into an interest in the everlasting covenant and made him partaker of its privileges. Hence it is that when the apostle Paul refers to the various covenants which God had made with men in Old Testament times, he styles them not "covenants of *stipulations"* but "covenants of *promise"* (Eph. 2:12).

Above we have pointed out that the continual additions which God made to His original revelation of mercy in Genesis 3:15 were, for a while, given mainly through the covenants He made with the fathers. It was a process of gradual development, issuing finally in the fulness of gospel grace; the substance of those covenants indicated the outstanding stages in this process. They are the great landmarks of God's dealings with men, points from which the disclosures of the divine mind expanded into increased and established truths. As revelations they exhibited in ever augmented degrees of fulness and clearness the plan of salvation through the mediation and sacrifice of the Son of God; for each of those covenants consisted of gracious promises *ratified by sacrifice* (Gen. 8:20 and 9:9; 15:9-11 and 18). Thus, those covenants were so many intimations of that method of mercy which took its rise in the eternal counsels of the divine mind.

Those divine revelations and manifestations of the grace decreed in the everlasting covenant were given out at important epochs in the early history of the world. Just as Genesis 3:15 was given immediately after the Fall, so we find that immediately following the Flood God solemnly renewed the covenant of grace with Noah. In like manner, at the beginning of the third period of human history, following the call of Abraham, God renewed it again, only then making a much fuller revelation of the same. It was now made known that the coming deliverer of God's people was to be of the Abrahamic stock and that all the families of the earth should be blessed in Him—a plain intimation of the calling of the Gentiles and the bringing of the elect from all nations into the family of God. In Genesis 15:5, 6, the great requirement of the covenant—namely, faith—was then more fully made known.

Unto Abraham God gave a remarkable pledge of the fulfillment of His covenant promises in the striking victory which He granted him over the federated forces of Chedorlaomer. This was more than a hint of the victory of Christ and His seed over the world: carefully compare Isaiah 41:2, 3, 10, 15. Genesis 14:19, 20 supplies proof of what we have just said, for upon returning from his memorable victory, Abraham was met by Melchizedek (type of Christ) and was *blessed* by him. A further revelation of the contents of the covenant of grace was granted unto Abraham in Genesis 15, where in the vision of the smoking furnace which passed through the midst of the sacrifice, an adumbration was made of the *sufferings* of Christ. In the miraculous birth of Isaac, intimation was given of the *supernatural birth* of Christ, the promised Seed. In the deliverance of Isaac from the altar, representation was made of the *resurrection* of Christ (Heb. 11:19).

Thus we may see how fully the covenant of grace was revealed and confirmed unto Abraham the father of all them that believe, by which he and his descendants obtained a clearer sight and understanding of the great Redeemer and the things which were to be accomplished by Him. And therefore did Christ take notice of this when He said, "Abraham rejoiced to see my day, and he saw it, and was glad" (John 8:56). These last words clearly intimate that Abraham had a definite spiritual apprehension of those things. Under the Sinaitic covenant a yet fuller revelation was made by God to His people of the contents of the everlasting covenant: the tabernacle, and all its holy vessels; the high priest, his vestments, and service; and the whole system of sacrifices and ablutions, setting before them its blessed realities in typical forms, they being patterns of heavenly things.

Thus, before seeking to set forth the everlasting covenant itself in a specific way, we have first endeavored to make clear the relation borne to it of the principal covenants which God was pleased to make with different men during the Old Testament era. Our sketch of them has necessarily been brief, for we shall take them up separately and consider them in fuller detail in the succeeding chapters. Yet sufficient has been said, we trust, to demonstrate that, while the terms of the covenants which God made with Noah, with Abraham, with Israel at Sinai, and with David, are to be understood, first, in their plain and *natural* sense, yet it should be clear to any anointed eye that they have a second and higher meaning—a *spiritual* content. The things of earth have been employed to represent heavenly things. In other words, those subordinate covenants need to be contemplated in both their letter and spirit.

Coming now more directly to the present aspect of our theme, let it be pointed out that, as there is no one verse in the Bible which expressly affirms there are three divine persons in the Godhead, coeternal, coequal, coglorious; nevertheless, by carefully comparing Scripture with Scripture we know that such is the case. In like manner, there is no one verse in the Bible which categorically states that the Father entered into a formal agreement with the Son: that on His executing a certain work, He should receive a certain reward. Nevertheless, a careful study of different passages obliges us to arrive at this conclusion. Holy Scripture does not yield up its treasures to the indolent; and as long as the individual preacher is willing to let Dr. Scofield or Mr. Pink do his studying for him, he must not expect to make much progress in divine things. Ponder Proverbs 2:1-5!

There is no one plot of ground on earth on which will be found growing all varieties of flowers or trees, nor is there any part of the world in which may be secured representatives of every variety of butterflies. Yet by expense, industry, and perseverance, the horticulturalist and the natural historian may gradually assemble specimens of every variety until they possess a complete collection. In like manner, there is no one chapter in the Bible in which *all* the truth is found on any subject. It is the part of the theologian to diligently attend unto the various hints and the more definite contributions scattered throughout Scripture on any given theme, and carefully classify and coordinate them. Alas, those genuine and independent theologians (those unfettered by any human system) have well-nigh disappeared from the earth.

The language of the New Testament is very explicit in teaching us the true light in which the plan of mercy is to be viewed, and in showing the saint that he is to regard all his spiritual blessings and privileges as coming to him out of the everlasting covenant. It speaks of "the eternal purpose which God purposed in Christ Jesus our Lord" (Eph. 3:11). Our covenant oneness with Christ is clearly revealed in Ephesians 1:3-5, that marvelous declaration reaching its climax in 1:6: "to the praise of the glory of his grace, wherein he hath made us accepted in the beloved." "Accepted *in* the beloved" goes deeper and means far more than "accepted *through* him." It denotes not merely a recommendatory passport from Christ, but *a real union with Him,* whereby we are incorporated into His mystical body, and made as truly partakers of His righteousness as the members of the physical body partake of the life which animates its head.

In like manner, there are many, many statements in the New Testament concerning Christ Himself which are only pertinent and intelligible in the light of His having acted in fulfillment of a covenant agreement with the Father. For example, in Luke 22:22 we find Him saying, "And truly the Son of man goeth *as it was determined":* "determined" when and where but in the everlasting covenant! Plainer still is the language in John 6:38, 39: "For I came down from heaven, not to do mine own will, but the will of him that sent me: and this is the Father's will which hath sent me, that of all which he hath given me I should lose nothing, but should raise it up again at the last day." Three things are there to be seen: (1) Christ had received a certain charge or commission from the Father; (2) He had solemnly engaged and undertaken to execute that charge; (3) the end contemplated in that arrangement was not merely the announcement of spiritual blessings, but the actual bestowal of them upon all who had been given to Him.

Again, from John 10:16 it is evident that a specific charge had been laid upon Christ. Referring to His elect scattered among the Gentiles He did not say "them also I *will* bring," but "them also I *must* bring." In His high priestly prayer we hear Him saying, "Father, *I will* that they also whom thou hast given me, be with me, where I am" (John 17:24). There Christ was claiming something that was *due* Him on account of or in return for the work He had done (v. 4). This clearly presupposes both an arrangement and a promise on the part of the Father. It was the surety putting in His claim. Now a claim necessarily implies a preceding promise annexed to a condition to be performed by the party to whom the promise is made, which gives a right to demand the reward. This is one reason why Christ, immediately afterward, addressed God as "righteous Father," appealing to His faithfulness in the agreement.

Again, the parallel which is drawn between Adam and Christ in Romans 5:12-19 and I Corinthians 15:20-23, 45-47 can be satisfactorily interpreted only on the principle that Adam and Christ were representative and federal heads of those whom the one involved in sin and death and for whom the other has secured righteousness and eternal life. "In hope of eternal life, which God, that cannot lie, promised before the world began" (Titus 1:2). But how could God promise eternal life before the world began on any other hypothesis than that of a compact with the Son acting in behalf of and for the benefit of His people? In Hebrew 3:2 it is said that "the Apostle and High Priest of our profession . . . was faithful to him that appointed him." Now just as "obedience" implies a precept, so "faithfulness" presupposes a trust; that is, a pledge that a certain thing shall be done in accordance with the directions given him.

11

The everlasting covenant or covenant of grace is that mutual agreement into which the Father entered with His Son before the foundation of the world respecting the salvation of His elect, Christ being appointed the mediator, He willingly consenting to be their head and representative. That there is a divine covenant to which Christ stands related, and that the great work which He performed here on earth was the discharge of His covenant office, is very plain from many Scriptures, first of all, from the covenant *titles* which He bears. In Isaiah 42:6 we hear the Father saying to the Son: "I the Lord have called thee in righteousness, and will hold thine hand, and will keep thee, and give thee *for a covenant* of the people, for a light of the Gentiles." As a covenantee in it, Christ is thus "given" unto His people, as the pledge of all its blessings (cf. Rom. 8:32). He is the representative of His people in it. He is, in His own person and work, the sum and substance of it. He has fulfilled all its terms, and now dispenses its rewards.

In Malachi 3:1 Christ is designated "the *messenger* of the covenant," because He came here to make known its contents and proclaim its glad tidings. He came forth from the Father to reveal and publish His amazing grace for lost sinners. In Hebrews 7:22 Christ is denominated "the *surety* of a better covenant." A surety is one who is legally constituted the representative of others, and thereby comes under an engagement to fulfill certain obligations in their name and for their benefit. There is not a single legal obligation which the elect owed unto God but what Christ has fully and perfectly discharged; He has paid the whole debt of His insolvent people, settling all their liabilities. In Hebrews 9:16 Christ is called "the *testator*" of the covenant or testament, and this, because to Him belong its riches, to Him pertain its privileges; and because He has, in His unbounded goodness, bequeathed them as so many inestimable legacies unto His people.

Once more, in Hebrews 9:15 and 12:24 Christ is styled "the *mediator* of the new covenant*," because it is by His efficacious satisfaction and prevailing intercession that all its blessings are now imparted to its beneficiaries. Christ now stands between God and His people, advocating their cause (I John 2:1) and speaking a word in season to him that is weary (Isa. 50:4). But how could Christ sustain such offices as these unless the covenant had been made with Him (Gal. 3:17) and the execution of it had been undertaken by Him (Heb. 10:5-7)? "Now the God of peace, which brought again from the dead our Lord Jesus, that great shepherd of the sheep, *through the blood of the everlasting covenant*" (Heb. 13:20): that one phrase is quite sufficient to establish the fact that an organic connection existed between the covenant of grace and the sacrifice of Christ. In response to Christ's execution of its terms, the Father now says to Him, "By the blood of thy covenant I have sent forth thy prisoners [those given to Him before the foundation of the world, but in Adam fallen under condemnation] out of the pit wherein is no water" (Zech. 9:11).

The covenant relationship which the God-man mediator sustains unto God Himself is that which alone accounts for and explains the fact that He so frequently addressed Him as "my God." Every time our blessed Redeemer uttered the words "my God" He gave expression to His covenant standing before the God-head. It must be so; for considering Him as the Second Person of the Trinity, He *was* God, equally with the Father and the Holy Spirit. We are well aware that we are now plunging into deep waters; yet if we hold fast to the very words of Scripture we shall be safely borne through them, even though our finite minds will never be able to sound their infinite depths. "Thou art *my God* from my mother's belly" (Ps. 22:10), declared the Savior. From the cross He said, "My God." On the resurrection morning He spoke of "my God" (John 20:17). And in the compass of a single verse (Rev. 3:12) we find the glorified Redeemer saying "my God" no less than four times.

What has been pointed out in the above paragraph receives confirmation in many other Scriptures. When renewing His covenant with Abraham, Jehovah said: "I will establish my covenant between me and thee, and thy seed after thee in their generations, for an everlasting covenant, *to be a God unto* thee and to thy seed after thee" (Gen. 17:7). *That* is the great covenant promise: to be a God unto any one signifies that He will supply all their need (Phil. 4:19)—spiritual, temporal, and eternal. It is true that God is the God of all men, inasmuch as He is their Creator, Governor and Judge; but He is the God of His people in a much more blessed sense. "For this is the covenant that I will make with the house of Israel after those days, saith the Lord: I will put my laws into their mind, and write them in their hearts; and *I will be to them a God,* and they shall be to me a people" (Heb. 8:10). Here again we are shown that it is with respect unto *the covenant* that, in a special way, God is the God of His people.

Before leaving Hebrews 8:10 let us note the blessed tenor of the covenant as expressed in the words immediately following: "And they shall not teach every man his neighbor, and every man his brother, saying, Know the Lord: for all shall know me, from the least to the greatest. For I will be merciful to their unrighteousness, and their sins and their iniquities will I remember no more" (vv. 11, 12). What conditions are there here? What terms of fulfillment are required from impotent men? None at all: it is all promise from beginning to end. So too in Acts 3:25 we find Peter saying, "Ye are the children of the prophets, and of the covenant which God made with our fathers." Here *the* covenant (not "covenants") is referred to generally; then it is specified particularly: "saying unto Abraham, And in thy seed shall all the kindreds of the earth"—be laid under conditions? No; be required to perform certain works? No; but, "shall be blessed," without any regard to qualifications or deeds of their own—entitled by virtue of their interest in what was performed for them by their covenant head

Let us consider now the various features of the everlasting covenant.

1. The Father covenanted with Christ that He should be the federal head of His people, undertaking for them, freeing them from that dreadful condemnation wherein God foresaw from eternity they would fall in Adam. This alone explains why Christ is denominated the "last Adam," the "second man" (I Cor. 15:45, 47). Let it be very carefully noted that in Ephesians 5:23 we are expressly told "Christ is the head of the church, and He is the saviour of the body." He could not have been the Savior unless He had first been the head; that is, unless He had voluntarily entered into the work of suretyship by divine appointment, serving as the representative of His people, taking upon Him all their responsibilities and agreeing to discharge all their legal obligations; putting Himself in the stead of His insolvent people, paying all their debts, working out for them a perfect righteousness,

and legally meriting for them the reward or blessing of the fulfilled law.

It is to that eternal compact the apostle makes reference when he speaks of a certain "covenant that was confirmed before of God in [or "to"] Christ" in Galatians 3:17. There we behold the covenant parties: on the one side, God, in the Trinity of His persons; and on the other side Christ, that is, the Son viewed as the God-man mediator. There we learn of an agreement between Them: a covenant or con-tract, and that confirmed or solemnly agreed upon and ratified. There too, in the immediate context, we are shown that Christ is here viewed not only as the executor of a testament bequeathed to the saints by God, or that salvation was promised to us through Christ, but there twice over we are specifically told (v. 16) that the promises were made *to* Abraham's "seed, which is *Christ*"! Thus we have the clearest possible Scriptural proof that the everlasting covenant contained something which is promised by God to Christ Himself.

Most blessedly were several features of the everlasting covenant typed out in Eden. Let us consider these features:

1. Christ was set up (Prov. 8:23) in the eternal counsels of the three-one Jehovah as the head over and heir of all things: the figure of His headship is seen in the Creator's words to Adam, "have *dominion over* the fish of the sea," and so forth (Gen. 1:28). There we behold Him as the lord of all creation and head of all mankind. But, second, Adam was *alone:* among all the creatures he ruled, there was not found a help-meet for him. He was solitary in the world over which he was king; so Christ was alone when set up by God in a past eternity. Third, a help-meet was provided for Adam, who was one in nature with himself, as pure and holy as he was, in every way suitable to him: Eve became his wife and companion (Gen. 2:21-24). Beautifully did that set forth the eternal marriage between Christ and His church (Eph. 5:29-32). Let it be carefully noted that Eve was married to Adam, and was pure and holy, *before* she fell; so it was with the church (Eph. 1:3-6). (For much in this paragraph we are indebted to a sermon by J. K. Popham.)

2. In order for him to execute His covenant engagement it was necessary for Christ to assume human nature and be made in all things like unto His brethren, so that He might enter their place, be made under the law, and serve in their stead. He must have a soul and body in which He was capable of suffering and being paid the just wages of His people's sins. This explains to us that marvelous passage in He-brews 10:5-9, the language of which is most obviously couched in covenant terms: the whole displaying so blessedly the voluntary en-gagement of the Son, His perfect readiness and willingness in acquiesc-

ing to the Father's pleasure. It was at the incarnation Christ fulfilled that precious type of Himself found in Exodus 21:5. Out of love to His Lord, the Father, and to His spouse the church, and His spiritual children, He subjected Himself to a place of perpetual servitude.

3. Having voluntarily undertaken the terms of the everlasting covenant, a special economical *relationship* was now established between the Father and the Son—the Father considered as the appointer of the everlasting covenant, the Son as the God-man mediator, the head and surety of His people. Now it was that the Father became Christ's "Lord" (Ps. 16:2, as is evident from vv. 9, 11; Mic. 5:4), and now it was that the Son became the Father's "servant" (Isa. 42:1; cf. Phil. 2:7), undertaking the work appointed. Observe that the clause "took upon him the form of a servant" *precedes* "and was made in the likeness of men." This explains His own utterance "as the Father *gave me commandment,* even so I do" (John 14:31; cf. 10:18; 12:49). This accounts for His declaration, "My Father is greater than I" (John 14:28), wherein our Savior was speaking with reference to the covenant engagement which existed between the Father and Himself.

4. Christ died in fulfillment of the covenant's requirements. It was absolutely impossible that an innocent person—absolutely considered as such—should suffer under the sentence and curse of the law, for the law denounced no punishment on any such person. Guilt and punishment are related; and where the former is not, the latter cannot be. It was because the Holy One of God was *relatively* guilty, by the sins of the elect being imputed to Him, that He could righteously be smitten in their stead. Yet even that had not been possible unless the spotless substitute had first assumed the office of suretyship; and that, in turn, was only legally valid because of Christ's federal headship with His people. The sacrifice of Christ owes all its validity from the covenant: the holy and blessed Trinity, by counsel and oath, having appointed it to be the true and only propitiation for sin.

So too it is utterly impossible for us to form any clear and adequate idea of what the Lord of glory died to achieve if we have no real knowledge of the agreement in fulfillment of which His death took place. What is popularly taught upon the subject today is that the atonement of Christ has merely *provided an opportunity* for men to be saved, that it has opened the way for God to justly pardon any and all who avail themselves of His gracious provision. But that is only a part of the truth, and by no means the most important and blessed part of it. The grand fact is that Christ's death was the *completion* of His agreement with the Father, which guarantees the salvation of all who were named in it—not one for whom He died can possibly miss heaven: John 6:39. This leads us to consider—

5. That on the ground of Christ's willingness to perform the work stipulated in the covenant, certain promises were made to Him by the Father: first, promises concerning Himself; and second, promises concerning His people. The promises which concerned the Mediator Himself may be summarized thus. First, He was assured of divine enduement for this discharge of all the specifications of the covenant (Isa. 11:1-3; 61:1; cf. John 8:29). Second, He was guaranteed the divine protection under the execution of His work (Isa. 42:6; Zech. 3:8, 9; cf. John 10:18). Third, He was promised the divine assistance unto a successful conclusion (Isa. 42:4; 49:8-10; cf. John 17:4). Fourth, those promises were given to Christ for the stay of His heart, to be pleaded by Him (Ps. 89:26; 2:8); and this He did (Isa. 50.8-10, cf. Heb. 2:13). Fifth, Christ was assured of success in His undertaking and a reward for the same (Isa. 53:10, 11; Ps. 89:27-29; 110:1-3; cf. Phil. 2:9-11). Christ also received promises concerning His people. First, that He should receive gifts for them (Ps. 68:18; cf. Eph. 4:10, 11). Second, that God would make them willing to receive Him as their Lord (Ps. 110:3; cf. John 6:44). Third, that eternal life should be theirs (Ps. 133:3; cf. Titus 1:2). Fourth, that a seed should serve Him, proclaim His righteousness, and declare what He had done for them (Ps. 22:30, 31). Fifth, that kings and princes should worship Him (Isa. 49:7).

Finally, let it be pointed out that this compact made between the Father and the Son on behalf of the whole election of grace is variously designated. It is called an *"everlasting* covenant" (Isa. 55:3) to denote the perpetuity of it, and because the blessings in it devised in eternity past will endure forever. It is called a "covenant of *peace"* (Ezek. 34:25; 37:26) because it secures reconciliation with God, for Adam's transgression produced enmity, but by Christ the enmity has been removed (Eph. 2:16), and therefore is He denominated the "Prince of Peace" (Isa. 9:6). It is called the "covenant of *life"* (Mal. 2:15), in contrast from the covenant of works which issued in death, and because life is the principal thing pledged in it (Titus 1:2). It is called the *"holy* covenant" (Luke 1:72), not only because it was made by and between the persons of the Holy Trinity, but also because it secures the holiness of the divine character and provides for the holiness of God's people. It is called a *"better* covenant" (Heb. 7:22) in contrast from the Sinaitic arrangement, wherein the national prosperity of Israel was left contingent on *their own* works.

PART TWO

The Adamic Covenant

I

It is of vital importance for a right understanding of much in God's Word to observe the relation which Adam sustained to his posterity. Adam was not only the common parent of mankind, but he was also their federal head and representative. The whole human race was placed on probation or trial in Eden. Adam acted not for himself alone, but he transacted for all who were to spring from him. Unless this basic fact be definitely apprehended, much that ought to be relatively clear to us will be shrouded in impenetrable mystery. Yea, we go further, and affirm that, until the federal headship of Adam and God's covenant with him in that office be actually perceived, we are without the key to God's dealings with the human race, we are unable to discern man's relation to the divine law, and we appreciate not the fundamental principles upon which the atonement of Christ proceeded.

"Federal headship" is a term which has almost entirely disappeared from current religious literature—so much the worse for our moderns. It is true that the expression itself does not verbally occur in Scripture; yet like the words *Trinity* and *the divine incarnation,* it is a necessity in theological parlance and doctrinal exposition. The principle or fact which is embodied in the term "federal headship" is that of *representation.* There have been but two federal heads: Adam and Christ, with each of whom God entered into a covenant. Each of them acted on behalf of others, each legally represented a definite people, so much so that all whom they represented were regarded by God as being *in* them. Adam represented the whole human race; Christ represented all those whom the Father had, in His eternal counsels, given to Him.

When Adam stood in Eden as a responsible being before God, he stood there as a federal head, as the legal representative of all his posterity. Hence, when Adam sinned, all for whom he was standing are accounted as having sinned; when he fell, all whom he represented fell; when he died, they died. So too was it with Christ. When He came to this earth, He, too, stood in a federal relationship to His own people; and when He became obedient unto death, all for whom He was acting were accounted righteous; when He rose again from the dead, all whom He represented rose with Him; when He ascended on high, they were regarded as ascending with Him. "For as in Adam all die, even so in Christ shall all be made alive" (I Cor. 15:22).

The relationship of our race to Adam or Christ divides men into two classes, each receiving nature and destiny from its respective head. All the individuals who comprise these two classes are so identified with their heads that it has justly been said, "There have been but two men in the world, and two facts in history." These two men are Adam and Christ; the two facts are the disobedience of the former, by which many were made sinners, and the obedience of the latter, by which many were made righteous. By the former came *ruin,* by the latter came *redemption;* and neither ruin nor redemption can be Scripturally apprehended except as they are seen to be accomplished by those representatives, and except we understand the relationships expressed by being "in Adam" and "in Christ."

Let is be expressly and emphatically affirmed that what we are here treating of is purely a matter of divine revelation. Nowhere but in Holy Scripture do we know anything about Adam, or of our relation to him. If it be asked how the federal constitution of the race can be reconciled with the dictates of human reason, the first answer must be, it is not for us to reconcile them. The initial inquiry is not whether federal headship be reasonable or just, but, is it a fact revealed in the Word of God? If it is, then reason must bow to it and faith humbly receive it. To the child of God the question of its justice is easily settled: we know it to be just, because it is a part of the ways of the infinitely holy and righteous God.

Now the fact that Adam *was* the federal head of the human race, that he *did* act and transact in a representative capacity, and that the judicial consequences of his actings *were* imputed to all those for whom he stood, is clearly revealed in God's Word. In Romans 5 we read: "Wherefore, as by one man sin entered into the world, and death by sin; and so death passed upon all men, in whom all sinned" (v. 12); "through the offence of one many be dead" (v. 15); "the judgment was by one to condemnation" (v. 16); "by one man's offence death reigned" (v. 17); "by the offence of one, judgment came upon all men to condemnation" (v. 18); "by one man's offence many were made [legally constituted] sinners" (v. 19). The meaning of these declarations is far too plain for any unprejudiced mind to misunderstand. It pleased God to deal with the human race *as represented in and by Adam.*

Let us borrow a simple illustration. God did not deal with mankind as with a field of corn, where each stalk stands upon its own individual root; but He dealt with it as with a tree, all the branches of which have one common root and trunk. If you strike with an axe at the root of a tree, the whole tree falls—not only the trunk, but also the branches: all wither and die. So it was when Adam fell. God permitted Satan to lay the axe at the root of the tree, and when Adam fell, all his posterity fell with him. At one fatal stroke Adam was severed from communion with his maker, and as the result "death passed upon all men."

Here, then, we learn what is the formal ground of man's judicial condemnation before God. The popular idea of *what* renders man a sinner in the sight of heaven is altogether inadequate and false. The prevailing conception is that a sinner is one who commits and practices sin. It is true that this is the *character* of a sinner, but it certainly is not that which primarily *constitutes* him a sinner. The truth is that every member of our race enters this world a guilty sinner before he ever commits a single transgression. It is not only that he possesses a sinful nature, but he is directly "under condemnation." We are legally constituted sinners neither by what we are nor by what we are doing, but by the disobedience of our federal head, Adam. Adam acted not for himself alone, but for all who were to spring from him.

On this point the teaching of the apostle Paul is plain and unambiguous. The terms of Romans 5:12-19, as we have shown above, are too varied and distinct to admit of any misconception: that it is on account of their sin in Adam, men, in the first instance, are accounted guilty and treated as such, as well as partake of a depraved nature. The language of I Corinthians 15:22 is equally unintelligible except on the supposition that both Adam and Christ sustained a *representative* character, in virtue of which the one involved the race in guilt and ruin, and the other, by His obedience unto death, secured the justification and salvation of all who believe in Him. The actual condition of the human race, throughout its history, confirms the same: the apostle's doctrine supplies the only adequate explanation of the universal prevalence of sin.

The human race is suffering now for the sin of Adam, or it is suffering for nothing at all. This earth is the scene of a grim and awful tragedy. In it we see misery and wretchedness, pain and poverty, decay and death, on every side. None escape. That "man is born unto trouble as the sparks fly upward" is an indisputable fact. But what is the explanation of it? Every effect must have a previous cause. If we are not being punished for Adam's sin, then, coming into this world, we are "children of wrath," alienated from God, corrupt and depraved, and on the broad road which leadeth to destruction, *for nothing at all!* Who would contend that this was better, more satisfactory, then the Scriptural explanation of our ruin?

But it will be said, It was unjust to make Adam our federal head. How so? Is not the principle of representation a fundamental one in human society? The father is the legal head of his children during their minority: what he does, binds the family. A business house is held responsible for the transactions of its agents. The heads of a state are vested with such authority that the treaties they make are binding upon the whole nation. This principle is so basic it cannot be set aside. Every popular election illustrates the fact that a constituency will act through a representative and be bound by his acts. Human affairs could not continue, nor society exist without it. Why, then, be staggered at finding it inaugurated in Eden?

Consider the alternative. "The race must have either stood in a full grown man, with a full-orbed intellect, or stood as babies, each entering his probation in the twilight of self-consciousness, each deciding his destiny before his eyes were half-opened to what it all meant. How much better would that have been? How much more just? But could it not have been some other way? There was no other way. It was either the baby or it was the perfect, well-equipped, all-calculating man—the man who saw and comprehended everything. That man was Adam" (G. S. Bishop). Yes, Adam, fresh from the hands of his creator, with no sinful ancestry behind him, with no depraved nature within. A man made in the image and likeness of God, pronounced by Him "very good," in fellowship with heaven. Who could have been a more suitable representative for us?

This has been the principle on which and the method by which God has acted all through. The posterity of Canaan were cursed for the single transgression of their parent (Gen. 9). The Egyptians perished at the Red Sea as the result of Pharaoh's wickedness. When Israel became God's witness in the earth it was the same. The sins of the fathers were to be visited upon the children: in consequence of Achan's one sin the whole of his family were stoned to death. The high priest acted on behalf of the whole nation. Later, the king was held accountable for the conduct of his subjects. One acting on behalf of others, the one responsible for the many, is a basic principle both of human and divine government. We cannot get away from it; wherever we look, it stares us in the face.

Finally, let it be pointed out that the sinner's salvation is made to depend upon the same principle. Beware, my reader, of quarreling with the justice of this law of representation. This principle wrecked us, and this principle alone can rescue us. The disobedience of the first Adam was the judicial ground of our condemnation; the obedience of the last Adam is the legal ground on which God alone can justify the sinner. The substitution of Christ in the place of His people, the imputation of their sins to Him and of His righteousness to them, is the cardinal fact of the gospel. But the principle of being saved by what another has done is only possible on the ground that we are lost through what another did. The two stand or fall together. If there had been no covenant of works there could have been no death in Adam, there could have been no life in Christ.

"By one man's disobedience many were made sinners" (Rom. 5:19). Here is cause for humiliation which few think about. We are members of a cursed race, the fallen children of a fallen parent, and as such we enter this world "alienated from the life of God" (Eph. 4:18), with nothing in us to prompt unto holy living. Oh, that God may reveal to you, dear reader, your connection with the first Adam, that you may realize your deep need of clinging to the last Adam. The world may deride this doctrine of representation and imputation, but that only evidences it to be of God. If the gospel (the genuine gospel) were welcomed by all, that would prove it was of human manufacture; for only that is acceptable to fallen man which is invented by fallen man. That the wise of this world scoff at the truth of federal headship, when it is faithfully presented, only goes to manifest its divine origin.

"By the offence of one judgment came upon all men *to condemnation*" (Rom. 5:18). In the day that Adam fell, the frown of God came upon all His children. The holy nature of God abhorred the apostate race. The curse of the broken law descended upon all Adam's posterity. It is only thus we can account for the universality of depravity and suffering. The corruption which we inherit from our parents is a great evil, for it is the source of all our personal sins. For God to allow this transmission of depravity is to inflict *a punishment*. But how could God punish all, unless all were guilty? The fact that all do share in this common punishment proves that all sinned and fell in Adam. Our depravity and misery are not, as such, the appointment of the Creator, but are instead the retribution of the Judge.

"By one man's disobedience many were made sinners" (Rom. 5:19). The word "made" in that verse calls for a definition and explanation. It does not refer directly and primarily to the fact that we inherit from Adam a corrupt and sinful nature—that we learn from other Scriptures. The term "were made sinners" is a forensic one, and refers to our being *constituted guilty* in the sight of God. A parallel case is found in II Corinthians 5:21: "He hath made him to be sin for us, who knew no sin." Clearly those words "made him [Christ] to be sin" cannot refer to any change which our Lord underwent in His nature or character. No, rather the blessed Savior so took His people's place before God that He was treated and dealt with as guilty: their sins were not *imparted,* but *imputed* to Him.

Again, in Galatians 3:13 we read that Christ was *"made* a curse for us": as the substitute of God's elect, He was judicially regarded as beneath the condemnation of the law. Our guilt was legally transferred to Christ: the sins we committed, He was regarded as responsible for; what *we* deserved, *He* endured. In like manner, Adam's offspring were *"made* sinners" by their head's disobedience: the legal consequences of their representative's transgression were charged to their account. They were judicially constituted guilty, because the guilt of Adam's sin was charged to them. Hence we enter this world not only with the heritage of a corrupt nature, but "under condemnation." We are by nature "children of wrath" (Eph. 2:3), for "the wicked are estranged from the womb" (Ps. 58:3)—separated from God and exposed to His judicial displeasure.

II

In the preceding chapter we pointed out at some length that when Adam stood in Eden as a responsible being before his creator, he stood there as the federal head of our race, that he legally transacted on the behalf of all his posterity, that in the sight of the divine law we were all so absolutely identified with him as to be accounted "in Adam." Hence what he did, all are regarded as having done: when he sinned, we sinned; when he fell, we fell; when he died, we died. The language of Romans 5:12-19 and I Corinthians 15:22 is so plain and positive on this point as to leave no valid room for any uncertainty. Having viewed, then, the representative office or position which Adam occupied, we turn to consider the covenant which God made with him at that time. But before so doing, let us observe how admirably equipped Adam was to fill that eminent office and transact for all his race.

It is exceedingly difficult, if not altogether impossible in our present state, for us to form any adequate conception of the most excellent and glorious endowment of man in his first estate. Negatively, he was entirely free from sin and misery: Adam had no evil ancestry behind him, no corruption within him, nothing in his body to distress him. Positively, he was made in the image and likeness of God, indwelt by the Holy Spirit, endued with a wisdom and holiness to which Christians are as yet, in themselves, strangers. He was blest with unclouded communion with God, placed in the fairest of environments, given dominion over all creatures here below, and graciously provided with a suitable helpmate. Fair as the morning was that blissful heritage into which Adam was estated. Made "upright" (Eccles. 7:29) and endowed with full ability to serve, delight in, and glorify his creator.

Though pronounced by God Himself as "very good" (Gen. 1:31) on the day of his creation, Adam was, nevertheless, a creature, and as such subject unto the authority of the One who had given him being. God governs all rational beings by law, as the rule of their obedience to Him. To that principle there is no exception, and in the very nature of things cannot be, for God must enforce His rights as Lord over all. Angels (Ps. 103:20), unfallen man, fallen men, redeemed men—all are subject to the moral government of God. Even the beloved Son, when He became incarnate, was "made under the law" (Gal. 4:4). Moreover, in the case of Adam his character was not yet confirmed, and therefore, like the angels, he must be placed on probation, subjected to trial, to see whether or no he would render allegiance to the Lord his maker.

Now the law which God gave to Adam, under which He placed him, was threefold: natural, moral, and positive. By the first we mean that subjection to his creator—acting for His honor and glory—was constituted the very law of his being. Being created in the image and likeness of God, it was his very nature to delight himself in the Lord and reproduce (in a creaturely measure) God's righteousness and holiness. Just as the animals are endowed with a nature or instinct which prompts them to choose and do that which makes for their well-being, so man in his pristine glory was endued with a nature which prompted him to do that which is pleasing unto God and that which promoted his own highest interests—the remains of which appear in fallen man's rationality and conscience.

By the "moral" law which was given to Adam by God, we mean that he was placed under the requirements of the Ten Commandments, the summary of which is "Thou shalt love the Lord thy God with all thy heart, with all thy mind, and with all thy strength, and thy neighbour as thyself." Nothing less than that was due unto Adam's maker, and nothing short of it became him as an upright creature. By "positive" law we mean that God also placed certain restrictions upon Adam which had never occurred to him from either the light of nature or from any moral considerations; instead, they were sovereignly appointed by God and were designed as a special test of Adam's subjection to the imperial will of his King. The term "positive law" is employed by theologians not as antithetical to "negative," but in contrast from those laws which are addressed to our moral nature: prayer is a "moral" duty: baptism is a "positive" ordinance.

This threefold law under which Adam was placed may be clearly discerned in the brief records of Genesis 1 and 2. The marriage between Adam and Eve illustrates the first: "Therefore shall a man leave his father and his mother, and shall cleave unto his wife, and they shall be one flesh" (Gen. 2:24). Any infraction of the marital relationship is a violation of the very law of *nature*. The institution and consecration of the Sabbath exemplifies the second: "And God blessed the seventh day and sanctified it, because that in it he had rested from all his work" (2:3): a procedure that would be inexplicable except as furnishing the ground for a like procedure on the part of man, for otherwise the hallowing and benediction spoken of must have lacked both a proper subject and a definite aim. In every age man's observance of the holy Sabbath has been made the supreme test of his moral relation to the Lord. The command for Adam to care for the garden ("dress and keep it": Gen. 2:15) demonstrates the third aspect, the *positive:* even in the unfallen state man was not to be idle and shiftless.

From the above it is plainly evident that there was the distinct recognition of an outward revelation to Adam of those three great branches of duty which appertain to man in every possible condition of mortal existence, and which unitedly comprehend every obligation upon man in this life; namely, what he owes to God, what he owes to his neighbor, and what he owes to himself. Those three embrace everything. The sanctification of the Sabbath, the institution of marriage, and the command to dress and keep the garden were revealed as outward ordinances, covering the three classes of duties, each of supreme importance in its own sphere: the spiritual, the moral, and the natural. Those intrinsic elements of divine law are immutable: they preceded the covenant of works, and would have remained had the covenant been kept—as they have survived its breach.

But there was need for something of a still more specific kind to test man's adherence to the perfect rectitude incumbent upon him; for in Adam humanity was on trial, the whole race not only having been potentially created in him, but being federally represented by him. "The question, therefore, as to its proper decisiveness, must be made to turn on conformity to an ordinance at once reasonable in its nature and specific in its requirements—an ordinance which the simplest should understand and respecting which no uncertainty could exist whether it had been broken or not. Such in the highest degree was the appointment respecting the tree of knowledge of good and evil, forbidden of God to be eaten on pain of death—an appointment positive in its character, in a certain sense arbitrary, yet withal perfectly natural" (P. Fairbairn, *The Revelation of Law in Scripture*).

Adam was now subjected to a simple and specific test as to whether the will of God was sacred in his eyes. Nothing less than perfect conformity of heart and unremitting obedience in act to the whole revealed will of God could be required of man. The command not to eat of the fruit of a certain tree was now made the decisive test of his general obedience. The prohibitory statute was a "positive" precept. It was not sinful per se to eat of the tree of the knowledge of good and evil, but only so because God had forbidden it. It was, therefore, a more suitable test of faith and obedience than a "moral" statute would have been, submission being required for no other reason than the sovereign will of God. At the same time let it be clearly observed that, disobedience of that "positive" precept certainly involved defiance of the "moral" law, for it was a failure to love God with all the heart, it was contempt of divine authority, it was coveting that which God had forbidden.

On the basis of the threefold constitution under which God had placed Adam—amenable to natural, moral, and positive law; on the basis of his threefold responsibility—to perform the duty which he owed unto God, unto his neighbor, unto himself; and on the basis of the threefold equipment with which he had been endowed—created in the image of God, pronounced "very good," indwelt by the Holy Spirit, and thus fully furnished to discharge his responsibility, God entered into a solemn compact with him. Clothed in dignity, intelligence, and moral excellence, Adam was surrounded on every side by exquisite beauty and loveliness. The occupant of Eden was more a being of heaven than of earth: an embodiment of wisdom, purity, and uprightness. God Himself deigned to visit and cheer him with His presence and blessing. In body perfectly sound; in soul completely holy; in circumstances blissfully happy.

The ideal fitness of Adam to act as the head of his race, and the ideal circumstances under which the decisive test was to be made, must forever shut every fair and honest mouth against objecting to the arrangement God proposed to Adam, and the fearful consequences which his sad failure have brought down upon us. It has been well said, "Had we been present—had we and all the human race been brought into existence at once—and had God proposed to us, that we should choose one of our number to be our representative that he might enter into covenant with him on our behalf—should we not, with one voice, have chosen our first parent for this responsible office? Should we not have said, 'He is a perfect man and bears the image and likeness of God,—if any one is to stand for us let him be the man'; *Now,*—since the angels who stood for themselves, fell—why should we wish to stand for ourselves. And if it be reasonable that one stand for us—why should we complain, when God has chosen the same person for this office, that *we* would have chosen, had we been in existence, and capable of choosing ourselves?" (G. S. Bishop).

"But of the tree of the knowledge of good and evil, thou shalt not eat of it: for in the day that thou eatest thereof thou shalt surely die" (Gen. 2:17). The contracting parties in this covenant were God and Adam. First, God as supreme Lord, prescribing what was equitable: God as *goodness* itself, promising communion with Himself—in which man's happiness principally lies—while treading the path of obedience and doing that which was well-pleasing to his maker; but God also as *justice* itself, threatening death upon rebellion. Second, Adam considered both as man and as the head and representative of his posterity. As man, he was a rational and responsible being, endowed with sufficient powers to fulfill all righteousness, standing not as a feeble babe but a fully developed man—a fit and fully qualified subject for God to enter into covenant with him. As head of the race, he was now called upon to transact in the nature and strength with which the Creator had so richly furnished him.

Yet it is clear that the covenant of works proceeded on the assumption that man in his original condition—though "made upright"—was capable of falling, just as the covenant of grace proceeds on the assumption that man, though fallen and depraved, is—through Christ—capable of being restored. "God made man male and female, with righteousness and true holiness, having the law of God in their hearts, and power to fulfil it; and yet under a possibility of transgressing, being left to the liberty of their will, which was subject to change" (Westminster Confession of Faith). In the closing words of that quotation some light is cast upon that mysterious question, How could a sinless creature *first sin?* How could one made "upright" fall? How could one whom God Himself had pronounced "very good" give ear to the devil, apostatize, and drag down himself and his posterity to utter ruin?

While in our present state perhaps it is not possible for us to fully solve this profound problem, yet it is our conviction that we may perceive the direction in which the solution lies. In the first place, Adam was *mutable* or subject to change. Necessarily so, for mutability and creaturehood are correlative terms. There is only One "with whom is no variableness, neither shadow of turning" (James 1:17). The essential attributes of God are incommunicable: for the Deity to bestow omniscience, omnipotence, or immutability on others would not be to bring into existence creatures, but would be raising up gods, equal with Himself. Therefore, while Adam was a perfect creature, he was but a creature, mutable and not immutable; and being mutable, he was subject to change either for the better or for the worse, and hence, liable to fall.

In the second place, Adam was constituted a *responsible* being, a moral agent, being endowed with a free will, and therefore he was capable of both obedience and disobedience. Moreover, though the first man was endowed with both natural and spiritual wisdom amply sufficient for all his needs, leaving him entirely without excuse if he made a false and foolish choice, nevertheless, he was but fallible, for infallibility pertains unto God alone, as Job 4:18 more than hints. Therefore, being fallible, Adam was capable of erring, though to do so was culpable to the highest degree. Mutability and fallibility are the conditions of existence of every creature; and while they are not blemishes, yet they are potential dangers, which can only be prevented from working ruin by the creature constantly looking to the Creator for his upholding grace.

In the third place, as a responsible being, as a moral agent, as one who was endowed with free will, Adam had necessarily to be *placed on probation,* submitted to a real test of his fealty unto God, before he was *confirmed,* or given an abiding standing in his creature perfections. Because Adam was a creature, mutable and fallible, he was entirely dependent upon his creator; and therefore he must be put on trial to show whether or no he would assert his independency, which would be open revolt against his maker and the repudiation of his creaturehood. Every creature must necessarily come under the moral government of God, and for free agents that necessarily implies and involves two possible alternatives—subjection or insubordination. The absolute dominion of God over the creature and the complete dependence and subjection of the creature to God, holds good in every part of the universe and throughout all ages. The inherent poison in every error and evil is the rejection of God's dominion and of man's dependence upon his maker, or the assertion of his independency.

Being but mutable, fallible, and dependent, the noblest and highest creature of all is *liable to* fall from his fair estate, and can only be preserved therein by the sovereign power of his creator. Being endowed with free will, man was capable of both obedience and disobedience. Had He so pleased, God could have upheld Adam, and that without destroying his accountability or infringing upon his liberty; but unless Adam had been left to his own creature wisdom and strength, there had been no trial of his responsibility and powers. Instead, God offered to man the opportunity of being confirmed as a holy and happy creature, secured on the condition of his own personal choice; so that his probation being successfully closed, he had been granted a firm standing before God. But God permitted Adam to disobey, to make way for the more glorious obedience of Christ; suffered the covenant of works to be broken that the far better covenant of grace might be administered.

III

Before entering into detail upon the nature and terms of the compact which God made with Adam, it may be well to obviate an objection which some are likely to make against the whole subject; namely, that since the word *covenant* is not to be found in the historical account of Genesis, therefore to speak of the Adamic covenant is naught but a theological invention. There is a certain class of people, posing as ultraorthodox, who imagine they have a reverence and respect for Holy Writ as the final court of appeal which surpasses that of their fellows. They say, Show me a passage which expressly states God made a covenant with Adam, and that will settle the matter; but until you can produce a verse with the exact term "Adamic covenant" in it, I shall believe no such thing.

Our reason for referring to this paltry quibble is because it illustrates a very superficial approach to God's Word which is becoming more and more prevalent in certain quarters, and which stands badly in need of being corrected. Words are only counters or signs after all (different writers use them with varying latitude, as is sometimes the case in Scripture itself); and to be unduly occupied with the shell often results in a failure to obtain the kernel within. Some Unitarians refuse to believe in the tri-unity of God, merely because no verse can be found which categorically affirms there are "three Persons in the Godhead" or where the word *Trinity* is used. But what matters the absence of the mere word itself, when three distinct divine persons are clearly delineated in the Word of truth! For the same reason others repudiate the fact of the total depravity of fallen man, which is the height of absurdity when Scripture depicts him as corrupt in *all* the faculties of his being.

Surely I need not to be told that a certain person has been born again if all the evidences of regeneration are clearly discernible in his life; and if I am furnished with a full description of his immersion, the mere word *baptism* does not make it any more sure and definite to my mind. Our first search, then, in Genesis, is not for the term *covenant*, but to see whether or not we can trace the outlines of a solemn and definite pact between God and Adam. We say this not because the word itself is never associated with our first parents—for elsewhere it is—but because we are anxious that certain of our readers may be delivered from the evil mentioned above. To dismiss from our minds all thoughts of an Adamic covenant simply because the term itself occurs not in Genesis 1 to 5 is to read those chapters very superficially and miss much which lies only a little beneath their surface.

Let us now remind ourselves of the essential elements of a covenant. Briefly stated, any covenant is a mutual agreement entered into by two or more parties, whereby they stand solemnly bound to each other to perform the conditions contracted for. Amplifying that definition, it may be pointed out that the terms of a covenant are (1) there is a stipulation of something to be done or given by that party proposing the covenant; (2) there is a restipulation by the other party of something to be done or given in consideration; (3) those stipulations must be lawful and right, for it can never be right to engage to do wrong; (4) there is a penalty included in the terms of agreement, some evil consequence to result to the party who may or shall violate his agreement—that penalty being added as a security.

A covenant then is a disposition of things, an arrangement concerning them, a mutual agreement about them. But again we would remind the reader that words are but arbitrary things; and we are never safe in trusting to a single term, as though from it alone we could collect the right knowledge of the thing. No, our inquiry is into the thing itself. What are the matters of *fact* to which these terms are applied? Was there any moral transaction between God and Adam wherein the above mentioned four principles were involved? Was there any proposition made by God to man of something to be done by the latter? any stipulation of something to be given by the former? any agreement of both? any penal sanction? To such interrogations every accurate observer of the contents of Genesis 1 to 3 must answer affirmatively.

"But of the tree of the knowledge of good and evil, thou shalt not eat of it: for in the day that thou eatest thereof thou shalt surely die" (Gen. 2:17). Here are all the constituent elements of a covenant: (1) there are the contracting parties, the Lord God and man; (2) there is a stipulation enjoined, which man (as he was duty bound) engaged to perform; (3) there was a penalty prescribed, which would be incurred in case of failure; (4) there was by clear and necessary implication a reward promised, to which Adam would be entitled by his fulfillment of the condition; (5) the "tree of life" was the divine seal or ratification of the covenant, as the rainbow was the seal of the covenant which God made with Noah. Later, we shall endeavor to furnish clear proof of each of these statements.

"We here have, in the beginning of the world, distinctly placed before us, as the parties to the covenant, the Creator and the creature, the Governor and the governed. In the covenant itself, brief as it is, we have concentrated all those primary, anterior, and eternal principles of truth, righteousness, and justice, which enter necessarily into the nature of the great God, and which must always pervade His government, under whatever dispensation; we have a full recognition of His authority to govern His intelligent creatures, according to these principles, and we have a perfect acknowledgment on the part of man, that in all things he is subject, as a rational and accountable being, to the will and direction of the infinitely wise and benevolent Creator. No part of a covenant therefore, in its proper sense, is wanting" (R. B. Howell, *The Covenant,* 1855).

There was, then, a formal compact between God and man concerning obedience and disobedience, reward and punishment, and where there is a binding law pertaining to such matters and an agreement upon them by both parties concerned, there is a covenant (cf. Gen. 21:27, and what precedes and follows Gen. 31:44). In this covenant Adam acted not as a private person for himself only, but as the federal head and representative of the whole of his posterity. In that capacity he served alone, Eve not being a federal head jointly with him, but was included in it, she being (later, we believe) formed out of him. In this Adam was a type of Christ, with whom God made the everlasting covenant, and who at the appointed time acted as the head and representative of His people: as it is written, "over them that had not sinned after the similitude of Adam's transgression, who is the figure of him that was to come" (Rom. 5:14).

The most conclusive proof that Adam did enter into a covenant with God on the behalf of his posterity is found in the penal evils which came upon the race in consequence of its head's disobedience. From the awful curse which passed upon all his posterity we are compelled to infer the legal relation which existed between Adam and them, for the Judge of all the earth, being righteous, will not punish where there is no crime. "Wherefore as by one man sin entered into the world, and death by sin; and so death passed upon all men, for that [or "in whom"] all sinned" (Rom. 5:12). Here is the fact, and from it we must infer the preceding cause of it: under the government of a righteous God, the suffering of holy beings unconnected with sin is an impossibility. It would be the very acme of injustice that Adam's sin should be the cause of death passing on all men, unless all men were morally and legally connected with him.

That Adam stood as the federal head of his race and transacted for them, and that all his posterity were contemplated by God as being morally and legally (as well as seminally) in Adam, is clear from almost everything that was said to him in the first three chapters of Genesis. The language there used plainly intimates that it was spoken to the whole human race, and not to Adam as a single individual, but spoken to *them* and of *them*. The first time "man" is mentioned it evidently signifies all mankind, and not Adam alone: "And God said, Let us make *man* and let *them* have dominion over the fish of the sea, and over the fowls of the air, and over the cattle, and over [not simply "the garden of Eden," but] *all the earth*" (Gen. 1:26). All men bear the name of their representative (as the church is designated after its head: I Cor. 12:12), for the Hebrew for "every man" in Psalm 39:5, 11 is "all Adam"—plain evidence of their being one in the eye of the law.

In like manner, what God said to Adam after he had sinned, was said to and of all mankind; and the evil to which he was doomed in this world, as the consequence of his transgression, equally falls upon his posterity: "Cursed is the ground for thy sake, in sorrow thou shalt eat of it all the days of thy life. In the sweat of thy face shalt thou eat bread, till thou return unto the ground: for out of it wast thou taken: for dust thou art, and unto dust shalt thou return" (Gen. 3:17, 19). As this sentence "unto dust shalt *thou* return" did not respect Adam only, but all his descendants, so the same language in the original threat had respect unto all mankind: "in the day thou eatest thereof *thou* shalt surely die." This is reduced to a certainty by the unequivocal declarations of Romans 5:12 and I Corinthians 15:22. The curse came upon all; so the sin must have been committed by all.

The terms of the covenant are related in or are clearly inferable from the language of Genesis 2:17. That covenant demanded perfect obedience as its condition. Nor was that in any way difficult: one test only was instituted by which that obedience was to be formally expressed; namely, abstinence from the tree of the knowledge of good and evil. God had endowed Adam, in his creation, with a perfect and universal rectitude (Eccles. 7:29), so that he was fully able to respond to all requirements of his maker. He had a full knowledge of God's will concerning his duty. There was no bias in him toward evil: having been created in the image and likeness of God, his affections were pure and holy (cf. Eph. 4:24). How simple and easy was the observance of the obligation! How appalling the consequences of its violation!

"The tendency of such a Divine precept is to be considered. Man is thereby taught, 1. that God is Lord of all things; and that it is unlawful for man even to desire an apple, but with His leave. In all things therefore, from the greatest to the least the mouth of the Lord is to be consulted, as to what He would, or would not have done by us. 2. That man's true happiness is placed in God alone, and nothing is to be desired but with submission to God, and in order to employ it for Him. So that it is *He* only, on whose account all things appear good and desirable to man. 3. Readily to be satisfied without even the most delightful and desirable things, if God so command: and to think there is much more good in obedience to the Divine precept than in the enjoyment of the most delightful thing in the world. 4. That man was not yet arrived at the utmost pitch of happiness, but to expect a still greater good, after his course of obedience was over. This was hinted by the prohibition of the most delightful tree, whose fruit was, of any other, greatly to be desired; and this argued some degree of imperfection in that state in which man was forbid the enjoyment of some good" (*The Economy of the Covenants,* H. Witsius, 1660).

Unto that prohibitive statute was annexed a promise. This is an essential element in a covenant: a reward being guaranteed upon its terms being fulfilled. So here: "In the day that thou eatest thereof thou shalt surely die" necessarily implies the converse—"If thou eatest not thereof thou shalt surely live." Just as "Thou shalt not steal" inevitably involves "thou shalt conduct thyself honestly and honorably," just as "rejoice in the Lord" includes "murmur not against Him," so according to the simplest laws of construction the threatening of death as a consequence of eating, affirmed the promise of life to obedience. God will be no man's debtor: the general principle of "in keeping of them [the divine commandments] there is great reward" (Ps. 19:11) admits of no exception.

A certain good, a spiritual blessing, in addition to what Adam and Eve (and their posterity in him) already possessed, was assured upon his obedience. Had Adam been without a promise, he had been without a well-grounded hope for the future, for the hope which maketh not ashamed is founded upon the promise (Rom. 4:18, etc.). As Romans 7:10 so plainly affirms: "the commandment which was ordained to life," or more accurately (for the word *ordained* is supplied by the translators) "the commandment which was unto life"—having life as the reward for obedience. And again, "the law is not of faith: but, The man that doeth them shall live in them" (Gal.

3:12). But the law was "weak through the flesh" (Rom. 8:3), Adam being a mutable, fallible, mortal creature.

Against what has been said above it is objected, Adam was already in possession of spiritual life; how, then, could life be the reward promised for his obedience? It is true that Adam was in the enjoyment of spiritual life, being completely holy and happy; but he was on probation, and his response to the test God gave him—his obedience or disobedience to His command—would determine whether that spiritual life would be continued or whether it would be forfeited. Had Adam complied with the terms of the covenant, then he would have been confirmed in his creature standing, in the favor of God toward him, in communion with his maker, in the happy state of an earthly paradise; he would then have passed beyond the possibility of apostasy and misery. The reward, or additional good, which would have followed Adam's obedience was a state of inalienable blessedness both for himself and his posterity.

The well-informed reader will observe from the above that we are not in accord with H. Witsius and some other prominent theologians of the Puritan period, who taught that the reward promised Adam upon his obedience was the heavenly heritage. Their arguments upon this point do not seem to us at all conclusive, nor are we aware of anything in Scripture which may be cited in proof thereof. An inalienable title to the earthy paradise is, we think, what the promise denoted. Rather was it reserved for the incarnate Son of God, by the inestimable worth of His obedience unto death, to merit for His people everlasting bliss on high. Therefore we are told that He has ushered in "a better covenant" with "better promises" (Heb. 8:6). The last Adam has secured, both for God and for His people, more than was lost by the defection of the first Adam.

IV

In the previous chapters we have seen that at the beginning man was "made upright" (Eccles. 7:29), which language necessarily implies a law to which he was conformed in his creation. When anything is made regular or according to rule, the rule itself is obviously presupposed. The law of Adam's being was none other than the eternal and indispensable law of righteousness, the same which was afterwards summed up in the Ten Commandments. Man's uprightness consisted in the universal rectitude of his character, his entire conformity to the nature of his maker. The very nature of man was then fully able to respond to the requirements of God's revealed will, and his response thereto was the righteousness in which he stood.

It was also shown that man was, in Eden, placed on probation: that as a moral being his responsibility was tried out. In other words, he was placed under the moral government of God; and being endowed with a free will, he was capable of both obedience or disobedience—his own free choice being the determining factor. As a creature, he was subject to his creator; as one who was indebted to God for all he was and had, he was under the deepest obligation to love Him with all his heart, and serve Him with all his might; and perfectly was he fitted so to do. Thus created, and thus qualified, it pleased the Lord God to constitute Adam the federal head and legal representative of his race; and as occupying that character and office, God entered into a solemn covenant or agreement with him, promising a reward upon the fulfillment of certain conditions.

It is true that the actual "covenant" does not occur in the Genesis record, in connection with the primordial transaction between God and man, but the facts of the case present all the constituent elements of a covenant. Brief as is the statement furnished in Genesis 2:17, we may clearly discern concentrated in it those eternal principles of truth, righteousness, and justice which are the glory of God's character, and which necessarily regulate His government in all spheres and in all ages. There is an avowal of His authority to govern the creature of His hands, a revelation of His will as to what He requires from the creature, a solemn threat of what would surely follow upon his disobedience, with a clearly implied promise of reward for obedience. One test only was stipulated, by which obedience was to be formally expressed: abstinence from the fruit of the one forbidden tree.

"The covenant of works was in its nature fitted, and designed to give, and did give uninterrupted happiness, as long as its requisitions were observed. This is true throughout the whole moral universe of God, for man is not the only being under its government. It is the law of angels themselves. To their nature, no less to man's while in a state of holiness, it is perfectly adapted. Those of them who 'have kept their first estate,' are conformed perfectly to all its demands. They meet and satisfy them fully by love; fervent love to God, and to all their celestial associates. Heaven is pervaded consequently with the unbroken harmonies of love. And how unspeakably happy! 'The man' said Paul, 'that doeth these things, shall *live* by them' (Rom. 10:5). His bliss is unfading" (R. B. Howell, 1855).

God, then, entered into a covenant with Adam, and all his posterity in him, to the effect that if he obeyed the one command not to eat of the tree of the knowledge of good and evil, he should receive as his reward an indefectibility of holiness and righteousness. Nor was that transaction exceptional in the divine dealings with our race; for God has made covenants with other men, which have vitally affected their posterity: this will appear when we take up His covenant with Noah and Abraham. The compact which the Lord God entered into with Adam is appropriately termed "the covenant of works" not only to distinguish it from the covenant of grace, but also because under it life was promised on condition of perfect obedience, which obedience was to be performed by man in his own creature strength.

We come now to consider *the penal sanction* of the covenant. This is contained in the words "In the day thou eatest thereof thou shalt surely die" (Gen. 2:17). Here was made known the terrible penalty which would most certainly follow upon Adam's disobedience, his violation of the covenant. All the blessings of the covenant would instantly cease. Transgression of God's righteous law would not only forfeit all blessings, but would convert them into so many fountains of wretchedness and woe. The covenant of works provided no mediator, nor any other method of restoration to the purity and bliss which was lost. There was no place given for repentance. All was irrevocably lost. Between the blessing of obedience and the curse of disobedience there was no middle ground. So far as the terms of the covenant of works was concerned, its inexorable sentence was: "The soul that sinneth, it shall die."

"But of the tree of the knowledge of good and evil, thou shalt not eat of it: for in the day that thou eatest thereof thou shalt surely die" (Gen. 2:17). It is to be duly noted what God here threatened was the direct consequence and immediate punishment of sin, to be inflicted only upon the rebellious and disobedient. That death which now seizes fallen man is no mere natural calamity, but a penal infliction. It is not a "debt" which he owes to "nature," but a judicial sentence which is passed upon him by the divine judge. Death has come in because our first parent, our federal head and representative, took of the forbidden fruit, and for no other reason. It was altogether meet to God's authority and holy will that there should be an unmistakable connection between sin and its punishment, so that it is impossible for any sinner to escape the wages of sin, unless another should be paid them in his stead—of which the covenant of works contained no hint.

"But of the tree of the knowledge of good and evil, thou shalt not eat of it: for in the day that thou eatest thereof thou shalt surely die," or, as the margin renders it, "dying thou shalt die." That dread threat was couched in general terms. It was not said, "thou shalt die physical-

ly," nor "thou shalt die spiritually," but simply "thou shalt surely
die." The absence of any modifying adverb shows that the term *death*
is here taken in its widest scope, and is to be defined according to
whatever Scripture elsewhere signifies by that term. It is the very
height of presumption for us to limit *what God has not limited.* Far be
it from us to blunt the sharp point of the divine threatening. The
"dying thou shalt die"—which expresses more accurately and forcibly
the original Hebrew—shows the words are to be taken in their full
emphasis.

First, *corporeal* death, the germs of which are in our bodies from
the beginning of their existence, so that from the moment we draw
our first breath, we begin to die. And how can it be otherwise, seeing
that we are "shapen in iniquity" and "conceived in sin" (Ps. 51:5)!
From birth our physical body is indisposed, and entirely unfitted for
the soul to reside in eternally; so that there must yet be a separation
from it. By that separation the good things of the body, the "pleasures
of sin" on which the soul so much dotes, are at once snatched away;
so that it becomes equally true of each one, "Naked came I out of my
mother's womb [the earth] and naked shall I return thither" (Job
1:21). God intimated this to Adam when He said, "Till thou return
unto the ground: for out of it wast thou taken: for dust thou art, and
unto dust shalt thou return" (Gen. 3:19).

Second, "by death is here understood all that lasting and hard
labour, that great sorrow, all the tedious miseries of this life, by which
life ceases to be *life,* and which are the sad harbingers of certain death.
To these things man is condemned: see Gen. 3:16-19—the whole of
that sentence is founded on the antecedent threatening of Gen. 2:17.
Such miseries Pharaoh called by the name 'death' (Ex. 10:17). David
called his pain and anguish 'the bands (sorrows) of death' (Psa.
116:3): by those 'bands' death binds and fastens man that he may
thrust them into and confine them in his dungeon. As 'life' is not
barely to live, but to be happy; so, 'death' is not to depart this life in a
moment, but rather to languish in a long expectation, dread and
foresight, of certain death, without knowing the time which God has
foreordained" (H. Witsius).

Third, "death" in Scripture also signifies spiritual death, or the
separation of the soul from God. This is what the apostle called "being
alienated from the life of God" (Eph. 4:18), which "life of God"
illuminates, sanctifies, and exhilarates the souls of the regenerate. The
true life of the soul consists of wisdom, pure love, and the rejoicing of
a good conscience. The spiritual death of the soul consists in folly, evil
lustings, and the rackings of an evil conscience. Therefore when
speaking of those who were "alienated from the life of God," the

apostle at once added, "Through the ignorance that is in them, because of the blindness of their heart: who being past feeling have given themselves over unto lasciviousness." Thus, the unregenerate are totally incapacitated for communion with the holy and living God.

"But I would more fully explain the nature of this (spiritual) death. Both living and dead bodies have motion. But a living body moves by *vegetation,* while it is nourished, has the use of its senses, is delighted, and acts with pleasure. Whereas, the dead body moves by *putrifaction* to a state of dissolution, and to the production of loathesome animals. And so in the soul, spiritually alive, there is motion, while it is fed, repasted, and fattened with Divine delights, while it takes pleasure in God and true wisdom; while, by the strength of its love, it is carried to and fixed on that which can sustain the soul and give it a sweet repose. But a dead soul has no feeling; that is, it neither understands truth, nor loves righteousness, but wallows and is spent in the sink of concupiscence, and brings forth the worms of impure thoughts, reasonings and affections" (H. Witsius).

Fourth, *eternal* death is also included in Genesis 2:17. The preludes of this are the terrors of an evil conscience, the soul deprived of all divine consolation, and often an anguished sense of God's wrath, under which it is miserably pressed down. At physical dissolution the soul of the sinner is sent into a place of torments (Luke 16:23-25). At the end of the world, the bodies of the wicked are raised and their souls are united thereto, and after appearing before the great white throne they will be cast into the lake of fire, there to suffer for ever and ever the "due reward of their iniquities." The wages of sin is death, and that the word *death* there involves and includes eternal death is unmistakably plain from the fact that it is placed in direct antithesis with "eternal life": Romans 6:23. The same appears again in Romans 5:21, which verse is the summing up of verses 12-20.

Let us now pause for a moment and review the ground already covered. First, we have seen the favorable and happy state in which Adam was originally created. Second, we have contemplated the threefold law under which he was placed. Third, we have observed that he stood in Eden as the federal head and legal representative of all his posterity. Fourth, we have pointed out that all the constituent elements of a formal covenant are clearly observable in the Genesis record: there were the contracting parties—the Lord God and Adam; there was the stipulation enjoined—obedience; there was the penalty attached—death upon disobedience; there was the necessarily implied promise of reward—an immutable establishment in holiness and an inalienable title to the earthly paradise.

In order to follow out the logical sequence, we should, properly, examine next the *"seal"* of the covenant; that is, the formal symbol and stamp of its ratification; but we will postpone our consideration of that until our next chapter, which will conclude what we have to say upon the Adamic covenant. Instead, we will pass on to *Adam's consent* unto the compact which the Lord God set before him. This may be inferred, first of all, from the very law of his nature: having been made in the image and likeness of God, there was nothing in him contrary to His holy will, nothing to oppose His righteous requirements: so that he *must* have readily attended.

"Adam, being holy, would not refuse to enter into a righteous engagement with his Maker: and being intelligent, would not decline an improvement in his condition" (W. Sledd): an "improvement" which, upon his fulfillment of the terms of the covenant, would have issued in being made immutably holy and happy, so that he would then have had spiritual life as indefectible, passing beyond all point of apostasy and misery. The only other possible alternative to Adam's freely consenting to be a party to the covenant would be his refusal, which is unthinkable in a pure and sinless being. Eve's words to the serpent in Genesis 3:2, 3 make it plain that Adam had given his word not to disobey his maker. We quote from another who has ably handled this point:

"The *voluntary assent* of the parties, which is in every covenant: one party must make the proposition: God proposed the terms as an expression of His will, which is an assent or agreement. God's commanding man not to eat, is His consent. As to man, it has been already observed, he could not without unreasonable opposition to his Creator's will, refuse any terms which the wisdom and benevolence of God would allow Him to proffer. Hence we should conclude, Adam must most cheerfully accede to the terms. But this the more readily, when their nature is inspected—when he should see in them every thing adapted for his advantage, and nothing to his disadvantage.

"The same conclusion we deduce from an inspection of the Scripture history. For 1, there is not a hint at any thing like a refusal on the part of Adam, before the act of violation. The whole history is perfectly consistent with the supposition that he did cheerfully agree. 2. It is evident that Eve thought the command most reasonable and proper. She so expressed herself to the serpent, giving God's commandment as a reason of her abstinence. This information she must have derived from her husband, for she was not created at the time the covenant was given to Adam. We hence infer Adam's *consent*. 3. Adam was, after his sin, abundantly disposed to excuse himself: he cast the blame upon the woman, and indirectly upon God, for giving her to him. Now most assuredly, if Adam could in truth have said, I never *consented* to abstain—I never agreed to the terms proposed—I have broken no pledge—he would have presented this apology or just answer to God; but according to Scripture he offered no such apology. Can any reasonable man want further evidence of his consent? Even this may be had, if he will. 4. Look at the consequences. The penal evils *did* result: sorrow and death *did* ensue; and hence, because God is righteous, we infer the legal relations. The Judge of all the earth would not punish where there is no crime" (Geo. Junkin, 1839).

V

We will now consider the *seal* which the Lord God made upon the covenant into which He entered with the federal head of our race. This is admittedly the most difficult part of our subject, and for that reason, the least understood in most circles today. So widespread is the spiritual ignorance which now prevails that, in many quarters, to speak of "the seal" of a covenant is to employ an unintelligible term. And yet the seal is an intrinsic part and an essential feature in the various covenants which God made. Hence, our treatment of the Adamic covenant would be quite inadequate and incomplete did we fail to give attention to one of the objects which is given a central place in the brief Genesis record. Mysterious as that object appears, light is cast on it by other passages. Oh, that the Holy Spirit may be pleased to guide us into the truth thereon!

"And out of the ground made the Lord God to grow every tree that is pleasant to the sight, and good for food; the tree of life also in the midst of the garden, and the tree of knowledge of good and evil" (Gen. 2:9). First of all, let it be said emphatically that we regard this verse as referring to two real and literal trees: the very fact that we are told they were "pleasant to the sight" obliges us to regard them as tangible and visible entities. In the second place, it is equally obvious from what is said of them that those two trees were extraordinary ones, peculiar to themselves. They were placed "in the midst of the garden"; and from what is recorded in connection with them in Genesis 3, it is clear that they differed radically from all the other trees in Eden. In the third place, we cannot escape the conclusion that those literal trees were vested with a symbolical significance, being designed by God to give instructions to Adam, in the same way as others of His positive institutions now do unto us.

"It hath pleased the blessed and almighty God, in every economy of His covenants, to confirm, by some sacred symbols, the certainty of His promises and at the same time to remind man in covenant with Him of his duty" (H. Witsius). Examples of that fact or illustrations of this principle may be seen in the *rainbow* by which God ratified the covenant into which He entered with Noah (Gen. 9:12, 13), and *circumcision* which was the outward sign of confirmation of the covenant entered into with Abraham (Gen. 17:9, 11). From these cases, then, we may perceive the propriety of the definition given by A. A. Hodge: "A seal of a covenant is an outward visible sign, appointed by God as a pledge of His faithfulness, and as an earnest of the blessings promised in the covenant." In other words, the seal of the covenant is an external symbol, ratifying the validity of its terms, as the signatures of two witnesses seal a man's will.

Now as we have shown in previous chapters, the language of Genesis 2:17 not only pronounced a curse upon the disobedient partaking of the fruit of the tree of knowledge of good and evil, but by necessary implication it announced a blessing upon the obedient noneating thereof. The curse was death, with all that that involved and entailed; the blessing was a continuance and confirmation in all the felicity which man in his pristine innocency enjoyed. In His infinite condescension the Lord God was pleased to confirm or seal the terms of His covenant with Adam—contained in Genesis 2:17—by a symbolic and visible emblem ratifying the same; as He did to Noah by the rainbow, and to Abraham by circumcision. With Adam, this confirmatory symbol consisted of "the tree of life" in the midst of the garden.

A seal, then, is a divine institution of which it is the design *to signify the blessings* promised in the covenant, and to give assurance of them to those by whom its terms have been fulfilled. The very name of this symbolic (yet real) tree at once intimated its design: it was "the tree *of life.*" Not, as some have erroneously supposed, that its fruit had the virtue of communicating physical immortality—as though anything material could do that. Such a gross and carnal conception is much more closely akin to the Jewish and Mohammedan fables, than to a sober interpretation of spiritual things. No, just as its companion (yet contrast) was to Adam "the tree of the knowledge of good and evil"—of "good" while he preserved his integrity and of "evil" as soon as he disobeyed his maker—so this other tree was both the symbol and pledge of that spiritual life which was inseparably connected with his obedience.

"It was chiefly intended to be a sign and seal to Adam, assuring him of the continuance of life and happiness, even to immortality and everlasting bliss, through the grace and favour of his Maker, upon

condition of his perseverance in his state of innocency and obedience"
(M. Henry). So far from its being a natural means of prolonging
Adam's physical life, it was a sacramental pledge of endless life and
felicity being secured to him as the unmerited reward of fidelity. It
was therefore an object for faith to feed upon—the physical eating to
adumbrate the spiritual. Like all other signs and seals, this one was not
designed to confer the promised blessing, but was a divine pledge given
to Adam's faith to encourage the expectation thereof. It was a visible
emblem to bring to remembrance what God had promised.

It is the fatal error of Romanists and other ritualists that signs and
seals actually convey grace of themselves. Not so: only as faith is
operative in the use of them are they means of blessing. Romans 4:11
helps us at this point: "And he received the *sign* of circumcision, a *seal*
of the righteousness of the faith which he had yet being uncircumcised; that he might be the father of all them that believe, though they
be not circumcised; that righteousness might be imputed unto them
also." Unto Abraham, circumcision was both a sign and a seal: a sign
that he had previously been justified, and a seal (pledge) that God
would make good the promises which He had addressed to his faith.
The rite, instead of conferring anything, only confirmed what Abra
ham already had. Unto Abraham, circumcision was the guarantee that
the righteousness of faith which he had (before he was circumcised) should come upon or be imputed unto believing Gentiles.

Thus as the rainbow was the confirmatory sign and seal of the
covenant promises God had made to Noah, as circumcision was the
sign and seal of the covenant promises God had made to Abraham, so
the tree of life was the sign and seal of the covenant promises He had
made to Adam. It was appointed by God as the pledge of His
faithfulness, and as an earnest of the blessings which continued fidelity would secure. Let it be expressly pointed out that, in keeping with
the distinctive character of this present antitypical dispensation—when
the substance has replaced the shadows—though baptism and the
Lord's Supper are divinely appointed ordinances, yet they are not
seals unto the Christian. The seal of "the new covenant" is *the Holy
Spirit Himself* (see II Cor. 1:22; Eph. 1:13; 4:30)! The gift of the
blessed Spirit is the earnest or guaranty of our future inheritance.

The references to the "tree of life" in the New Testament confirm
what has been said in the above paragraphs. In Revelation 2:7 we hear
the Lord Jesus saying, "To him that overcometh will I give to eat of
the tree of life, which is in the midst of the paradise of God." Those
words express a promise of eternal life—the perfection and consummation of holiness and happiness—couched in such terms as obviously
allude to Genesis 2:9. This is the first of seven promises made by

Christ to the overcomer of Revelation 2 and 3, showing that this immutable gift (eternal life) is the foundation of all the other inestimable blessings which Christ's victory has secured as the inheritance of those who by His grace are faithful unto death. Each victorious saint shall eat of "the tree of life"; that is, be unchangeably established in a state of eternal felicity and bliss.

"And the Lord God said, behold, the man is become as one of us, to know good and evil: and now, lest he put forth his hand, and take also of the tree of life, and eat, and live for ever: Therefore the Lord God sent him forth from the garden of Eden, to till the ground from whence he was taken. So he drove out the man; and he placed at the east of the garden of Eden Cherubims, and a flaming sword, which turned every way, to keep the way of the tree of life" (Gen. 3:22-24). This is the passage which carnal literalists have wrested to the perversion of the symbolical and spiritual significance of the seal of the covenant. By God's words "lest he put forth his hand and take also of the tree of life, and eat, and live for ever," they conclude that the property of that tree was to bestow physical immortality. We trust the reader will bear with us for mentioning such an absurdity; yet, inasmuch as it has obtained a wide hearing, a few words exposing its fallacy seem called for.

It was not the mere eating of the fruit of the tree of the knowledge of good and evil which was able of itself to impart any knowledge; rather was it that by taking of its fruit contrary to God's command, Adam and Eve obtained experimental acquaintance with the knowledge of evil *in themselves,* that is, by experiencing the bitterness of God's curse, as previously through their obedient abstinence, they had a personal knowledge of good, that is, by experiencing the sweetness of God's blessing. In like manner, the mere eating of the tree of life could no more bestow physical immortality than feeding upon the heavenly manna immortalized the Israelites in the wilderness. Both of those trees were symbolical institutions, and by the sight of them Adam was reminded of the solemn yet blessed contents of the covenant of which they were the sign and the seal.

To suppose that the Lord God was apprehensive that our fallen parents would now eat of the tree of life and continue forever their earthly existence, is the very height of absurdity; for His sentence of death had already fallen upon them. What, then, did His words connote? First, had Adam remained obedient to God, had he been confirmed in a state of holiness and happiness, spiritual life would have become his inalienable possession—the divine pledge of which was this sacramental tree. But now that he had broken the covenant, he had forfeited all right to its blessings. It must be carefully borne in mind that by his fall Adam lost far more than physical immortality. Second, God banished Adam from Eden "lest" the poor, blinded, deceived man—now open to every error—should suppose that by eating of the tree of life, he might regain what he had irrevocably lost.

"So he drove out the man; and he placed at the east of the garden of Eden Cherubims, and a flaming sword, which turned every way, to keep the way of the tree of life" (Gen. 3:24). Unspeakably solemn is this: thereby our first parent was prevented from profanely appropriating what did not belong to him, and thereby he was made the more conscious of the full extent of his wretchedness. His being driven out from the presence of the tree of life, and the guarding of the way thereto by the flaming sword, plainly intimated his irrevocable doom. Contrary to the prevailing idea, I believe that Adam was eternally lost. He is mentioned only once again in Genesis, where we read: "And Adam lived an hundred and thirty years, and begat a son in *his own likeness*" (5:3). He is solemnly *missing* from the witnesses of faith in Hebrews 11! He is uniformly presented in the New Testament as the fountainhead of death, as Christ is of life (Rom. 5:12-19; I Cor. 15:22).

In its deeper significance, the tree of life was an emblem and type of Christ. "The tree of life signified the Son of God, not indeed as He is Christ and Mediator (that consideration being peculiar to *another* covenant), but inasmuch as He is the life of man in every condition, and the fountain of all happiness. And how well was it spoken by one who said, that it became God from the first to represent, by an outward sign, *that person* whom He loves, and for whose glory He has made and does make all things; that man even then might acknowledge Him as such. Wherefore Christ is called 'the Tree of Life' (Rev. 22:2). What indeed He now is by His merit and efficacy, as Mediator, He would have always been as the Son of God; for, as *by Him* man was created and obtained an animal life, so, in like manner, he would have been transformed by Him and blessed with a heavenly life. Nor could He have been the life of the sinner, as Mediator, unless He had likewise been the life of man in his holy state, *as God;* having life in Himself, and being life itself" (H. Witsius).

Here, then, we believe was the first symbolical foreshadowment of Christ, set before the eyes of Adam and Eve in their sinless state; and a most suitable and significant emblem of Him was it. Let us consider these prefigurements.

1. Its very name obviously pointed to the Lord Jesus, of whom we read, "In him was life, and the life was the light of men" (John 1:4). Those words are to be taken in their widest latitude. All life is resident in Christ—natural life, spiritual life, resurrection life, eternal life. "For

to me to live is Christ" (Phil. 1:21) declares the saint: he lives *in* Christ (II Cor. 5:17), he lives *on* Christ (John 6:50-57), he shall for all eternity live *with* Christ (I Thess. 4:17).

2. The position it occupied: "in the midst of the garden" (Gen. 2:9). Note how this detail is emphasized in Revelation 2:7, "in the midst of the paradise of God," and "in the midst of the street" (Rev. 22:2), and compare "in the midst of the elders stood a Lamb" (Rev. 5:6). Christ is the center of heaven's glory and blessedness.

3. In its sacramental significance: In Eden the symbolic tree of life stood as the seal of the covenant, as the pledge of God's faithfulness, as the ratification of His promises to Adam. So of the antitype we read, "For all the promises of God in him [Christ] are yea, and in him [Christ] Amen, unto the glory of God by us" (II Cor. 1:20). Yes, it is in Christ that all the promises of the everlasting covenant are sealed and secured.

4. Its attractiveness: "pleasant to the sight and good for food" (Gen. 2:9). Superlatively is that true of the Savior: to the redeemed He is "fairer than the children of men" (Ps. 45:2), yea, "altogether lovely" (Song of Sol. 5:16). And when the believer is favored with a season of intimate communion with Him, what cause he has to say, "His fruit was sweet to my taste" (Song of Sol. 2:3).

5. From the symbolical tree of life the apostate rebel was excluded (Gen. 3:24); likewise from the antitypical tree of life shall every finally impenitent sinner be separated: "Who shall be punished with everlasting destruction *from the presence* of the Lord, and from the glory of His power" (II Thess. 1:9).

"Blessed are they that do his commandments, that they may have right to the tree of life, and may enter in through the gates into the city" (Rev. 22:14). Here is the final mention of the tree of life in Scripture—in marked and blessed contrast from what is recorded in Genesis 3:22-24. There we behold the disobedient rebel, under the curse of God, divinely excluded from the tree of life; for under the old covenant no provision was made for man's restoration. But here we see a company under the new covenant, pronounced "blessed" by God, having been given the spirit of obedience, that they might have the right to enjoy the tree of life for all eternity. That "right" is threefold: the right which divine promise has given them (Heb. 5:9), the right of personal meetness (Heb. 12:14), and the right of evidential credentials (James 2:21-25). None but those who, having been made new creatures in Christ, do His commandments, will enter the heavenly Jerusalem and be eternally regaled by the tree of life.

VI

This primordial compact or covenant of works was that agreement into which the Lord God entered with Adam as the federal head and representative of the entire human family. It was made with him in a state of innocency, holiness, and righteousness. The terms of that covenant consisted in perfect and continuous obedience on man's part, and the promise of confirming him in immutable holiness and happiness on God's part. A test was given whereby his obedience or disobedience should be evidenced. That test consisted of a single positive ordinance: abstinence from the fruit of the tree of the knowledge of good and evil, so named because so long as Adam remained dutiful and faithful, he enjoyed that inestimable "good" which issued from communion with his maker, and because as soon as he disobeyed he tasted the bitter "evil" which followed the loss of communion with Him.

As we have seen in the previous chapters, all the essential elements of a formal covenant between God and Adam are clearly to be seen in the Genesis record. A requirement was made—obedience; a penal sanction was attached—death as the penalty of disobedience; a reward was promised upon his obedience—confirmation in life. Adam consented to its terms; the whole was divinely sealed by the tree of life—so called because it was the outward sign of that life promised in the covenant, from which Adam was excluded because of his apostasy, and to which the redeemed are restored by the last Adam (Rev. 2:7). Thus Scripture presents all the prime features of a covenant as co-existing in that constitution under which our first parent was originally placed.

Adam wickedly presumed to eat the fruit of the forbidden tree, and incurred the awful guilt of violating the covenant. In his sin there was a complication of many crimes: in Romans 5 it is called the "offence," "disobedience," "transgression." Adam was put to the test of whether the will of God was sacred in his eyes, and he fell by preferring his own will and way. He failed to love God with all his heart; he had contempt for His high authority; he disbelieved His holy veracity; he deliberately and presumptuously defied Him. Hence, at a later date, in the history of Israel, God said, "But they *like Adam* have *transgressed the covenant,* they have dealt treacherously against me" (Hos. 6:7, margin). Even Darby (notes on Hosea, in *Synopsis,* vol. 2, p. 472) acknowledged, "It should be rendered 'But they like Adam have transgressed the covenant.'"

It is to this divine declaration in Hosea 6:7 the apostle makes reference, when of Adam he declares that he was "the figure of him that was to come." Let it be duly noted that Adam is not there viewed in his creation state simply, but rather as he is related to an offspring whose case was included in his own. As the vicar of his race Adam disobeyed the Eden statute in their room and stead, precisely as Christ, the "last Adam" (I Cor. 15:45), obeyed the moral law as the representative of His people in their room and stead. "By *one man* sin entered into the world" (Rom. 5:12). This is a remarkable statement calling for the closest attention. Eve sinned too; she sinned *before* Adam did; then why are we not told that "by *one woman* sin entered into the world"?—the more so seeing that she is, equally with Adam, a root of propagation.

Only one answer is possible to the above question: because Adam was the one public person or federal head that represented us, and not she. Adam was the legal representative of Eve as well as of his posterity, for she was taken out of him. Remarkably is this confirmed by the historical record of Genesis 3: upon Eve's eating of the forbidden fruit no change was evidenced; but as soon as Adam partook, "the eyes of them *both* were opened, and they knew that they were naked" (Gen. 3:7). This means that they were instantly conscious of the loss of innocency, and were ashamed of their woeful condition. The eyes of a convicted conscience were opened, and they perceived their sin and its awful consequences: the sense of their bodily nakedness only adumbrating their spiritual loss.

Not only was it by Adam (rather than by Eve) that sin entered into the world, "the judgment was by *one* [offence] to condemnation, but the free gift is of many offences unto justification" (Rom. 5:16). The fact that Eve is entirely omitted from Romans 5:12-19 shows that it is the guilt of our federal head being imputed to us which is there in view, and not the depravity of nature which is imparted; for corruption has been directly derived through her as much as from Adam. The fact that it was by Adam's one offense that condemnation has come upon all his posterity, shows that his subsequent sins are not imputed to us; for by his original trangression he lost the high honor and privilege conferred upon him: in the covenant being broken, he ceased to be a public person, the federal head of the race.

Man's defection from his primordial state was purely voluntary and from the unconstrained choice of his own mutable and self-determining will. Adam was "without excuse." By eating of the forbidden fruit, he broke, first, the law of his very being, violating his own nature, which bound him unto loving allegiance to his maker: self now took the place of God. Second, he flouted the law of God, which requires perfect and unremitting obedience to the moral Governor of the world: self had now usurped the throne of God in his heart. Third, in trampling upon the positive ordinance under which he was placed, he broke the covenant, preferring to take his stand alongside of his fallen wife.

"Every man at his best estate is altogether vanity" (Ps. 39:5). Thus was Adam. In full-grown manhood, with every faculty perfect, amid ideal surroundings, he rejected the good and chose the evil. He was not deceived: Scripture declares he was not—I Timothy 2:14. He knew well what he was doing. "Deliberately he wrecked himself and us. Deliberately he jumped the precipice. Deliberately he murdered unnumbered generations. Like many another who has loved 'not wisely but too well,' he would not lose his Eve. He chose her rather than God. He determined he would have her if he went to Hell with her" (G. S. Bishop). Direful were the consequences: the death sentence fell upon Adam the day in which he sinned, though for the sake of his posterity the full execution of it was delayed.

As Romans 5:12 declares, "Wherefore as by one man [the first man, the father of our race] sin [guilt, criminality, condemnation] entered [as a solemn accuser in the witness stand] into the world [not into "the universe," for that had previously been defiled by the rebellion of Satan and his angels; but the world of fallen humanity], and death [as a judicial infliction] by sin [the original offense], and so death [as the divine punishment] passed [as the penal sentence from the Judge of all the earth], upon all men, [none, not even infants, being exempted], in whom [the correct rendering—see margin] all have sinned"—that is, sinned in the "one man," the federal head of the race, the legal representative of the "all men"; note, not all now "sin," nor all are inherently "sinful" (though sadly true), but "in whom all have sinned" in Eden.

Direful and dreadful as was the outcome of the Adamic covenant, yet we may, with awe, perceive and admire the divine wisdom in the same. Had God permitted and enabled Adam to stand, all his posterity had been eternally happy. Adam had then been in a very real sense their savior, and while enjoying everlasting bliss, all his posterity would have exclaimed, "For all this we are indebted to our first parent." Ah, what anointed eye can fail to discern that *that* would have been far too great a glory for any finite creature to have borne. Only the last Adam was entitled to and capable of sustaining such an honor. Thus, the first man, who was of the earth, earthy, must fall, so as to make way for the second man, who is "the Lord from heaven."

It must also be pointed out that, in taking this way of staining human pride (involving the dreadful fall of the king of our race), displaying His own infinite wisdom, and securing the glory of His beloved Son (so that in all things He has "the pre-eminence"), God made not the slightest infraction of His justice. In decreeing and permitting Adam's fall, with the consequent imputation of the guilt of his offense unto all his posterity, God has wronged no man. This needs to be emphatically insisted upon and plainly pointed out, lest some in their blatant haughtiness should be guilty of charging the Most High with unfairness. God is inflexibly righteous, and all His ways are right and just. Nor is the one which we are now considering any exception; and this will be seen, once it is rightly understood.

In saying that the guilt of Adam's offense is imputed to all his posterity, we do not mean the human race is now suffering for something in which they had no part, that innocent creatures are being condemned for the act of another which cannot rightly be laid to their account. Let it be clearly understood that God punishes none for Adam's personal sin, but only for his own sin in Adam. The whole human race had a federal standing in Adam. Not only was each of us seminally in his loins the day God created him, but each of us was legally represented by him when God instituted the covenant of works. Adam acted and transacted in that covenant not merely as a private being, but as a public person; not simply as a single individual, but as the surety and sponsor of his race. Nor is it lawful for us to call into question the meetness of that arrangement: all God's works are perfect, all His ways are ordered by infinite wisdom and righteousness.

Of necessity the creature is subject to the Creator, and his loyalty and fealty must be put to the proof. In the nature of the case only two alternatives were possible: the human family must either be placed on probation in the person of a responsible and suitable head and representative, or each individual member must enter upon his probation for himself. Once again we quote the words of Bishop: "The race must have either stood in a full-grown man, with a full-orbed intellect, or stood as babies, each entering his probation in the twilight of self-consciousness, each deciding his destiny before his eyes were half-opened to what it all meant. How much better would that have been? How much more just? But could it not have been some other way? There was no other way. It was either the baby or it was the perfect, well-equipped, all-calculating man—the man who saw and comprehended everything. That man was Adam."

The simplest and most satisfactory way of reconciling with human reason the federal constitution which was given to Adam, is to recognize it was of divine appointment. God cannot do what is wrong. It must therefore have been right. The principle of representation is inseparable from the very constitution of human society. The father is the legal representative of his children during their minority, so that what he does binds his family. The political heads of a nation represent the people, so that their declarations of war or treaties of peace bind the whole commonwealth. This principle is so fundamental that it cannot be set aside: human affairs could not move nor society exist without it. Founded in man's nature by the wisdom of God, we are compelled to recognize it; and being of *His* appointment we dare not call into question its rightness. If it was unjust for God to impute to us Adam's guilt, it must equally have been so to impart to us his depravity; but seeing God has righteously done the latter, we must vindicate Him for doing the former.

The very fact that we go on breaking the covenant of works and disobeying the law of God, shows our oneness with Adam under that covenant. Let that fact be duly weighed by those who are inclined to be captious. Our complicity with Adam in his rebellion is evidenced every time we sin against God. Instead of challenging the justice which has charged to our account the guilt of the first human transgression, let us seek grace to repudiate Adam's example, standing out in opposition to his insubordination by gladly taking upon us the easy yoke of God's commandments. Finally, let it again be pointed out that if we were ruined *by another*, Christians are redeemed *by Another*. By the principle of representation we were lost, and by the same principle of representation—Christ transacting for us as our surety and sponsor—we are saved.

In what sense is the covenant of works abrogated? and in what sense is it still in force? We cannot do better than subjoin the answers of one of the ablest theologians of the last century. "This Covenant having been broken by Adam, not one of his natural descendants is ever able to fulfil its conditions, and Christ having fulfilled all of its conditions in behalf of all His own people, salvation is offered now on the condition of faith. In *this* sense the Covenant of Works having been fulfilled by the second Adam is henceforth abrogated under the Gospel.

"Nevertheless, since it is founded upon the principles of immutable justice, it still binds all men who have not fled to the refuge offered in the righteousness of Christ. It is still true that 'he that doeth these things shall live by them,' and 'the soul that sinneth it shall die.' This law in *this* sense remains, and in consequence of the unrighteousness of men condemns them, and in consequence of their absolute inability to fulfil it, it acts as a schoolmaster to bring them to Christ. For he having fulfilled alike its condition wherein Adam failed, and its penalty which Adam incurred, He has become the end of this covenant for righteousness to every one that believeth, who in Him is regarded and treated as having fulfilled the covenant, and merited its promised reward" (A. A. Hodge).

It only remains for us now to point out wherein the Adamic covenant adumbrated the everlasting covenant. While it be true that the covenant of works and the covenant of grace are diametrically opposed in their character—the one being based upon the principle of do and live, the other on live and do—yet there are some striking points of agreement between them.

That engagement which the Father entered into with the Mediator before the foundation of the world was foreshadowed in Eden in the following respects.

1. Adam, the one with whom the covenant was made, entered this world in a manner that none other ever did. Without being begotten by a human father, he was miraculously produced by God; so with Christ.

2. None but Adam of the human family entered this world with a pure constitution and holy nature; so was it with Christ.

3. His wife was taken out of him, so that he could say, "This is now bone of my bones, and flesh of my flesh" (Gen. 2:23); of Christ's bride it is declared, "We are members of his body, of his flesh, and of his bones" (Eph. 5:30).

4. Adam voluntarily took his place alongside of his fallen wife. He was not deceived (I Tim. 2:14), but had such a love for Eve that he could not see her perish alone; just so Christ voluntarily took on Himself the sins of His people (cf. Eph. 5:25).

5. In consequence of this, Adam fell beneath the curse of God; in like manner Christ bore the curse of God (cf. Gal. 3:13).

6. The father of the human family was their federal head; so is Christ, the "last Adam," the federal head of His people.

7. What Adam did is imputed to the account of all those whom he represented; the same is true of Christ. "For as by one man's disobedience many were made sinners, so by the obedience of one shall many be made righteous" (Rom. 5:19).

PART THREE

The Noahic Covenant

I

Noah is the connecting link between "the world that then was," which "being overflowed with water, perished," and the earth which now is "reserved unto fire against the day of judgment and perdition of ungodly men" (II Peter 3:6, 7). He lived upon both, was preserved from the awful judgment which swallowed up the former, and given dominion over the latter in its pristine state. A period of sixteen centuries intervened between the covenant of works which God entered into with Adam and the covenant of grace which He made with Noah. So far as Scripture informs us, no other covenant was instituted by the Lord during that interval. There were divine revelations, divine promises and precepts—in fact, the antediluvians enjoyed very much more light from heaven than they are commonly credited with. But during those early centuries, where grace abounded, sin did much more abound, until "God looked upon the earth, and, behold, it was corrupt; for all flesh had corrupted his way upon the earth" (Gen. 6:12).

"The longsuffering of God waited in the days of Noah, while the ark was a preparing" (I Peter 3:20), and "space" was granted the ungodly to turn from their wickedness. Enoch prophesied, "Behold, the Lord cometh with ten thousands of his saints, to execute judgment upon all, and to convince all that are ungodly among them of all their ungodly deeds, which they have ungodly committed, and of their hard speeches which ungodly sinners have spoken against him" (Jude 14, 15). Noah too was "a preacher of righteousness" (II Peter 2:5), and therefore must have warned his hearers that "the wrath of God is revealed from heaven against all ungodliness and unrighteousness of men, who hold the truth in unrighteousness" (Rom. 1:18). But it was all to no avail: "Because sentence against an evil work is not executed

65

speedily, therefore the heart of the sons of men is fully set in them to do evil" (Eccles. 8:11). The evil continued to increase, till the divine patience was thoroughly exhausted. The threatened punishment came, the ungodly were swept from the earth, and the first great period in the world's history closed in judgment.

The facts briefly stated above require to be carefully kept in mind, for they throw not a little light upon the covenant which the Lord God made with Noah. They explain the reason for the transaction itself, and impart at least some aid toward a right conception of the particular form it took. The background of that covenant was divine judgment: drastic, unsparing, effectual. Every individual of the ungodly race perished: the great Deluge completely relieved the earth of their presence and crimes. In due time the water subsided, and Noah and his family came from their place of refuge to people the earth afresh. It is scarcely possible for us to form any adequate conception of the feelings of Noah on this occasion. The terrible and destructive visitation, in which the hand of God was so manifest, must have given him an impression of the exceeding sinfulness of sin and of the ineffable holiness and righteousness of God such as he had not previously entertained.

"In one respect the world seemed to have suffered material loss by the visitation of the deluge. Along with the agents and instruments of evil there had also been swept away by it the emblems of grace and hope—paradise with its tree of life and its cherubim of glory. We can conceive Noah and his household, when they first left the ark, looking around with melancholy feelings on the position they now occupied, not only as being the sole survivors of a numerous offspring, but also as being themselves bereft of the sacred memorials which bore evidence of a happy past, and exhibited the pledge of a yet happier future. An important link of communion with Heaven, it might well have seemed, was broken by the change thus brought through the deluge on the world" (P. Fairbairn).

As I pointed out many years ago in my *Gleanings in Genesis*, the contents of Genesis 4, though exceedingly terse, intimate that from the time of Adam onward, there was a specific place where God was to be worshiped. When we are told in verses 3 and 4 that Cain and Abel "*brought* an offering unto the Lord," the implication is clear that they came to some particular location of His appointing. When we read that Abel brought "the firstling of his flock *and the fat thereof*," we cannot escape the conclusion that there was an altar where the victim must be offered and upon which its fat must be burned. These necessary inferences receive clear corroboration in the words of verse 16, "And Cain *went out from* the presence of the Lord," which can hardly mean less than that he was formally pro-

hibited from the place where the presence of Jehovah was symbolically manifest. That place of worship appears to have been located at
the east of the Garden of Eden.

In their commentary on Genesis, Jamieson, Fausset, and Brown
translate the last verse of chapter 3 as follows: "And he [God] dwelt
at the east of the Garden of Eden between the Cherubim, as a
Shekinah [a fire tongue or fire sword] to keep open the way to the
tree of life." The same thought is presented in the Jerusalem Targum.
Thus it would seem, that when man was excluded from the garden,
God established a mercy-seat, protected by cherubim, the fire tongue
or sword being the emblem of His presence, and whosoever would
worship Him must approach that mercy-seat with a bloody sacrifice
We may add that the Hebrew word "shaken," which in Genesis 3:24 is
rendered "placed," is defined in Young's concordance "to tabernacle"; eighty-three times in the Old Testament it is translated "to
dwell," as in Exodus 25:8, and so forth.

The signal and sovereign mercy which God had displayed toward
Noah must have deeply affected him. He would be strongly constrained to give some sweet expression to the overwhelming emotions
of his heart. Accordingly, his very first act on taking possession of the
new earth was to engage in a service of solemn worship: "And Noah
builded an altar unto the Lord: and took of every clean beast, and of
every clean fowl, and offered burnt offerings on the altar" (Gen.
8:20). Nothing could have been more becoming and appropriate: it
was an acknowledgment of his deep obligations to the Lord, an
expression of gratitude for the rich grace shown him, an intimation of
his sense of personal unworthiness, an exercise of faith in the promised Seed through whom alone divine blessings were conferred, and an
avowal of his determination to consecrate himself to God and walk
before Him in humble obedience.

It was in connection with this act of worship that the Lord God
now entered into a covenant with the new head of the race; but before
examining its terms, let us further ponder the circumstances in which
Noah now found himself, and try to form some idea of the thoughts
which must then have exercised his mind. "However remarkable the
deliverance he had experienced, whatever the conclusions he might
have been warranted to draw from it in regard to the certainty of the
Divine favour towards himself, and however ardent his gratitude in the
view of the great mercy of which he had been the recipient, he was
still a man, and his novel situation could hardly fail to awaken anxiety
and apprehension on several distinct grounds. He and his family were
few in number, and with very slender means of shelter and defense in
their reach. His condition was far from secure.

"Although the natural disposition of the animals preserved with him in the ark had been by Divine power brought under restraint, he could not be ignorant that, when again left at large, their natural tempers and the instinctive ferocity of some of them would be resumed; and multiplying, in a more rapid ratio than his own family, he might probably have distrusted his ability to cope with them, and might have anticipated the likelihood of perishing before their destructive violence. He knew, too, that the heart of man was full of evil, and that however his naturally bad propensities may have been awed by the fearful catastrophe from which he had recently escaped, the effect of it was not likely to be lasting; the time he might well fear would come—and that at no distant period—when the sinful tendencies of the heart would acquire strength, would be excited by temptation, and soon issue in the most disastrous consequences.

"He must have had a distinct and painful remembrance of those sins of lawlessness and violence with which he had been familiar in the old world. He might reasonably dread their repetition, and look forward to times when human life would be held cheap, and when wanton passion would not scruple to sacrifice it in the furtherance of its selfish purposes, unrestrained by any competent authority, and only feebly checked by the dread of revenge. The prospect would have been anything but cheering, and it cannot be thought surprising that he should have contemplated it with feelings of concern and dismay. He could form his views of the future simply from what he knew of the past, and his memory could recall little but what was painful and distressing" (John Kelly, 1861).

But more; Noah had not only witnessed the outbreakings of human depravity in its worst forms, he had also seen the failure of all the religious means employed to restrain the same. Outside of his own little family, the worship of God had entirely ceased, the preaching of His servants was completely disregarded, and profligacy and violence universally prevailed. Even his building of the ark—"by the which he condemned the world" (Heb. 11:7)—had no effect upon the wicked. The divine warnings were openly flouted, until the Flood came and swept them all away. Nor had Noah any reason now to believe that human nature had undergone any radical change for the better, or that sin had been eradicated from the hearts of the few survivors of the Deluge. As Noah reflected upon the past, his anticipations of the future must have been anxious and gloomy.

What assurance could he have that the evil propensities of fallen men would not again break out in works just as heinous as any performed by those who had found a watery grave? Would not men still be impatient against divine restraints, and treat the divine warnings with reckless contempt? Were such fears realized, should the corruption of the human heart once more develop in enormities and unlimited crimes, then what else could be expected than a repetition of the judgment which he had just survived? And where could such a recurrence of crime and punishment end? Did there not seem but one likely answer: the Almighty, in His righteous indignation, would utterly exterminate a guilty race which refused to be reclaimed. Such fears would not be the bogies of unwarrantable pessimism, but the natural and logical conclusions to be drawn from what had already transpired upon the theater of this earth. It is only by thus entering into the exercises of Noah's heart that we can really appreciate the pertinency of that assurance which Jehovah now gave him.

But as we endeavor to follow the thoughts which must have presented themselves to our patriarch's mind, we must not overlook one bright ray of comfort which doubtless did much to relieve the darkness of his trepidations. When God had declared unto Noah, "And, behold, I, even I, do bring a flood of waters upon the earth, to destroy all flesh, wherein is the breath of life, from under heaven, and every thing that is in the earth shall die," He also added, *"But with thee will I establish my covenant"* (Gen. 6:17, 18). That gracious promise provided a resting place for his poor heart during the dreary days and months when he had been shut up in the ark, and must also have imparted some cheer as he now stood upon the judgment-swept and desolate earth. Yet, who that has any personal experience of the fierce assaults made by carnal reasonings (unbelief) can doubt but what Noah's faith now met with a painful conflict as it sought to withstand the influence of gloom and anxiety.

Some readers may consider that we have gone beyond due bounds in what has been said above, and that we have drawn too much upon our own imagination. But Scripture says, "As in water face answereth to face, so *the heart of man to man*" (Prov. 27:17). How had you felt, dear reader, had you been in Noah's place? What had been my thoughts, had I been circumstanced as he was? Would we have had no such fears as those we have sought to describe? Had we anticipated the unknown future without any such dark forebodings? Could we have passed through such a fearful ordeal, and have returned to an earth from which the last of our former companions had been swept away, without wondering if the next storm of divine judgment would not quite complete its awful work? Would we, only eight all told, have been quite confident that the wild beasts would leave us unmolested? Why, it is just this very mental background which enables us to appreciate the tender mercy in what God now said unto Noah.

"And God blessed Noah, and his sons, and said unto them, Be fruitful, and multiply, and replenish the earth. And the fear of you and dread of you [why such repetition, but for the sake of emphasis?] shall be upon every beast of the earth, and upon every fowl of the air, upon all that moveth upon the earth, and upon all the fishes of the sea; into your hand are they delivered. Every moving thing that liveth shall be meat for you; even as the green herb have I given you all things. But flesh with the life thereof, which is the blood thereof, shall ye not eat. . . . And God spake unto Noah, and to his sons with him, saying, And I, behold, I establish my covenant with you, and with your seed after you; And with every living creature that is with you, of the fowl, of the cattle, and of every beast of the earth with you; from all that go out of the ark, to every beast of the earth. And I will establish my covenant with you; neither shall all flesh be cut off any more by the waters of a flood, neither shall there any more be a flood to destroy the earth" (Gen. 9:1-4, 8-11). What does such language imply? What fears were such gracious declarations designed to calm? What other conclusions can logically be drawn from these verses than those that we have sketched in the preceding paragraphs? To me, at least, an endeavor to place myself in Noah's position and follow out the thoughts most likely to engage his mind, has caused me to admire as never before the suitability of the divine revelation then given to Noah.

That which we have assayed to do in this first chapter on the Noahic covenant has been to indicate its background, the occasion of it, and why it took the particular form it did. Just as the various Messianic prophecies, given by God at different times and at wide intervals, were suited to the local occasions when they were first made, so it was in the different renewals of His covenant of grace. Each of those renewals—unto Abraham, Moses, David and so forth— adumbrated some special feature of the everlasting covenant into which God had entered with the Mediator; but the immediate circumstances of each of those favored men molded, or gave form to, each particular feature of the eternal agreement which was severally shadowed forth unto them. We trust that the reader will now the better perceive the reasons why God gave unto Noah the particular statements recorded in Genesis 9.

II

Having contemplated the occasion when the Lord God entered into covenant with Noah, the unspeakably solemn circumstances which formed its background, we are now almost ready to turn our attention to the covenant itself and examine its terms. The covenants which the Lord established at successive intervals with different parties were substantially one, embracing in the main the same promises and receiving similar confirmation. The Sinaitic covenant—although it possessed peculiar features which distinguished it from all others—was no exception. They were all of them revelations of God's gracious purpose, exhibited at first in an obscure form, but unfolding according to an obvious law of progress: each renewal adding something to what was previously known, so that the path of the just was as the shining light, which shone more and more unto the perfect day, when the shadows were displaced by the substance itself.

We are not to suppose that the divine promises, of which the covenant was the expression and confirmation, were not previously known. The antecedent history shows otherwise. The declaration made by Jehovah to the serpent in Genesis 3:15, while it announced his doom, clearly intimated mercy and deliverance unto the woman's "seed"—an expression which is by no means to be restricted to Christ personally, but which pertains to Christ mystically, that is, to the head *and* His body, the church. The divine institution of sacrifices opened a wide door of hope to those who were convicted of their sinful and lost condition by nature, as the recorded case of Abel clearly shows (Heb. 11:4). The spiritual history of Enoch, who walked with God and before his translation received testimony that he pleased Him (Heb. 11:5), is a further evidence that the very earliest of the saints were blessed with considerable spiritual light, and were granted an insight into God's eternal counsels of grace.

There is a word in Genesis 5:28, 29 which we should carefully ponder in this connection. There we read that "Lamech lived an hundred eighty and two years, and begat a son: and he called his name Noah, saying, This same shall comfort us, concerning our work and toil of our hands, because of the ground which the Lord hath cursed." This is the first mention of Noah in Scripture, and there is no doubt he had his name prophetically given him. His name signifies "Rest," and was bestowed upon him by his father in the confident expectation that he would prove more than an ordinary blessing to his generation: he would be the instrument of bringing in that which would speak peace and inspire hope in the hearts of the elect—for the "us" and "our" (spoken by a believer) obviously refer to the godly line.

The words of the believing Lamech had respect unto what had been said in Genesis 3:15, and were also undoubtedly a prophecy which looked forward to Christ Himself, in whom it was to receive its antitypical fulfillment, for *He* is the true rest-giver (Matt. 11:28) and deliverer from the curse (Gal. 3:13). The full scope and intent of Lamech's prophetic language is to be understood in the light of those blessings which were pronounced on Noah by God *after* the Flood— blessings which, as we shall see, were infinitely more precious than that which their mere letter conveys. They were blessings to proceed through the channel of the everlasting covenant of grace and by means of the redemption which is in Christ Jesus. The proof of this is found in the fact that they were pronounced *after* sacrifice had been offered. This requires us to glance again at Genesis 8:20-22.

"And Noah builded an altar unto the Lord, and took of every clean beast, and of every clean fowl, and offered burnt offerings *on the altar*" (v. 20). The typical teaching of this carries us much further than that which was foreshadowed by Abel's offering. Here, for the first time in Scripture, mention is made of the "altar." The key which unlocks the meaning of this is found in Matthew 23:19—"the altar that sanctifieth the gift." And what was the altar which sanctified the supreme gift? Why, the Person of Christ Himself: it was *who* He was that rendered acceptable and efficacious *what* He did. Thus, while the offering of Abel pointed forward to the sacrifice of Christ, the altar of Noah adumbrated the One who offered that sacrifice; His person being that which gave infinite value unto the blood which He shed.

"And the Lord smelled a sweet savour" (v. 21). Here again our present type rises much higher than that of Abel's: in the former case it was the *manward* aspect which was in view; but here it is the *godward* that is brought before us. Blessed indeed is it to learn what the sacrifice of Christ obtained for His people—deliverance from the wrath to come, securing an inheritance in Heaven forever; but far more blessed is it to know what that sacrifice meant unto Him to whom it was offered. In the sacrifice of Christ, God Himself found that which was "a sweet savour," with which He was well pleased, that which not only met every requirement of His righteousness and holiness, but also which satisfied His heart.

"And the Lord said in his heart, I will not again curse the ground any more for man's sake; for the imagination of man's heart is evil from his youth; neither will I again smite any more every thing living, as I have done" (v. 21). The unusual words "The Lord said in his heart" emphasize the effect which the "sweet savour" of the sacrifice had upon Him. The remainder of the verse appears, at first sight, to mar the unity of the passage; for it seems to bear no direct relation

unto what immediately precedes or follows. But a more careful
pondering of it reveals its pertinency. The reference to human depravity comes in here with a solemn significance, intimating that the
waters of judgment had in nowise changed the corruption of fallen
man's nature, and announcing that it was not because of any change in
the flesh for the better that the Lord now made known His thoughts
of peace and blessing. No, it was solely on the ground of the sweet
smelling sacrifice that He dealt in grace.

The blessings which were included in the benedictions which God
pronounced upon Noah and his sons were granted on a new foundation, on the basis of a grant quite different from any revelation or
promise which the Lord gave to Adam in his unfallen condition, even
on the ground of that covenant of grace which He had established
with the Mediator before ever the earth was. That eternal charter
anticipated Adam's offense, and provided for the deliverance of God's
elect from the curse which came in upon our first parent's sin; yea,
secured for them far greater blessings than any which pertained to the
earthly paradise. It is of great importance that this fact should be
clearly grasped: namely, that it was on the sure foundation of the
everlasting covenant of grace that God here pronounced blessing upon
Noah and his sons—as He did later on Abraham and his seed.

What has just been pointed out would have been more easily
grasped by the average reader had the chapter break between Genesis
8 and 9 been made at a different point. Genesis 8 should close with
verse 19. The last three verses of Genesis 8 as they stand in our Bibles
should begin chapter 9, and then the immediate connection between
Noah's sacrifice and the covenant which the Lord made with him
would be more apparent. The covenant was Jehovah's response to the
offering upon the altar. That offering was "a sweet savour" to Him,
clearly pointing to the offering of Christ. Christ's sacrifice was not yet
to be offered for over two thousand years; so the satisfaction which
Noah's typical offering gave unto Jehovah must have pointed back to
the everlasting covenant, in which the great sacrifice was agreed upon.

Noah's passing safely through the Flood, in the ark, was a type of
salvation itself. For this statement we have the authority of Holy Writ:
see I Peter 3:20, 21. Noah and his sons were delivered from the wrath
of God which had destroyed the rest of the world, and they now
stepped out onto what was, typically, resurrection ground. Yes, the
earth having been swept clean by the besom of divine judgment, and a
fresh start now being made in its history, it was virtually *new-creation*
ground onto which the saved family came as they emerged from the
ark. Here is another point in which our present type looked unto
higher truths than did the types which had preceded it. It is in

connection with the *new* creation that the inheritance of the saints is found (I Peter 1:3, 4). We are therefore ready now to consider the blessing of the typical heirs.

"And God blessed Noah and his sons" (Gen. 9:1). This is the first time that we read of God *blessing* any since the Fall had occurred. Before sin entered the world we read that "male and female created he them: and God blessed them" (Gen. 1:27, 28). No doubt there is both a comparison and a contrast suggested in these two verses. First, and from the natural viewpoint, God's blessing of Noah and his sons was the formal announcement that the same divine favor which the Creator had extended to our first parents should now rest upon the new progenitors of the human race. But second, and more deeply, this blessing of Noah and his sons *after* the offering upon the altar, and in connection with the covenant, denoted their blessing upon a new basis. Adam and Eve received blessing on the ground of their creature purity; Noah and his sons (as the representatives of the entire election of grace) received blessing on the ground of their acceptance and perfection *in Christ*.

"And God blessed Noah and his sons, and said unto them, Be fruitful, and multiply, and replenish the earth. And the fear of you and the dread of you shall be upon every beast of the earth, and upon every fowl of the air, upon all that moveth upon the earth, and upon all the fishes of the sea; into your hand are they delivered. Every moving thing that liveth shall be meat for you; even as the green herb have I given you all things" (Gen. 9:1-3). These verses (together with the closing ones of chap. 8) introduce us to the beginning of a new world. In several respects it resembles the first beginning: there was the divine blessing upon the heads of the human family; there was the renewed command for the propagation of the human species—the earth having been depopulated; and there was the promise of the subjection of the lower creatures to man. But there was one great and vital difference, which has escaped the notice of most of the commentators: *all now rested on the covenant of grace.*

This difference is indeed radical and fundamental. Adam was placed as lord over the earth on the ground of the covenant of works. His tenure was entirely a conditional one, his retention thereof depending wholly upon his own conduct. Consequently, when he sinned he not only forfeited the blessing and favor of his creator, but lost his dominion over the creature; and as a discrowned monarch he was sent forth to play the part of a common laborer in the earth (Gen. 3:17-19). But here we see man reinstated over the lost inheritance, not on the basis of creature responsibility and human merits, but on the basis of divine grace—for Noah "found *grace* in the eyes of the Lord"

(Gen. 6:8); not on the foundation of creature doings, but on the foundation of the excellency of that sacrifice which satisfied the heart of God. Consequently it was as the children of *faith* that the heirship of the new world was given to Noah and his seed.

"Man now rises, in the person of Noah, to a higher place in the world; yet not simply as man, but as a child of God, standing in faith. His faith had saved him amid the general wreck of the old world, to become in the new a second head of mankind, and an inheritor of earth's domain, as now purged and rescued from the pollution of evil. He is 'made heir,' as it is written in Hebrews, 'of the righteousness which is by faith,'—heir, that is, of all that properly belongs to such righteousness, not merely of the righteousness itself, but also of the world, which in the Divine purpose it was destined to possess and occupy. Hence, as if there had been a new creation, and a new head brought in to exercise over it the right of sovereignty, the original blessing and grant to Adam was substantially renewed to Noah and his family: Gen. 9:1-3. Here, then, the righteousness of faith received direct from the grace of God the dowry that had been originally bestowed upon the righteousness of nature—not a blessing merely, but a blessing coupled with the heirship and dominion of the world" (P. Fairbairn).

"Howbeit that was not first which is spiritual, but that which is natural; and afterward that which is spiritual" (I Cor. 15:46). Though these words have reference immediately to the bodies of the saints, yet they enunciate a cardinal principle in the ways of God in the outworking of His eternal purpose. Divine grace cannot clearly appear as *grace* until it shines forth from the dark background of man's sin and ruin. It was therefore requisite that the covenant of works with Adam should precede the covenant of grace with Noah. The failure of the first man did but make way and provide a suitable foil for the triumph of the Second Man—whom Noah clearly foreshadowed, as his name and the prophetic utterance of his father concerning him plainly announced. The more clearly this be grasped the easier will it be to perceive the deeper meaning of the Noahic covenant.

Everything was now clearly placed on a fresh footing and established upon a new basis. This fact throws light upon or brings out the significance of several details which, otherwise, are likely to be passed by unappreciated. For example, that "*eight* souls were saved by water" (I Peter 3:20), for in the language of Bible numerics eight speaks of *a new beginning*. Hence, too, the reverent student of Holy Writ, who delights to see the finger of God in its minutest details, will regard as something more than a coincidence the fact that the word *covenant* is found in connection with Noah just eight times: Genesis

6:18; 9:9, 11, 12, 13, 15, 16, 17. It is to be carefully noted that the entire emphasis is upon the Lord's making a covenant with Noah, and not of Noah with God: He was the initiator and sole compactor. In it there were no conditions stipulated, no "ifs" interposed; all was of grace—free, pure, unchangeable.

The blessed promises recorded in Genesis 8:22 and 9:2, 3 were all well calculated to still the fears of Noah's heart and establish his confidence. Therein he was graciously assured that in God's full view of the evil which still remained in the heart of man, a similar judgment, at least to the same extent, would never again be repeated; that not only would man be preserved on the earth, but that also the whole animal creation should be in subserviency to his use. By these divine assurances his fears were effectually relieved—adumbrating the fact that God delights to bring His children, sooner or later, into the full assurance of faith, and of confidence and joy in His presence.

III

In the previous chapter we intimated that the blessings contained in the benediction which the Lord pronounced upon Noah and his sons were infinitely more precious than the mere letter conveys. In order to attain a right understanding of the various covenants which God made with different men, it is highly essential that we carefully distinguish between the literal and the figurative, or the outward form and its inner meaning. Only thus shall we be able to separate between what was merely local and evanescent, and that which was more comprehensive and enduring. There was connected with each covenant that which was literal or material, and also that which was mystical or spiritual; and unless this be duly noted, confusion is bound to ensue. Yea, it is at this very point that many have erred—particularly so with the Abrahamic and Sinaitic covenants.

Literalists and futurists have been so occupied with the shell or letter, that they have quite missed the kernel or spirit. Allegorizers have been so much engaged with the figurative allusions, they have often failed to discern the historical fulfillment. Still others have so arbitrarily juggled the two, that they have carried out and applied neither consistently. It is, therefore, of the utmost importance that we use the best possible care in seeking to distinguish between the carnal and the spiritual, the transient and the eternal, what pertains to the earthly and what adumbrated the heavenly in the several covenants. The reader should already have been prepared, in some measure at least, to follow us in what we are now saying, by what was brought out in our examination of the Adamic covenant.

When studying the Adamic covenant we discovered the need for throwing upon the Genesis record the light of later Scripture, finding in the Prophets and Epistles that which helped to open the meaning of the historical narrative. We saw the necessity of regarding Adam as something more than a private individual—namely, as a public head or federal representative. We learned that the language of Genesis 2:17 conveyed not only a solemn threat, but, by necessary implication, also contained a blessed promise. We also perceived that the "death" there threatened was something far more dreadful than physical dissolution. We ascertained from other passages that while the "tree of life" in the center of the garden was a real and tangible one, yet it also possessed an emblematic significance, being the seal of the covenant. Let us seek to keep in mind these principles as we proceed to our consideration of the other covenants.

Each covenant that God made with men shadowed forth some element of the everlasting covenant which He entered into with Christ before the foundation of the world on behalf of His elect. The covenants which God made with Noah, Abraham, and David as truly exhibited different aspects of the compact of grace as did the several vessels in the tabernacle typify certain characteristics of the person and work of Christ. Yet, just as those vessels also had an immediate and local use, so the covenants respected what was earthly and carnal, as well as what was spiritual and heavenly. This dual fact receives illustration and exemplification in the covenant which is now before us. That which was literal and external in it is so obvious and well known that it needs no enlarging upon by us here. The sign and seal of the covenant—the rainbow—and the promise connected therewith were tangible and visible things, which the senses of men have verified for themselves from then till now. But is that all there was to the Noahic covenant?

The note made upon the Noahic covenant in the Scofield Bible reads as follows: "The elements of: (1) The relation of man to the earth under the Adamic Covenant is confirmed (Gen. 8:21). (2) The order of nature is confirmed (Gen. 8:22). (3) Human government is established (Gen. 9:1-6). (4) Earth is secured against another universal judgment by water (Gen. 8:21; 9:11). (5) A prophetic declaration is made that from Ham will descend an inferior and servile posterity (Gen. 9:24, 25). (6) A prophetic declaration is made that Shem will have a peculiar relation to Jehovah (Gen. 9:26, 27). All Divine revelation is made through Semitic men, and Christ, after the flesh, descends from Shem. (7) A prophetic declaration is made that from Japheth will descend the 'enlarged' races (Gen. 9:27). Government, science, and art, speaking broadly, are and have been Japhetic, so that history is the indisputable record of the exact fulfilment of these declarations." This is a fair sample of the superficial contents to be found in this popular catch-penny, and we strongly advise our readers not to waste their money in purchasing or their time in perusing the same.

Asking our readers' pardon for so doing, let us glance for a moment at the above summary. The last three items in Scofield's "Elements" do not belong at all to the Noahic covenant, having no more connection with it than does that which is recorded in Genesis 9:20-23. The first four elements Mr. S. mentions all concern that which is mundane and political. The whole is a lifeless analysis of the letter of the passage. There is absolutely nothing helpful in it. No effort is attempted at interpretation: no mention is made of the significant and blessed connection there is between the offering on the altar (8:20) and the Lord's covenant with Noah: no notice is taken of the new foundation upon which the divine grant is made: no hint is given of the precious typical instruction of the whole: and the thought does not seem to have entered the editor's mind that there was anything mystical or spiritual in the covenant.

Was there no deeper meaning in the promises than that the earth should never again be destroyed by a flood, that so long as it existed its seasons and harvests were guaranteed, that the fear of man should be upon all the lower creatures? Had those things no spiritual import? Assuredly they have, and in them may be clearly discerned—by those favored with anointed eyes—that which adumbrated the contents of the everlasting covenant. Noah and his family had been wondrously saved from the wrath of God, which had destroyed the rest of the race. Now that the world was to be restored from its ruined state, what more suitable occasion than that for a fuller revelation of various aspects of the believer's so-great salvation! It was ever God's way in Old Testament times to employ the event of some *temporal* deliverance of His people, to renew His intimation of the great *spiritual* deliverance and restoration by Christ's redemption. Who can doubt that it was so here, immediately after the Flood?

It seems pitiable that at this late date it should be necessary to labor a point which ought to be obvious to all God's people. And obvious it would be, at least when pointed out to them, were it not that so many have had dust thrown into their eyes by carnal "dispensationalists" and hucksters of "prophecy." Alas, that I myself once had my own vision dimmed by them, and even now I often have to exert myself in order to refuse to look at things through their colored spectacles. That there were temporal benefits bestowed upon Noah and his seed in Jehovah's covenant grant is just as sure as that Noah built a tangible altar and offered real sacrifices thereon. But to confine those benefits to the temporal, and ignore (or deny) their spiritual import, is as excuseless as would be a failure to discern Christ and His sacrifice in what Noah presented and which was a "sweet savour" unto God.

Yet so dull of spiritual comprehension are many of God's own people, so prejudiced and stupified are they by the opiates which false teachers have ministered to them, we must perforce proceed slowly, and take nothing for granted. Therefore, before we seek to point out the various typical, mystical, and spiritual features of the Noahic covenant, we must first establish the fact that something more than the temporary interests of this earth or the material well-being of its inhabitants was involved in what God said to our patriarch in Genesis 9. Nor is this at all a difficult matter. Leaving for our closing chapter the contemplation of later Scriptures which cast a radiant glow upon the seal of the covenant, the rainbow, we turn to one passage in the prophets which clearly contains all that can be required by us.

In Isaiah 54:5-10 we read: "Fear not; for thou shalt not be ashamed; neither be thou confounded, for thou shalt not be put to shame; for thou shalt forget the shame of thy youth, and shalt not remember the reproach of thy widowhood any more. For thy Maker is thy husband; the Lord of hosts is his name; and thy Redeemer the Holy One of Israel: The God of the whole earth shall he be called. For the Lord hath called thee as a woman forsaken and grieved in spirit, and a wife of youth, when thou wast refused, saith thy God. For a small moment have I forsaken thee, but with great mercies will I gather thee. In a little wrath I hid my face from thee for a moment; but with everlasting kindness will I have mercy on thee, saith the Lord thy Redeemer. For this is as the waters of Noah unto me: for as I have sworn that the waters of Noah should no more go over the earth; so have I sworn that I would not be wroth with thee, nor rebuke thee."

The connection of Isaiah 54 with the preceding chapter (on the atonement) suggests that gospel times are there in view, which is confirmed by the use Paul makes of it in Galatians 4:27, and so forth. The church, under the form of the Israelitish theocracy, is pictured as a married woman, who (like Sarah) had long continued barren. Comparatively few of the real children of God had been raised up among the Jews. At the time of Christ's advent pharisaical formality and Sadducean infidelity were well-nigh universal, and this was a sore grief unto the little remnant of genuine saints. But the death of Christ was to introduce better times, for many from among the Gentiles would then be saved. Accordingly, the barren woman is exhorted to break forth into singing, faith being called upon to joyfully anticipate the promised blessings. Gracious assurances were given that her hope should not be confounded.

True, the church was then at a low ebb and seemingly deserted by the Lord Himself, but the hiding of His face was only temporary, and He would yet gather an increasing number of children into His family, and that with "great mercy" and with "everlasting kindness." God's engagements to this effect were irrevocable, as His covenant testified. In the days of that patriarch the Lord had contended with the world in great wrath for a whole year, the "waters of Noah" having completely destroyed it. Nevertheless, He returned in "great mercy," yea, with "everlasting kindness," as His covenant with Noah attested. Though the world has often been highly provoking to God since then, yet He has faithfully kept His promise, and will continue doing so unto the end. In like manner there is often much in His people to displease and try God's patience, but He will not utterly cast them *off* (Ps. 89:34).

Here in Isaiah 54 the Noahic covenant is appealed to in proof of the perpetuity of God's gracious purpose in the midst of His sore chastenings. There we find definite interpretation of its original import, confirming what we said in the earlier paragraphs. The prophet Isaiah was announcing God's mercy to the church in future times, and he adduces His oath unto Noah as a sure pledge of the promised grace—an assurance of its certain bestowment, notwithstanding the afflictions which the people of God were then enduring and of the low condition to which they had been reduced. The unalterableness of the one is appealed to in proof of the unalterableness of the other. How plainly this shows that the covenant with Noah not only afforded a practical demonstration of the unfailing faithfulness of God in fulfilling its temporal promise to the world, but also that the church was the chief object and subject concerned in it.

Why did the Lord promise to preserve the earth until the end of time, so that it should not again be destroyed by a flood? The answer is, *Because of the church;* for when the full number of the elect have been gathered out of every clime and brought (manifestatively) into the body of Christ, the world will come to an end. That the Noahic covenant has a clear connection with the everlasting covenant (called in Isaiah 54 "the covenant of peace" because based upon reconciliation effected) and that it has a special relation to the church, is abundantly evident from what the prophet there says of it: "For this [namely, 'with everlasting kindness will I have mercy on thee'] is as the waters of Noah unto me: for as I have sworn that the waters of

Noah shall no more go over the earth, so have I sworn that I would not be wroth *with thee*"—the church.

From all that has been said it should now be abundantly clear that, while the *literal* aspect of the promises made to Noah concerned the *temporal* welfare of the earth and its inhabitants yet their *mystical* import had respect unto the *spiritual* well-being of the church and its members. This same twofoldedness will come before us again yet more plainly, when we consider the rainbow, which was the sign and seal of the Noahic covenant. It seems strange that those who perceived that the laws which God gave unto Israel respecting the eating only of fishes with scales and fins and animals which divided the hoof and chewed the cud, had not only a temporal or hygienic value, but a mystical or spiritual meaning as well, should have failed to discern that the same dual feature holds good in respect to all the details of the Noahic covenant.

Once this key is firmly grasped by us, it is not difficult to reach the inner contents contained in the benediction which the Lord pronounced after He had smelled the sweet savor of Noah's offering. The guarantee that the earth should not again be destroyed by a flood (as the Adamic earth had been) pointed to the eternal security of the saints—a security assured by the vastly superior position which is now theirs from what they had in Adam, namely, their inalienable portion in Christ. The promise that while the earth remained seedtime and harvest should not fail, contained as its inner kernel the divine pledge that as long as the saints were left below, God would supply all their need "according to his riches in glory by Christ Jesus." The fact that those blessings were promised after Noah and his family had come on to resurrection and new-creation ground, foreshadowed the blessed truth that the believer's standing is no longer "in the flesh."

Noah is the figure of Christ. First, as the remover of the curse from a corrupted earth, and as the rest-giver to those who, with sorrow of heart and sweat of the brow, had to till and eat of it (Gen. 5:29; Matt. 11:28). Second, as the heir of the new earth, wherein there shall be "no more curse" (Gen. 8:21; Rev. 22:3). Third, as the one into whose hands all things were now delivered (Gen. 9:2; John 17:2; Heb. 1:2). Noah's sons or seed were the figure of the church. With him they were "blessed" (Gen. 9:1; cf. Eph. 1:3). With him they were given dominion over all the lower creatures: so the saints have been made "kings and priests unto God" (Rev. 1:6) and shall "reign with him" (II Tim. 2:12). With him they were bidden to be "fruitful" and "bring forth abundantly" (Gen. 9:7): so Christians are to abound in fruit and in every good work. The fact that this covenant was an absolute or unconditional one tells us of the immutability of our blessings in Christ.

IV

"While the earth remaineth, seedtime and harvest, and cold and heat, and summer and winter, and day and night shall not cease" (Gen. 8:22). These promises were made by God upward of four thousand years ago; and the unfailing fulfillment of them annually, all through the centuries, affords a striking demonstration of His faithfulness. Moreover, in their fulfillment we have exemplified a fact which is generally lost sight of by the world today; namely, that behind nature's "laws" is nature's *Lord*. Skepticism would now shut God out of His own creation. A casual observance of nature's "laws" reveals the fact that they are not uniform in their operation; and therefore if we had not Scripture, we would be without any assurance that the seasons might not radically change and the whole earth again be inundated. Nature's "laws" did not prevent the Deluge in Noah's days. How then should they hinder a recurrence of it in ours? How blessed for the child of God to listen to this guarantee of his Father!

See here also the aboundings of God's mercy in proceeding with us by way of a covenant, binding Himself with a solemn oath that He would never again destroy the earth by water. He might well have exempted the world from this calamity and yet never have told men that He would thus act. Had He not granted such assurance, the remembrance of the Deluge would have been like a sword of terror suspended over their heads. But in His great goodness, the Lord sets the mind of His creatures at rest upon this score, by promising not to repeat the Flood. Thus does He deal with His people: "That by two immutable things [His revealed purpose of grace and His covenant oath] in which it was impossible for God to lie, we might have a strong consolation, who have fled for refuge to lay hold upon the hope set before us" (Heb. 6:18).

" 'I will not again curse the ground any more for man's sake' (Gen. 8:21), was the word of God to Noah, when accepting the first offering presented to Him on the purified earth. It is, no doubt, to be understood relatively; not as indicating a total repeal of the evil, but only a mitigation of it; yet such a mitigation as would render the earth a much less afflicted and more fertile region than it had been before. This again indicated that, in the estimation of Heaven, the earth had now assumed a new position; that by the action of God's judgment upon it, it had become hallowed in His sight, and was in a condition to receive tokens of the divine favor, which had formerly been withheld from it" (P. Fairbairn). We pointed out the mystical significance of Genesis 8:21 in our last chapter.

"And God spake unto Noah, and to his sons with him, saying, And

I, behold, I establish my covenant with you, and with your seed after you; and with every living creature that is with you, of the fowl, of the cattle, and of every beast of the earth with you; from all that go out of the ark, to every beast of the earth. And I will establish my covenant with you: neither shall all flesh be cut off any more by the waters of a flood; neither shall there any more be a flood to destroy the earth. And God said, This is the token of the covenant which I make between me and you, and every living creature that is with you, for perpetual generations: I do set my bow in the cloud, and it shall be for a token of a covenant [literally, "My bow I have set in the cloud, and it shall be for a covenant sign"] between me and the earth. And it shall come to pass when I bring a cloud over the earth, that the bow shall be seen in the cloud: and I will remember my covenant, which is between me and you and every living creature of all flesh; and the waters shall no more become a flood to destroy all flesh" (Gen. 9:8-15).

The above words contain the fulfillment of the promise which the Lord had given to Noah in Genesis 6:18, and amplify what He had said in Genesis 8:21, 22. That which we shall now concentrate upon is the "token" or "sign" of the covenant. There is no doubt whatever in our own mind it was now that the rainbow appeared for the first time in the lower heavens, for the purpose of allaying men's fears against the calamity of another universal flood and to provide them with a visible pledge in nature for the performance of her existing order and constitution; for had this divine marvel appeared before unto the antediluvians, it would have possessed no special and distinctive meaning and message after the Flood. The fact that the rainbow was an entirely new phenomenon, something which was quite unknown to Noah previously, supplies a striking demonstration of the silent harmony of Scripture; for it is clear from Genesis 2:6 that no rain had fallen before the Flood!

The first rain was sent in divine judgment; but now God turns it into a blessing. The sunshine of heaven falls upon the rain on earth, and lo, the beautiful rainbow! How blessedly suited, then, was the rainbow to serve as the sign of the covenant which God had made with Noah. "There is an exact correspondence between the natural phenomenon it presents and the moral use to which it is applied. The promise in the covenant was not that there should be no future visitations of judgment upon the earth, but that they should not proceed to the extent of again destroying the world. In the moral, as in the natural sphere, there might still be congregating vapours and descending torrents; indeed, the terms of the covenant imply that there should be such, and that by means of them God would not fail to testify His displeasure against sin, and keep in awe the workers of inquity. But there should be no second deluge to diffuse universal ruin; mercy should always so far rejoice against judgment.

"Such in the field of nature is the assurance given by the rainbow, which is formed by the lustre of the sun's rays shining on the dark cloud as it recedes; so that it may be termed, as in the somewhat poetical description of Lange, 'the sun's triumph over the floods; the glitter of his beams imprinted on the rain-cloud as a mark of subjection'! How appropriate an emblem of that grace which should always show itself ready to return after wrath! Grace still sparing and preserving, even when storms of judgment have been bursting forth upon the guilty! And as the rainbow throws its radiant arch over the expanse between heaven and earth, uniting the two together again as with a wreath of beauty, after they have been engaged in an elemental war, what a fitting image does it present to the thoughtful eye of the essential harmony that still subsists between the higher and the lower spheres! Such undoubtedly is its symbolic import, as the sign peculiarly connected with the covenant of Noah; it holds out, by means of its very form and nature, an assurance of God's mercy, as engaged to keep perpetually in check the floods of deserved wrath, and continue to the world the manifestation of His grace and goodness" (P. Fairbairn).

But God's bow in the clouds was not only an assurance unto men at large that no more would the world be destroyed by a flood, it was also the seal of confirmation of the covenant which God had made with the elect seed, the children of faith. Blessed it is to know that, not only *our* eyes, but *His* too are upon the bow; and thus this gives us fellowship with Himself in that which tells of the storm being over, of peace displacing turmoil, of the dark gloom now being irradiated by the shining of the sun. It was the rain which broke up the light into its separate rays, now reflected in the bow: the blue or heavenly ray, the yellow or golden ray, the crimson ray of atonement. Thus it is in the everlasting covenant that God is fully revealed as light and as love, as righteous yet merciful, merciful yet righteous. The covenant of grace is beautifully expressed in the rainbow. For the following nine points on this covenant we are indebted to a sermon by Ebenezer Erskine, preached about 1730.

1. It is of God's ordering: "I have set my bow in the clouds." So the covenant of grace is of God's ordering: "I have made a covenant with my chosen" (Ps. 89). Though it be our duty to "take hold of" the covenant (Isa. 56:4), and to come under engagements through the grace thereof, yet we have no part in appointing or ordering it. The covenant of grace could no more have been made by man, than he can form a bow in the clouds.

2. The bow was set in the clouds upon God's smelling a sweet savor in Noah's sacrifice; so that the covenant of grace is founded upon and sealed with the blood of the Lamb—a reminder thereof being set before us every time we sit down to partake of the Lord's Supper.

3. The rainbow is a divine security that the waters should return no more to destroy the earth; so the covenant of grace guarantees against the deluge of God's wrath, that it shall never return again to destroy any soul that by faith flees to Christ (Isa. 54:9).

4. It is the sun which gives being to the rainbow. Remove it from the firmament and there could not be its glorious reflection in the clouds. So Christ, the Sun of righteousness, gives being to the covenant of grace. He is its very life and substance: "I will preserve thee and give thee for a covenant of the people" (Isa. 49:8).

5. Although the arch of the bow is high above us, reaching to the heaven, yet the ends of it stoop down and reach to the earth. Just so it is with the covenant of grace: although the great covenant Head be in heaven, yet, through the gospel, He stoops down to men upon earth—"The word is nigh thee" (Rom. 10:6-8).

6. God's bow in the clouds is very extensive, reaching from one end of heaven to the other; so His covenant of grace is wide in its reach, stretching back to eternity past and reaching forward to eternity future, embracing some out of every nation and kindred, and tribe and tongue.

7. As the rainbow is a security against a universal deluge, so it is also a prognostic of refreshing showers of rain to the thirsty earth. So the bow of the covenant which encircles the throne of God (Rev. 4:3) not only secures against vindictive wrath, but gives assurance of the rain—the Spirit's influences.

8. The visible appearance of the rainbow is but of a short continuance, for usually it appears only for a few minutes and then vanishes. So the sensible and lively views which the believer gets of the covenant of grace are usually of brief duration.

9. Although the rainbow disappears, and that for a long while together, yet we do not conclude therefrom that God's covenant is broken or that a flood will come and destroy the earth. So too the saint may not now be favored with a sensible sight of the covenant of grace; yet the remembrance of former views thereof will keep the soul from fears of wrath.

The following paragraph is quoted from our work *Gleanings in Genesis.* "There are many parallels between the rainbow and God's grace. As the rainbow is the joint-product of storm and sunshine, so grace is the unmerited favour of God appearing on the dark background of the creature's sin. As the rainbow is the effect of the sun shining on the drops of rain in a cloud, so Divine grace is manifested

by God's love shining through the blood shed by our blessed Redeemer. As the rainbow is the telling out of the varied hues of the
white light, so the *'manifold* grace of God' (I Pet. 4:10) is the ultimate
expression of God's heart. As nature knows nothing more exquisitely
beautiful than the rainbow, so heaven itself knows nothing that
surpasses in loveliness the wondrous grace of God. As the rainbow is
the union of heaven and earth—spanning the sky and reaching down to
the ground—so grace in the one Mediator has brought together God
and man. As the rainbow is a public sign of God hung out in the
heavens that all may see it, so 'the grace of God that bringeth salvation
hath appeared to all men' (Titus 2:11). Finally, as the rainbow has
been displayed throughout all the past forty centuries, so *in the ages
to come* God will show forth 'the exceeding riches of His grace in His
kindness toward us through Christ Jesus' (Eph. 2:7)."

The later references in Scripture to the rainbow are inexpressibly
blessed. Thus, in the visions of the glory of God which Ezekiel was
favored with at the beginning of his ministry, we find part of the
imagery thus described, "As the appearance of the bow that is in the
cloud in the day of rain, so was the appearance of the brightness
round about" (Ezek. 1:28). It is to be duly noted that this verse
comes in at the close of one of the most awe-inspiring representations
of heavenly things to be found in Scripture. It is a vision of the
ineffable holiness of God, hence the presence of the cherubim. There
is then the fervid appearance of metallic brightness and flashes of
liquid flame, which shone forth from all parts of the vision. Then
wheels of vast proportion are added to the cherubim: wheels full of
eyes, speaking of the terrible energy which was going to characterize
the divine providences. Above all was the throne of God, on which He
Himself sat in human form.

It is well known that at the time of this vision the people of Israel
were in a most distressed condition. Those amongst whom Ezekiel
prophesied were in captivity, and the ruin of their country was nigh at
hand. How blessed, then, was the introduction here of the sign of the
rainbow into this vision! It intimated that the purpose and promises of
divine grace were sure. Though God's judgment would fall heavily
upon the guilty nation, yet because of the elect remnant therein, it
would not be utterly cast off; and after the storm had passed, times of
restoration and peace would follow. It was the divine assurance, for
faith to rest upon and enjoy, that what Jehovah had pledged in the
covenant would be made good.

"And there was a rainbow round about the throne in sight like unto
an emerald" (Rev. 4:3). The canopy of God's throne is a rainbow. We
understand this vision in Revelation 4 to have immediate reference to

the glorious exercise of divine grace under the New Testament economy. There is a manifest allusion in it to Genesis 9: it signifies that God deals with His people according to His covenant engagements. Its emerald or green color denotes that, because of the faithfulness of Him who sits upon the throne of grace, His covenant is ever the same, ever fresh, without any shadow of turning. "Its surrounding the throne denoted that the holiness, and justice of God, and all His dispensations as the Sovereign of all worlds, had respect to His covenant of peace and engagements of love, which He had ratified to His believing people, and harmonized with them" (T. Scott).

Thus the Noahic covenant served to bring out in a new light, and establish on a firmer basis, the unfailing faithfulness of Jehovah and the immutability of His purpose. An assurance to that effect was specially needed just after the Flood, for it was over that basic truth that the judgment of the Deluge had seemed to cast a shadow. But the promises made to Noah, solemnly given in covenant form and sealed by the token of the rainbow, effectually reestablished confidence and stands out still—after all these many centuries—as one of the grand events in God's dealings with men; assuring us that, however the sins of the world may provoke the justice of God, the purpose of His grace unto His chosen people stands unalterably sure.

PART FOUR

The Abrahamic
Covenant

I

We shall now consider one of the most illustrious characters set before us in the pages of Holy Writ, one who is expressly designated "the friend of God" (James 2:23), and from whom Christ Himself derives one of His titles, "the son of Abraham" (Matt. 1:1). Not only was he the one from whom the favored nation of Israel sprang, but he is also "the father of all them that believe" (Rom. 4:11). It is scarcely consonant with our present design to review here the remarkable life of this man; yet the history of Abraham—in its broad outlines, at least—is so closely bound up with the covenant which Jehovah made with him, that it is hardly possible to give any exposition of the latter without paying more or less attention to the former. Nevertheless, we shall be obliged to pass by many interesting episodes in his varied experience if our discussion of the Abrahamic covenant is to be kept within anything like reasonable bounds.

A period of more than three hundred years passed from the time that the Lord made the covenant with Noah and the appearing of Abraham upon the stage of sacred history. We may here note briefly two things which occurred in that period, and we do so because of the bearing which they have and the light they throw upon our present subject. The first of these is the remarkable prophecy uttered by Noah in Genesis 9:25-27. Passing by the sad incidents which immediately preceded and gave rise to the prediction, we would observe particularly its pronouncements as they intimated the future development of God's purpose of grace. This comes out first in the "Blessed be the Lord God of Shem," or as it should more properly be rendered, "Blessed be [or "Praised be"] Jehovah, the God of Shem." This is the first time in Scripture that we find God calling Himself the God of any particular person; moreover, it was *as Jehovah* He should be related to Shem.

Jehovah is God made known in *covenant* relationship: it is God in His manifested personality as taking subjects into His free favor; it is God granting a revelation of His institutions for redemption. These were to be the specific portion of Shem—in sharp contrast from the curse pronounced upon Ham; not of Shem simply as an individual, but as the head of a distinct section of the human race. It was with that section God was to stand in the nearest relation: it was a spiritual distinction which they were to enjoy: a covenant relation, a priestly nearness. A special interest in the divine favor is what was denoted in this primitive prediction concerning Shem. His descendants were to be the line through which the divine blessing was to flow: it was among them that Jehovah was to be known, and where His kingdom was to be set up and established.

"God shall enlarge Japheth, and he [Japheth] shall dwell in the tents of Shem." The obvious meaning of the first clause is, God would give Japheth a numerous posterity, with widely extended territories, which has been fulfilled in the fact that they have not only gained possession of all Europe, North and South America, and Australia, but likewise a large portion of Asia. The stock of Japheth was to be the most energetic and ambitious of Noah's descendants, giving themselves to colonization and diffusive operations, pushing their way and establishing themselves far and wide. But it is the second clause of Genesis 9:27 we are now more concerned with: "and he shall dwell in the tents of Shem"—he was to enjoy fellowship in the high spiritual privileges of Shem. Japeth was to come under the divine protection and be admitted to the blessings which were the peculiar but not exclusive portion of Shem.

Throwing the light of the New Testament upon this ancient prophecy, we find it clearly announced that it was through the line of Shem that the gifts of grace and the blessings of salvation were more immediately to flow. Yet so far from them being confined unto that section of the human family, the larger portion of it (Japheth) would also share their good. The Shemites were to have them firsthand, but the descendants of Japheth were also to participate in them. "The exaltation of Shem's progeny into the nearest relationship to God, was not that they might keep the privilege to themselves, but that first getting it, they should admit the sons of Japheth, the inhabitants of the isles, to share with them in the boon, and spread it as wide as their scattered race should extend" (P. Fairbairn).

Here, then, in this early prediction through Noah we have the germ of what is more fully developed in later Scripture. It was only by entering the tents of Shem that Japheth could enter the place where divine blessing was to be found, which, in the language of the New Testament is only another way of saying that *from the Jews would salvation flow forth unto the Gentiles.* But before we develop that thought a little further, we would mention a very striking point brought out by E. W. Hengstenberg in his most suggestive three-volume work on *The Christology of the Old Testament.* Amid his dry and technical notes on the Hebrew text, he shows how that "as the reaction against Ham's sin had *originated with Shem* (Gen. 9:23), Japheth only joining himself in it; so in the future, the rich home of salvation and piety would be with Shem, to whom Japheth, in the felt need of salvation, should come near."

"And he [Japheth] shall dwell in the tents of Shem." The earth was to be possessed and peopled by the three sons of Noah. Of them, Shem was the one selected to be the peculiar channel of divine gifts and communications; but these were to be not for his own exclusive benefit, but rather to the end that others might share in the blessing. The kingdom of God was to be established in Shem, but Japheth should be received into its community. Therein was intimated not only that "salvation is of the Jews" (John 4:22), but also the mystery of Romans 11:11, and so forth. Though "salvation is of the Jews," nevertheless, Gentiles should be partakers of it. Though Shem alone be the real root and trunk, yet into their tree the Gentiles should be "grafted!" Though he appeared to speak dark words, yet, by the Holy Spirit, Noah was granted amazing light and was given a deep insight into the secret counsels of the Most High.

The connection between what we have briefly dwelt upon above with our present subject is so obvious that few words are called for in connection therewith. The remarkable prophecy of Noah began to receive its historical unfolding when the Lord announced to the patriarch, "In thee shall all families of the earth be blessed" (Gen. 12:3). Abraham was of the stock of Shem (Gen. 11:1, 23, 26), and he was now made the depository of the divine promises (Gal. 3:16); yet God's blessing was to be confined neither to himself nor to his lineal descendants, but "all families of the earth" were to be the gainers thereby. Yet, notwithstanding, it was only through Abraham that the Gentiles were to be advantaged: "*In thee* shall all families of the earth be blessed"—the central promise in the Abrahamic covenant. What was that but reaffirming, in more specific detail, "God shall enlarge Japheth, and he shall dwell *in the tents of Shem*"? How perfect is the harmony of God's wondrous Word!

The second thing to be noted, which happened during the interval between the Noahic and the Abrahamic covenants, and which clearly had a bearing upon the latter, is the incident recorded in Genesis 11—namely, the building and overthrow of the tower of Babel. It is a great mistake to regard that event as an isolated occurrence; rather is it to be considered as the heading up of an evil course and movement. Of the events which transpired from the Deluge to the call of Abraham—embracing an interval of over four centuries—the information we possess is brief and summary, yet enough is recorded to show that the character of man is unchanged, the same in principle and practice as it had been before the Flood. It might perhaps have been expected that so terrible a judgment would have left upon the survivors and their descendants for many generations a deep and salutary impression, which would have acted as a powerful restraint upon their evil propensities. Alas, what is man!

Even in the family of Noah, and while the remembrance of the awful visitation of God's wrath was still fresh in their minds, there were indications which testified to both the existence and exercise of sinful dispositions, which the recent judgment had failed to eradicate or even curb. The sad failure of Noah himself, and the wicked behavior of his son on beholding the fall of his father, afforded awful proof that the evil which is in the heart of fallen man is so deeply rooted and so powerful that nothing external, no matter how frightful, can subdue it; and supplied a distinct foreboding of what was soon made manifest on a wider scale and in a much worse form. Idolatry itself quickly found an entrance and speedily established itself among the inhabitants of the earth in their dispersion. Joshua 27:2 gives us more than a hint of this, while Romans 1:21-23 casts a flood of light upon that dark situation.

Within a short time after the Deluge, human depravity resumed its old course and manifested itself in open defiance of heaven. As the population of the earth increased, evil schemes of ambition began to be entertained; and soon there appeared on the scene one who took the lead in wickedness. He is first brought before us in Genesis 10:8: "Nimrod: who began to be a mighty one in the earth." It is to be noted that he belonged to the line of Ham, upon which the divine curse had been pronounced, and significantly enough "Nimrod" means "the Rebel"—suitable title for the one who headed a great confederacy in open revolt against God. This confederacy is described in Genesis 11; and that it was an organized revolt against Jehovah is clear from the language of Genesis 10:9: "Nimrod, the mighty hunter *before the Lord.*" If that expression be compared with "The earth also [in the days of Noah] was corrupt *before God,*" the impression conveyed is that this "Rebel" pursued his impious and ambitious designs in brazen defiance of the Almighty.

Four times over we find the word *mighty* connected with Nimrod. First, in Genesis 10:8 it said that "he *began to be* a mighty one in the earth," which suggests that he struggled for the preeminence, and by force of will and ability obtained it; the "mighty one *in the earth*" intimates conquest and subjection, becoming a leader and ruler over men. This is confirmed by "the beginning of his kingdom was Babel" (Gen. 10:10), so that he reigned as a king. In the previous verse we are told, "He was a mighty hunter before the Lord: wherefore it is said, Even as Nimrod the mighty hunter before the Lord"—the reference probably is to his being a hunter *of men*. In so brief a description the repetition of those words "mighty hunter before the Lord" are significant. The word for "mighty" is *gibbor*, and is translated in the Old Testament "chief" and "chieftain." In I Chronicles 1:10 we are told, "And Cush begat Nimrod: he began to be mighty upon the earth." The Chaldee paraphrase of this verse says, "Cush begat Nimrod, who began to prevail in wickedness, for he slew innocent blood and rebelled against Jehovah."

"And the beginning of his kingdom was *Babel*" (Gen. 10:10). Here is the key to the first nine verses of chapter 11. In the language of that time "Babel" meant "the gate of God" (see Young's *Concordance*); but afterwards, because of the divine judgment inflicted there, it came to mean "confusion." By coupling together the various hints which the Holy Spirit has here given us, it seems quite clear that Nimrod organized not only an imperial government over which he presided as king, but that he also introduced a new and idolatrous worship, most probably demanding—under pain of death—that divine honors be paid his own person. As such he was an ominous and striking type of the Antichrist. "Out of that land he went forth into Assyria [margin], and builded Nineveh, and the city Rehoboth, and Calah," and so forth (vv. 11, 12). From these statements we gather the impression that Nimrod's ambition was to establish a world empire.

Though Nimrod is not mentioned by name in Genesis 11, it is clear from 10:10 that he was the "chief" and "king" who organized and headed the movement and rebellion there described. "And they said, Go to, let us build us a city and a tower, whose top may reach unto heaven; and let us make us a name, lest we be scattered abroad upon the face of the whole earth." Here is discovered a concerted effort in most blatant defiance of God. He had said, "Be fruitful and multiply, *and replenish the earth*" (9:1); but Nimrod and his followers deliberately refused to obey that divine command, given through Noah, saying, "Let us make us a name *lest we be scattered abroad* upon the face of the whole earth."

It is clear from Genesis 10 that Nimrod's ambition was to establish a world empire. To accomplish this, two things were necessary. First, a center of unity, a city-headquarters; and second, a motive for the inspiration and encouragement of his fellows. The first was secured in "the beginning of his kingdom was Babel" (10:9); the second was supplied in the "let us make us a name" (11:4), which intimated an inordinate desire for fame. Nimrod's aim was to keep mankind together under his leadership—"lest we be scattered abroad." The idea suggested by the "tower"—considered in the light of its whole setting—was that of strength, a stronghold; while its name, "the gate of God," tells us that Nimrod was arrogating to himself divine honors. In it all, we may discern Satan's initial attempt to forestall the purpose of God concerning His Christ, by setting up a universal ruler of men of *his* providing.

The response of heaven was swift and drastic. "And the Lord said, Behold, the people is one, and they have all one language; and this they begin to do: and now nothing will be restrained from them, which they have imagined to do. Go to, let us go down, and there confound their language, that they may not understand one another's speech. So the Lord scattered them abroad from thence upon the face of all the earth: and they left off to build the city. Therefore is the name of it called Babel; because the Lord did there confound the language of all the earth" (11:6-9). Once again the human race had been guilty of open apostasy. Therefore did God intervene in judgment, bringing to naught the ambitious scheme of Nimrod, confounding the speech of his subjects, and scattering them abroad on the face of the earth.

The effect of God's intervention was the origination of the different nations and the formation of "the world" as it continued up to the time of Christ. It was then that men were abandoned to their own devices, when God "suffered all nations to walk in their own ways" (Acts 14:16). Then was executed that terrible judicial hardening, when "God also gave them up to uncleanness," when "God gave them up unto vile affections," when "God gave them over to a reprobate mind" (Rom. 1:24, 26, 28). Then and thus it was that the way was cleared for the next stage in the outworking of the divine plan of mercy; for where sin had abounded, grace was now to superabound. Having abandoned (temporarily) the nations, God now singled out one man, Abraham, from whom the chosen nation was to spring.

II

"And therefore will the Lord *wait* that he may be gracious" (Isa. 30:18)—wait until the most suited time, wait until the stage is prepared for action, wait until there is a fit background for Him to act from; wait, very often, until man's extremity has been reached. "When the *fulness of time* was come, God sent forth his Son" (Gal. 4:4). Winter's frosts and snows must do their work before vegetation is ready to bud and blossom. As it is in the material creation, so it is in the realm of divine providence. There is a wonderful order in all God's works, an all-wise timing of the divine actions. Not that the Almighty is hampered or hindered by finite creatures of the dust, but that His wondrous ways may be the more admired by those who are granted spirituality to discern them. "Great and marvellous are thy works, Lord God Almighty; just and true are thy ways, thou King of saints" (Rev. 15:3).

Having dealt in *judgment* at Babel, God was then pleased to manifest His *grace*. This has ever been, and will ever be, true of all God's dealings. According to His infinite wisdom, judgment (which is God's "strange" work) only serves to prepare the way for a greater and grander outflow of His redeeming love. Having abandoned (temporarily) the nations, God now singled out the man from whom the chosen nation was to spring. Later, God's rejection of Israel resulted in the enriching of the Gentiles. And we may add, that the judgment of the great white throne will be followed by the new heaven and new earth, wherein righteousness shall dwell and upon which the tabernacle of God shall be with men. Thus it was of old: the overthrow of the tower of Babel and the dispersion of Nimrod's impious followers were succeeded by the call of Abraham, through whom, ultimately, the divine blessing should flow to all the families of the earth.

The lesson to be learned here is a deeply important one: the connection between Genesis 11 and 12 is highly significant. The Lord God determined to have a people of His own by the calling of grace, a people which should be taken into privileged nearness unto Himself, and which should show forth His praises; but it was not until all the claims of the natural man had been repudiated by his own wickedness, not until his utter worthlessness had been clearly exhibited, that divine clemency was free to flow forth on an enlarged scale. Sin was suffered to abound in all its hideousness, before grace superabounded in all its blessedness. In other words, it was not until the total depravity of men had been fully demonstrated, first by the antediluvians and then again by the concerted apostasy at Babel, that God now dealt with Abraham in sovereign grace and infinite mercy.

That it was grace, grace alone, sovereign grace, which called Abraham to be the friend of God, appears clearly from his natural state and circumstances when the Lord first appeared to him. Abraham belonged not to a pious family where Jehovah was acknowledged and honored; instead his progenitors were idolaters. It seems that once more "all flesh had corrupted his way in the earth." The house from which Abraham sprang was certainly no exception to the rule; for we read, "Your fathers dwelt on the other side of the flood in old time, even Terah the father of Abraham and the father of Nachor, and they *served other gods*" (Josh. 24:2). There was nothing whatever, then, in the object of the divine choice to commend him unto God, nothing in Abraham that merited His esteem. No, the *cause* of election is always to be traced to the discriminating will of God; for election itself is "of grace" (Rom. 11:5) and therefore it depends in no wise upon any worthiness in the object, either present or foreseen. If it did, it would not be "of grace."

That it was not at all a matter of any goodness or fitness in Abraham which moved the Lord to single him out to be the special object of His high favor is further seen from Isaiah 51:1, 2: "Look unto the rock whence ye are hewn, and to the hole of the pit whence ye are digged. Look unto Abraham your father, and unto Sarah that bare you." While it be true that God never acts capriciously or at random, nor arbitrarily—that is, without some wise and good reason for what He does—yet the spring of all His actions is His own sovereign pleasure. The moment we ascribe any of God's exercises unto aught *outside* of Himself, we are guilty not only of impiety, but of affirming a gross absurdity. The Almighty is infinitely self-sufficient, and can no more be swayed by the creatures of His own hand, than an entity can be influenced by nonentities. Oh, how vastly different is the Deity of Holy Writ from the "God" which present-day Christendom dreams about!

"The God of glory appeared unto our father Abraham, when he was in Mesopotamia, before he dwelt in Haran. And said unto him, Get thee out of thy country, and from thy kindred, and come into the land which I will shew thee" (Acts 7:2, 3). The divine title employed here is a remarkable one, for we regard it as intimating that the shekinah itself was manifested before Abraham's wondering gaze. God always suits the revelation which He makes of Himself according to the effect which is to be produced. Here was a man in the midst of a heathen city, brought up in an idolatrous home. Something vivid and striking, supernatural and unmistakable, was required in order to suddenly change the whole course of his life. "The God of glory"—in blessed and awesome contrast from the "other gods" of his sires—

"appeared unto our father Abraham." It was probably the first of the theophanic manifestations, for we never read of God appearing to Abel or Noah.

If our conclusion be correct that this was the earliest of all the theophanic manifestations (God appearing in human form: cf. Gen. 32:24; Josh. 5:13, 14; etc.) that we read of in the Old Testament, which anticipated the incarnation itself, as well as marked the successive revelations of God to men; and if this theophany was accompanied by the resplendent glory and majesty of the shekinah, then great indeed was the privilege now conferred upon the son of Terah. Nothing in him could possibly have merited such an amazing display of divine grace. The Lord was here "found" of one that "sought him not" (Isa. 65:1), as is the case with each of all those who are made the recipients of His everlasting blessing; for "there is none that seeketh after God" (Rom. 3:11). It is not the lost sheep which seeks the Shepherd, but the Shepherd who goes after it, and reveals Himself unto it in all His love and grace.

God said unto Abraham: "Get thee out of thy country, and from thy kindred, and come into the land which I will show thee." Those were the terms of the divine communication originally received by our patriarch. This command from the Most High came to Abraham in Mesopotamia, in the city of Ur of the Chaldeans, which was situated near the Persian Gulf. It was a call which demanded absolute confidence in and full obedience to the word of Jehovah. It was a call for definite separation from the world. But it was far more than a bare command issuing from the divine authority: it was an effectual call which demonstrated the efficacy of divine grace. In other words, it was a call accompanied by the divine power, which wrought mightily in the object of it. This is a distinction which is generally lost sight of today: there are two kinds of the divine call mentioned in Scripture, the one which falls only on the outward ear and produces no definite effect; the other which reaches the heart, and moves unto a real response.

The first of these calls is found in such passages as, "Unto you, O men, I call; and my voice is to the sons of men" (Prov. 8:4), and "For many be called" (Matt. 20:16). It reaches all who come under the sound of God's Word. It is a call which presses upon the creature the claims of God, and the call of the gospel, which reveals the requirements of the Mediator. This call is universally unheeded: it is unpalatable to fallen human nature, and is rejected by the unregenerate: "I have called, and ye refused" (Prov. 1:24); "And they all with one consent began to make excuse" (Luke 14:18). The second of these calls is found in such passages as "Whom he called, them he also

justified" (Rom. 8:30); "Called you out of darkness into his marvellous light" (I Peter 2:9).

The first call is general; the second, particular. The first is to all who
come under the sound of the Word; the second is made only to the
elect, bringing them from death unto life. The first makes manifest the
enmity of the carnal mind against God; the second reveals the grace of
God toward His own. It is by the effect produced that we are able to
distinguish between them. "He calleth his own sheep by name, and
leadeth them out. And when he putteth forth his own sheep, he goeth
before them, and the sheep follow him: for they know his voice"
(John 10:3, 4)—follow the example which He has left them (I Peter
2:21). They follow Him along the path of self-denial, of obedience, of
living to the glory of God. Here, then, is the grand effect wrought
upon the soul when it receives the effectual call of God: the understanding is illuminated, the conscience is convicted, the hard heart is
melted, the stubborn will is conquered, the affections are drawn out
unto Him who before was despised.

Such an effect as we have just described is supernatural: it is a
miracle of divine grace. The proud Pharisee is humbled into the dust;
the stout-hearted rebel is brought into subjection; the lover of pleasure
is now made a lover of God. He who before kicked defiantly against
the pricks, bows submissively and cries, "Lord, what wouldest Thou
have me to do?" But let it be said emphatically, nothing but the
immediate power of God working upon the heart can produce such
a blessed transformation. Neither financial losses, family bereave-
ments, nor a dangerous illness can effect it. Nothing external will
suffice to change the depraved heart of fallen man. He may listen to
the most faithful sermons, the most solemn warnings, the most win-
some invitations, and he will remain unmoved, untouched, unless the
Spirit of God is pleased to first quicken him into newness of life.
Those who are spiritually dead can neither hear, see, nor feel *spiritually*.

Now it is this effectual call that Abraham was the subject of when
Jehovah suddenly appeared to him in Ur of Chaldea. This is evident
from the effect produced in him. He was bidden to "get thee out of
thy country, and from thy kindred, and come into the land which I
will show thee" (Acts 7:3). Think of what that involved: to forsake
the land of his birth, to sever the nearest and dearest of all natural ties,
to make a complete break with his old manner of life, and step out
on what appeared to carnal reason to be an uncertain venture. What
was his response? "By faith Abraham, when he was called to go out
into a place which he should after receive for an inheritance, obeyed;
and he went out, not knowing whither he went" (Heb. 11:8). Ah, my

reader, *that* can only be satisfactorily accounted for in one way: almighty power had wrought within him; invincible grace had conquered his heart.

Before proceeding further, let us pause and take stock of our own souls. Have we experienced anything which at all corresponds to this radical change in the life of Abraham? Have you, have I, been made the subjects of a divine call which has produced a right-about-face in our lives? Have we been the subjects of a divine miracle, so that grace has wrought effectually upon our hearts? Have we heard something more than the language of Scripture falling upon our outward ears? Have we heard God Himself speaking in the most secret recess of our souls, so that it may be said, "The gospel came not unto you in word only, but also *in power,* and in the Holy Spirit, and in much assurance" (I Thess. 1:5)? Can it be said of us, "The word of God, which effectually worketh also in you that believe" (I Thess. 2:13)? Is the Word working effectually in us, so as to govern our inner and outer man, so as to produce an obedient walk, and issue in fruit to God's glory?

Though the response made by Abraham to the call which he had received from the Lord clearly demonstrated that a miracle of divine grace had been wrought within him, nevertheless, God suffered sufficient of the "flesh" to appear in him so as to evidence that he was still a sinful and failing creature. While regeneration is indeed a wonderful and blessed experience, yet it is only the beginning of God's "good work" in the soul (Phil. 1:6), and requires His further operations of sanctification to carry it forward to completion. Though a new nature is imparted when the soul is brought from death unto life, the old nature is not removed; though the principle of holiness is communicated, the principle of sin is neither annihilated nor exterminated. Consequently, there is not only a continual conflict produced by these contrary principles, but their presence and exercise prevent the soul from fully attaining its desires and doing as it would (Gal. 5:17).

Abraham's obedience to the divine command was both partial and tardy. God had bidden him to leave his own country, separate from his kindred, and "come into the land" which He would show him (Acts 7:3). His failure is recorded in Genesis 11:31: "And Terah took Abram his son, and Lot the son of Haran his son's son, and Sarai his daughter in law, his son Abram's wife; and they went forth with them from Ur of the Chaldees, to go into the land of Canaan; and they came unto Haran, and dwelt there." He left Chaldea; but instead of leaving behind his kindred, his father and nephew accompanied him. This was the more excuseless because Isaiah 51:2 expressly declares that God had called Abraham "alone." It is significant to note that the word

"Terah" means "delay," and such his presence occasioned Abraham, for instead of entering the land of Canaan at once, he stopped short at Haran, and there he remained for five years until Terah died (Gen. 11:32; 12:4, 5).

And why did the Lord suffer the "flesh" in Abraham to mar his obedience? To indicate to his spiritual children that absolute perfection of character and conduct is not attainable in this life. We do not call attention to this fact so as to encourage loose living or to lower the exalted standard at which we must ever aim, but to cheer those who are discouraged because their honest and ardent efforts after godliness so often fall below that standard. Again; there is only One who has walked this earth in perfect obedience to God in thought and word and deed, and that not occasionally, but constantly and uninterruptedly; and He must "have the pre-eminence in all things." Therefore God will not suffer Christ's glory to be reduced by fashioning others to honor Him as *He* did. Finally, God's permitting the flesh to exist and be active in Abraham further magnified the divine grace, by making it still further manifest that it was through no excellency in him that he had been called.

"Then came he out of the land of the Chaldeans, and dwelt in Haran: and from thence, when his father was dead, he removed him into this land" (Acts 7:4). Though God had suffered the flesh in Abraham to mar his obedience, yet He would not allow it to completely triumph. Divine grace is not only magnified by the unworthiness of its object, but it is glorified in triumphing over the flesh and producing what is contrary thereto. The hindrance to Abraham's obedience was removed, and now we see him actually entering the place to which God had called him.

III

The first thing recorded of Abraham after he had actually entered the land of Canaan is the Lord's appearing unto him and his building an altar: "And Abram passed through the land unto the place of Sichem, unto the plain of Moreh. And the Canaanite was then in the land. And the Lord appeared unto Abram, and said, Unto thy seed will I give this land: and there builded he an altar unto the Lord" (Gen. 12:6, 7). There are several details here which claim our attention.

1. Abraham did not settle down and enter into possession of the land, but "passed through it," as Acts 7:5 tells us: "And he gave him none inheritance in it, no, not so much as to set foot on."

2. The presence there of "the Canaanite"—to challenge and contest the possession of it. So it is with the believer: the flesh, the devil, and the world unite in opposing his present enjoyment of the inheritance unto which he has been begotten; while hosts of wicked spirits in the heavenlies wrestle with those who are partakers of the heavenly calling (Eph. 6:12).

3. "The Lord appeared unto Abram." He had done so originally as the "God of glory," when He revealed Himself to the patriarch in Chaldea. There is no intimation of Abraham receiving any further revelation from God during his delay at Haran; but now that God's call had been fully obeyed, he was favored with a fresh manifestation of Him.

And now Abraham's obedience is rewarded. At the beginning the Lord had said, "Get thee out of thy country and from thy kindred, and from thy father's house, unto a land that I will *show* thee" (Gen. 12:1); now He declared, "Unto thy seed will I *give* this land" (v. 7). This brings before us a most important principle in the ways of God, which has often been lost sight of by men who only stress one side of the truth. That principle is that divine grace never sets aside the requirements of divine righteousness. God never shows mercy at the expense of His holiness.

God is "light" as well as "love," and each of these divine perfections is exemplified in all His dealings with His people. Moreover, in the exercise of His sovereignty God never enforces the responsibility of the creature; and unless we keep both of these steadily in view, we not only become lopsided, but lapse into real error. The grace of God must not be magnified to the beclouding of His righteousness, nor His sovereignty pressed to the exclusion of human accountability. The balance can only be preserved by our faithfully adhering to Scripture. If we single out favorite verses and ignore those which are unpalatable to the flesh, we are guilty of handling the Word of God deceitfully, and fall under the condemnation of "according as ye have not kept my ways, but have been partial in the law" (Mal. 2:9). The principles of law and gospel are not contradictory, but supplementary, and neither can be dispensed with except to our irreparable loss.

What has been pointed out above supplies the keys to a right understanding of the Abrahamic covenant; and unless those dual principles be steadily kept before us in our contemplation of the same, we are certain to err. Some writers when referring to the Abrahamic covenant speak of it as "a covenant of pure grace," and such it truly

was; for what was there about Abraham to move the God of glory to
so much as notice him? Nevertheless, it would be equally correct to
designate the Abrahamic covenant "a covenant of righteousness," for
it exemplified the principles of the divine *government* as actually as it
made manifest the benignity of the divine *character*. Other writers
have referred to the Abrahamic covenant as an "unconditional one,"
but in this they erred, for to talk of "an unconditional covenant" is a
flat contradiction in terms. Suffer us to quote here from our first
chapter:

"Let us point out the *nature* of a covenant; in what it consists. 'An
absolute complete covenant is a voluntary convention, pact, or agreement between distinct persons, about the ordering and dispensing of
things in their power, unto their mutual concern and advantage' (J.
Owen). Blackstone, the great commentator upon English law, speaking
of the parts of a deed, says, 'After warrants, usually follow *covenants,*
or conventions, which are clauses of agreement, contained in a deed,
whereby either party may stipulate for the truth of certain facts, or
may bind himself to perform, or give something to the other' (Vol. 2,
p. 20). So he includes three things: the parties, the terms, the binding
agreement. Reducing it to still simpler language, we may say that a
covenant is the entering into of a mutual agreement, a benefit being
assured on the fulfillment of certain conditions."

We supplement by a quotation from H. Witsius: "The covenant
does, on the part of God, comprise three things in general. 1st. A
promise of consummate happiness in eternal life. 2nd. A designation
or *prescription* of the condition, by the performance of which, man
acquires a right to the promise. 3rd. A *penal sanction* against those
who do not come up to the prescribed condition. . . . Man becomes
the other party when he consents thereto: embracing the good promised by God, engaging to an exact observance of the condition required; and upon the violation thereof, voluntarily owning himself
obnoxious to the threatened curse."

Let it now be pointed out that in this chapter we are turning to
another side of the subject from what we have mainly dwelt upon in
the previous ones. In those we amplified what we said in the fourth
and fifth paragraphs of the second chapter. Having dwelt so largely
upon the divine sovereignty and grace aspects, we need to weigh
carefully the divine righteousness and human responsibility elements.
Having shown how the various covenants which God made with men
adumbrated the central features in the everlasting covenant which He
made with Christ, we are now required to consider how that in them
God maintained the claims of His righteousness by what He required
from the responsible agents with whom He dealt. It was not until after

Noah "did according to all that God commanded him" (Gen. 6:22) by preparing an ark "to the saving of his house" (Heb. 11:7), that God confirmed His "with thee will I establish my covenant" (Gen. 6:18) by "I establish my covenant" (9:9). Noah having fulfilled the divine stipulations, God was now prepared to fulfill His promises.

The same thing is clearly seen again in connection with Abraham. There is no hint in Scripture that the Lord entered into any covenant with him while he was in Ur of Chaldea. Instead, the land of Canaan was then set before him *provisionally:* "The Lord said unto Abram, Get thee out of thy country, and from thy kindred and from thy father's house, unto a land *that I will* show thee" (Gen. 12:1). The order there is unmistakably plain. First, God acted in grace, sovereign grace, by singling out Abraham from his idolatrous neighbors, and by calling him to something far better. Second, God made known the requirements of His righteousness and enforced Abraham's responsibility by the demand there made upon him. Third, the promised reward was to follow Abraham's response to God's call. These three things are conjoined in Heb. 11:8: "By faith Abraham, when he was called [by divine grace] to go out into a place which he should after receive for an inheritance [the reward], obeyed [the discharge of his responsibility] ; and he went out, not knowing whither he went."

Nor does what has just been said in anywise conflict with what was pointed out in previous chapters. The above elements just as truly shadowed forth another fundamental aspect of the everlasting covenant as did the different features singled out from the Adamic and the Noahic. In the everlasting covenant, God promised a certain reward unto Christ upon His fulfilling certain conditions—executing the appointed work. The inseparable principles of law and gospel, grace and reward, faith and works, were most expressly conjoined in that compact which God entered into with the Mediator before the foundation of the world. Therein we may behold the "manifold wisdom of God" in combining such apparent opposites; and instead of carping at their seeming hostility, we should admire the omniscience which has made the one the handmaid of the other. Only then are we prepared to discern and recognize the exercise of this dual principle in each of the subordinate covenants.

Not a few writers supposed they magnified the grace of God and honored the Mediator when affirming that Christ Himself so fulfilled the conditions of the covenant and so met every requirement of God's righteousness that His people have been entirely freed of all legal obligations, and that nothing whatever is left for them to do but express their gratitude in lives well-pleasing to Him. It is far easier to make this mistake than it is to expose it. It is true, blessedly true,

gloriously true, that Christ did perfectly discharge His covenant engagements, magnified the law and made it honorable, that God received from Him a full satisfaction for all the sins of His people. Yet
that does not mean that the law has been repealed, that God rescinds
His righteous claims upon the creature, or that believers are placed in a
position of privilege from which obligation is excluded; nor does it
involve the idea that saints are freed from covenant duties. Grace
reigns, but it reigns "through righteousness" (Rom. 5:21) and not at
the expense of it.

Christ's obedience has not rendered ours unnecessary: rather has it
rendered ours acceptable. In that sentence lies the solution to the
difficulty. The law of God will accept nothing short of perfect and
perpetual obedience; and such obedience the Surety of God's people
rendered, so that He brought in an everlasting righteousness which is
reckoned to their account. Yet that is only one half of the truth on
this subject. The other half is not that Christ's atonement has inaugurated a regime of lawlessness or license, but rather has it placed its
beneficiaries under additional obligations. But more: it had procured
the needed grace to enable those beneficiaries to discharge their
obligations—not perfectly, but nevertheless, acceptably to God. And
how? By securing that the Holy Spirit should bring them from death
unto life, impart to them a nature which delights in the law, and work
in them both to will and to do of God's good pleasure. And what is
God's good pleasure for His people? The same as it was for His
incarnate Son: to be perfectly conformed to the law in thought and
word and deed.

God has one and the same standard for the head and the members
of His church; and therefore we are told, "he that saith he abideth in
him ought himself also so to walk, even as he walked" (I John 2:6). In
I Peter 2:21 we read, "Christ also suffered for us." With what end in
view? That we might be relieved from all obligation to God? That we
might pursue a course of lawlessness under the pretense of magnifying
"grace"? No, indeed; but rather "leaving us an example that ye should
follow his steps." And what is the nature of that example which Christ
has left us? What, but "fulfilling the law" (Matt. 5:17), loving the
Lord His God with all His heart and mind and strength, and His
neighbor as Himself? But in order to do this there must be a nature in
harmony with the law and not enmity against it. Could Christ declare,
"I delight to do thy will, O my God: yea, thy law is within my heart"
(Ps. 40:8), so can each of His redeemed and regenerated people say, "I
delight in the law of God after the inward man," (Rom. 7:22). And
were there nothing else in them but the new man they would render
perfect obedience to the law. Such is their honest desire, but the
presence of the old man thwarts them.

The everlasting covenant was, in its nature and contents, a mixed one, for the principles of both law and grace were operative therein. It was grace pure and simple which ordained that any from Adam's fallen race should be saved, as it was amazing and infinite grace that provided the Son of God should become incarnate and serve as their surety. But it was law pure and simple that the Surety should earn and purchase their salvation by His rendering unto God a perfect satisfaction on their behalf. Christ was "made under the law" (Gal. 4:4). His whole life was perfectly conformed to the precepts of the law, and His death was an enduring of the penalty of the law; and all of this was in fulfillment of His covenant engagements. In like manner, these two principles of grace and law are operative in connection with the administration of the everlasting covenant—that is, in the application of its benefits to those on whose behalf Christ transacted. "Do we then make void the law through faith? God forbid: yea, we establish the law" (Rom. 3:31).

The work of Christ has released the believer from the law as a procuring cause of his justification, but it has in nowise abolished it as his rule of life. Divine grace does not set aside its recipient's responsibility, nor does the believer's obedience render grace any the less necessary. God requires obedience (conformity to His law) from the Christian as truly as He does from the non-Christian. True, we are not saved *for* (because of) our obedience; yet it is equally true that we cannot be saved *without* it. Unless Noah had heeded God and built the ark, he had perished in the Flood; yet it was by the goodness and power of God that the ark was preserved. It is through Christ, and Christ alone, that the believer's obedience is acceptable to God. But it may be asked, Will God accept an imperfect obedience from us? The answer is yes, if it be sincere; just as He is pleased to answer our poor prayers when presented in the all-meritorious name of His Son.

Once again we would point out that any covenant necessarily signifies a *mutual* agreement, with terms to be carried out by both parties. A vivid but most solemn example of this is found in the case of Judas and the chief priests of the Jews, concerning whom we read: "they covenanted with him for thirty pieces of silver" (Matt. 26:15). That is to say, in return for his fulfilling the contract to betray his Master into their hands, they would pay him this sum of money, which, in Acts 1:18, is denominated "the reward of iniquity." It is only by paying close attention to all the expressions used in Scripture of God's covenant and of our relation thereto, that we can obtain a right and full conception thereof. We read of those "that *take hold of* my covenant" (Isa. 56:4, 6); "that thou shouldest *enter into* covenant with the Lord thy God" (Deut. 23:12); "those that have *made* a covenant with me by sacrifice" (Ps. 50:5); "mercy and truth unto such as *keep* his covenant and his testimonies" (Ps. 25:10); "be ye *mindful* always of his covenant" (I Chron. 16:15); "Ye *break* my covenant" (Lev. 26:15); "them that *forsake* the holy covenant" (Dan. 11:30).

Against what has been said above, it may be objected that this reduces the covenant of grace to one and the same level with the covenant of works. Not so, we reply; for though those covenants have something in common, yet there is a real and radical difference between them. Each of them maintains the claims of God's righteousness by enforcing the requirements of the law, but the covenant of works had no mediator, nor was any provision made for those who failed under it; whereas the covenant of grace supplies both. Moreover, under the covenant of works obedience was rendered unto an absolute God, whereas under the covenant of grace it is given to God in Christ, and there is a world of difference between those two things. The application of these principles to the case of Abraham we must consider next.

IV

In the application unto Abraham of those divine principles considered in the preceding chapter, it should be quite obvious that the law of his obedience was attended with both promises and threatenings, rewards and punishments, suited unto the goodness and holiness of God, and fitted for the discharge of his moral responsibility. It may be asked, Where is there any hint in Scripture of any provisos and terms attached to the Abrahamic covenant, or any clear statement that God stipulated any terms to him? Such a question is capable of several answers. In the first place, unless there *were* such provisos and terms, no covenant had been made at all. Second, the extreme brevity of the Genesis account must be borne in mind; and instead of expecting a full categorical statement, its fragmentary details need to be carefully pieced together. Third, Genesis 12:1 shows plainly that Canaan was first set before him *provisionally*.

In addition to what has just been said, we would point out what the Lord declared in connection with the sign and seal of this covenant: "the uncircumcised manchild whose flesh of his foreskin is not circumcised, that soul shall be cut off from his people: he hath broken my covenant" (Gen. 17:14). Here, then, it is clear that a condition was stipulated, the failure to meet which broke the covenant. Again, in Genesis 18:19 we find God saying, "For I know him, that he will command his children and his household after him, and they shall keep the way of the Lord, to do justice and judgment; that [in order that] the Lord may bring upon Abraham that which he hath spoken of him." Abraham had to "keep the way of the Lord," which is defined as "to do justice and judgment"; that is, walk obediently, in subjection to God's revealed will, if he was to receive the fulfillment of the divine promises. Once more, we read "Abraham obeyed my voice, and kept my charge, my commandments, my statutes, and my laws" (Gen. 26:5). Thus, while God dealt with Abraham in pure grace, it is plain that he was also placed under the law.

Some readers are likely to object, This is a wretched subversion of the glorious covenant of grace: by your "conditions," "terms," and "provisos" you reduce it to a contingency and uncertainty, instead of its being "ordered in all things and *sure.*" Our first rejoinder is that *we* have not introduced the conditions and provisos into the covenant; instead, they are so stated in Scripture. God did not make an absolute grant of Canaan unto Abraham when He first revealed Himself to him in Chaldea. Rather was he required to tread the path of obedience unto that land "which he should *after* receive for an inheritance." Nor does God make an absolute (or unconditional) grant of heaven when the sinner first believes in Christ. Instead, He requires him to walk the narrow way which alone leadeth unto life, and faithfully warns him that it is to his imminent peril if he converges therefrom.

It may be replied, But this is to leave all at an uncertainty. It all depends upon the angle from which you view it. Considered as the object of God's everlasting love, as chosen in Christ, as redeemed by Him, as indwelt and sealed by the Spirit, the believer's safely reaching heaven is placed beyond all peradventure. But consider the believer as a responsible agent, as still having the "flesh" in him, living in a world where he is beset by temptation on every side, called upon to "fight the good fight of faith" and to "lay hold on eternal life," and the matter appears in quite another light; and the one viewpoint is just as *real and actual* as is the other! The difficulty here as to whether or not the believer's "keeping" or "breaking" the covenant renders all insecure, is precisely the same as showing the consistency between divine *preservation* and Christian *perseverance.* Though the "ifs" of John 8:31 and Colossians 1:23 do not annul the promise of Philippians 1:6, nevertheless, they are there, and must be taken into account by us.

From the divine side, the covenant of grace is "ordered in all things and sure." There is not the slightest possibility of anything in it failing. Christ will "see of the travail of his soul and be satisfied," and not one of those given to Him by the Father before the foundation of the world will be lost. But that does not alter the fact that while the elect are left here in this world they are bidden to "make their calling and election sure" (II Peter 1:10), "if they may apprehend [lay hold of] that for which also they were apprehended of Christ Jesus" (Phil. 3:12). The covenant has provided for the communication of effectual grace to secure the saints' obedience and perseverance; yet that does not alter the fact that God still enforces His righteous claims upon them and deals with them as moral agents who are required to heed His warnings, obey His precepts, and use the means He has appointed for their preservation.

Some experience difficulty in fitting together those Scriptures which present eternal life as the present and inalienable possession of the believer with other passages that place it in the future and as only being attained unto by following a course of self-denial. Such verses as John 5:24 and Romans 6:23 are quite simple to them; but Romans 6:22; 8:13; Galatians 6:8; and Jude 21 they are at a loss to know what to do with. But there is nothing inconsistent between a believer acting from a principle of grace and life *already* communicated to him by the Holy Spirit, and his so acting that he *may* live. A man must be alive before he can eat; yet he must eat in order that he may live. Were he to cease entirely from the taking of food, would there be any life for him in a month's time? Neither would the Christian enter heaven if he entirely neglected the means of grace appointed for his spiritual preservation.

Of old, Moses said unto Israel, "The Lord thy God *will* circumcise thine heart, and the heart of thy seed, to love the Lord thy God with all thine heart, and with all thy soul, that thou mayest live" (Deut. 30:6). Was he, then, inconsistent when, at the close of the same address, he declared: "I call heaven and earth to record this day against you, that I have set before you life and death, blessing and cursing: therefore choose life, that both thou and thy seed *may* live: That thou mayest love the Lord thy God, and that thou mayest obey his voice, and that thou mayest cleave unto him: For he *is* thy life, and the length of thy days: that thou mayest dwell in the land which the Lord sware unto thy fathers, to Abraham, to Isaac, and to Jacob, to give them" (vv. 19, 20)? Was Moses there setting before them a "yea and nay gospel"? Emphatically, no; for he was the mouthpiece of Jehovah Himself. Nor was this appeal a "legal" one, but a strictly "evangelical" one. Alas, that so many today err, "not knowing the Scriptures." "Know therefore that the Lord thy God, He is God, the faithful God, which keepeth covenant and mercy with them that love him and keep his commandments to a thousand generations"—not merely from Moses till Christ (Deut. 7:9)—yes, and with no others. This verse is just as much a part of the holy and inspired Word of God as is Ephesians 2:8, 9; and the one is needed by us as much as the other.

It might be objected, This is bringing in a legalistic inducement and inculcating a mercenary spirit to put the believer upon using means in order to obtain his preservation, and setting before him heaven or eternal life as a reward for his faithfulness. In reply, let us quote from the renowned and evangelical Dutch theologian: "A mercenary baseness is certainly unworthy of the high-born sons of God, but their heavenly Father does not forbid them to have any regard to *their own* advantage in the exercise of holiness. David himself confesseth that, the judgments of the Lord are true and righteous altogether. 'By them is Thy servant warned, and *in keeping of them* there is great *reward*' (Psa. 19:9, 11). And the faith of Moses is commended because 'he had respect unto the recompense *of the reward*' (Heb. 11:26). Yea, *that* faith is required of all who come to God, that they '*must* believe that He is, and that He is a *Rewarder* of them that diligently seek Him'— Heb. 11:6" (from *Irenicon*, by H. Witsius, 1696).

To anticipate one more objection—not with any expectation of convincing the carping critic, but rather in the hope of helping some who are in a state of bewilderment from the one-sided teaching of our unhappy day—But does not all of the above inculcate the principle of human merit? No, for it is due alone to divine grace that the believer has had communicated to him a principle of obedience—a heart or nature which desires to please God. Furthermore, it is solely for Christ's sake that God so liberally rewards the sincere endeavors of His people, for apart from the Mediator and His merits, they could not be accepted by Him. Finally, there is no proportion whatever between the Christian's obedience and the reward he receives—the inheritance infinitely exceeding his poor efforts—any more than there was in God's giving Canaan to Abraham and his seed because he left Chaldea.

Coming closer now to our immediate theme, it should be pointed out that the Abrahamic covenant is not to be regarded as a thing apart, having no direct connection with what went before or what followed it; but rather is it to be viewed as a part of and a further step in the unfolding unto God's people of His eternal counsels. The call of Abraham was a most important step in the outworking of God's purpose. It was one of those remarkable epochs in the history of the church which produced a new order of things, in perfect keeping with, yet greatly in advance of, what had previously been communicated. The work of preparation for the appearance of the Messiah now assumed a more tangible form and entered on a phase bearing more visibly upon the attainment of the ultimate result. The line from which the promised Seed was to spring was now more definitely defined, while the scope of divine grace was more clearly revealed.

The declaration made by the Lord God in Eden after Adam's transgression, that the Seed of the woman should triumph over and destroy the serpent, had been the ground of the saints' faith and the object of their hope during the first two thousand years' history of the world. Until the time of Abraham, nothing more had been revealed concerning the person of the coming deliverer (so far as Scripture records) than that He was to be of the human race; but of what particular family, or even of which nation, no one was informed. Where men were to look for Him, whether in Egypt, in Babylon, or in some other land, did not yet transpire. But in the covenant which God made with Abraham, not only was the promise of a Savior renewed, but His family and place were now made known. For this great honor the "friend of God" was selected: to him it was revealed that the Messiah should spring from his stock, and that the land of Canaan would be the scene of His glorious mission.

Not only should the Abrahamic covenant be regarded as part of a greater whole rather than an isolated transaction, but attention must not be restricted to any single episode in the patriarch's life or God's dealings with him. We fully agree with John Kelly when he said, "If we would form an accurate estimate of that covenant, and of the truth which it was the means of revealing, we must not confine ourselves to any one particular transaction in which allusion is made to it, however important that transaction may have been. Our examination must embrace all the incidents recorded. We must bear in mind that everything that occurred to Abraham, from his call to the close of his life, was intended to explain and illustrate the nature of the Covenant."

It was not by one specific communication that the mind of God was fully disclosed unto Abraham. Several were made at different times, all relating to the same subject and unfolding the import of the covenant; while the character of Abraham himself—shaped by the various trials through which he was called to pass and molded by grace through faith—throws important light upon the conceptions which he entertained of what had been revealed to him. All these form one homogeneous whole; and from them, thus considered, we are to form our views of the covenant. When Abraham was first called by the Lord, a bare hint was given him of the divine purpose, which, under the Spirit's blessing, was the means of quickening his faith and producing the decision which he made. Yet only a glimpse was then afforded him of what God designed: it was not the formal establishment of the covenant. That event took place subsequently, after an interval of some years.

What has just been said appears to receive confirmation from Galatians 3:16, 17: "Now to Abraham and his seed was the promise made. He saith not, And to seeds, as of many; but as of one, and to thy seed, which is Christ. And this I say, that the covenant, that was confirmed before of God in Christ, the law, which was four hundred and thirty years after, cannot disannul, that it should make the promise of none effect." "Four hundred and thirty years" prior to the giving of the law at Sinai takes us back to the beginning of God's dealings with Abraham, recorded in Genesis 12, though the actual term covenant is not found in that chapter. It is not until we reach Genesis 15:18 that we find the transaction itself: "In that same day, the Lord made a covenant with Abram, saying, Unto thy seed have I given this land." Then in Genesis 17 we find the sign and seal of the covenant—circumcision—given. To the covenant there are other references in the chapters which follow: in Genesis 22 the covenant is confirmed. Thus, in fact, the covenant received important and successive enlargements during the intercourse which God, in infinite condescension, continued to have with His servant. Hebrews 6:13-18 links together the great promise of Genesis 12:3 and the oath of Genesis 22:15-18.

In our endeavor, then, to obtain a correct and comprehensive view of the divine transaction in the Abrahamic covenant, we are required to carefully examine all the information which the Genesis narrative supplies: the leading events in Abraham's own life (which are designed as a contribution for imparting an explanation), and the light which the New Testament casts upon them both, and regard all in its entire unity as illustrative of the covenant. To confine ourselves to one passage, however important it may seem to be, would be doing injustice to the subject. It is failure at this point which has resulted in so many superficial, inadequate, and one-sided discussions of the same by various writers. Those who approach the examination and consideration of the Abrahamic covenant (or any other Scriptural theme) with a single pet theory or idea in their minds, which they are determined to establish at all costs, cannot expect to obtain a right and full view of the covenant as a whole.

We shall, then, regard the Abrahamic covenant as a striking advance in the development of God's gracious purpose toward men, and yet as only a part of a greater and grander whole. In so doing, what will claim our special attention is, What was the particular nature and what the amount of the truth, which it was the means of revealing? Upon these points a very wide diversity of opinion obtains, both among the older and more recent writers. Exactly what did the Abrahamic covenant make manifest to the minds and hearts of God's people of old? And how far does the same apply to us now? The proper answers to these questions must be drawn from Holy Writ itself, fairly interpreted. Perhaps our best course is to single out the leading particulars, and then comment thereon as each may seem to require.

V

"Now the Lord had said unto Abram, Get thee out of thy country, and from thy kindred, and from thy father's house, unto a land that I will show thee: And I will make of thee a great nation, and I will bless thee, and make thy name great; and thou shalt be a blessing: And I will bless them that bless thee, and curse him that curseth thee: and in thee shall all the families of the earth be blessed" (Gen. 12:1-3). In this simple narrative we have the original promise made to Abraham that the Messiah should come of his family. This divine pledge was made to the patriarch when he was only a little short of seventy-five years of age. It was given at a point in human history halfway between the creation of the first Adam and the incarnation of the last Adam— that is, two thousand years after the entrance of sin into the world and two thousand years before the advent of the Savior.

The first great purpose of the Abrahamic covenant was to make known the stock from which the Messiah was to spring. This was the most prominent aspect of truth revealed in it: the appearing of the promised Seed in Abraham's own line. The primary intimation of this was given to the patriarch when God first appeared to him: "In thee shall all the families of the earth be blessed." Two things are to be noted in the language there used. First, the "all families *of the earth* be blessed" obviously looks back to Genesis 3:17, for the *"all* families" was sufficiently definite to announce the international scope of the blessing. It is indeed very striking to observe that in Genesis 12:3 God did not use the word *eretz* (as in Gen. 1:1; 14:19; 18:25, etc.), but *adamah* (as in Gen. 3:17). The manifest link between "Cursed is the *ground*" (Gen. 3:17) would have been made more evident had Genesis 12:3 been rendered "in thee shall all families of the *ground* be blessed"—the curse was to be removed by Christ!

Second, the terms of this Messianic intimation were quite general in their character. Later, this original promise was repeated in more specific form: the "*in thee* shall all the families of the earth be blessed" being defined as "*in thy seed* shall all the nations of the earth be blessed." This illustrates an important principle which may be discerned throughout the divine revelation, namely, that of progressive unfolding: "first the blade, then the ear, after that the full corn in the ear" (Mark 4:28). This is evident here by a comparison of the far-reaching promises made to Abraham with the prophecies of Noah concerning his three sons. Jehovah was the God of Shem, yet Japheth should dwell in his tents (Gen. 9:26, 27); now He becomes known as "the God of Abraham," but all families of the ground should be blessed in him and his seed. What a striking advance was here made in the divine plan, by revealing the breadth of its meaning and the explicitness of its purpose!

"By his call Abraham was raised to a very singular pre-eminence and constituted in a manner the root and centre of the world's future history, as concerned the attainment of real blessing. Still, even in that respect, not exclusively. The blessing was to come chiefly to Abraham, and through him; but, as already indicated in the prophecy on Shem, others were to stand, though in a subordinate rank, on the same line—since those also were to be blessed who blessed him, that is, who held substantially the same faith, and occupied the same friendly relation to God. The cases of such persons in the patriarch's own day, as his kinsman Lot, who was not formally admitted into Abraham's covenant, and still more of Melchizedek, who was not even of Abraham's line and yet individually stood in some sense higher than Abraham himself, clearly showed, and were no doubt partly raised up for the purpose of showing, that there was nothing arbitrary in Abraham's position, and that the ground he occupied was to a certain extent common to believers generally.

"The peculiar honour conceded to him was, that the great trunk of blessing was to be of him, while only some isolated twigs or scattered branches were to be found elsewhere; and even these could only be found by persons coming, in a manner, to make common cause with him. In regard to himself, however, the large dowry of good conveyed to him in the Divine promise could manifestly not be realised through him personally. There could at the most be but a beginning made in his own experience and history: and the widening of the circle of blessing to other kindreds and regions, till it reached to the most distant families of the earth, must necessarily be affected by means of those who were to spring from him. Hence the original word of promise 'In thee shall all families of the earth be blessed,' was afterwards changed into 'In thy seed shall all the nations of the earth be blessed' " (P. Fairbairn).

It needs pointing out, though, that each of those expressions had its own specific significance and importance, and that they must be conjoined so as to bring out the full design of God in the calling of Abraham. The promised blessing was to be wrought out in its widest sense not by Abraham individually and immediately, but through him mediately, by means of the seed that should be given to him. This clearly implied that that seed must possess far higher qualities than any to be found in Abraham himself, since blessing from it would flow out so widely; yea, it only thinly veiled the truth that there should be a wondrous commingling of the divine with the human. Christ, then, as the essential kernel of the promise and the Seed of Abraham, rather than Abraham himself, was to have the honor of blessing all nations.

But what we have just called attention to by no means evacuates the force of the original "*in thee* shall all families of the earth be blessed"; for by so definitely connecting the good with Abraham himself as well as with his seed, the organic connection was marked between the one and the other. "The blessing to be brought to the world through his line had even in his time a present though small realisation—precisely as the kingdom of Christ had its commencement in that of David, and the one ultimately merged into the other. And so, in Abraham as the living root of all that was to follow, the whole and every part may be said to take its rise" (P. Fairbairn). Not only was Christ after the flesh "the son of Abraham" (Matt. 1:1), but every believer in Christ is of Abraham's seed (Gal. 3:29); and the entire company of the redeemed shall have their place and portion "with Abraham" in the kingdom of God (Matt. 8:11).

Other promises followed, such as "unto thy seed will I give this land" (Gen. 12:7), "to be a God unto thee and to thy seed after thee" (Gen. 17:7), and so forth, which we shall consider later. That which immediately concerns us is the meaning of the term "seed" in these passages. The Scripture which throws the most light thereon is Galatians 3:16, 17: "Now to Abraham and his seed were the promises made. He saith not, and to seeds, as of many; but as of one, and to thy seed, which is Christ. And this I say, that the covenant, that was confirmed before of God in Christ, the law, which was four hundred and thirty years after, cannot disannul, that it should make the promise of none effect." Yet strange to say, this passage has occasioned the commentators much trouble, no two of them agreeing in its interpretation. It is commonly regarded as one of the most abstruse passages in all the Pauline Epistles.

Matthew Henry says, "The covenant is made with Abraham and his Seed. And he (the apostle) gives us a very surprising exposition of that," but he attempts no detailed interpretation at all. J. N. Darby seeks to cut the knot by changing the apostle's "promises" to "the promise," restricting the reference to Genesis 22. Yet not only is the Greek in the plural number, but such an idea is plainly refuted by the "four hundred and thirty years after," which necessarily carries us back to Genesis 12. Albert Barnes discusses at great length what he terms "the perplexities of this very difficult passage of Scripture." But as usual, the commentators have created their own difficulties: partly by failing to take into full account the immediate context, and partly through a slavish adherence to "the letter," thereby missing the "spirit" of the verse.

"Now to Abraham and his seed were the promises made." Abraham was the "father" of a twofold "seed," a natural and a spiritual; and if we attend unto the context here, there is not the slightest difficulty in determining which of them the Holy Spirit has in view. In verse 6 He had said, "Even as Abraham believed God, and it was accounted to him for righteousness"; from which the conclusion is drawn, "Know ye therefore that they which are of faith, the same are the children of Abraham" (v. 7). What could be plainer than that? They which are "of faith," genuine believers, are "the children of Abraham": that is, his spiritual children—he being their "father" as the pattern to which they are conformed. In other words, sinners today are justified by God in precisely the same way as Abraham was—by faith.

"And the scripture, foreseeing that God would justify the heathen [Gentiles] through faith, preached before the gospel unto Abraham: In thee shall all nations be blessed. So then they which be of faith are blessed with faithful Abraham" (Gal. 3:8, 9). The same truth is here reaffirmed. In view of God's purpose to justify Gentiles by faith, He proclaimed that gospel to Abraham himself, saying, "In thee shall all nations be blessed." Let it be carefully noted that the Holy Spirit here quotes from Genesis 12, and *not* from Genesis 22. The same conclusion is again drawn: believers receive the identical spiritual blessing that Abraham did, namely, the righteousness of Christ imputed to their account, so that they now measure up to every requirement of the law. And that, because "Christ hath redeemed us from the curse of the law, being made a curse for us" (v. 13); this having opened the way "that the blessing of Abraham might come on the Gentiles through Jesus Christ; that we might receive the promise of the Spirit through faith" (v. 14).

"Brethren, I speak after the manner of men; Though it be but a man's covenant, yet if it be confirmed, no man disannulleth, or addeth thereto" (Gal. 3:15). But in the case before us we have far more than "a man's covenant"—we have a *divine* covenant, for God solemnly ratified His promises to Abraham by covenant. "Now to Abraham and his seed were the promises made" (v. 16). Now in the light of "the children of Abraham" (v. 7), "they which be of faith are blessed with faithful Abraham" (v. 9), and "that the blessing of Abraham might come on the Gentiles through Jesus Christ" (v. 14), "to Abraham and his seed" must mean "to Abraham and his *spiritual* seed were the promises made." Collateral proof of this is supplied by Romans 4:16, "Therefore it is of faith, that it might be by grace, to the end the promise might be sure to all the seed; not to that only which is of the law, but to that also which is of the faith of Abraham; who is the father of us all"; for it is only all of his *spiritual* seed who are assured of the blessings promised.

"He saith not, And to seeds, as of many; but as of one, And to thy seed, which is Christ" (Gal. 3:16). This is the clause which many have found so perplexing. They have pointed out that, both in the Old Testament and the New, the term "seed" often refers to descendants *without* limitation, just as the word *posterity* does with us. Furthermore, it is a fact, which a use of the concordance will amply confirm, that this term "seed" is never used in the plural at all to denote a posterity, the singular form being constantly employed for that purpose; indeed the plural form of the word never occurs except here in Galatians 3:16. This presents a problem for which no literalist can supply any satisfactory solution, which plainly intimates that it was not with the surface meaning of the term the apostle was here treating.

"The force of his reasoning here depends not on the mere dictionary *word* 'seed,' but upon the great scriptural *idea* which, more and more clearly in Old Testament revelation, becomes manifested through that word—the idea of an individual person, who should sum up in Himself the covenant people as well as (for them) the covenant blessings, that is, the promised Messiah, *Christ*" (Jas. MacGregor, on Galatians, 1879). This is the only writer we are acquainted with who has indicated the direction in which we must look for the true explanation of the apostle's terms, namely, not in their merely literal signification, but in the spiritual concept which they embodied—just as the term "christ" literally signifies "anointed," but is employed as the special title of the Savior, and is given to Him not as a private but public person, including both the Head and members of the church (I Cor. 12:12).

"He saith not, And to seeds, as of many; but as of one, And to thy seed, which is Christ." To sum up. The promises of God were never by human procreation, the other by divine regeneration. But the promises were not made to both of his seeds, but to one of them only, namely, the spiritual, the mystical "Christ"—the Redeemer and all who are legally and vitally united to Him. Thus the antithesis drawn by the apostle is between the *unity* of the "seed" in contrast from the *diversity* of the "seeds." This had been strikingly shadowed forth on the earth plane. Abraham had two sons; but one of them, Ishmael, was excluded from the highest privileges: "In *Isaac* shall thy seed be called" (Gen. 21:12). But those words did not signify, All the descendants of Isaac are destined unto heavenly bliss; rather do they affirm that it was from Isaac that the promised Messiah would, according to the flesh, descend.

Later, the line of Messiah's descent was more definitely restricted; for of Isaac's two sons, Esau was rejected and Jacob was chosen as the progenitor of Christ. Out of Jacob's twelve sons, Judah was selected as the tribe from which the promised Seed should issue. Out of all the thousands of Judah, the family of Jesse was the one honored to give birth to the Savior (Isa. 11:1). Of Jesse's eight sons (I Sam. 16:10, 11), David was appointed to be the father of the Messiah. Thus we may see that as time went on, the channel through which Abraham's Seed should issue was more definitely narrowed down and defined, and therein and thereby God gradually made it known how His original promises to Abraham were to receive their fulfillment. The *limitation* of these promises was evidenced by the rejection of Ishmael, and then of Esau, which clearly intimated that all of Abraham's descendants were not included therein; until, ultimately, it was seen that their *fulfillment* was received in Christ Himself and those united to Him.

Had the promises of God to Abraham embraced both branches of his family including Ishmael as well as Isaac, then some other term than "seed" would have been used. But God so ordered that so different were the circumstances of their births and future lives, so diverse were the prophecies respecting them, and so utterly dissimilar were the two races that sprang from them, that in Scripture the descendants of Ishmael ceased to be spoken of as the posterity of Abraham. And therein God adumbrated the wide gulf which separated the natural descendants of Abraham (the Jews) from his spiritual children (Christians), and has thereby rendered excuseless our confounding the one with the other when looking for the fulfillment of the promises. The promises were limited originally, and that limitation was evidenced more clearly by successive revelations, until it was shown that none but Christ (and those united to Him) were included: "And to thy seed, which is Christ" (mystical)!

"He saith not, And to seeds, as of many; but as of one, And to thy seed, which is Christ." To sum up. The promises of God were never made to all the descendants of Abraham, like so many different kinds of "seed," but were limited to the spiritual line, that is, to "Christ" mystical. Hence the unbelieving descendants of Jacob were as much excluded from those promises as were the posterity of Ishmael and Esau. Contrariwise, believing Gentiles, one with Christ in the everlasting covenant, were as truly embraced by them, as were Isaac and Jacob and all the godly Israelites.

VI

What was before us in the last chapter is of fundamental importance: not only to a right understanding of the Abrahamic covenant itself, but also for a sound interpretation of much of the Old Testament. Once it is clearly recognized that *the type merges into the antitype,* that believers in Christ are Abraham's "children" (Rom. 4:16; Gal. 3:7), citizens of the free and heavenly Jerusalem (Gal. 4:16; Eph. 2:19; Rev. 21:2, 14), the "circumcision" (Phil. 3:3), the "Israel of God" (Gal. 6:16; Eph. 2:12, 13), the "comers unto Mount Zion" (Heb. 12:22), it will be found that we have a reliable guide for conducting us through the mazes of prophecy, without which we are sure to lose ourselves in inextricable confusion and uncertainty. This was common knowledge among the saints in days gone by, but alas a generation succeeded them boasting they had new light, only to plunge themselves and their followers into gross darkness.

The promises of God to Abraham and his seed were never made to his natural descendants, but belonged to those who had a like faith with him. It could not be otherwise, "For all the promises of God in him [Christ] are yea, and in him amen, unto the glory of God by us" (II Cor. 1:20). All the "promises" (not "prophecies") of God are made *in Christ;* that is, all the blessings promised are placed in the hands of the Mediator, and none who are out of Christ can lay claim to a single one of them. All who are out of Christ are out of God's favor; and therefore the divine threatenings, and not the promises, are their portion. Here, then, is our reply to those who complain, "You apply to the church all the good things of the Old Testament, but the bad ones you relegate to the Jews." Of course we do; the *blessings* of God pertain to all who are in Christ; the *curses* of God to all—Jews or Gentiles—who are out of Christ.

Thus, the unbelieving descendants of Jacob were as much excluded from the Abrahamic promises as were the posterity of Ishmael and

Esau; whereas those promises belonged as really and truly to believing Gentiles as they did to Isaac, Jacob, and Joseph. But alas this basic truth, so clearly revealed in Scripture, is repudiated by "dispensationalists," who are perpetuating the error of those who opposed Christ in the days of His flesh. When He spoke of the spiritual freedom which He could bestow, His unregenerate hearers exclaimed, "We be Abraham's seed, and were never in bondage to any man" (John 8:33). When He made mention of His Father, the carnal Jews answered, "Abraham is our father"; to which the Savior replied, "If ye were Abraham's children, ye would do the works of Abraham" (John 8:39). Alas, alas, that so many of our moderns know not *who are* "Abraham's children."

The vital importance of what we sought to present in the last chapter will appear still more evident when it be pointed out that believers in Christ have *a joint heritage with Abraham,* as well as a common standing before God. But many will at once object to this, That cannot be; why, the inheritance of Abraham and his seed was an earthly one—it was the land of Canaan which God promised them! Our first answer is, Such was the firm belief of those who crucified the Lord of glory; such is still the conviction of all the "orthodox" Jews on earth today—Jews who despise and reject the Christ of God. Are *they* safe guides to follow? To say the least, professing Christians who share this view are not in very good company! The very fact that this idea is so widely entertained among Jews who have not the Spirit of God, should raise a strong suspicion in those claiming to have spiritual discernment.

Our second answer is that, If the inheritance of Abraham was an earthly one, namely, the land of Canaan, then most certainly the Christians' inheritance is an earthly one too, for we are all joint heirs with Abraham. Are you, my reader (no matter what you may have received from "deep students of prophecy"), prepared to settle this question by the plain teaching of Holy Scripture? If you are, it may quickly be brought to a simple issue: "And if ye be Christ's, then are ye Abraham's seed, *and heirs* according to the promise" (Gal. 3:29). What could be clearer than that: "If children, then heirs" (Rom. 8:17)—if children of God, then heirs of God; and in like manner, if children of Abraham, then heirs of and with Abraham. There is no legitimate escape from that obvious conclusion.

In the last verse of Galatians 3 the apostle drew the unavoidable inference from the premises which he had established in the context. Let us return for a moment to Galatians 3:16, and then observe what follows. There the plain statement is made: "Now to Abraham and to his seed were the promises made"; and, as we fully proved in our last chapter, the reference is to his spiritual seed. But as though to remove all possible uncertainty, the Holy Spirit has added: "and to thy seed, which is Christ"—Christ mystical as in I Corinthians 12:12 and Colossians 1:24; that is, Christ Himself and all who are united to Him. Thus there is no room left for a shadow of doubt as to whom the Abrahamic promises belonged—his carnal seed being expressly excluded in the "he saith not, and to seeds, as of many."

"And this I say, that the covenant, that was confirmed before of God in Christ, the law, which was four hundred and thirty years after, cannot disannul, that it should make the promise of none effect" (Gal. 3:17). The only difficulty lies in the words "in Christ." Inasmuch as "the covenant" here mentioned was confirmed only four hundred and thirty years before the law (at Sinai), the reference cannot be to the everlasting covenant—which *was* "confirmed" by God in Christ ere the world began (Titus 1:2, etc.). Hence we are obliged to adopt the rendering given by spiritual and able scholars: "the covenant that was confirmed before of God *concerning* Christ"—just as *eis Christon* is translated *"concerning* Christ" in Ephesians 5:32 and *eis auton* is rendered *"concerning* him" in Acts 2:25. Here, then, is a further word from God that His covenant with Abraham concerned Christ, that is, Christ mystical—Abraham's "Seed."

Now the special point that the apostle was laboring in Galatians 3 was that the promises given by God to Abraham (which were solemnly "confirmed" by His covenant oath) were given centuries before the Sinaitic economy was established; and that inasmuch as God is faithful so that His word cannot be broken (v. 15), then there could be nothing in connection with the giving of the law that would to the slightest degree invalidate what He was pledged to bestow: "The law, which was four hundred and thirty years after, cannot disannul, that it should make the promise of none effect." Be it observed that here "the promise" is in the singular number, the reason for this being that the apostle was about to confine himself to one particular promise, namely, that which respected the inheritance (v. 18).

"For if the inheritance be of the law, it is no more of promise: but God gave it to Abraham by promise" (v. 18). The inheritance was given to Abraham by God long before the law. The question now before us is, What was the inheritance which God gave to Abraham? Easily answered, replies someone: Genesis 12:7, 13:15, and so forth tell us it was "the land of Canaan"; and when God said "this land" He means that, and nothing else. Not quite so fast, dear friend. When a young believer reads Exodus 12, with its varied details of the slaying of the lamb, and the promise of shelter beneath its blood, and wonders what is the spiritual significance thereof, by far his best course is to turn to the New Testament, and prayerfully search for the answer. Eventually he will find that answer in I Corinthians 5:7: "Christ *our passover* is sacrificed for us."

When the young believer reads Leviticus 16, describing the elaborate ritual which the high priest of Israel was required to observe on the annual day of atonement, and is concerned to discover the spiritual meaning of the same, the ninth chapter of Hebrews will give him much light thereon. In like manner, those reading the historical account in Genesis 14 of Melchizedek, the king of Salem and priest of the Most High God, bringing forth bread and wine and blessing Abraham, to whom the patriarch paid tithes, may learn from Hebrews 7 that Melchizedek supplied a striking foreshadowment of the Lord Jesus in His official character. Now let us point out two things which are common to all these three examples. First, the New Testament teaching thereon in nowise reduces those important Old Testament incidents to mere allegories: it neither repudiates their historicity nor evacuates their literality. Second, but the New Testament does reveal that those Old Testament events possessed a higher meaning than their literal significance, that the historical was but a shadowing forth on earth of that which has its reality or antitype in heaven.

Why not, then, apply this same principle to God's promise to give the land of Canaan to Abraham and his seed? Since believers in Christ are Abraham's children and "heirs according to the promise," then it clearly follows that they are interested in *all* that was said or promised to him. It is a great mistake to regard certain of the Abrahamic promises as being simply of a temporal kind and restricted to his natural descendants, and that others were of a celestial character and pertained to his spiritual seed. The fact is that the outward and the temporal never existed by itself nor for itself, but was appointed as an adumbration of the spiritual and eternal, and as a means for the obtaining thereof. The outward and the temporal must be consistently viewed throughout as the shell and shadow of the spiritual and eternal.

Nor is the establishing of this important principle left in any doubt as it applies to the subject of the inheritance of Abraham and his seed. In chapter 11 of Hebrews we find the patriarchs themselves identifying their prospects of a future inheritance with ours. "By faith he sojourned in the land of promise, as in a strange country, dwelling in tents with Isaac and Jacob, the heirs with him of the same promise: For he looked for a city which hath foundations, whose builder and maker is God. These all died in faith, not having received the promises, but having seen them afar off, and were persuaded of them, and embraced them, and confessed that they were strangers and pilgrims on the earth. For they that say such things declare plainly that they seek a country. And truly, if they had been mindful of that country from whence they came out, they might have had opportunity to have returned. But now they desire a better country, that is, a heavenly: wherefore God is not ashamed to be called their God, for he hath prepared for them a city" (vv. 9-16). How clear it is from these verses that they looked beyond the literal purport of the promises, unto a heavenly and eternal inheritance, namely, to the same described in I Peter 1:4.

We are not now concerned with considering the immediate ends which were served by the natural descendants of Abraham occupying the earthly Canaan—a consideration parallel with the temporal advantages enjoyed by those who lived under the literal exercise of the Aaronic priesthood. Whatever be or be not the future of Palestine in relation to the Jews, even though they again occupy it for a thousand years, certain it is that the promise of God that Abraham and his seed should have "the land of Canaan for an *everlasting* possession" (Gen. 17:8) has not, will not, and cannot be fulfilled in his natural posterity; for that land, in common with the whole earth, is to be destroyed! No, rather are we now concerned with the spiritual and antitypical meaning thereof.

Our third answer, then, to the oft-made affirmation that the inheritance of Abraham and his seed was an earthly one, is that it is repudiated by Scripture itself. Was the inheritance of Moses an earthly one? No, indeed; for of him we read, "Esteeming the reproach of Christ greater riches than the treasures in Egypt: for he had respect unto the recompence of the reward" (Heb. 11:26). Was the inheritance of David an earthly one? No, indeed; for after his kingdom was established, he declared, "Hold not thy peace at my tears, for I am a stranger with thee; and a sojourner, as all my fathers were" (Ps. 39:12); and again, "I am a stranger in the earth" (Ps. 119:19). The "land of Canaan" is no more to be understood in a carnal way than the "seed" of Abraham is to be regarded as his natural posterity. The land of Canaan was no more given to the Jews after the flesh than the "blessing of Abraham" (namely, the Holy Spirit—Galatians 3:14) has come upon them.

"For the promise, that he should be the heir of the world, was not made to Abraham, or to his seed, through the law, but through the righteousness of faith" (Rom. 4:13). Observe two things: first, it was promised that Abraham should be not merely "the heir of Palestine," but "of the world"; and second, this promise was made to Abraham *and* "to his seed," which "seed" is defined in Romans 4:12 as those who "walk in the steps of that faith" which their "father Abraham" had. In perfect harmony with this our Lord declared, "Blessed are the meek, for they shall inherit [possess, have dominion over, enjoy] *the earth*" (Matt. 5:5). If literalists have cast such a shadow over this verse that some readers find it hard to understand, then we suggest that they ponder it in the light of I Corinthians 3:21-23 and I John 5:4! In concluding this important chapter we feel that we cannot do better than give the spiritual Calvin's comments on Romans 4:13, which are a refreshing contrast from the carnalizings of "dispensationalists."

"Since he now speaks of eternal salvation, the apostle seems to have somewhat unseasonably led his readers to 'the world'; but he includes generally under this word 'world,' *the restoration* which was expected through Christ. The chief thing was indeed the restoration of life; it was yet necessary that the fallen state of the whole world should be repaired. The apostle, in Heb. 1:2, calls Christ the Heir of all the good things of God; for the adoption which we obtain through His favour restores to us the possession of the inheritance which we lost in Adam; and as under the type of the land of Canaan, not only the hope of a heavenly life was exhibited to Abraham, but also the full and complete blessing of God, the apostle rightly teaches us that *the dominion of the world* was promised to him. Some taste of this the godly have in the present life, for how much soever they may at times be oppressed with want, yet as they partake with a peaceable conscience of those things which God has created for their use, and as they enjoy through His mercy and good-will His earthly benefits no otherwise than as pledges and earnests of eternal life, their poverty does in no degree prevent them from acknowledging heaven and the earth, and the sea, *as their own possessions.*

"Though the ungodly swallow up the riches of the world, they can yet call nothing as their own; but they rather snatch them as it were by stealth; for they possess them under the curse of God. It is indeed a great comfort to the godly in their poverty, that though they fare slenderly, they yet steal nothing of what belongs to another, but receive their lawful allowance from the hand of their heavenly Father, until they enter on the full possession of their inheritance, when all creatures shall be made subservient to their glory; for both heaven and earth shall be renewed for this end,—that according to their measure they may contribute to render glorious the kingdom of God." It will repay the reader to reread the above and meditate thereon as a helpful opening up of Romans 4:13, with its application to us.

VII

In the last two chapters on this most interesting subject we sought to establish the basic fact that the promises of God to Abraham were never made to his natural descendants, but rather to his spiritual seed—that is, to those possessing a like faith with his. Consequently, the unbelieving posterity of Jacob were as much excluded from the spiritual blessings of the covenant as were the offspring of Ishmael and Esau. Then we sought to show, by an appeal to Romans 4:13-16; Galatians 3:16-18, 29; and Hebrews 11:9-16 that all who belong to Christ have a joint heritage with Abraham. At the close of the preceding chapter we endeavored to dispose of the objection that the inheritance promised to Abraham was merely an earthly one. Before proceeding further, we make a suggestive quotation from the writings of Robert Haldane.

"The land of Canaan was a type of the heavenly country. It was the inheritance given by promise to Abraham and his posterity: as his descendants after the flesh inherited the one, so his spiritual seed shall inherit the other. Canaan was the land of rest, after the toils and dangers of the wilderness. To make it a fit inheritance, and an emblem of that inheritance which is undefiled, and into which there shall in no wise enter any thing that defileth, neither whatsoever worketh abomination, it was cleared of the ungodly inhabitants. As the introduction of the people of Israel into that land was not effected by their own power or efforts (Josh. 24:12; Psa. 44:4), but by the unmerited goodness and power of God; so the children of God do not obtain possession of the heavenly inheritance by their own power or efforts, but by the free grace and power of God (Rom. 9:16). As those who believed not were excluded from Canaan, so all unbelievers will be excluded from Heaven. As Moses could not lead the people of Israel into Canaan, that honour being reserved for Joshua, so it is not by the law that the people of God shall enter Heaven, but by the Gospel of Jesus Christ, the true Joshua. No other country on earth could have been selected as a fitter emblem of Heaven: it is called in Scripture 'the pleasant land', 'the glory of all lands,' 'a land flowing with milk and honey.' "

Not only was Palestine a striking and beautiful type of heaven, but the promise of the heavenly Canaan was couched under the promise of the earthly Canaan. The patriarchs themselves so understood it, as is abundantly evident from Hebrews 11. "By faith Abraham, when he was called to go out into a place which he should after receive for an inheritance, obeyed" (v. 8). That place which he was to afterward receive for an inheritance could not be the earthly Canaan, for we are distinctly told that God "gave him none inheritance in it, not so much as to set his foot on" (Acts 7:5), and in the absence of any Scriptural statement to that effect, it would seem most incongruous to suppose that after spending four thousand years in heaven, the patriarch, after the resurrection, will again reside upon earth. No, his hope concerned a "heavenly country" (Heb. 11:14, 16); yet no promise concerning it is found anywhere in the Old Testament unless it be the real kernel inside the promise of the earthly Canaan. That *our* "hope" is the same as Abraham's is clear from Hebrews 6:17-19.

In addition to the two great promises which our patriarch received— that in him should all the families of the earth be blessed and the inheritance be secured to them—was the still greater and yet more comprehensive assurance "to be a God unto thee and to thy seed after thee . . . I will be their God" (Gen. 17:7, 8). This divine declaration was designed to make known the infinitely condescending relation which Jehovah meant to sustain to His believing people, and to encourage them in the exercise of strong confidence in Him. It was a new revelation to Abraham of the gracious intercourse which He would maintain with them; for so far as Scripture records, no similar word had been given to any of the saints which preceded. Here, then, was a further and fuller unfolding of the divine communications under the Abrahamic covenant, a distinct advance upon what had been previously revealed.

When the Most High promises to be a God unto any, it is in effect declaring that He takes them into His favor and under His protection; that He will be their portion, and that there is nothing good—with a wise respect to their welfare—which He will withhold from them. All there is of evil which needs to be averted, all there is of real good that can suitably be bestowed, is included in this grand assurance. Our finite minds are incapable of defining the capacity of God to bless, or to adequately comprehend all that such a statement includes. Its application is not limited to this life only, but also looks forward to the never-ending ages of eternity. The great Jehovah is solemnly pledged to guide, guard, glorify His covenant people: "My God shall supply all your need, according to his riches in glory by Christ Jesus" (Phil. 4:19).

Now each of the promises to Abraham receives a double fulfill- ment: a "letter" and a "spirit" or, as we prefer to designate them, a carnal and a spiritual. "Thou shalt be a father of many nations . . . and kings shall come out of thee" (Gen. 17:4, 6). In addition to the Israelites, Abraham was the father of the Ishmaelites and the various children of Keturah (Gen. 25:1, 2). But these were all born after the flesh (Gal. 4:23), and were only a figure of the real seed, the spiritual.

This is clear from, "Therefore it is by faith, that it might be by grace, to the end the promise might be sure to all the seed: not to that only which is of the law, but that also which is of the faith of Abraham, who is *the father of us all*—as it is written, I have made thee *a father of many nations*" (Rom. 4:16, 17). Thus, in the truest and highest sense Abraham was the father of believers, whether Jews or Gentiles, and of them only. In John 8:39 and 44 Christ emphatically denied that Abraham was the father of the unbelieving Jews of His day.

"And I will establish my covenant between me and thee and thy seed after thee in their generations, for an everlasting covenant" (Gen. 17:7). The making good of this was adumbrated when Israel after the flesh was taken into covenant by Jehovah at Sinai, whereby He formally became their God and acknowledged them as His people (Exod. 19:5, 6; Lev. 26:12, etc.). But the actual and ultimate accomplishment of Genesis 17:7 is in connection with the spiritual Israel, Abraham's children by faith, and this by a "better covenant": for with the true house of Israel He says, "I will put my laws into their mind, and write them in their hearts; and I will be to them a God, and they shall be to me a people . . . I will be merciful to their unrighteousnesses, and their sins and their iniquities will I remember no more" (Heb. 8:10, 12).

"And I will give unto thee, and to thy seed after thee, the land wherein thou art a stranger, all the land of Canaan, for an everlasting possession" (Gen. 17:8). Israel's conquest and occupation of the earthly Canaan in the days of Joshua was the figurative and lower fulfillment of this promise. As we have already shown, its spiritual realization lies in the possession of the "better country" which those who are of the faith of Abraham shall eternally inherit. Thus it was that the patriarchs themselves understood this promise, as is unmistakably evident from Hebrews 11:9:16: their faith was more especially directed to the "heavenly country," of which the earthly was but an emblem.

The same truth was brought out clearly in our Lord's reasoning with the Sadducees, who denied all that was spiritual. "Now that the dead are raised, even Moses showed at the bush, when he calleth the Lord the God of Abraham, and the God of Isaac, and the God of Jacob" (Luke 20:37). The covenant promises taught the patriarchs that their resurrection and glorification was necessary to the fulfillment of them. That the "Canaan" in which they were to dwell after the resurrection was to be, not on earth, but in heaven, is equally plain from the previous part of this same conversation of Christ: "The children of this world [the earthly Canaan in which the Sadducees then were] marry and are given in marriage; but they who shall be counted worthy to obtain that world [the heavenly Canaan] and the resurrection from the dead, [to prepare them for it] neither marry nor are given in marriage; neither can they die any more, for they are equal unto the angels" (vv. 34-36).

The apostle Paul gave an exposition of the covenant promises in perfect accord with what we have just considered from the lips of the Lord Jesus. In his defense before King Agrippa, he hesitated not to say, and that in the presence of the Jewish leaders (Acts 25:7): "I stand and am judged for the hope of the promise made of God unto our fathers: unto which promise our twelve tribes, instantly serving day and night, hope to come. For which hope's sake, king Agrippa, I am accused of the Jews" (Acts 26·6, 7). And what was that promise? Their unimpeded and happy enjoyment of the land of Palestine? No, indeed; but "why should it be thought a thing incredible with you, that God should raise the dead?" (v. 8). So also, when before Felix, he declared: "I confess unto thee, that after the way that they [the unbelieving Jews] call heresy, so worship I the God of my fathers, believing all things which are written in the law and in the prophets. And have hope toward God, which they themselves also allow, that there shall be a resurrection of the dead, both of the just and of the unjust" (Acts 24:14, 15).

But where is the promise made unto the fathers of the resurrection from the dead "written *in the law*"? The answer is, nowhere, unless it be *in the covenant promises* made to Abraham and repeated to Isaac and Jacob; nor is it there, except in the sense in which they have now been explained. God will raise from the dead all the spiritual seed of Abraham, and will give them "for an everlasting possession" that Canaan above, of which the Canaan on earth was the appointed emblem and shadow. Rightly did James Haldane point out that "One great means by which Satan has succeeded in corrupting the Gospel, has been the blending [we may add "the confusing"] of the literal and spiritual fulfillment of these promises—thus confounding the old and new covenants. This is seen in the attempts made to apply to the carnal 'seed' of believers (Christians) the promises made to the spiritual 'seed of Abraham.' "

We are not unmindful that some of our readers are likely to object strongly to what they would term this "spiritualizing" method of interpreting Scripture. But let it be pointed out that this giving to the covenant promises both a "letter" and "spirit" significance is not a theory formed to serve a purpose: it is in keeping with and required by every part of the Old Testament dispensation, wherein the things of earth were employed to shadow forth heavenly realities, types pointing forward to antitypes. Take for example the temple: it was "the house of God" in the letter, but Christ and His church are so in the spirit. To now call any earthly building "the house of God" is as far below the sense which that expression bears when it is applied to the church of Christ, as calling the nation of Israel the "people of God" was far below the meaning of that phrase when applied to the spiritual Israel (Gal. 6:16).

Things are said of the house of God in the letter which only fully suit the spirit. Solomon declared, "I have surely built thee a house to dwell in, a settled place for thee to abide in forever" (I Kings 8:13). Now the incongruity of supposing that He whom "the heaven of heavens cannot contain" should dwell in any earthly and material house forever, as "a settled habitation," is only removed by referring it to the spirit. Christ's body (personal and mystical) is the only "temple" (John 2:19, 21; Eph. 2:18-22) of which this is fully true. This is not open to argument: God did not "dwell forever" in the temple built by Solomon, for it was destroyed thousands of years ago; but in His *spiritual* temple it is accomplished to its utmost extent. According to the same principle must the covenant promises be interpreted: the temporal things promised therein being but images of those "better things" which God promised to bestow upon Abraham's believing children.

Reviewing the ground now covered, let us point out that the first great purpose of the covenant was to make known *the stock* from which the Messiah was to spring. Second, this covenant revealed that God's ultimate design was the *worldwide* diffusion of the benefits it announced. Before Nimrod, the whole race spoke one language and had an easy intercourse with each other. But upon the confusion of tongues, they were divided and scattered abroad, and were all alike fast falling into a state of confirmed defection from God. When Abraham was called, and his family selected as a people to whom God was to communicate a knowledge of His will and attach (by sovereign grace) to His service, it would be natural to infer that the rest of the nations were totally and finally abandoned to their own evil devices, and that only the one favored nation would participate in the triumphs of the future deliverer. It is instructive to note how this logical but erroneous conclusion was anticipated by God from the beginning, and refuted by the very terms of the covenant which He made with Abraham.

The patriarch and his descendants were· indeed set apart from all others; peculiar privileges and blessings of the highest value were conferred upon them; but at the very conferring of them the Lord gave an express intimation that those privileges were confined to them in trust, and that the Israelitish theocracy was only a temporary arrangement, for in Abraham would *"all* families of the earth be blessed." Thus clear announcement was made that the time would come when the middle wall of partition would be broken down and all restrictions removed, and the blessings of Abraham be extended to a far wider circle. The external arrangements of the covenant were simply a necessity for a time, with the object of securing grander and more comprehensive results. "In thy seed shall all nations of the earth be blessed" (Gen. 22:18) was a definite publication of the international scope of the divine mercy.

Thus, the Abrahamic covenant, taken as a whole, not only defined the particular line from which the Messiah was to spring, announced the needful (temporal) arrangements in preparation for His appearing, and the extent to which His glorious work was destined to reach; but it placed in a clearer light the relation which (in consequence of it) God condescended to sustain to His redeemed people; and it supplied a striking intimation and typification of the nature of the blessings, which, in virtue of that relation, He designed to confer upon them. It was a wonderful enlargement of revelation; it was the gospel in figure, and is so regarded in the New Testament (John 8:56; Gal. 3:8). The apostle Paul refers to the Abrahamic covenant again and again as foreshadowing and illustrating the privileges bestowed upon Christians, and of the principle on which those privileges are conferred—a faith which is evidenced by obedience.

VIII

The grand promises of the Abrahamic covenant, as originally given to the patriarch, are recorded in Genesis 12:2, 3, 7. The covenant itself was solemnly ratified by sacrifice, thus making it inviolable, in Genesis 15:9-21. The seal and sign of the covenant, circumcision, is brought before us in Genesis 17:9-14. The covenant was confirmed by divine oath in Genesis 22:15-18, which provided a ground of "strong consolation" (Heb. 6:17-19). There were not two distinct and diverse covenants made with Abraham (as the older Baptists argued), the one having respect to spiritual blessings and the other relating to temporal benefits. The covenant was one, having a special spiritual object, to which the temporal arrangements and inferior privileges enjoyed by the nation of Israel were strictly subordinated, and necessary only as a means of securing the higher results contemplated.

It is true that the contents of the covenant were of a mixed kind, involving both the natural descendants and the spiritual seed of Abraham, its promises receiving a minor and major fulfillment. There was to be a temporary accomplishment of those promises to his natural offspring here on earth, and there was to be an eternal realization of them to his spiritual children in heaven. Unless this twofoldness of the contents of the covenant be steadily borne in mind, it is impossible to obtain a right and clear view of them. Nevertheless it is highly essential that we distinguish sharply between the two, lest we fall into the error of others who insist that the spiritual blessings belonged not only to the natural seed of Abraham, but to the offspring of Christians as well. Spiritual blessings cannot be communicated by carnal propagation.

Nothing could more clearly establish what has just been pointed out than, "For they are not all Israel, which are of Israel: neither because they are the *seed* of Abraham, are they all *children:* but, in Isaac shall thy seed be called. That is, they which are the children of the flesh, these are not the children of God: but the children of the promise are counted for the seed" (Rom. 9:6-8). All of Abraham's descendants did not participate in the spiritual blessings promised to him, for to some of them Christ said, "Ye shall die in your sins" (John 8:24), which was shadowed forth in the fact that Ishmael and Esau were excluded from even the temporal privileges enjoyed by the offspring of Isaac and Jacob. Nor do all the children of Christians enter into the spiritual privileges promised to Abraham, but only those which were eternally chosen unto salvation; and who they are cannot be known until they believe: "Know ye therefore that they which are of faith, the same are the children of Abraham" (Gal. 3:7).

Let us point out in the next place that Abraham's covenant was strictly peculiar to himself; for neither in the Old Testament nor in the New is it ever said that the covenant with Abraham was made on behalf of all believers, or that it is given to them. The great thing that the covenant secured to Abraham was that he should have a seed, and that God would be the God of that seed; but Christians have no divine warrant that He will be the God of their seed, nor even that they shall have any children at all. As a matter of fact, many of them have no posterity; and therefore they cannot have the covenant of Abraham. The covenant of Abraham was as peculiar to himself as the one God made with Phinehas, "And he shall have it, and his seed after him, even the covenant of an everlasting priesthood" (Num. 25:13), and as the covenant of royalty which God made with David and his seed (II Sam. 7:12-16). In each case a divine promise was given *securing a posterity;* and had no children been born to those men, then God had broken His covenant.

Look at the original promises made to Abraham: "And I will make of thee a great nation, and I will bless thee, and make thy name great; and thou shalt be a blessing. And I will bless them that bless thee, and curse him that curseth thee; and in thee shall all families of the earth be blessed" (Gen. 12:2, 3). Has God promised every Christian that He will make of him a "great nation"? or that He will make his "name great"—celebrated like the patriarch's was and is? or that in him "all the families of the earth shall be blessed"? Surely there is no room for argument here: the very asking of such questions answers them. Nothing could be more extravagant and absurd than to suppose that any such promises as these were made to us.

If God fulfills the covenant with Abraham and his seed to every believer and his seed, then He does so in accord with the terms of the covenant itself. But if we turn to and carefully examine its contents, it will at once appear that they were not to be fulfilled in the case of all believers, in addition to Abraham himself. In that covenant God promises that Abraham should be "a father of many nations," that "kings shall come out of thee," that "I will give thee and to thy seed after thee, the land wherein thou art a stranger, all the land of Canaan, for an everlasting possession" (Gen. 17:5-8). But Christians are not made the fathers of many nations; kings do not come out of them; nor do their descendants occupy the land of Canaan, either literally or spiritually. How many a godly believer has had to mourn with David: "Although my house be not so with God; yet he hath made with me an everlasting covenant, ordered in all things and sure, for this is all my salvation" (II Sam. 23:5).

The covenant established no spiritual relation between Abraham and his offspring; still less does it establish a spiritual relation between every believer and his babes. Abraham was not the spiritual father of his own natural offspring, for spiritual qualities cannot be propagated by carnal generation. Was he the spiritual father of Ishmael? Was he the spiritual father of Esau? No, indeed; instead, Abraham was "the father of all them that believe" (Rom. 4:11). So far as his natural descendants were concerned, Scripture declares that Abraham was "the father of circumcision to them who are not of the circumcision only, but who also walk in the steps of that faith of our father Abraham, which he had being yet uncircumcised" (Rom. 4:12). What could be plainer? Let us beware of adding to God's Word. No theory or practice, no matter how venerable it be or how widely held, is tenable, if no clear Scripture can be found to warrant and establish it.

The question may be asked, But are not Christians under the Abrahamic covenant? In the entire absence of any word in Scripture affirming that they are, we answer No. The blessing of Abraham has indeed "come on the [believing] Gentiles through Jesus Christ" (Gal.

3:14), and what this blessing is, the very same verse tells us—namely, "that we might receive the promise of the Spirit *through faith.*" That blessing consists not in creating spiritual relations between believers and their infant offspring, but is for themselves, in response to the exercise of their faith. Plainer still is Galatians 3:9 in defining for us what the "blessing of Abraham" is which has come upon the Gentiles: "So then they which be of faith are blessed with faithful' Abraham." And again, "Know ye therefore that they which are of faith, the same are the children of Abraham" (v. 7). The only spiritual children of Abraham are such as have faith.

We must now turn to and consider *the seal* of the covenant. "And God said unto Abraham, Thou shalt keep my covenant therefore, thou, and thy seed after thee in their generations. This is my covenant which ye shall keep between me and you and thy seed after thee: Every man-child among you shall be circumcised. And ye shall circumcise the flesh of your foreskin; and it shall be a token of the covenant betwixt me and you. And he that is eight days old shall be circumcised among you, every man-child in your generations, he that is born in the house, or bought with money of any stranger, which is not of thy seed. He that is born in thy house, and he that is bought with thy money, must needs be circumcised; and my covenant shall be in your flesh for an everlasting covenant. And the uncircumcised man-child whose flesh of his foreskin is not circumcised, that soul shall be cut off from his people; he hath broken my covenant" (Gen. 17:9-14).

In seeking to ascertain the significance of the above passage, we cannot do better than throw upon it the light of the New Testament. There we are told, "And he [Abraham] received the sign of circumcision, a seal of the righteousness of the faith which he had yet being uncircumcised: that he might be the father of all them that believe, though they be not circumcised: that righteousness might be imputed unto them also" (Rom. 4:11). The first observation we would make upon this verse is that it definitely establishes the *unity* of the Abrahamic covenant, for in Romans 4:3 the apostle had quoted from Genesis 15—where the word *covenant* occurs for the first time in connection with Abraham; and now he refers us to Genesis 17, thereby intimating it is one and the same covenant in both chapters. The main difference between the two chapters is that the one gives us more the divine side (ratifying the covenant), the other the human side (the keeping of the covenant, or obedience to the divine command).

The next thing we would observe is that circumcision was "a seal of the righteousness of the faith which he had." Again we would say, Let us be on our guard against adding to God's Word, for nowhere does

Scripture say that circumcision was a seal to anyone but to Abraham himself; and even in his case, so far was it from communicating any spiritual blessing, it simply confirmed what was already promised to him. As a seal from God, circumcision was a divine pledge or guaranty that from him should issue that seed which would bring blessing to all nations, and that, on the same terms as justifying righteousness had become his—by faith alone. It was not a seal of his faith, but of that righteousness which, in due time, was to be wrought out by the Messiah and Mediator. Circumcision was not a memorial of anything which had already been actualized, but an earnest of that which was yet future—namely, of that justifying righteousness which was to be brought in by Christ.

But did not God enjoin that all the males of Abraham's household, and in those of his descendants, should also be circumcised? He did, and in that very fact we find definite confirmation of what has just been said above. What did circumcision seal to Abraham's servants and slaves? Nothing. "Circumcision neither signed nor sealed the blessings of the covenant of Abraham to the individuals to whom it was by Divine appointment administered. It did not imply that they who were circumcised were accounted the heirs of the promises, either temporal or spiritual. It was not applied to mark them individually as heirs of the promises. It did not imply this even to Isaac and Jacob, who are by name designated heirs with Abraham. *Their* interest in the promises was secured *to them* by God's expressly giving *them* the covenant, but was *not* represented in their circumcision. Circumcision marked no character, and had an individual application to no man but Abraham himself. It was the token of this covenant; and as a token or sign, no doubt applied to every promise in the covenant, but it did not designate the individual circumcised as having a personal interest in these promises. The covenant promised a numerous seed to Abraham; circumcision, as the token of that covenant, must have been a sign of this; but it did not sign this *to any other*. Any other circumcised individual, except Isaac and Jacob, to whom the covenant was given by name, might have been *childless*.

"Circumcision did not import to any individual that any portion of the numerous seed of Abraham should descend through *him*. The covenant promised that all nations should be blessed in Abraham—that the Messiah should be his descendant. But circumcision was no sign *to any other* that the Messiah should descend from him,—even to Isaac and Jacob this promise was peculiarly given, *and not implied in their circumcision*. From some of Abraham's race, the Messiah, according to the covenant, must descend, and circumcision was a sign of this: but this was not signed by circumcision to any one of all his race. Much less could circumcision 'sign' this to the strangers and slaves who were not of Abraham's posterity. To such, even the temporal promises were not either 'signed' or sealed by circumcision. The covenant promised Canaan to Abraham's descendants, but circumcision could be no sign of this to the strangers and slaves who enjoyed no inheritance in it" (Alexander Carson, 1860).

That circumcision did not seal anything to anyone but to Abraham himself is established beyond shadow of doubt by the fact that circumcision was applied to those who had no personal interest in the covenant to which it was attached. Not only was circumcision administered by Abraham to the servants and slaves of his household, but in Genesis 17:23 we read that he circumcised Ishmael, who was expressly excluded from that covenant! There is no evading the force of that, and it is impossible to reconcile it with the views so widely pervading upon the Abrahamic covenant. Furthermore, circumcision was not submitted to voluntarily, nor given with reference to faith, it was compulsory, and that in every instance: "He that is born in thy house, and he that is bought with thy money must needs be circumcised" (Gen. 17:13)—those refusing, being "cut off from his people" (v. 14). How vastly different was that from Christian baptism!

It may be asked, If, then, circumcision sealed nothing to those who received it, except in the one case of Abraham himself, then why did God ordain it to be administered to all his male descendants? First, because it was the mark He selected to distinguish from all other nations that people from whom the Messiah was to issue. Second, because it served as a continual reminder that from the Abrahamic stock the promised Seed would spring—hence, soon after He appeared, circumcision was set aside by God. Third, because of what it typically foreshadowed. To be born naturally of the Abrahamic stock gave a title to circumcision and the earthly inheritance, which was a figure of their title to the heavenly inheritance of those born of the Spirit. The servants and slaves in Abraham's household "bought with money" beautifully adumbrated the truth that those who enter the kingdom of Christ are "bought" by His blood.

It is a mistake to suppose that baptism has come in the place of circumcision. As that which supplanted the Old Testament sacrifices was the one offering of the Savior, as that which superseded the Aaronic priesthood was the high priesthood of Christ, so that which has succeeded circumcision is the spiritual circumcision which believers have in and by Christ: "In whom also ye are circumcised with the circumcision made without hands, in putting off the body of the sins of the flesh, by the circumcision of Christ" (Col. 2:11)—how simple! how satisfying! "Buried with him in baptism, wherein also ye are risen with him" (v. 12) is *something additional:* it is only wresting Scripture to say these two verses mean "Being buried with him in baptism, ye are circumcised." No, no; verse 11 declares the Christian circumcision is "made *without* hands," and baptism is administered *by* hands! The circumcision "made without hands in putting off [judicially, before God] the body of the sins of the flesh" has taken the place of the circumcision made *with* hands. The circumcision of Christ has come in the place of the circumcision of the law. Never once in the New Testament is baptism spoken of as the seal of the new covenant; rather is the Holy Spirit the seal: see Ephesians 1:13; 4:30.

To sum up. The grand design of God's covenant with Abraham was to make known that through him should come the One who would bring blessing to all the families of the earth. The promises made to him were to receive a lower and a higher fulfillment, according as he was to have both natural and spiritual children—for "kings shall come out of thee" (Gen. 17:6) compare Revelation 1:6; for "thy seed shall possess the gate of his enemies" (Gen. 22:17) compare Colossians 2:15; Romans 8:37; I John 5:4. Abraham is called a "father" neither in a federal nor in a spiritual sense, but because he is the head of the faith clan the prototype to which all believers are conformed. Christians are not under the Abrahamic covenant, though they are "blessed with him" by having their faith counted unto righteousness. Though New Testament believers are not under the Abrahamic covenant, they are, because of their union with Christ, heirs of its spiritual inheritance.

It only remains for us now to point out wherein the Abrahamic covenant adumbrated the everlasting covenant. First, it proclaimed the international scope of the divine mercy: some out of all nations were included in the election of grace. Second, it made known the ordained stock from which the Messiah and Mediator was to issue. Third, it announced that faith alone secured an interest in all the good God had promised. Fourth, in Abraham's being the father of all believers was shadowed forth the truth that Christ is the Father of His own spiritual seed (Isa. 53:10, 11). Fifth, in Abraham's call from God to leave his own country and become a sojourner in a strange land, was typed out Christ's leaving heaven and tabernacling upon earth. Sixth, as the "heir of the world" (Rom. 4:13), Abraham foreshadowed Christ as "the heir of all things" (Heb. 1:2). Seventh, in the promise of Canaan to his seed we have a figure of the heavenly inheritance which Christ has procured for His people.

(It seems a sad tragedy that the people of God are so divided on the subject of baptism. Though we have strong convictions on the subject we have refrained from pressing—or even presenting—them in this study. But it seemed impossible to deal faithfully with the Abrahamic covenant without making some slight reference thereto. We have sought to write temperately in the above chapter, avoiding harsh expressions and needless reflections. We trust the reader will kindly receive it in the spirit in which it is written.)

PART FIVE

The Sinaitic Covenant

I

We have now arrived at a stage of our subject which we fear is not likely to be of much interest to many of our readers; yet we would ask them to kindly bear with us for the sake of those who *are* anxious to have a systematic exposition thereof. We write, therefore, for those who desire answers to such questions as the following: What was the precise nature of the covenant which God entered into with Israel at Sinai? Did it concern only their temporal welfare as a nation, or did it also set forth God's requirements for the individual's enjoyment of eternal blessings? Was a radical change now made in God's revelation to men and what He demanded of them? Was an entirely different "way of salvation" now introduced? Wherein is the Sinaitic covenant related to the others, particularly to the everlasting covenant of grace and to the Adamic covenant of works? Was it in harmony with the former, or a renewal of the latter? Was the Sinaitic covenant a simple or a mixed one: did it have only a "letter" significance pertaining to earthly things or a "spirit" as well, pertaining to heavenly things? What specific contribution did it make unto the progressive unfolding of the divine plan and purpose?

We deem it of great importance that a clear conception be obtained of the precise nature and meaning of that august transaction which took place at Sinai, when Jehovah proclaimed the Ten Commandments in the hearing of Israel. No one who has given any due attention thereto can fail to perceive that it marked a memorable epoch in the history of that people. But it was far more than that: it possessed a much deeper and broader significance—it was the beginning of a new era in the history of the human race, being a momentous step in that series of divine dispensations toward fallen mankind. Yet it must be frankly acknowledged that the subject is as difficult as

141

it is important: the great diversity of opinion which prevails among the theologians and divines who have studied the subject is proof thereof. Yet this is no reason why we should despair of obtaining light thereon. Rather should it cause us to cry to God for help, and to prosecute our inquiry cautiously, humbly, and carefully.

What was the precise character of the transaction which Jehovah entered into with Israel at Sinai? That there *was* a bona fide covenant made on that occasion cannot be gainsaid. The term is actually used in Exodus 19:5: "Now therefore, if ye will obey my voice indeed, and keep my covenant, then ye shall be a peculiar treasure unto me above all people." So again we read, "And he took the book of the covenant, and read in the audience of the people: and they said, All that the Lord hath said will we do, and be obedient. And Moses took the blood, and sprinkled it on the people, and said, Behold, the blood of the covenant, which the Lord hath made with you concerning all these words" (Exod. 24:7, 8). Years after, when rehearsing God's dealings with Israel, Moses said, "The Lord our God made a covenant with us in Horeb" (Deut. 5:2). Not only is the word *covenant* used, but the transactions at Sinai contained all the elements of a covenant: the contracting parties were the Lord God and Israel; the condition was, "If ye will obey my voice indeed"; the promise was, "Ye shall be unto me a kingdom of priests and a holy nation" (Exod. 19:6); the penalty was the curses of Deuteronomy 28:15, and so forth.

But what was the nature and design of that covenant? Did God mock His fallen creatures by formally renewing the (Adamic) covenant of works, which they had already broken, under the curse of which all by nature lay, and which He knew they could not keep for a single hour? Such a question answers itself. Or did God do with Israel then as He does with His people now: first redeem, and then put under law as a rule of life, a standard of conduct? But if that were the case, why enter into this formal "covenant"? Even Fairbairn virtually cuts the knot here by saying that the form of a covenant is of no consequence at all. But this covenant form at Sinai is the very thing which requires to be accounted for. Christians are not put under the law as a *covenant,* though they are as a *rule.* No help is to be obtained by dodging difficulties or by denying their existence; they must be fairly and prayerfully grappled with.

There is no doubt in my mind that many have been led astray when considering the typical teaching of Israel's history and the antitype in the experience of Christians, by failing to duly note the contrasts as well as the comparisons between them. It is true that God's deliverance of Israel from the bondage of Egypt blessedly foreshadowed the redemption of His elect from sin and Satan; yet let it not be forgotten that the majority of those who were emancipated from Pharaoh's slavery perished in the wilderness, not being suffered to enter the promised land. Nor are we left to mere reasoning at this point: it is placed upon inspired record that "behold, the days come saith the Lord, when I will make a *new* covenant with the house of Israel and with the house of Judah: not according to the covenant that I made with their fathers, in the day when I took them by the hand to lead them out of the land of Egypt; because they continued not in my covenant, and I regarded them not, saith the Lord" (Heb. 8:8, 9). Thus we have divine authority for saying that God's dealings with Israel at Sinai were not a parallel with His dealings with His people under the gospel, but a contrast!

H. Witsius took the view that the Sinaitic compact was neither, formally, the covenant of grace nor the covenant of works, but a national covenant which presupposed them both, and that it promised "not only temporal blessings . . . but also spiritual and eternal." So far so good. But when he states (bk. 4, sec. 4, par. 43-45) that the condition of this covenant was "a sincere, though not, in every respect, a perfect obedience of His commands," we certainly cannot agree. Witsius held that the Sinaitic covenant differed from the covenant of works—which made no provision or allowance for the acceptance of a sincere though imperfect obedience; and that it differed from the covenant of grace, since it contained no promises of strength to enable Israel to render that obedience. Though plausible, his position is not only erroneous but highly dangerous. God never promised eternal life to men on the condition of an imperfect but sincere obedience—that would overthrow the whole argument of Romans and Galatians.

Thomas Bell (1814) in his heavy work on *The Covenants* insists that "the covenant of works was delivered from Sinai, yet as subservient to the Covenant of Grace." Such an accurate thinker was bound to feel the pressure of those difficulties which such a postulate involves, yet he took a strange way of getting out of them. Appealing to Deuteronomy 29:1, Bell argued that God made "two distinct covenants with Israel," and that "the one made in Moab was the Covenant of Grace," and that "the two covenants mentioned in Deut. 29:1 are as opposite as the righteousness of the law and the righteousness of faith." We will not here attempt to show the unsatisfactoriness and untenability of such an inference; suffice it to say there is less warrant for it than to conclude that God made two totally distinct covenants with Abraham (in Genesis 15 and 17): the covenant at Moab was a renewal of the Sinaitic, as the ones made with Isaac and Jacob were of the original one with Abraham.

Quite a different idea has been advanced by those known as the Plymouth Brethren. Darby (who had quite a penchant for novelties) advanced the theory that at Sinai Israel made a fatal blunder, deliberately abandoning the ground of receiving all from God on the basis of pure grace, and in their stupidity and self-sufficiency agreeing henceforth to *earn* His favors. The idea is that when God rehearsed His merciful dealings with them (Exod. 19:4) and then added, "Now therefore if ye will obey my voice indeed and keep my covenant, then ye shall be a peculiar treasure unto me above all people," that Israel was guilty of perverting His words, and evidenced their carnality and pride by saying, "All that the Lord hath spoken, we will do." Those are regarded as most disastrous words, leading to most disastrous results; for it is supposed that, from this time, God entirely changed His attitude toward them.

In his *Synopsis,* Darby concludes his remarks on Exodus 18 and opens 19 by saying, "But having thus terminated the course of grace the scene changes entirely. They do not keep the feast on the mount, whither God, as He had promised, had led them—had 'brought them, bearing them as on eagles' wings, to Himself.' He proposes a condition to them: If they obeyed His voice, they should be His people. The people—instead of knowing themselves, and saying, 'We dare not, though bound to obey, place ourselves under such a condition, and risk our blessing, yea, make sure of losing it'—undertake to do all that the Lord has spoken. The blessing now took the form of dependence, like Adam's on the faithfulness of man as well as of God. . . . The people, however, are not permitted to approach God, who hid Himself in the darkness."

C. H. Mackintosh, in his comments on Exodus 19, says, "It [the scene presented at the end of 18] was but a brief moment of sunshine in which a very vivid picture of the kingdom was afforded; but the sunshine was speedily followed by the heavy clouds which gathered around that 'palpable mount,' where Israel, in a spirit of dark and senseless legality, abandoned His covenant of pure grace for man's covenant of works. Disastrous movement! A movement fraught with the most dismal results. Hitherto as we have seen no enemy could stand before Israel—no obstacle was suffered to interrupt their onward and victorious march. Pharaoh's hosts were overthrown, Amalek and his people were discomfitted with the edge of the sword; all was victory, because God was acting on behalf of His people in pursuance of His promise to Abraham, Isaac and Jacob.

"In the opening verses of the chapter now before us, the Lord recapitulates His actions toward Israel in the following touching and beautiful language: see Ex. 29:3-6. Observe, it is *'My voice'* and *'My covenant.*' What was the utterance of that 'voice'? and what did that 'covenant' involve? Had Jehovah's voice made itself heard for the purpose of laying down the rules and regulations of a severe and unbending lawgiver? By no means. It had spoken to demand freedom for the captive, to provide a refuge from the sword of the destroyer, to make a way for the ransomed to pass over, to bring down bread from heaven, to draw forth water out of the flinty rock;—such had been the gracious and intelligible utterance of Jehovah's 'voice' up to the moment at which 'Israel camped before the mount.'

"And as to His 'covenant,' it was one of unmingled grace. It proposed no condition, it made no demands, it put no yoke on the neck, no burden on the shoulder. When 'the God of glory appeared unto Abraham' in Ur of the Chaldees, He certainly did not address him in such words as thou shalt do this, and thou shalt not do that, ah, no; such language was not according to His heart. It suits Him far better to place 'a fair mitre' upon a sinner's head than to put a 'yoke upon his neck.' His word to Abraham was '*I will give.*' The land of Canaan was not to be purchased by man's doings, but to be given by God's grace. Thus it stood; and in the opening of the Book of Exodus we see God coming down in grace to make good His promise to Abraham's seed. . . . However, Israel was not disposed to occupy this blessed position."

As so many have been misled by this teaching, we will digress for a moment and show how utterly un-Scriptural it is. It is a serious mistake to say that in the Abrahamic covenant God "proposed no conditions, and made no demands, it put no yoke on the neck." As we pointed out in our chapters thereon when studying the Abrahamic covenant, attention is not to be confined unto one or two particular passages; but the whole of God's dealings with that patriarch are to be taken into consideration. Did not God say to Abraham: "Walk before me, and be thou upright, and I will make a covenant between me and thee" (Gen. 17:1)? Did He not say: "For I know him, that he will command his children and his household after him, and they shall keep the way of the Lord, to do justice and judgment; that [in order that] the Lord may bring upon Abraham that which he hath spoken of him" (18:19)? Abraham had to "keep the way of the Lord," which is defined as "to do justice and judgment"—that is, to walk obediently, in subjection to God's revealed will—if he was to receive the fulfillment of the divine promises.

Again: did not the Lord expressly confirm His covenant to Abraham by oath in saying: "By myself have I sworn, saith the Lord, for because thou hast done this thing, and hast not withheld thy son, thine only son, That in blessing I will bless thee," and so forth (22:16,

17). It is true, blessedly true, that God dealt with Abraham in pure grace; but it is equally true that He dealt with him as a responsible creature, as subject to the divine authority and placed him under law. At a later date, when Jehovah renewed the covenant to Isaac, He said: "I will make thy seed to multiply as the stars of heaven, and will give unto thy seed all these countries; and in thy seed shall all the nations of the earth be blessed [the original covenant promise] because that Abraham obeyed my voice, and kept my charge, my commandments, my statutes, and my laws" (Gen. 26:4, 5). That is clear enough; and nothing could be plainer that God introduced *no change* in His dealings with Abraham's descendants when He said to Israel at Sinai, "Now therefore, if ye will obey my voice indeed, and keep my covenant, then ye shall be a peculiar treasure unto me above all people" (Exod. 19:5).

Equally clear is it from Scripture that the nation of Israel was itself under law before they reached Sinai: "If thou wilt diligently hearken to the voice of the Lord thy God, and wilt do that which is right in his sight, and will give ear to his commandments and keep all his statutes, I will put none of these diseases upon you" (Exod. 15:26). Is it not strange to see men ignoring such plain passages? Lest the quibble be raised that the reference to God's "commandments and statutes" in that passage was *prospective*—that is, in view of the law which was shortly to be given them—note the following, "Behold, I will rain bread from heaven for you; and the people shall go out and gather a certain rate every day, that I may prove them, whether they will walk in my law, or no" (Exod. 16:4). The meaning of this is explained in "tomorrow is the rest of the holy Sabbath unto the Lord" (16:23). Alas for their response: "There went out some of the people on the seventh day to gather" (v. 27). Now mark carefully God's complaint: "How long refuse ye to keep my commandments and my laws?" (16:28). So the reference in 16:4 was not prospective, but retrospective: Israel was *under law* long before they reached Sinai!

But in further rebuttal of the strange theory mentioned above, we would ask, Was it not the Lord Himself who took the initiative in this so-called abandonment of the Abrahamic covenant? For it was *He* who sent Moses to the people with the words (Exod. 19:5) which manifestly sought to evoke an affirmative reply! Again, we ask, If their reply proceeded from carnal pride and self-sufficiency, if it displayed an intolerable arrogancy and presumption, why did it call forth no formal rebuke? So far from the Lord being displeased with Israel's promise, He said to Moses: "Lo, I come unto thee in a thick cloud, that the people may hear when I speak with thee, and believe thee forever" (19:9). Again: why, at the rehearsal of this transaction, did Moses say, "The Lord said unto me, I have heard the voice of the words of this people, which they have spoken unto thee; they have well said all that they have spoken," and then breathed the wish, "O that there were such an heart in them, that would fear me, and keep all my commandments always, that it might be well with them, and with their children forever" (Deut. 5:28, 29).

How utterly excuseless and untenable is this theory (which has been accepted by many and echoed in the Scofield Bible) in the light of the plain facts of Holy Writ. Had Israel acted so madly and presumptuously, would the Lord have gone through all the formalities of a covenant transaction (Exod. 24:3-8)? Had the words uttered by Him, and responded to by the people, been based on impossible conditions on the one side and palpable lies on the other, a covenant would be unthinkable. Finally, let it be carefully observed that so far from God pronouncing a judgment upon Israel for their promise at Sinai, He declared that, on their performance of the same, they would be peculiarly honored and blessed (Exod. 23:27-29; Deut. 6:28).

II

In approaching the study of the Sinaitic covenant, several things need attending to. First, it is to be viewed in connection with all that had preceded it (particularly the earlier covenants), rather than regarded as an isolated transaction: only thus can its details be seen in their proper perspective. Second, it is to be pondered in relation to the eternal purpose of God, and the gradual and progressive unfolding thereof which He gave unto His people: there was something more in it than what is merely temporal and evanescent. Third, the full light of the later communications from God must not be read back into it; nevertheless, the direct references to the Mosaic dispensation in the New Testament are to be carefully weighed in connection therewith.

Let us start, then, by considering what had preceded the Sinaitic covenant. Confining ourselves to that which relates the closest to our present inquiry, let us remind ourselves that under the preceding covenant God had made it known that the promised Messiah and Redeemer should spring from the line of Abraham. Now, clearly, that necessitated several things. The existence of Abraham's descendants as a separate people became indispensable, so that Christ's descent could be undeniably traced and the leading promise of that covenant clearly verified. Moreover, the isolation of Abraham's descendants (Israel) from the heathen was equally essential for the preservation of the knowledge and worship of God in the earth, until the fulness of time should come and a higher dispensation succeed. In pursuance of this, to Israel were committed the living oracles, and amongst them the ordinances of divine worship were authoritatively established.

It was not until the large family of Jacob had developed (seventy-five souls: Acts 7:14) that the Abrahamic covenant, in its natural aspect, began to bud toward fulfillment. There was then a fair prospect of their progressive increase; yet considerable time would be required before they could attain that augmentation in numbers which would justify their political organization as a separate nation and put them into a condition to occupy the promised inheritance. In order for that, the providence of God gave them a temporary settlement in Egypt, which was greatly to their advantage. A season in the midst of the most learned nation of antiquity afforded the Israelites an opportunity of obtaining instruction in many important branches of knowledge, of which they took advantage, as their subsequent history shows; while the fact that "every shepherd was an abomination to the Egyptians" (Gen. 46:34) kept the two nations apart religiously, so that to a considerable extent the Hebrews were preserved from idolatry. Later, the cruel bondage they experienced there made them glad to leave.

In Egypt, the descendants of Abraham had multiplied so extensively that by the time of the great Exodus there were probably at least two million souls. If, then, they were to be organized into a nation, and brought into proper subjection to God, it was necessary that He should make a full revelation of His will for them, giving them laws and precepts for the regulation of all phases of their corporate and individual lives; and, above all, prescribe the nature and requirements of the divine worship. This is what Jehovah graciously did at Sinai. There, God gave Israel a full declaration of His claims upon them and what He required of them, providing a "constitution" which had in view naught but their own good and the glorifying of His great name; the whole being ratified by a solemn covenant. This was a decided advance on all that had gone before, and marked another step forward in the unfolding of the divine plan.

But at this point we are faced with a formidable difficulty, namely, the remarkable diversity in the representation found in later Scripture respecting the tendency and bearing of the law on those who were subject to it. On the one hand, we find a class of passages which represent the law as coming expressly from Israel's redeemer, conveying a benign aspect and aiming at happy results. Moses extolled the condition of Israel as, on this very account, surpassing that of all other people: "For what nation is there so great, who hath God so nigh unto them, as the Lord our God is in all things that we call upon him for? And what nation is there so great, that hath statutes and judgments so righteous as all this law, which I set before you this day?" (Deut. 4:7, 8). The same sentiment is echoed in various forms in the Psalms. "He showed his word unto Jacob, his statutes and his judgments unto Israel. He hath not dealt so with any nation; and as for his judgments, they have not known them" (147:19, 20). "Great peace have they which love thy law, and nothing shall offend them" (119:165).

But on the other hand, there is another class of passages which appear to point in the very opposite direction. In these the law is represented as a source of trouble and terror—a bondage from which it is true liberty to escape. "The law worketh wrath" (Rom. 4:15); "the strength of sin is the law" (I Cor. 15:56). In II Corinthians 3:7, 9 the apostle speaks of the law as "the ministration of death, written and engraven in stones," and as "the ministration of condemnation." Again, he declares, "For as many as are of the works of the law are under the curse" (Gal. 3:10). "Stand fast therefore in the liberty wherewith Christ hath made us free, and be not entangled again with the yoke of bondage. Behold, I Paul say unto you, that if ye be circumcised, Christ shall profit you nothing. For I testify again to every man that is circumcised, that he is a debtor to do the whole law" (Gal. 5:1-3).

Now it is very obvious that such diverse and antagonistic representations could not have been given of the law in the same respect, or with the same regard, to its direct and primary aim. We are obliged to believe that both these representations are true, being alike found in the volume of inspiration. Thus it is clear that Scripture requires us to contemplate the law from more than one point of view, and with regard to different uses and applications of it. What those different viewpoints are, and what the varied uses and applications of the law, will be pointed out later on. For the present, we confine ourselves to a consideration of the place which the law holds in the *Mosaic* economy. This is surely the only logical order to follow, for it is the happier class of representation which are found in the Pentateuch, occupying the foreground; while the others come in afterward, and must be noticed by us subsequently.

"The *national covenant* with Israel was here (Ex. 19:5) meant; the charter upon which they were incorporated, as a people, under the government of Jehovah. It was an engagement of God, to give Israel possession of Canaan, and to protect them in it: to render the land fruitful, and the nation victorious and prosperous, and to perpetuate

His oracles and ordinances among them; so long as they did not, as a people, reject His authority, apostatize to idolatry, and tolerate open wickedness. These things constitute a forfeiture of the covenant; as their national rejection of Christ did afterwards. True believers among them were *personally* dealt with according to the Covenant of Grace, even as true Christians now are; and unbelievers were under the Covenant of Works, and liable to condemnation by it, as at present: yet, *the national covenant* was not strictly either the one or the other, but had something in it of the nature of each.

"The national covenant *did not* refer to the final salvation of individuals: nor was it broken by the disobedience, or even idolatry, of any number of them, provided this was not sanctioned or tolerated by public authority. It was indeed *a type* of the covenant made with true believers in Christ Jesus, as were all the transactions with Israel; but, like other types, it 'had not the very image,' but only 'a shadow of good things to come.' When, therefore, *as a nation,* they had broken this covenant, the Lord declared that He would make 'a *new* covenant with Israel, putting His law,' not only in their hands, but 'in their inward parts'; and 'writing it,' not upon tables of stone, 'but in their hearts; forgiving their iniquity and remembering their sin no more' (Jer. 31:32-34; Heb. 8:7-12; 10:16, 17). The Israelites were under a dispensation of mercy, and had outward privileges and great advantages in various ways for salvation: yet, like professing Christians, the most of them rested in these, and looked no further. The outward covenant was made with the Nation, entitling them to outward advantages, upon the condition of outward national obedience; and the covenant of Grace was ratified *personally* with true believers, and sealed and secured *spiritual* blessings to them, by producing a holy disposition of heart, and spiritual obedience to the Divine law. In case Israel kept the covenant, the Lord promised that they should be to Him 'a peculiar treasure.' 'All the earth' (Ex. 19:5) being the Lord's, He might have chosen any other people instead of Israel: and this implied that, as His choice of them was gratuitous, so if they rejected His covenant, He would reject them, and communicate their privileges to others; as indeed He hath done, since the introduction of the Christian dispensation" (Thomas Scott).

The above quotation contains the most lucid, comprehensive, and yet simple analysis of the Sinaitic covenant which we have met with in all our reading. It draws a clear line of distinction between God's dealings with Israel as a nation, and with individuals in it. It shows the correct position of the everlasting covenant of grace and the Adamic covenant of works in relation to the Mosaic dispensation. All were born under the condemnation of their federal head (Adam), and while they continued unregenerate and in unbelief, were under the wrath of God; whereas God's elect, upon believing, were treated by Him then, as individuals, in precisely the same way as they are now. Scott brings out clearly the character, the scope, the design, and the limitation of the Sinaitic covenant: its character was a supplementary combination of law and mercy; its scope was national; its design was to regulate the temporal affairs of Israel under the divine government; its limitation was determined by Israel's obedience or disobedience. The typical nature of it—the hardest point to elucidate—is also allowed. We advise the interested student to reread the last four paragraphs.

Much confusion will be avoided and much help obtained if the Sinaitic economy be contemplated separately under its two leading aspects, namely, as a system of religion and government designed for the immediate use of the Jews during the continuance of that dispensation; and then as a scheme of preparation for another and better economy, by which it was to be superseded when its temporal purpose had been fulfilled. The first design and the immediate end of what God revealed through Moses was to instruct and order the life of Israel, now formed into a nation. The second and ultimate intention of God was to prepare the people, by a lengthy course of discipline, for the coming of Christ. The character of the Sinaitic covenant was, in itself, neither purely evangelical nor exclusively legal: divine wisdom devised a wondrous and blessed comingling of righteousness and grace, justice and mercy. The requirements of the high and unchanging holiness of God were clearly revealed; while His goodness, kindness, and long-suffering were also as definitely manifested. The moral and the ceremonial law, running together side by side, presented and maintained a perfect balance, which only the corruption of fallen human nature failed to reap the full advantage of.

The covenant which God made with Israel at Sinai required outward obedience to the letter of the law. It contained promises of *national* blessing if they, as a people, kept the law; and it also announced national calamities if they were disobedient. This is unmistakably clear from such a passage as the following: "Wherefore it shall come to pass, if ye hearken to these judgments, and keep and do them, that the Lord thy God shall keep unto thee the covenant and the mercy which he sware unto thy fathers: And he will love thee, and bless thee, and multiply thee: he will also bless the fruit of thy womb, and the fruit of thy land, thy corn, and thy wine, and thine oil, the increase of thy kine, and the flocks of thy sheep, in the land which he sware unto thy fathers to give thee. Thou shalt be blessed above all people: there shall not be male or female barren among you, or among your cattle. And the Lord will take away from thee all sickness, and will put none of the evil diseases of Egypt, which thou knowest, upon thee; but will lay them upon all them that hate thee. And thou shalt consume all the people which the Lord thy God shall deliver thee" (Deut. 7:12-16).

In connection with the above passage notice, first, the definite reference made to God's "mercy," which proves that He did not deal with Israel on the bare ground of exacting and relentless law, as some have erroneously supposed. Second, observe the reference which the Lord here made unto His oath to their fathers, that is Abraham, Isaac, and Jacob; which shows that the Sinaitic covenant was based upon, and not divorced from, the Abrahamic—Israel's occupation of Canaan being the "letter" fulfillment of it. Third, if, as a nation, Israel rendered unto their God the obedience to which He was entitled as their King and Governor, then He would love and bless them—under the Christian economy there is no promise that He will love and bless any who live in defiance of His claims upon them! Fourth, the specific blessings here enumerated were all of a temporal and material kind. In other passages God threatened to bring upon them plagues and judgments (Deut. 28:15-65) for disobedience. The whole was a compact promising to Israel certain outward and national blessings on the condition of their rendering to God a general outward obedience to His law.

The tenor of the covenant made with them was, "Now therefore, if ye will obey my voice indeed, and keep my covenant, then ye shall be a peculiar treasure unto me above all people; for all the earth is mine, and ye shall be unto me a kingdom of priests, and a holy nation" (Exod. 19:5, 6). "Behold, I send an Angel before thee, to keep thee in the way, and to bring thee into the place which I have prepared. Beware of him, and obey his voice, provoke him not; for he will not pardon your transgressions: for my name is in him. But if thou shalt indeed obey his voice, and do all that I speak; then I will be an enemy unto thine enemies, and an adversary unto thine adversaries" (Exod. 23:20-22). Nevertheless, a provision of mercy was made where true repentance for failure was evidenced: "If they shall confess their iniquity, and the iniquity of their fathers, with their trespass which they trespassed against me, and that also they have walked contrary unto me; and that I also have walked contrary unto them, and have brought them into the land of their enemies: if then their uncircumcised hearts be humbled, and they then accept of the punishment of their iniquity: Then will I remember my covenant with Jacob, and also my covenant with Isaac, and also my covenant with Abraham. . . . These are the statutes and judgments and laws which the Lord made between him and the children of Israel in Mount Sinai by the hand of Moses" (Lev. 26:40-42, 46).

The Sinaitic covenant in no way interfered with the divine administration of either the everlasting covenant of grace (toward the elect) nor the Adamic covenant of works (which all by nature lie under); it being in quite another region. Whether the individual Israelites were heirs of blessing under the former, or under the curse of the latter, in no wise hindered or affected Israel's being as a people under this national regime, which respected not inward and eternal blessings, but only outward and temporal interests. Nor did God in entering into this arrangement with Israel mock their impotency or tantalize them with vain hopes, any more than He does so now, when it still holds good that "righteousness exalteth a nation; but sin is a reproach to nations" (Prov. 14:34). Though it be true that Israel miserably failed to keep their national engagements and brought down upon themselves the penalties which God had threatened, nevertheless, the obedience which He required of them was not obviously and hopelessly impracticable: nay, there were bright periods in their history when it was fairly rendered, and the fruits of it were manifestly enjoyed by them.

III

Considered as a part of the gradual and progressive unfolding of God's eternal purpose, the Sinaitic transaction marked a decided step forward upon the Abrahamic covenant, while it was also a most suitable scheme of preparation for Christianity; considered separately by itself, the Sinaitic transaction was the giving of a system of government designed for the immediate use of the Jews. These two leading aspects must be kept distinct if hopeless confusion is to be avoided. It is of the second we continue to treat, namely the Sinaitic covenant as it pertained strictly to the nation of Israel. It announced certain outward and temporal blessings on the condition that Israel as a people remained in subjection to their divine King, while it threatened national curses and calamities if they rejected His scepter and flouted His laws. This supplies the key to the entire history of the Jews.

As an example and exemplification of what has just been said, take the following, "Wherefore say unto the children of Israel, I am the Lord, and I will bring you out from under the burdens of the Egyptians, and I will rid you out of their bondage, and I will redeem you with a stretched out arm, and with great judgments; And I will take you to me for a people, and I will be to you a God: and ye shall know that I am the Lord your God, which bringeth you out from under the burdens of the Egyptians. And I will *bring you in unto the land,* concerning the which I did sware to give it to Abraham, to Isaac, and to Jacob; and I will give it you for a heritage: I am the Lord" (Exod. 6:6-8). Now that passage has presented a formidable difficulty to those who have thoughtfully pondered it, for scarcely any of the adults whom God brought out of Egypt ever entered Canaan! How, then, is this to be explained?

Thus: first, that promise concerned Israel *as a people,* and did not by any means necessarily imply that all, or even any of that particular generation were to enter Canaan. The divine veracity was not sullied: forty years later the nation *did* obtain the promised inheritance. Second, other passages must be compared with it. In Exodus 6 no express condition was mentioned in connection with the promise, not even the believing of it. Yet, so far as that generation was concerned, this, as the sequel clearly shows, was implied; for if it had been an absolute, unconditional promise to that generation, it must have been performed, otherwise God had failed to make good His word. That the promise to that generation was suspended upon their faith is plain from Hebrews 3:18, 19. Third, therein we see the contrast: the fulfillment of every condition is secured for us in and by Christ.

The Sinaitic covenant, then, was a compact promising to Israel as a people certain material and national blessings on the condition of their rendering to God a general obedience to His laws. But at this point it may be objected that God, who is infinitely holy and whose prerogative it is to search the heart, could never be satisfied with an outward and general obedience, which in the case of many would be hollow and insincere. The objection is pertinent and presents a real difficulty: how can we meet it? Very simply: this would be true of *individuals* as such, but not necessarily so where *nations* are concerned. And why not, it may be asked? For this reason: because nations as such have only a temporary existence; therefore they must be rewarded or punished in this present world, or not at all! This being so, the kind of obedience required from them is lower than from individuals, whose rewards and punishments shall be eternal.

But again it may be objected, Did not the Lord declare, "I will take you to me for a people, and I will be to you a God" (Exod 6:7)? Is there not something far more spiritual implied there than a national covenant, something in its terms which could not be exhausted by merely outward and temporal blessings? Once more we must insist upon drawing a broad line between what pertains to individuals and what is applicable to nations. This objection would be quite valid if that promise described the relation of God to the individual soul, but the case is quite different when we remember the relation in which God stands to a nation as such! To ascertain the exact purport and scope of the divine promises to Israel as a people we must take note of the actual engagements which we find He entered into with them as a nation. This is quite obvious, yet few theologians have followed it out consistently when dealing with what is now before us.

Let it next be pointed out that the view we have propounded above (and in the preceding chapter) of the nature and scope of the Sinaitic covenant, agrees fully with the statements made regarding it in the New Testament, the most important of which is found in Hebrews 8, where it is contrasted from the better and new covenant under which Christians are now living. At first view it may appear that the antithesis drawn between the two covenants in Hebrews 8 is so radical that it must be an opposition between the covenant of works made with Adam and the covenant of grace made with believers under the gospel; in fact, several able commentators so understand it. But this is quite a mistake, and one which carries serious implications, for error on one point affects, more or less, the whole of our theological thinking. A little reflection should quickly determine this matter.

In the first place, the people of God, even before the incarnation of Christ, were not under the broken covenant of works, with its inevitable curse, but enjoyed the blessings of the everlasting covenant which God had made with their surety before the foundation of the world. In the second place, such a view of the Sinaitic covenant (i.e., making it a repetition of the one entered into with Adam) would be in flat contradiction to what is said in the Epistle to the Galatians, where it is specifically declared that, whatever may have been God's purpose in the giving of the law, it was not meant to and could not annul the promises made to Abraham or supersede the previous method of salvation by faith which was revealed to that patriarch. But if we understand the apostle (and remember he was addressing Jews in the Hebrews Epistle) to be drawing a contrast between the *national* covenant made with their fathers at Sinai, and the far higher and better covenant into which Jews and Gentiles are brought by faith in Christ, then we get a satisfactory explanation of Hebrews 8 and one that brings it into complete harmony with Galatians 3.

Observe carefully what is said in Hebrews 8 to be the characteristic difference between the new and the old economies: "I will put my laws into their minds and write them *in their hearts*" (v. 10). No promise in any wise comparable to this was given at Sinai. But the absence of any assurance of the Spirit's internal and effectual operations was quite in keeping with the fact that the Mosaic economy required not so much an inward and spiritual, as an outward and natural obedience to the law, which for them had nothing higher than temporal sanctions. This is a fundamental principle which has not received the consideration to which it is entitled: it is vital to a clear understanding of the radical difference which obtains between Judaism and Christianity. Under the former God dealt with one nation only; now He is manifesting His grace to elect individuals scattered among all nations. Under the former He simply made known His requirements; in the latter He actually produces that which meets His requirements.

Galatians 3 shows plainly that the Sinaitic covenant was subsidiary to the promises given to Abraham concerning his Seed: "Wherefore then serveth the law [i.e., the entire legal economy]? It was *added* because of transgressions, till the seed should come to whom the promise was made" (v. 19). Thus it is clear that from the first the Mosaic economy was designed to be but *temporary,* to last only from the time of Israel's sojourn in the wilderness till Christ. It was needed because of their "transgressions." The children of Israel were so intractable and perverse, so prone to depart from God, that without such a divinely provided hedge, they would have lost their national identity, mixing themselves with the surrounding nations and becoming sunk in their idolatrous ways. The Holy Spirit was not then so largely given that, by the potent influences of His grace, such a disastrous issue would have been prevented. Therefore a temporary arrangement, such as Judaism provided, was essential to preserve a pure stock from which the promised Messiah should issue; and *this* end the Sinaitic covenant, with its promises and penalties, did effect!

But there was another and deeper reason for the legal economy. Though the Sinaitic compact was not identical with the covenant of works made with Adam, yet, in some respects, it closely resembled it: it was analogous to it, only on a lower plane. During the fifteen hundred years which elapsed between Sinai and Bethlehem, God carried out a practical demonstration with the two great divisions of the human race. The Gentiles were left to the light of nature: they were "suffered to walk in their own ways" (Acts 14:16; cf. 17:26-30), and this in order to supply an answer (for men) to the question, "Can fallen man, in the exercise of his own unaided reason and conscience find out God, and raise himself to a higher and better life?" One has only to consult the history of the great nations of that period—the Egyptians, Babylonians, Persians, Greeks, and Romans—to see the hopelessness of such an attempt. Romans 1:21-31 gives the inspired comment thereon.

Running parallel with God's suffering all nations (the Gentiles) to walk in their own ways, was another experiment (speaking from the human side of things, for from the divine side "Known unto God are *all* his works from the beginning of the world": Acts 15:18), conducted on a smaller scale, yet quite as decisive in its outcome. The Jews were placed under a covenant of law to supply an answer to this further question, "Can fallen man, when placed in most favorable circumstances, win eternal life by any doings of his own? Can he, even when separated from the heathen, taken into outward covenant with God, supplied with a complete divine code for the regulation of his conduct, conquer indwelling sin and act so as to secure his acceptance with the thrice holy God?" The answer furnished by the history of Israel is an emphatic negative. The lesson supplied thereby for all succeeding generations of the human race is written in unmistakable language: If Israel failed under the national covenant of outward and general obedience, how impossible it is for any member of Adam's depraved offspring to render spiritual and perfect obedience!

In the spirit of it, the Sinaitic covenant contained the same moral law as the law of nature under which Adam was created and placed in Eden—the tenth commandment giving warning that something more than outward things were required by God. Yet only those who were divinely illumined could perceive this—it was not until the Holy Spirit applied that tenth commandment in power to the conscience of Saul of Tarsus that he first realized that he was an inward transgressor of the law (Rom. 7:7, etc.). The great bulk of the nation, blinded by their self-sufficiency and self-righteousness, turned the Sinaitic compact into the covenant of works, elevating the handmaid into the position of the married wife—as Abraham did with Hagar. Galatians 4 reveals that, while the Sinaitic covenant was regarded as subservient to the covenant of grace, it served important practical ends; but when Israel perversely elevated it to the place which the better covenant was designed to hold, it became a hindrance and the fruitful mother of bondage.

The grievous error into which so many of the Jews fell concerning the design of God in giving them His law has been perpetuated, though in a modified form, by some of our own theologians. This is due to their failure to properly recognize the condition of Israel at Sinai. But once we see what they already possessed, it rules out of court the idea of the law being intended to convey the same to them. When was it that they received from God His law? Not while they were still in the land of Pharaoh, nor while they were on the Egyptian side of the Red Sea, but after they had been completely delivered from their taskmasters. It is clear then beyond contradiction, from the very time of its introduction, that the law was not given to Israel in order to deliver them from evil or as a procurer of blessing. It could not have for its design the delivering of them from death or the obtaining of God's favor, for such blessings were already theirs.

It is of great importance to keep distinctly in view what the law was never designed to effect. If we exalt it to a position which it was never meant to occupy, or expect benefits from it which it was never fitted to yield, then we shall not only err in our own reckonings, but deprive ourselves of any clear knowledge of the dispensation to which it belonged. It was in order to define the negative side of the law—what it was *not* intended to procure—that the apostle declared: "And this I say, the covenant, that was confirmed before of God concerning Christ, the law, which was four hundred and thirty years after, cannot disannul, that it should make the promise of none effect. For if the inheritance be of the law, it is no more of promise: but God gave it to Abraham by promise" (Gal. 3:17, 18). This is decisive, yet perhaps a few words of explanation will enable the reader to more easily grasp its purport.

It was because the Jews had, for the most part, come to regard their obedience to the law as constituting their title to the inheritance, and because certain of the Judaizers were beginning to corrupt the Galatian converts with the leaven of their self-righteousness, that the apostle was here moved by the Spirit to check this evil, and to expose the basic error from which it proceeded. He presses upon them the Scriptural facts of the nature and design of Jehovah's covenant with Abraham, which he declares was "confirmed before of God concerning Christ." The covenant promise made to Abraham is said to be "concerning Christ," first, because it had preeminent regard to Him; and second, because it had in view the covenant of redemption which He was to establish. The particular point which the apostle now emphasized was, that the Abrahamic covenant expressly conferred on his posterity, as God's *free gift,* the inheritance of the land of Canaan—which entailed their deliverance from the land of bondage and their safe passage through the wilderness, which were necessary in order for them to enter and take possession thereof.

Thus the apostle made it unmistakably clear that Israel's title to Canaan could not possibly need to be reacquired by a law righteousness performed by them personally, for in such a case the law would revoke the covenant of promise, and thereby the latter revelation which God made at Sinai would overthrow the foundation of what He had laid in His promises to Abraham. That the Lord never meant for the law to interfere with the gifts and promises of the Abrahamic covenant is abundantly clear from what He said to Israel immediately before the law was formally announced from Sinai: "Ye have seen what I did unto the Egyptians, and how I bare you on eagles' wings, and brought you unto myself. Now therefore, if ye will obey my voice indeed, and keep my covenant, then ye shall be a peculiar treasure unto me above all people: for all the earth is mine: and ye shall be unto me a kingdom of priests, and a holy nation" (Exod. 19:4-6).

From the above quotation it will be seen that God addressed Israel as already standing in such a blessed relation to Him as evidenced for them an interest in His love and faithfulness. He appealed to the proofs which He had given of this, as being not only sufficient to set their hearts at rest, but also to encourage them to expect whatever might still be needed to complete their felicity. "Now therefore, if ye will obey my voice": not because ye *have* obeyed it have I wrought so mightily for you: but these things have been done that ye might render me loving and loyal subjection. So too He prefaced the Ten Commandments with "I am the Lord thy God which have brought thee out of the land of Egypt, out of the house of bondage" (Exod. 20:2). He rests His claims to their obedience on the grace that He had already bestowed upon them.

(For much in the early paragraphs of this chapter we are indebted to an able discussion of the character of the Sinaitic covenant by Robert Balfour, which appeared in the *British and Foreign Evangelical Review* of July 1877.)

IV

When God established His covenant with Abraham He said to him, "Know of a surety that thy seed shall be a stranger in a land that is not theirs, and shall serve them; and they shall afflict them four hundred years. And also that nation, whom they shall serve will I judge; and afterwards shall they come out with great substance" (Gen. 15:13, 14). Accordingly, when the time approached for the execution of judgment on their oppressors, the servitude of Israel had reached its extreme point, and the bitterness of their bondage had awakened in their minds an earnest desire for deliverance. Their discipline was an essential part of their preparation for the benefits which God designed to bestow upon them. Contemporaneously with those events, Moses was raised up as the instrument of their deliverance, and was divinely qualified for the work assigned him.

Moses, acting under divine directions and by a series of remarkable judgments upon Egypt, extorted from Pharaoh a reluctant permission for their departure from his land, with all their possessions. Those judgments were designed not only to afford a practical confutation of the idolatry of the Egyptians and a retribution for their cruel oppression of God's people, but more particularly an open vindication of the supremacy of Jehovah in the sight of the surrounding nations, and at the same time to influence the hearts of the people themselves so as to induce a heartfelt acknowledgment of God, and a prompt and cheerful obedience to Him. Assuredly, no course could have been more fitted to accomplish those ends. The manifestations of divine power Israel had witnessed, the marked separation between them and the Egyptians—being preserved from the plagues which smote their oppressors and their miraculous escape from the judgment which overwhelmed the Egyptians at the Red Sea—were well suited to create deep and lasting effects upon them.

Those impressive events all indicated God's interposition for their deliverance in a manner to which it was impossible that even the blindest among them could have been insensible. They were well calculated to awaken a deep conviction of the divine presence in their midst in a special manner. Such manifestations of God's power, faithfulness, and grace on their behalf ought to have produced in them a ready compliance with every intimation of His holy will. He had dealt with them as He had dealt with no other people. How much they needed those object lessons, and how little they really benefited from them, their future conduct shows.

Their moral conditions the Lord well knew—their faintheartedness, their perversity, their unbelief. In order to more effectually prepare them for the immediate future, as well as of formally establishing that covenant by which He indicated the relation which He was graciously pleased to sustain toward them and the principles by which His future dealings with them would be regulated, He led them through the wilderness and brought them to Sinai. There the Lord granted a fresh manifestation of His glory: amidst thunderings and lightnings, flames and smoke, He delivered to them the Ten Words. The object of God in that solemn transaction was clearly intimated in the language He addressed to them immediately before (see Exod. 19:5, 6). But although the law of the Ten Commandments constituted the leading feature of the Sinaitic covenant and gave to the entire transaction its distinctive character, yet we must conclude that it was limited thereto.

It is true that God added no more to the Ten Commandments at that time, not because there was nothing more to be revealed, but because the people in terror entreated that Moses might be the medium of all further communications (Deut. 5:24-27). Accordingly we find the law itself was followed by a number of statutes (Exod. 21-23), which were in part explanatory of the great principles of the law and in part enjoining the ordinances for the regulation of their worship—which later received much enlargement. Both the basic law and the subsidiary statutes were immediately put on permanent record, and the whole sealed by "the book of the covenant" being read in the audience of the people and blood being sprinkled on them (Exod 24:4-8). It was to that solemn ratification of this covenant which the apostle makes reference in Hebrews 9:18-20—it was substantially a repetition of the same significant ceremony which attended the establishment of the earlier covenants.

Thus it is clear that while the Ten Commandments was the most prominent and distinctive feature of the Sinaitic covenant, yet it embraced the entire body of the statutes and judgments which God gave Moses for the government of Israel, as well in their civil as in their religious capacity. They formed one code, in which the moral law and the ceremonial law were blended in a way peculiar to the special constitution under which the nation of Israel was placed. Speaking generally, the civil had a religious and the religious a civil aspect, in a sense found nowhere else. All the particulars of that code were not equally important: some things were vital to it, the violation of which involved the practical renunciation of the covenant; others were subordinate, enjoined because necessary as means of attaining the grand end in view. Yet were they all parts of the one covenant, demanding a prompt and sincere obedience.

In the above paragraphs we have purposely gone back to the beginnings of God's dealings with Israel as a nation, in order to show once more how unique was the Mosaic economy, that there was much connected with it which, in the very nature of the case, has no parallel under the present gospel order of things. The Sinaitic covenant was the foundation of that *political constitution* which the people of Israel enjoyed: in consequence thereof Jehovah sustained a special relation to them. He was not only the God of all the earth (Exod. 19:5), but, in a peculiar sense, the King and Legislator of Israel. Any attempt on their part to change the divinely instituted system of law, given for their government, was expressly forbidden: "Ye shall not add unto the words which I command you, neither shall ye diminish aught from it, that ye may keep the commandments of the Lord your God" (Deut. 4:2). That code was complete in itself—that is, as considered in relation to the particular condition of that people for whose government it was intended.

"It is of great importance to the right interpretation of many passages in the O.T., that this particular be well understood and kept in view. Jehovah is very frequently represented as the Lord and God of all the ancient Israelites; even where it is manifest that the generality of them were considered as destitute of internal piety, and many of them as enormously wicked. How, then, could He be called *their* Lord and *their* God, in distinction from His relation to Gentiles (whose Creator, Benefactor, and Sovereign He was), except on the ground of the *Sinai* covenant? He was *their* Lord as being their Sovereign, whom, by a federal transaction they were bound to obey, in opposition to every political monarch who should at any time presume to govern them by laws of his own. He was *their* God, as the only Object of holy worship; and whom, by the same National covenant, they had solemnly engaged to serve according to His own rule, in opposition to every Pagan idol.

"But that National relation between Jehovah and Israel being long since dissolved, and the Jew having no prerogative above the Gentile; the nature of the Gospel economy and of the Messiah's kingdom absolutely forbids our supposing that either Jews or Gentiles are warranted to call the Universal Sovereign *their* Lord or their God, if they do not yield willing obedience to Him and perform *spiritual* worship. It is, therefore, either for want of understanding, or of considering the nature, aspect, and influence of the Sinai Constitution, that many persons dream of the New Covenant in great numbers of places where Moses and the Prophets had no thought of it, but had the Convention at Horeb directly in view. It is owing to the same ignorance, or inadvertency, that others argue from various passages in the O.T. for justification before God by their own obedience, and against the final perseverance of real saints.

"Again, as none but real Christians are the subjects of our Lord's kingdom, neither adults nor infants can be members of the Gospel Church in virtue of an *external* covenant or a *relative* holiness. A striking disparity this, between the Jewish and the Christian Church. A barely *relative* sanctity [that is, a sanctity accruing from belonging to the nation of God's choice, A.W.P.] supposes its possessors to be the people of God in a merely external sense; such an external people supposes an external covenant, or one that relates to exterior conduct and temporal blessings; and an external covenant supposes an external king. Now an external king is a political sovereign, but *such is not* our Lord Jesus Christ, nor yet the Divine Father.

"Under the Gospel Dispensation, these peculiarities have *no* existence. For Christ has not made an external covenant with any people. He is not the king of any particular nation. He dwells not in a temple made with hands. His throne is in the heavenly sanctuary, nor does He afford His visible presence in any place upon earth. The partition-wall between Jews and Gentiles has long been demolished: and, consequently, our divine Sovereign does not stand related to any people or to any person so as to confer a relative sanctity, or to produce an *external* holiness.

"The covenant made at Sinai having long been obsolete, all its peculiarities are vanished away: among which, relative sanctity [that is, being accounted externally holy, because belonging to the nation separated unto God, A.W.P.] made a conspicuous figure. That National Constitution being abolished, Jehovah's political sovereignty is at an end. The Covenant which is now in force, and the royal relation of our Lord to the Church, are *entirely spiritual.* All that external holiness of persons, of places, and of things, which existed under the old economy, is gone for ever; so that if the professors of Christianity do not possess a real, *internal* sanctity, they have none at all. The National confederation at Sinai is expressly contrasted in Holy Scripture with the new covenant (see Jer. 31:31-34; Heb. 8:7-13), and though the latter manifestly provides for internal holiness, respecting all the covenantees, yet it says not a word about relative sanctity" (Abraham Booth, 1796).

Jehovah, then, was King in Israel: His authority was supreme. He gave them the land in which they dwelt; settled the conditions on which they held it; made known the laws they were required to obey; and raised up from time to time, as they were demanded, leaders and judges, who for a season exercised, under God, authority over them. This is what is signified by the term *theocracy*—a government adminis- tered, under certain limitations, directly by God Himself. Such a relation as Jehovah sustained toward Israel, condemning all idolatry and demanding their separation from other nations, largely regulated the legislation under which they were placed. So far as righteousness between man and man was concerned, there was of course much which admitted of a universal application, resting on common and unalterable principles of equity; but there were also many enactments which derived their peculiar complexion from the special circumstances of the nation. The most cursory examination of the Pentateuch suffices to show this.

The Books of Moses reveal the singular provisions made for a self-sustaining nation, carefully fenced around and protected from moral danger from without, so far as civil arrangements could effect this end. Encouragement was indeed given to such strangers as might, on the renunciation of idolatry, become converts to the faith of Israel and settle amongst them, though they were not permitted to have any share in the earthly inheritance; but all connection and ensnaring alliances with any people beyond their own confines were rigorously guarded against. The law of jubilee, which secured to each family a perpetual interest in the property belonging to it; the restrictions on marriage; the practical discouragement of commerce; the hindrances placed in the way of aggressive warfare—in the prohibition of cavalry, then the chief strength of armies: these were all of a restricted character and illustrated that special exclusiveness of Judaism.

The nature of God's immediate government of Israel involved a special providence as essential to its administration. It is true that eternal rewards and punishments were not employed for this purpose, because nations, as such, have no hereafter. In the Judgment men will be dealt with not according to their corporate but in their individual capacity. Yet it must not be inferred that Israel had no knowledge of a future state, for they had; but that knowledge could not be formally employed to enforce their civil obedience. Social relations are an affair of this world, and the laws which regulate them must find their sanctions in considerations bearing on the mere interests of this present life. Accordingly, God, as the political head of Israel, by special and extraordinary providences, intimated His approval or displeasure as their conduct called for. Prosperity, peace, and an abundance of material things were the rewards of national obedience; wars, famines, and pestilences were the punishment of their sin. The whole history of the nation shows with what uniformity the course of this intimation was pursued toward them.

Such, then, was the nature and design of the constitution conferred upon Israel; yet it must be remembered that the great benefits it involved were not the fruit of the Sinaitic covenant. True, their continued enjoyment of them depended on their obedience to that covenant; but their original bestowment was the effect of the Abrahamic covenant. Of this fact they were definitely reminded by Moses: "The Lord did not set his heart upon you, nor choose you, because ye were more in number than any people: for ye were the fewest of all people; but because the Lord loved you, and because he would keep the oath which he had sworn *unto your fathers*" (Deut 7:7, 8). In keeping therewith we find that when serious crises arose because of their sins, those who interceded before God in their behalf sought forgiveness on the ground of the promises made to Abraham (see Exod. 32:13; Deut. 9:27; II Kings 13:23).

By undeserved and sovereign grace the Israelites were chosen to be the people of God, and their obedience was not intended to purchase advantages and immunities not already possessed, but rather to preserve to them the possession of what God had already bestowed. This is what indicates the place which the moral law occupied in regard to the nation at large. It proceeded on the recognition of their *existing relation to God:* He had chosen, redeemed, and made them His people; and now it was their privilege and duty to live in subjection to Him. It set before them the character and conduct which that existing relation required from them, and on which its perpetuation, with all the advantages connected with it, depended. "And ye shall be holy unto me, for I the Lord am holy, and have severed you from other people, that ye should be mine" (Lev. 20:26). At the same time it was the standard to which their political code was adjusted, so far as their circumstances allowed.

The place which the moral law occupied, the express terms in which love to God was enforced as its leading principle (Deut. 6:5), and the solemn circumstances under which it was given, were all fitted to teach the people that something more was required from them than a mechanical performance of duties—something in their heart and inward state, without which no service they were capable of performing could meet the approval of the Holy One. To suppose that a mere external conformity to the law was all that was expected from the people is to overlook the plainest statements and the most obvious facts recorded in the Old Testament. God required truth "in the *inward* parts" (Ps. 51:6), and scores of passages revealed the fact that nothing but a right state of heart toward Him could secure the service He commanded. Nothing but the blindness which sin occasioned could have made the Israelites insensible to this basic truth, otherwise the charges brought against them by Christ had been quite groundless and pointless; it had been meaningless for Him to denounce them for making clean the outside while they were full of corruption within.

V

The moral law (the Ten Commandments), which formed so prominent and distinctive a feature of the Sinaitic covenant, was accompanied by much which was of an *evangelical* nature. This consisted not so much in the announcement of what was absolutely new, as in giving greater fulness, precision, and significancy, to what had been already revealed. It is true that this was communicated largely through the medium of symbols; yet the instruction imparted by them was at once most impressive and adapted to the condition of Israel. While in Egypt, they were not in a situation which admitted of any extension of the means of worship. But now that they were about to take their place as an independent nation, in a country of their own, the time had arrived for the formal appointment of those institutions and ordinances which the regulation of their religious life required. Moreover, this was rendered the more needful from the prominence which the moral law was given in that economy.

Designed to be subservient to the great purposes of the previous covenant, it was requisite that the law should be counterbalanced by a more full and instructive disclosure of the grand truths which that covenant embraced, in order that the law might not override and neutralize them. We must always bear in mind that the Abrahamic covenant was in nowise superseded or placed in abeyance by the revelation given through Moses; it was still in unabated force. The law was, in reality, an "addition" to it and designed to more effectually secure its objects. It was therefore fitting that the grace and mercy made known to Abraham should receive such enlargement and illustration as might make the law not a hindrance, but the handmaid, to the believing reception of its truth. The *grace* of the Abrahamic covenant and the *law* of Moses had an important mutual relation. They threw light on one another, and in combination were designed to secure a common end.

It was, then, the Levitical institutions which supplied the enlarged instruction that the circumstances of the nation now rendered necessary. First and foremost were the directions given for the public manifestation of that fellowship and intercourse with God which it was the privilege of Israel to enjoy. A sanctuary was to be erected, the pattern of which was revealed to Moses in the mount, and the materials for which were to be supplied by the freewill offerings of the people—intimating that all must be regulated by the divine will, but that only a free and spontaneous worship from them was acceptable. The tabernacle was at once a pledge that God dwelt in their midst, and a visible means of enjoying that communion with Him to which He had graciously admitted them: it was a perpetual memorial of it, and a help to train them to those more spiritual apprehensions of the worship of God which the gospel alone has fully revealed and realized.

A priesthood was appointed, and one which presented a marked contrast from those which existed in other nations. Among the heathen, the priesthood was a distinct caste, a body of men standing apart from and even in antagonism to those for whom they officiated; and characterized by all the pride and tyrannical tendencies which caste distinctions engender. But the Hebrew priesthood belonged to all the people, representing them in their divine calling. One family alone, Aaron's, was permitted to enter the sacred precincts of the Lord's house and officiate for them. When the high priest entered the holy of holies he bore the names of all the tribes on his breastplate, and confessed all their transgressions. Thus the high honor of being permitted to draw nigh unto God was impressively taught the people, the sanctity of His house was emphasized, and the hindrance which sin imposed was borne testimony to.

An elaborate system of sacrifices was enjoined. These were not only incorporated with the institutions of worship, but were explanatory of their importance and design. They were appointed to expiate the guilt of offenses committed, with the express declaration that "the life of the flesh is in the blood, and I have given it to you upon the altar to make an atonement for your souls" (Lev. 17:11). A day was set apart annually for atonement to be formally made for the sins of the people (Lev. 16), and the elaborate services of it were so arranged as to concentrate therein, in the most impressive manner, the various lessons which the sacrifices inculcated. That those sacrifices could not, in themselves, take away sins, their frequent repetition indicated; and the fact that there were certain sins for which no sacrifices were provided, further showed their limitation. Nevertheless, they gave assurance that God was gracious, furnished a ground of hope, and supplied an inducement for them to unreservedly surrender themselves to their God, who was both righteous and merciful.

The special design of prolonging these chapters is to seek to help those who have been deceived by "dispensationalists," and others who have been misled by unwarrantable conclusions drawn from Old Testament premises. What has been pointed out above should make it evident that they are quite wrong who suppose that the Mosaic economy was a pure covenant of works which gave no hope to transgressors. God never made a promulgation of law to sinful men in order to keep them under mere law, without also setting before them the grace of the covenant of redemption, by which they might escape the wrath which the law denounced. The awful curse of Deuteronomy 27:26 must not be magnified to the exclusion of the wondrous blessing of Numbers 6:24-27. The justice of the moral law was tempered by the mercy of the ceremonial law, and the "severity" of the Sinaitic constitution was modified by the "goodness" of the Abrahamic covenant being still administered.

"The legal and evangelical dispensations have been but different dispensations of the same Covenant of Grace and of the blessings thereof. Though there is now a greater degree of light, consolation, and liberty, yet if Christians are now under a kingdom of grace where there is pardon upon repentance, the Lord's people under the Old Testament were (as to the reality and substance of things) also under a kingdom of *grace*" (James Fraser). "Moreover, brethren, I would not that ye should be ignorant, how that all our fathers were under the cloud, and all passed through the sea; and were all baptized unto Moses in the cloud and in the sea; and did all eat the same spiritual meat and did all drink the same spiritual drink; for they drank of that spiritual Rock that followed them: and that Rock was Christ" (I Cor. 10:1-4). In the light of that passage as a whole, being "baptized unto Moses" can only mean that he is there set forth as the minister of grace, the typical savior who had led them out of Egypt.

The tabernacle, the priesthood, and the Levitical offerings were really an amplification and explanation of the grace revealed in the promises of the Abrahamic covenant. The place which the moral law held in the Mosaic economy and its relation to that grace is clearly defined in, "Wherefore, then, serveth the law? It was *added* because of transgressions, till the seed should come" (Gal. 3:19). At Sinai God did not give the law as a message explaining how justification could be obtained by obedience thereto, for such obedience as it required was impossible to fallen man. In such a case, the law had not been "added" to the "promise," but would be in direct opposition to it. The previous verse makes it clear that if the law had been set up for such an end, it had completely disannulled the promise: "For if the inheritance be of the law, it is no more of promise; but God gave it to Abraham *by promise*" (v. 18).

So far, then, from the Mosaic economy canceling the Abrahamic promises, it was added thereto. Had that economy been one exclusively of works (as some of our moderns imagine), then the whole of Israel had been damned the first day it was instituted. Had it been a strict regime of law, untempered by mercy, then no pardon had been available (which flatly contradicts Lev. 26:40-46), and in such a case the Sinaitic covenant could not have been reckoned among Israel's *blessings* (Rom. 9:4). The word "added" in Galatians 3:19 proves that the dispensation of law was not established as a thing distinct by itself alone, but was an appendix to the grace of the Abrahamic covenant. In other words, the moral law and the ceremonial law which accompanied it were given with evangelical ends: to show sinners their need of Christ, and to indicate how He would meet that need.

Again: had the law been promulgated in divine wrath, with the object of its issuing in naught but death, then it had been in the hand of an *executioner,* and not as Galatians 3:19 states, "in the hand of a *mediator,*" whose office is to effect reconciliation. This supplies the key to and explains that much disputed and little understood statement in the next verse, "Now a mediator is not of one, but God is one" (v. 20). "God is one" signifies that His purpose and design is *the same* in both the Abrahamic and Sinaitic covenants; in other words, the law was published with a gracious end in view. Therefore when the apostle proceeds to ask the definite question, "Is the law then against the promises of God" (i.e., does it clash with or annul the gracious revelation made to Abraham), the emphatic answer is, "God forbid" (v. 21).

In the preceding chapter we affirmed that the Sinaitic covenant was a compact promising the Israelites as a people certain material and national blessings, on the condition of their rendering to God a general obedience to His law. Let it now be pointed out that something higher was required to achieve *individual communion* with the Lord. This is clear from such a passage as, "Lord, who shall abide in thy tabernacle? who shall dwell in thy holy hill? He that walketh uprightly, and worketh righteousness, and speaketh the truth in his heart. He that backbiteth not with his tongue, nor doeth evil to this neighbor, nor taketh up a reproach against his neighbour" (Ps. 15:1-3). No loose or mechanical compliance with the requirements of the law would suffice: God's glory is inseparably bound up with the interests of righteousness, and there can be no righteousness where the heart is divorced from Him.

In like manner we read again, "Who shall ascend into the hill of the Lord? or who shall stand in his holy place? He that hath clean hands, and a pure heart; who hath not lifted up his soul unto vanity, nor sworn deceitfully: he shall receive the blessing from the Lord" (Ps. 24:3-5). Here was described the character of the true worshipers of God, as contradistinguished from hypocrites. The ascending into the hill of the Lord, standing in his holy place, and abiding in his tabernacle is but figurative language to express spiritual access and spiritual fellowship with the Most High. It is striking to note that both of these searching passages were delivered at a time when the tabernacle service was about to be renewed (by Solomon) with increased splendor. Plainly they were designed as a *warning* to the people that whatever regard was paid to the solemnities of public worship, it could avail them nothing if there was not first practical righteousness in the offerer of it.

It is to be particularly observed that in the above passages it was not so much the righteousness of the law in general that the psalmist pressed for, as that establishing of *the second table,* because hypocrites and formalists have so many ways of counterfeiting the works of the first table. The same principle was pressed by the prophets again and again. "What hast thou to do to declare my statutes, or that thou shouldest take my covenant in thy mouth? Seeing thou hatest instruction, and castest my words behind thee. When thou sawest a thief, then thou consentedst with him, and hast been a partaker with adulterers. Thou givest thy mouth to evil, and thy tongue framest deceit. Thou sittest and speakest evil against thy brother; thou slander-est thine own mother's son" (Ps. 50:16-20). And yet in their blindness and self-complacency they had dared to talk of God's statutes and prate about His covenant. But no outward adherence to the worship of Jehovah could be accepted while the divine commands were tram-pled underfoot.

Isaiah was still more severe in his denunciations. He encountered those who feigned great respect for the temple, multiplying their offerings, treading the holy courts, keeping the feasts with much diligence, and making "many prayers." Yet he addressed them as the "rulers of Sodom" and as the "people of Gomorrah," and affirmed that their sacrifices and religious performances were nauseating to God, that His soul hated such pretensions, and that He would not hearken to their prayers because they oppressed the needy and ground down the fatherless and the widow (Isa. 1:10-17). There was no sincerity in their devotions: to pose as pious in the house of the Lord while iniquity filled their own dwellings was a grievous offense. Hence, he told them that their altar gifts were "lying offerings" (so "vain oblations" of v. 13 should be rendered), and that the whole of their worship was an abomination in the sight of the Holy One.

In like manner we hear Jeremiah saying, "Amend your ways and your doings, and I will cause you to dwell in this place. Trust ye not in lying words, saying, The temple of the Lord, The temple of the Lord, The temple of the Lord, are these. For if ye thoroughly amend your ways and your doings; if ye thoroughly execute judgment between a man and his neighbour; if ye oppress not the stranger, the fatherless, and the widow, and shed not innocent blood in this place, neither walk after other gods to your hurt; then will I cause you to dwell in this place that I gave to your fathers forever and ever" (7:2-8). Thus he exposed and condemned the blatant folly of those who trusted in the temple and its services for a blessing, when by their ungodliness and wicked works they had turned the temple into a resort of evil doers. Ezekiel too rebuked religious hypocrites, and showed how God could be satisfied with nothing less than that reality which was evidenced by practical righteousness between man and man (chaps. 18 and 33).

On the one hand, then, there was a godly remnant in Israel, who used the law "lawfully" (I Tim. 1:8) by causing its spirituality and holiness to cast them back on the grace and promises of the Abra-hamic covenant, turning to God as their redeemer and healer. It is in such passages as Psalm 119 we find their experience described. There was a realization of the excellence, the breadth, the height of the divine law; its suitability to man's condition; the blessedness of being conformed to its requirements; and the earnest longings of the pious heart after all that properly belongs to it. Those acknowledgments and aspirations are interspersed with confessions of backsliding, prayers for divine mercy and restoring grace, and fresh resolutions are formed in dependence upon divine aid to resist evil and strive after higher attainments in the righteousness which the law enjoins. In many other passages we find the consciousness of sin and moral weakness driving the soul to God for deliverance and help, especially in the appropriation of the gracious provision made in the sacrifices for expiation of guilt and restoration of peace to the troubled conscience.

On the other hand, there was a far greater number of the godless in Israel who made a wrong use of the law, perverting the design of the Sinaitic constitution, divorcing it from the Abrahamic covenant. These shut their eyes to the depths and spirituality of the law's requirements, for they were determined to attain unto a righteousness before God on a merely legal basis, and therefore they reduced the Decalogue to an outward performance of certain rules of conduct. This, of course, engendered a servile spirit, for where duties are not performed from high motives and grateful impulses, they necessarily become a burden and are discharged solely for the wages to be paid in return. Such a spirit actuated the scribes and Pharisees who were "hirelings" and not sons. Moreover, such a degradation of the law could only result in formality and hypocrisy. Finally, those who thus erred concerning the law's place and spirit could neither look rightly for the Messiah nor welcome Him when He appeared.

VI

As we have seen, that which preeminently characterized the Mosaic dispensation was the prominent and dominant position accorded to the law. Not only was that dispensation formally inaugurated by Jehovah Himself proclaiming the Decalogue from Sinai—the Exodus from Egypt and the journey across the wilderness being but introductory thereto—but those Ten Words were given the place of supreme honor. The tables of stone upon which they had been inscribed were assigned to the tabernacle. Now the most sacred vessel in the tabernacle, and that which formed the very center of all the services connected with it, was the ark. It was the special symbol of the Lord's covenant presence and faithfulness, for upon its cover was the throne on which He sat as King in Israel. Yet that ark was made on purpose to house the two tables of the law, and was called "the ark of the covenant" simply because it contained the agreed upon articles of the covenant. Thus those Ten Words were plainly recognized as containing in themselves the sum and substance of that righteousness which the covenant strictly required.

The very position, then, which the two tables of stone occupied, intimated most plainly that the observance of the law was God's great end in the establishment of Judaism. The law, perfect in its character and perpetual in its obligation, formed the foundation of all the symbolical institutions of worship which were afterwards imposed. As the center of Judaism was the tabernacle, so the center of the tabernacle was the law; for the sacred ark, which was enshrined in the holy of holies, had been built specially for the housing of it. Thus the thoughtful worshiper could scarcely fail to perceive that obedience to the law was the preeminent reason for which the Levitical economy was appointed. Every strictly religious rite and institution ordained by God through Moses was intended as a means to enforce the principles and precepts of the law, or as remedies to provide against the evils which inevitably arose from its neglect and violation.

The real relation which existed between the ceremonial and the moral law has not been sufficiently recognized, and therefore we will now consider at more length the true design and spiritual purpose of the Levitical code. The Decalogue itself was the foundation of the tabernacle service, all its symbolical ceremonies pointing to it as their common ground and center. In other words, the ceremonial institutions were entirely subservient to the righteousness which the law required. Let it be remembered that it was not until after the Sinaitic covenant had been formally ratified that the ritual of the Levitical system was given. Thus its very place in the history denotes that the ceremonial law is to be regarded not as of primary, but only of secondary moment in the constitution of God's kingdom in Israel. God had called Israel to occupy a place of peculiar nearness to Himself; so He first made known to them the great principles of truth and righteousness which were to regulate their lives, and then that there should be a visible bond of fellowship, by placing in their midst a dwelling place for Himself; appointing everything in connection therewith in such a manner as to impress them with the character of their King and of what became them as His subjects.

Most strikingly was the subserviency of the ceremonial to the moral law signified in connection with the divine appointments concerning the tabernacle. All was to be ordered according to the pattern shown to Moses in the mount, while the people were to signify their readiness to submit to God's will by contributing the required materials (Exod. 25:2-9). Now the first thing to be made was not the framework (walls) of the tabernacle itself, nor that which belonged to the outer court, but instead *the ark of the covenant* (Exod. 25:20-22), which was the repository of the Decalogue. The ark was given the precedence of everything else—altar, laver, lampstand, and table of shewbread. Thus it was plainly intimated that the ark was the most sacred piece of furniture pertaining to the house of God—the center from which all spiritual fellowship with the Lord was to proceed and derive its essential character. Thus an unmistakable link of connection between the ceremonial and the moral law, and the subordination of the one to the other, was impressed from the first on the very constitution of the tabernacle.

Now the chief lesson inculcated by the ceremonial law, proclaimed by numerous rites and ordinances, was that the holy and righteous have access to God's fellowship and blessing; whereas the unclean and wicked are excluded. But who constituted the one class, and who the other? Not simply those who observed, or refused to observe, the mere letter of the ceremonial law, but rather those who possessed in reality what was therein symbolized, and *that* was ascertained only in the light of God Himself. He had revealed His character in that law of moral duty which He took for the foundation of His throne and the center of His government in Israel. There the "line and plummet" of right and wrong, of holy and unholy in God's sight, was set up, and the Levitical code itself implied that very "line and plummet," and called men's attention to it by its manifold prescriptions concerning clean and unclean, defilement and purification.

The "divers washing" of the ceremonial law and its ever recurring atonements by blood pointed to existing impurities, but what many have failed to recognize is that those very impurities were such because at variance with the law of righteousness. "The Decalogue had pointed, by the predominantly negative form of its precepts, to the prevailing tendency in human nature to sin; and in like manner the Levitical code, by making everything that directly bore on generation and birth a source of uncleanness, perpetually reiterated in men's ears the lesson that corruption cleaved to them, that they were conceived in sin and brought forth in iniquity. The very institution of a separate order for immediate approach to God, and performing, in behalf of the community, the most sacred offices of religion, was a visible sign of actual shortcomings and transgressions among the people: it was a standing testimony that they were *not holy* after the lofty pattern of holiness exhibited in the law of Jehovah's throne.

"The distinction, also, between clean and unclean *in food,* while it deprived them of nothing that was required either to gratify the taste or minister nourishment to the bodily life—granted them, indeed, what was best adapted for both—yet served as a daily monitor in respect to the spiritual dangers that encompassed them and of the necessity of exercising themselves to a careful choosing between one class of things and another; reminded them of a good that was to be followed and of an evil to be shunned. And then there is a whole series of defilements springing from contact with what is emphatically the wages of sin—*death,* or death's livid image, the leprosy, which, wherever it alighted, struck a fatal blight in the organism of nature and rendered it a certain prey to corruption:—things, the very sight and touch of which, formed a call to humiliation, because carrying with them the mournful evidence, that, while sojourners with God, men still found themselves in the region of corruption and death" (*The Revelation of Law in Scripture,* by P. Fairbairn, 1869, to whom we are also indebted for other thoughts in this chapter).

In the light of what has been said above, it will be seen that "the law of carnal ordinances" contained most important instruction for the people—that is, not when considered by itself, but when regarded (according to its proper design) as an auxiliary to the Ten Commandments. But if the ceremonial law be isolated from them, and be regarded as possessing an independent use and value, then its message had flatly repudiated the truth; for in such case it had encouraged men to rely upon mere outward distinctions and rest in corporeal observances. But that had been contradictory rather than complementary of the Decalogue, for it throws all the emphasis upon the moral element, both in the divine character and the obedience which He requires from His people. Kept, however, in its proper place of subordination to the moral law, the Levitical code furnished most important instruction for Israel, keeping steadily before them the fact that sin brought defilement and shut out from fellowship with the Holy One.

That the Levitical ordinances had merely a subsidiary value, and that they derived all their importance from the connection in which they stood with the moral precepts of the law, is evident from other considerations. It is clearly demonstrated by the fact that when the special judgments of heaven were denounced against the covenant people, it never was for neglect of the ceremonial observances, but always for flagrant violations of the Ten Commandments. Let the reader carefully ponder the following passages in proof: Jeremiah 7:22-31; Ezekiel 8 and 18:1-3; Hosea 4:1-3; Amos 3:4-9; Micah 5 and 6. It is evident again from the fact that whenever the indispensable conditions of entrance to God's house and of abiding fellowship with Him are set forth, they are seen to be in conformity to the moral precepts, and not to the ceremonial observances (Pss. 15 and 24). Finally, it is evident from the fact that when the people exalted ceremonialism above practical obedience, the procedure was denounced as idolatry and the service rejected as a mockery (see I Sam. 15:22; Ps. 45:7; Isa. 1:2; Mic. 6:8).

Having dwelt upon the relation which existed between the ceremonial and the moral law—the one being strictly subservient to the other, the one reiterating the testimony of the other concerning holiness and sin—let us now consider another and quite different aspect of it. The Decalogue itself proclaimed the righteous requirements of the Lord, and therefore it made no allowance for disobedience and no provision for the disobedient: all it did was to threaten condemnation, and the awful penalty it announced could inspire nought but terror. But with the Levitical code it was quite otherwise: *there* was a mediatorial priesthood, *there* were sacrifices for obtaining forgiveness, *there* were ordinances of cleansing; and the design of these was to secure restoration of fellowship with God for those whose sins excluded them from His holy presence. Thus, while these ordinances were far from making light of sin, for those who repented and humbled themselves, they mercifully procured reconciliation to the lawgiver.

It should, however, be carefully noted that God imposed very definite limits to the scope of the expiatory sacrifices. And necessarily so: had there been no restrictions, had the way been open, at all times, for any one and every one, to obtain remission and cleansing, then the Levitical code had granted a corrupt and fatal license; for in that case men could have gone on in a deliberate course of evil, assured that further sacrifices would expiate their guilt. Therefore we see divine holiness tempering divine mercy, by appointing sacrifices for the sins of ignorance only, or for those defilements which were contracted unwittingly or unavoidably; whereas for flagrant and wilful transgressors of the Ten Commandments there remained nought but summary judgment. Thereby a gracious provision was made for what we may term sins of infirmity, while justice was meted out to the lawless and defiant.

The distinction to which we have just called attention, or the limitation made in the Levitical code for the obtaining of pardon, is clearly expressed in, "If any soul sin through ignorance, then he shall bring a she goat of the first year for a sin offering. And the priest shall make an atonement for the soul *that sinneth ignorantly,* when he sinneth by ignorance before the Lord, to make an atonement for him; and it shall be forgiven him. Ye shall have one law for him that sinneth through ignorance, both for him that is born among the children of

Israel, and for the stranger that sojourneth among them. But the soul that *doeth aught presumptuously* [with a high hand], whether he be born in the land, or a stranger, the same reproacheth the Lord; and that soul shall be cut off from among his people. Because he hath despised the word of the Lord, and hath broken his commandment, that soul shall utterly be cut off; his iniquity shall be upon him" (Num. 15:27-31).

But while there was this great difference between the ceremonial and the moral law—a merciful provision made for certain transgressors of it—yet we may clearly perceive how divine wisdom protected the Decalogue from dishonor, yea, by the very limitations of that provision upheld its righteous demands. "So that here, again, the Levitical code of ordinances *leant on* the fundamental law of the Decalogue, and did obeisance to its supreme authority. Only they who devoutly recognized this law, and in their conscience strove to walk according to its precepts, had any title to and interest in the provisions sanctioned for the blotting out of transgression. Then, as now, 'to walk in darkness' or persistently adhere to the practice of iniquity, was utterly incompatible with having fellowship with God—I John 1:6" (P. Fairbairn).

Yet, let it be pointed out, on the other hand, that God is sovereign, high above all law, and by no means tied by the restrictions which He has placed on His creatures. This grand truth ever needs to be clearly and boldly proclaimed, never more so than in our day, when such low and dishonoring views of God so widely prevail. When Jehovah made known Himself to Moses He said, "The Lord God, merciful and gracious, longsuffering, and abundant in goodness and truth; keeping mercy for thousands, forgiving iniquity and transgression and sin; and that will by no means clear the guilty: visiting the iniquity of the fathers upon the children" (Exod. 34:6, 7). That precious word was ever available to faith, as Numbers 14:17-20 and other passages blessedly show. True, even in this passage there is a solemn warning that justice will not forgo its claims, that obstinate rebels should meet their deserts. Yet that is given the second place, while grace occupies the foreground.

It was *that* which inspired relief in humble and penitent hearts: God is gracious. Thus, though at every point the Israelite was taught that sin is a most solemn and serious matter, and that neither the moral nor the ceremonial law made any provision of mercy where certain offenses were committed, yet that did not prevent the Lord dealing with them on a footing of pure grace. The revealed character of God opened a door of hope unto contrite souls, even when their case appeared utterly hopeless. A striking illustration of this is found in

Psalm 51. There we see David, after the commission of sins for which the law demanded the death penalty, and for which no Levitical sacrifice was of any avail (v. 16), acknowledging with a broken heart his heinous transgressions, casting himself on God's unconditional forgiveness (v. 1), and obtaining pardon from Him.

To give completeness to our present line of study, one other feature respecting the Levitical institutions requires to be noticed. Considered from one viewpoint the ceremonial oblations and ablutions were a real privilege of the Israelite, but from another they added to his obligations of duty—illustrating the fact that increased blessings always entail increased responsibility. The Levitical institutions were as truly legal enactments as were the Ten Commandments, and wiful violators of them were as much subject to punishment as those who profaned the Sabbath or committed murder (see Lev. 7:20; 17:4, 14; Num. 9:13).

The reason why those who transgressed the Levitical ordinances were subject to judgment was because the ceremonial statutes were invested with the same authority as were those commandments which pertained strictly to the moral sphere, and therefore to set them at nought was to dishonor the divine Legislator Himself. Moreover, it was to despise the means which He had graciously appointed—the only available means—for having guilt remitted and defilement removed, and which therefore remained unforgiven, yea, aggravated, by the despite that was done to the riches of God's mercy. Therein we may perceive a clear foreshadowing of that which pertains to the gospel, but our consideration of that must be deferred.

VII

The Sinaitic covenant needs to be studied from three independent viewpoints: (1) the relation which it sustains to the previous revelations which had been granted by God, being a marked advance thereon in the unfolding of His eternal purpose; (2) considered with regard to the peculiar relation in which it stood to the Jewish nation, furnishing as it did a unique constitution and a complete code for their guidance; (3) in its relation to the future, being admirably designed to pave the way for the advent of Christ and the dawn of Christianity. The first two of these have already engaged our attention; the third, which involves the most difficult aspects of our subject, we must now consider.

Until we had carefully contemplated the Mosaic economy as it related to the nation of Israel, their political and temporal welfare, we were not ready to view it in its wider and ultimate significance. God's first and immediate design in connection with the Sinaitic covenant was to furnish a "letter" fulfillment of the promises made to Abraham: to give him a numerous seed, to establish them in the land of Canaan, to preserve pure the stock from which the Messiah was to spring, to continue them there until Christ actually appeared in the flesh. Thus the Mosaic economy had served its purpose when the Son of God became incarnate. But, second, God's ultimate design under the Mosaic economy was to furnish a clear and full demonstration of the utter inability of fallen man, even under the most favorable conditions or circumstances, to meet His holy and righteous requirements; thereby making manifest the exceeding sinfulness of sin and the imperative need of an all-sufficient Savior.

From one standpoint it certainly appears that the Sinaitic covenant completely failed to achieve its object and that the whole of the Mosaic economy was a pathetic tragedy. In nowise did Israel as a nation conduct themselves as the beloved, called, and redeemed people of God. They rendered not to the moral law the obedience which it required, and the mercies of the ceremonial law they perverted to God's dishonor and their own spiritual undoing. Instead of the law leading sinners to Christ, "He came unto his own, and his own received him not" (John 1:11). Yet there is no failure with the Most High, no breakdown in His plan, no thwarting of His imperial will. The very failure of Israel only served to subserve the divine purpose, for it demonstrated the imperative need of something superior to that which Judaism, as such, supplied, and reserved for Christ the honor of bringing in that which is perfect.

In seeking to ascertain wherein the Mosaic economy paved the way for the introduction of Christianity, we shall notice, first, the imperfection or inadequacy of the provision supplied by Judaism; and second, briefly consider the typification and foreshadowment it made of the better covenant yet to be established. Though the order of things which was instituted by the Sinaitic covenant was a great advance upon that which obtained under the Abrahamic—for it not only supplemented the covenant of promise (which pledged the divine faithfulness to bestow every needed blessing) by the covenant of law, which bound Israel to yield that dutiful obedience to which the Lord was entitled; but it also brought the natural seed of Abraham into a relation of corporate nearness to the God of Abraham, providing in the tabernacle a visible representation that He was in their midst—yet it belonged unto a state of comparative immaturity and the relative twilight of divine revelation.

That which outstandingly characterized Judaism was that it concerned the outward and objective, rather than the inward and subjective. The Decalogue was written not upon the hearts of Israel, but upon tables of stone. It was a lord over them, demanding implicit submission, a schoolmaster to instruct them, but it supplied (as such) no power to produce obedience and no influence to move the secret springs of the heart. The same feature marked the Levitical institutions: they too were formally addressed to them from without, and pertained only to bodily exercises. The whole was an external discipline, in keeping with "a worldy sanctuary." True, what the law required was love; yet law as such does not elicit love. Fear was what predominated—the dread of suffering the wrath of an offended God, which the penalties of His law threatened on every hand.

It is true that great relief was provided by the ceremonial law, for provision was there made for obtaining forgiveness. The means for effecting this was the sacrifices—"the life-blood of an irrational creature, itself unconscious of sin, being accepted by God in His character of Redeemer for the life of the sinner. A mode of satisfaction no doubt in itself unsatisfactory, since there was no just correspondence between the merely sensuous life of an unthinking animal and the higher life of a rational and responsible being; in the strict reckoning of justice the one could form no adequate compensation for the other. But in this respect it was not singular; it was part of a scheme of things which bore throughout the marks of relative imperfection" (P. Fairbairn).

This same characteristic of relative imperfection appears on the tabernacle. A provisional arrangment was made whereby transgressors, otherwise excluded, might obtain the remission of their sins and enjoy again the privilege of fellowship with Jehovah; yet even here there was a conspicuous incompleteness, for though the reconciled were permitted to enter the outer court, yet they had no direct and personal access to the immediate presence chamber of the Lord. How far, far below the freedom of intercourse which all believers may now have with God, was the entrance of a few ministering priests into the courts of the tabernacle, with access to the holy of holies granted to one person alone, and to him only one day in the year! While the tabernacle itself, in dimensions but a hundred cubits by fifty cubits, and in materials composed of earthly and perishable things—how inadequate a representation of the dwelling place of Him who filleth heaven and earth!

The law exhibited the ineffable holiness of the divine character and bound Israel by covenant engagement to make that the standard after which they must seek to regulate all their conduct: "Ye shall be holy, for I the Lord your God am holy" (Lev. 9:2; cf. Exod. 19:6). But when it was enlightened and aroused by the lofty ideal of truth and duty thus presented before it, conscience would be but the more sensible of transgressions committed against the very righteousness required. The law is addressed to the conscience; and when once searched by it, men could not fail to perceive its extent and spirituality. Just in proportion as an Israelite's mind was honestly in exercise, he would come to understand that outward acts were far from being the only things which the law demanded, that it reached unto the thoughts and intents, affections and motives of the heart; he would find it, as the psalmist expressed it, "exceeding broad" (119:96). He might, indeed, have attempted to silence the deep and distressing sense of guilt thus awakened; but unless deceived, those attempts would have brought him no help.

The law, then, was far from inculcating or encouraging a spirit of self-righteousness. Instead of being a witness to which men could appeal in proof of their having met the requirements of God, it became an accuser, testifying against them of broken vows and violated obligations. Thereby it kept perpetually alive in the conscience a sense of guilt, and served to awaken in the hearts of those who really understood its spiritual meaning a feeling of utter helplessness and a sense of deep need. Goaded by the demands of a law which they were altogether incapable of fulfilling, their case must have seemed hopeless. Nor did the ordinances of the ceremonial law afford them any more than a very imperfect relief. To them it must have been apparent that "the blood of calves and of goats could not take away sins." A striking proof of this is furnished by the case of Isaiah; for upon beholding the manifested presence of Jehovah, he cried out, "Woe is me! for I am undone" (6:5)—clear evidence that his conscience was more oppressed by a sense of sin than comforted by the blessing of forgiveness.

Such a case as Isaiah's makes it plain that where there was an exercised heart (and there were such in Israel at every stage of their history), the holy law of God had produced convictions much too deep for the provisions of the ceremonial law "to make him that did the service perfect as pertaining to the conscience" (Heb. 9:2). But more emphatic still is the testimony supplied by the Psalms, which, be it remembered, were used in the public service of God, being designed to express the sentiments of all sincere worshipers. Not only do those Psalms extol the manifold perfections of the law (see especially the

19th and the 119th), but they also record the piercing accusations which it wrought. "For mine iniquites are gone over mine head: as a heavy burden they are too heavy for me. My wounds stink and are corrupt because of my foolishness. I am troubled; I am bowed down greatly: I go mourning all the day long. For my loins are filled with a loathsome disease, and there is no soundness in my flesh. I am feeble and sore broken: I have roared by reason of the disquietness of my heart. Lord, all my desire is before thee, and my groaning is not hid from thee" (38:4-9). "For innumerable evils have compassed me about: mine iniquities have taken hold upon me, so that I am not able to look up; they are more than the hairs of mine head: therefore my heart faileth me. Be pleased, O Lord, to deliver me; O Lord, make haste to help me" (40:12, 13).

Thus the divine law, by presenting a standard of perfect righteousness and by convicting men of their utter inability to meet its holy demands, prepared their minds for the coming Redeemer. This supplies the key to such passages as we have just quoted above. Awakened souls were made to feel iniquity cleaving to them like a girdle, and inward corruption like a deadly virus poisoning their very nature, breaking out continually in unholy tempers, defiling all they did or attempted, and thus destroying all hope of justification or acceptance with God on the ground of personal conformity to His requirements. Alive to the truth of an ineffably holy and infinitely perfect God, they were also alive to painful misgivings and fears of guilt; and hence their confessions of sin, sobs of penitence, and cries for mercy.

It was because the present deliverance furnished by the ceremonial law bore on it such marks of imperfection—the inadequacy of the blood of animals to atone for offenses so heinous, and the blessing secured being only a restored entrance to the outer court of the tabernacle—that it intimated a far better provision in the future; for nothing short of perfection could satisfy the One with whom they had to do. Because the Decalogue awakened a sense of guilt and alienation from the Lord which the ordinances of the ceremonial law could not perfectly remove, because wants and desires were aroused which could not then be more than partially satisfied, the Mosaic economy was well fitted to raise expectations in the bosom of the worshiper of some "better thing to come," disposing him to gladly receive the intimations of this which it was the part of prophecy to announce.

It was, then, the spiritual design of the law (in addition to its dispensational purpose—to restrain sin, etc.) to quicken conscience, to produce a deep sense of guilt, to slay the spirit of self-righteousness, to impart a pungent sense of personal helplessness, thereby moving exercised souls to look forward in faith and hope to the promised

Savior. That this was the effect produced by the law in an elect remnant, we have seen; that it ought to have been produced in all, cannot be fairly questioned. Thus, the law materially contributed to the right understanding of the dispensation under which Israel was placed, and was also a wise and gracious means for disciplining their faith to look onward to the future for the proper fulfillment of what their carnal ordinances only shadowed in type, thereby confirming the expectations which their ritual encouraged but could not, in the nature of things, satisfy.

The only course open to the awakened and exercised in Israel was to cast themselves unreservedly on the free mercy of God, in the sure hope that the future would reveal the perfect remedy and ransom when the promised Seed should appear, as the intimations of their figurative worship led them to expect, and by which all the exigencies of their case would be met. "Thus the Lord schooled them, fenced their path on every side, led them by the hand, and guided them to expect from the distant future what the present could not supply. Its convictions pointed to the relief which the Gospel alone was destined to furnish; it shut them up to the exercise of faith in the coming Redeemer" (John Kelly).

It is scarcely necessary for us to point out that God's order in the dispensations (i.e., the Mosaic preceding the Christian and paving the way for it) is precisely the same as His order now in connection with each truly converted soul. It still remains true that "by the law is the knowledge of sin" (Rom. 3:20), and the sinner must be searched and humbled by it before he will be brought heartily to rejoice in the message of the gospel. Not until the soul is conscious that it is under the law's sentence of death will it desire and appreciate the life that is to be found in Christ, and in Him alone—this the apostle Paul testified he found to be the case in his own experience (Rom. 7:7-10). The law is a perfect rule of righteousness; and when we measure ourselves by it, our innumerable shortcomings and sins are at once made apparent. When, then, an Israelite was quickened by the Spirit, he at once perceived the law's true character, became deeply sensible of his guilt, and longed for something higher and better than was then provided for his true consolation.

The same fundamental principle receives plain and striking exemplification on the opening pages of the New Testament. The way of the Redeemer was prepared by one who proclaimed with trumpet voice the law's righteousness, evoking the terrors of its threatenings: the ministry of John the Baptist must ever precede that of Christ. There will never be a genuine revival until we get back to this basic fact and act accordingly. The Lord Jesus Himself entered upon His blessed work of evangelization by unfolding the wise extent and deep spirituality of the law's requirements; for a large portion of the Sermon on the Mount (Matt. 5) was devoted to a clear and searching exposition of the law's righteousness, rescuing it from the false glosses of men and pressing its holy claims upon the multitudes. This is why that "sermon" is now so much hated by our moderns!

VIII

In the preceding chapter we sought to show how the inadequacy and imperfections of the Mosaic economy only served to pave the way for the introduction of Christianity. Such marks of imperfection were stamped on the very nature of the Levitical institutions; for they were, to a large extent, as the apostle termed them, "weak and beggarly elements" (Gal. 4:9). This was because it was then the comparative minority of the church, and the materials of a more spiritual economy did not exist. "The atonement was yet but prospective; the Holy Spirit did not operate as He does under the Gospel; and God's gracious designs as regards the redemption of our race (rather "of the elect") lay embedded and concealed in the obscure intimations that the Seed of the woman should bruise the Serpent's head and in the promises to Abraham. Nor were those defects perfectly remedied throughout the whole course of the dispensation. To the last the Jew walked in comparative darkness" (Litton's "Bampton" Lectures).

In the historical outworking of the economy, not only imperfection, but, as we all know, gross failure, characterized the entire history of Israel as a nation—ominously foreshadowed at the beginning, when Aaron lent himself to the awful idolatry of the golden calf at the very base of Sinai itself. In the vast majority, spirituality was so lacking and love to God beat so feebly in their hearts, that the requirements of the law were regarded as an oppressive yoke. Only too often, those who ought to have been the most exemplary in performing what was enjoined, and from their position in the commonwealth should have checked the practice of evil in others, were themselves the most forward in promoting it. Consequently, the predominating principle of the Mosaic economy—namely, the inseparable connection between obedience and blessing, transgression and punishment—was obscured, for souls which should have been "cut off" from the congregation as deliberate covenant breakers were allowed to retain their standing in the community and to enjoy its privileges.

It should be pointed out that this expression "that soul shall be cut off," which occurs so frequently in the Pentateuch, signifies something far more solemn and awful than does being "disfellowshipped from the church" today—such an explanation or definition on the part of not a few learned men is quite unpardonable. "That soul shall be cut off" refers primarily to God's act; for it occurs in connections and cases where those in human authority could not interfere, the violations of the law being *secret* ones (see Lev. 17:10; 18:29; 22:2). In fact, in a number of instances God expressly said, "*I* will cut off" (Lev. 20:3, 5, etc.). But where the act was open and the guilt known, God's decision was to be carried out by the community (as in Num. 15:30; Josh. 7:24-26). Yet even when Israel's judges or magistrates failed to enforce this, the guilty *were* cut off in God's judgment.

It was very largely through the failure of the responsible heads in Israel to execute the sentence of the law upon its open violators that the nation fell into such a low state, bringing down upon itself the providential judgments of Jehovah. Alas that history has repeated itself, for at no one point is the failure of Christendom more apparent than in the almost universal refusal of the so-called churches to enforce a Scriptural discipline upon its refractory members—sentiment and the fear of man have ousted a love of holiness and the fear of God. And just as surely, the consequence has been the same; though, in keeping with the more spiritual character of this dispensation, the divine judgments have assumed another form: error has supplanted truth, a company of godless worldings occupy the pulpits, so that those who long for bread are now being mocked with a stone.

Had Israel been faithful to their covenant engagement at Sinai, had they as a nation striven in earnest, through the grace offered them in the Abrahamic covenant, to produce the fruits of that righteousness required by the Mosaic, then, as another has beautifully experessed it, "delighting in the Law of the Lord and meditating therein day and night, in their condition they should assuredly have been 'like a tree planted by the rivers of water, that bringeth forth its fruit in his season, whose leaf doth not wither and whatsoever he doeth shall prosper.' " Canaan would then, indeed, have verified the description of "a land flowing with milk and honey." But alas, the law was despised, discipline was neglected, self-will and self-pleasing was rampant; and consequently, famines, pestilences, and wars frequently became their portion.

Just in proportion as practical holiness disappeared from Israel's midst, so was there a withdrawal of God's blessing. Israel's history in

Canaan never presented anything more than a most faulty display of that righteousness and prosperity which, like twin sisters, should have accompanied them all through their course. Yet again we would point out that Israel's failure by no means signified that the plan of the Almighty had been overthrown. So far from that, if the reader will turn to and glance at Deuteronomy 28 and 32 he will find that the Lord Himself predicted the future backslidings of the people, and from the beginning announced the sore afflictions which should come in consequence upon them. Thus, coincident with the birth of the covenant, intimations were given of its imperfect nature and temporal purpose: it was made clear that not through its provisions and agencies would come the ultimate good for Israel and mankind.

But it is high time that we now pointed out, second, wherein the *types* under the Mosaic economy prepared the way for the dawn of Christianity. A large field is here before us, but its ground has been covered so thoroughly by others that it is not necessary to do more than now call attention to its outstanding features. Ere doing so, let us again remind the reader that the Old Testament types were divinely designed to teach by way of contrast, as well as by comparison. The recognition of this important principle at once refutes the God-insulting theory that the types were defective and often misleading. The reason for this should be obvious: the antitypes far excelled the types in value. God is ever jealous of the glory of His beloved Son, and to Him was reserved the honor of producing and bringing in that which is perfect.

First, let us notice the special and *peculiar relation which Israel sustained to the Lord.* They were His chosen people, and He was their God in a way that He was the God of no others. It was as the descendants of Abraham, Isaac, and Jacob, as the children of promise, that God dealt with them from the beginning (see Exod. 2:24, 25; 6:5). It was in fulfillment of His holy promise to Abraham that "he brought forth his people with joy, his chosen with gladness" (Ps. 105:42, 43) from the cruel bondage of the land of Egypt. This basic fact must be steadily borne in mind when pondering all of God's subsequent dealings with them. Therein we find a perfect foreshadowment of God's dealings with His people today: each of them receives mercy on a covenant basis—the everlasting covenant made with Christ—and on the ground of it are they delivered from the power of Satan and translated into the kingdom of Christ.

Second, what we have just said above supplies the key to our right understanding of the *typical significance* of God's giving the Decalogue to Israel. The revelation of law at Sinai did not come forth in independence of what had preceded, as if it were to lay the foundation of something altogether new. It did not proceed from God considered simply as the Creator, exercising His prerogative to impose commands on the consciences of His creatures, which, with no other helps and endowments but those of mere nature, they were required with unfailing rectitude to fulfill. The history of Israel knows nothing of law in connection with promise and blessing. It was as the Redeemer of Israel that God announced the Ten Words, as being in a special sense "the Lord their God" (Exod. 20:2), proclaiming Himself therein to be the God of mercy as well as holiness (20:5, 6), and recognizing their title to the inheritance of Canaan as His own sovereign gift to them (20:12).

The law, then, was not given to Israel as a deliverer from evil, nor as the bestower of life. Its design was not to rescue from bondage, nor found a title to the favor and blessing of Jehovah, for all that was already Israel's (see Gal. 3:16-22). "So that grace here also took precedence of law, life of righteousness; and the covenant of law, assuming and rooting itself in the prior covenant of grace (the Abrahamic) only came to shut the heirs of promise up to that course of dutiful obedience toward God, and brotherly kindness toward each other, by which alone they could accomplish the higher ends of their calling. In *form* merely (viz., the Law now given as a covenant) was there anything new in this, not in *principle*. For what else was involved in the command given to Abraham. . . . 'I am the almighty God, walk before Me and be thou perfect' (Gen. 17:1)—a word which was comprehensive of all true service and righteous behaviour.

"But an advance *was* made by the entrance of the Law over such preceding calls and appointments, and it was this: the obligation to rectitude of life resting upon the heirs of promise was now thrown into a categorical and imperative form, embracing the entire round of moral and religious duty; yet, not that they might by the observance of this work themselves into a blissful relation to God, but that, as already standing in such a relation, they might walk worthy of it, and become filled with the fruits of righteousness, which alone could either prove the reality of their interest in God, or fulfil the calling they had received from Him" (P. Fairbairn).

Therein we have a striking exemplification of the relation which the law sustains to the people of God in all dispensations, most blessedly so in this Christian era. In every dispensation God has first revealed Himself unto His people as the giver of life and blessing and then as the requirer of obedience to His commands. Their obedience, so far from entitling them to justification, can never be acceptably rendered until they *are* justified. All the blessings of Israel were purely and solely of grace, received through faith. And what is faith but the acceptance of heaven's gifts, or the trusting in the record wherein those gifts are promised. The order of experience in the life of every saint, as it is so clearly set forth in the Epistle to the Romans (summed up in 12:1), is first participation in the divine mercy, and then, issuing from it, a constraining obligation to run in the way of God's commandments.

How could it be otherwise? Surely it is not more obvious than that it is impossible for fallen and depraved creatures, already lying under the divine condemnation and wrath, to earn anything at God's hands, or even to perform good works acceptable in His sight, until they have become partakers of His sovereign grace. Can they, against the tide of inward corruption, against the power of Satan and the allurements of the world, and against God's judicial displeasure, recover themselves and set out on a journey heavenward, only requiring the aid of the Spirit to perfect their efforts? To suppose such an absurdity betrays an utter ignorance of God's character in reference to His dealings with the guilty. If He "spared not his own Son" (Rom. 8:32), how shall He refuse to smite thee, O sinner! But, blessed be His name, He can, for His Son's sake, bestow eternal life and everlasting blessing on the most unworthy; but He cannot stoop to bargain with criminals about their acquiring a title to it, through their own defective services.

Third, if the circumstances of God's placing Israel under the law typified the fact that it was not given to unredeemed sinners in order for them to procure the divine favor, on the other hand, it is equally clear that it exemplifies the fact that the redeemed are placed under the law. Otherwise, one of the most important of all the divine transactions of the past (Exod. 19) would have no direct bearing upon us today. The Christian needs the law. First, to subdue the spirit of self-righteousness. Nothing is more calculated to produce humility than a daily measuring of ourselves by the exalted standard of righteousness required by the law. As we recognize how far short we come of rendering what unremitting love demands, we shall be constantly driven out of self unto Christ. Second, to restrain the flesh and hold us back from lawlessness. Third, as a rule of life, setting before us continually that holiness of heart and conduct which, through the power of the Spirit, we should be ever striving to attain.

Should it be objected that the believer has perfect freedom, and must not be entangled again in the yoke of bondage, the answer is, Yes, he is "free *to righteousness*" (Rom. 6:18); he is free to act as a servant of Christ, and not as a lord over himself. Believers are not free to introduce what they please into the service of God, for He is a jealous God, and will not suffer His glory to be associated with the vain imaginations of men; they are free to worship Him only in spirit and truth. "The freedom of the Spirit is a freedom only within the bounds of the Law" (P. Fairbairn). Subjection to the law is that which alone proves our title to the grace which is in Christ Jesus. None has any legitimate ground to conclude that he has savingly trusted in the Savior, unless he possesses a sincere desire and determination of heart to serve and glorify God. Faith is not a lawless sentiment, but a holy principle, its sure fruit being obedience. Love to God ever yields itself willingly to His requirements.

But let us now observe a conspicuous contrast in the type. At Sinai God said: "Now therefore, if ye will obey my voice indeed [as enunciated in the Ten Words] , and keep my covenant, then ye shall be a peculiar treasure unto me above all people. . . . Yet shall be unto me a kingdom of priests, and a holy nation" (Exod. 19:5, 6). There was a contingency: Israel's entering into those blessings turned upon their fulfillment of the condition of obedience. But the terms of the "new covenant," under which Christians live, are quite otherwise. Here there is no contingency, but blessed certainty; for the condition of it was perfectly fulfilled by Christ. Hence God now says, "I will make an everlasting covenant with them, that I will not turn away from them to do them good; but I will put my fear in their hearts, that they shall not depart from me" (Jer. 32:40); and, "I will put my Spirit within you, and cause you to walk in my statutes, and ye shall keep my judgments and do them" (Ezek. 36:27). Therein we may adore God for the antitype excelling the type: the *if* concerning Israel being displaced by His *shall.*

Yet in concluding our consideration of this branch of the subject, let us say very emphatically that the only ones who are entitled to draw comfort from those precious "shalls" of God, are they who correspond to the characters described in the immediate context. Jeremiah depicts them as those in whose hearts God puts His holy fear. If, then, the fear of God is not in me, if I do not stand in awe of His majesty and dread a despising of His authority, then I have no reason to conclude that I am numbered amongst those to whom the promises belong. Ezekiel describes those who "shall keep God's judgments and do them" as they from whom He takes away the stony heart and gives a heart of flesh. If, then, my heart is unresponsive to the divine voice and impenitent when I have disregarded it, then I am not one of the characters there delineated. Finally, God says of them, "I will put my laws into their minds and write them in their hearts" (Heb. 8:10). If, then, I do not "delight in the law of God after the inward man" and "serve the law of God" (Rom. 7:22, 25), then I have no part or lot in the better covenant.

IX

Continuing our survey of the typical teachings of the Mosaic economy as they anticipated and prepared the way for the establishing of
Christianity, we note, fourth, the *corporate character of Israel.* This
was a distinct line in the typical picture, and a feature in marked
advance of anything that had preceded. Under the previous covenants,
God treated only with particular persons; and throughout the history
associated therewith, everything was peculiarly individualistic. But at
Sinai the Lord established a formal bond between Himself and the
favored nation. It was then, for the first time, that we see the people
of God in an organized condition. It is true that they were divided
into twelve separate tribes; yet their union before God was most
blessedly evidenced when the high priest, as the representative of the
whole nation, ministered before Jehovah in the holy place with their
names inscribed on his breastplate.

Israel in their national capacity was a people set apart from all
others, and the degree in which they fulfilled the end of their separation foreshadowed the church of God, the true kingdom over which
the Messiah presides. Vain indeed is the claim of any church or
collection of churches, any party or "assemblies," that it or they are
either the antitype or the "representation" of the true church, though
this arrogant pretension is by no means confined to the Roman
hierarchy. The purest churches on earth are but most imperfect
shadows of that true kingdom wherein dwelleth righteousness. "The
true antitype is 'the Church of the Firstborn, whose names are written
in Heaven' (Heb. 12:23)—that willing and chosen people, the spiritual
seed of Abraham, of whom Christ is the Head, in whose character the
Law will be perfectly transcribed, and who will be all righteous, not in
profession merely, but in fact" (John Kelly).

That church will be revealed in its corporate character or collective
capacity only when Christ comes the second time "without sin unto
salvation," to conduct them to that inheritance which He hath prepared for them from the foundation of the world. Yet it is in the New
Testament, in those Scriptures which more especially pertain to the
Christian dispensation, that we find the clearest and fullest unfolding
of the people of God in their corporate character. It is there that the
body of Christ—the sum total of the elect, redeemed, regenerated
people of God of all ages—is revealed as the object of His love and the
reward of His sacrificial work. Though Christian churches are in
nowise the antitype of the commonwealth of Israel, nor the prototype
of the church in glory, yet in proportion as they are "Christian," they

supply a continuous testimony to the practical separation of God's people from this present evil world.

Fifth, the representation given of the blessed *truth of sanctification.* Though justification and sanctification cannot be separated, yet they may be distinguished. That is to say, though these divine blessings always go together, so that those whom God justifies He also sanctifies, still they are capable of being considered singly. When this be essayed, then they should be taken up in the order wherein they are presented to us in the Epistle to the Romans: in chapters 4 and 5 the apostle expounds the doctrine of justification, in chapters 6 to 8 he treats the various aspects of sanctification. This same order is observable in connection with the covenants: under the Abrahamic, the blessed truth of justification received clear illustration (Gen. 15:6); under the Sinaitic, the equally blessed truth of sanctification was plainly demonstrated. The same order is also exemplified in Israel's own history: they had been redeemed from Egypt before the great transaction at Sinai took place.

Now in order really to practice true holiness there must be a deliverance from the power of Satan and the dominion of sin, for none are free to serve God in newness of spirit until they have been emancipated from the old bondage of depravity. Thus, the deliverance of Israel from the serfdom and slavery of Pharoah laid the necessary foundation for them to enter the service of Jehovah. The grace which makes believers free from the dominion of sin supplies the strongest argument and motive imaginable to resist and mortify sin, and the greatest obligation to the practice of holiness. Most vividly was this adumbrated in Jehovah's dealings with the seed of Abraham, who had for so long groaned in the brick kilns of Egypt: the gracious deliverance from their merciless taskmasters placed them under deep obligations to render a grateful obedience to their Benefactor, which He accordingly emphasized in His preface to the Ten Commandments.

That which occurred at Sinai typified the santification of the church. The first words Jehovah addressed to Israel after they had reached the holy mount were, "Ye have seen what I did unto the Egyptians, and how I bare you on eagles' wings, and brought you unto myself" (Exod. 19:4). Here was their relative or *positional* sanctification: Israel had not only been separated from the heathen, but they were taken into a place of nearness to the Lord Himself. Then followed, "Now therefore if ye will obey my voice indeed and keep my covenant . . . ye shall be unto me a kingdom of priests and a holy nation." Next, Moses was bidden to "go unto the people, and sanctify them to-day and to-morrow, and let them wash their clothes" (Exod. 19:10): here there was a prefiguration of *practical* sanctification. In giving to them the law, God provided Israel with the rule of holiness, the standard to which all conduct is to be conformed. Finally, in sprinkling the blood upon the people (Exod. 24:8) there was shadowed forth that which is declared in, "Wherefore Jesus also, that he might sanctify the people with His own blood, suffered without the gate" (Heb. 13:12).

Sixth, *the teaching of the tabernacle* and the ceremonial institutions. And here we must distinguish between God's immediate design in connection with them and their ultimate purpose. The significance of the tabernacle and its worship can only be rightly understood when we apprehend the place given to it in connection with the ceremonial law. And, as we have shown in a previous chapter, the ceremonial law can only be understood when we clearly perceive its subordination to the moral law. The ceremonial law was an auxiliary of the moral, and the Levitical institutions were, in their primary aspect, an exhibition (by means of symbolical rites) of the righteousness enjoined in the Decalogue, by which the heart might be brought into some conformity therewith. Only by a clear insight, then, into the prior revelation of the Decalogue and of the prominent place it was designed to hold in the Mosaic economy, are we prepared to approach and consider that which was merely supplementary thereto.

It is failure to observe what has just been pointed out which leads to regarding the tabernacle and its service as too exclusively typical, causing recent writers to seek therein an adumbration of the person and work of Christ as the only reason for the things belonging thereto. This is not only a mistake, but it ignores the key to sound interpretation, for only as we perceive the *symbolical* design of the Levitical institutions are we prepared to understand their *typical* purport. The more fully the ceremonial parts of the Mosaic legislation were fitted to accomplish their prime end of enforcing the requirements of the Decalogue—setting forth the personal holiness it demanded and supplying the means for the removal of unholy pollutions—the more must they have tended to fulfill their ultimate design: by producing convictions of sin and by testifying to the defilement which it produced, the heart was prepared *for Christ!*

The sanctuary is not only called "the tabernacle of the congregation" (Exod. 40:2, 32, etc.) or as the Hebrew more literally signifies "the tent of meeting," but also "the tabernacle of the testimony" (Exod. 38:21, etc.) or "the tent of witness" (Num. 17:17, 18). The "witness" there borne conspicuously and continually, had respect more immediately to the ineffable holiness of God, and then by necessary implication to the fearful sinfulness of His people. The tables of stone in the ark "testified" to the righteous demands of the former, while they also witnessed in a condemnatory manner unto the latter. Thus, the meeting which God's people were to have with Him in His habitation was not simply for fellowship, but it also bore a prominent respect unto sins on their part (against which the law was ever testifying) and the means provided for their restoration to His favor and blessing.

"By the Law is the knowledge of sin" and Israel's sense of their shortcomings would be in exact proportion to the insight they obtained of its true spiritual meaning and scope. The numerous restrictions and services of a bodily kind which were imposed by the Levitical statutes, speaking (symbolically) as they did of holiness and sin, must have produced deeper impressions of guilt in those who honestly listened to them. "The law entered that the offence might abound" (Rom. 5:20); for while the ceremonial statutes were bidding men to abstain from sin, they were at the same time multiplying the occasions of offense. They made things to be sins which were not so before, or in their own nature—as the prohibition from certain foods, the touching of a carcass, manufacturing the anointing oil for personal use, and so forth. Thus it increased the number of transgressions and the burden upon the conscience.

Two things were thus outstandingly taught the Israelites. First, the ineffable holiness of God and the exalted standard of purity up to which He required His people to measure. Second, their own utter sinfulness, continually failing at some point or other to meet the divine requirements. To the thoughtful mind it must have appeared that there was a struggle which was continually being waged between God's holiness and the sinfulness of His creatures. And what would be the immediate outcome? Why, the oftener they were oppressed by a sense of guilt, the oftener would they resort to the blood of atonement. Necessarily so, for until sin was remitted and defilement removed they could not enter the holy habitation and commune with the Lord. How strikingly all of this finds its counterpart in the experience of the Christian! The more he is enlightened by the Holy Spirit, the more does he perceive his vileness and what a complete failure he is; and then the more is he made to appreciate the precious blood of Christ which "cleanseth from all sin."

Having viewed the tabernacle as "the tent of *witness*," a brief word now on it as "the tent of *meeting*." It was the place where God met with His people, and where they were permitted to draw nigh unto Him. This received its typical realization, first in Christ personally, when He "became flesh and tabernacled among us" (John 1:14), for in Him "dwelleth all the fulness of the Godhead bodily" (Col. 2:9). But second, it finds its realization in Christ mystical, for as the fulness of the Godhead dwells in Christ, so again He dwells in the church of true believers as His "fulness" (Eph. 1:23). The dwelling of God in the man Christ Jesus was not for Himself alone, but as the medium of intercourse between God and the church, and therefore is the church called "the house of God" (I Tim. 3:15) or "his habitation through the Spirit" (Eph. 2:21, 22). Thus the grand truth symbolized of old in the tabernacle and temple receives its antitypical realization not in Christ apart, but in Christ as the head of His redeemed, for through Him they have access to the Father Himself.

Seventh, *the significance of the promised land.* Canaan was the type of heaven, and therefore the constitution appointed for those who were to occupy it was framed with a view of rendering the affairs of time an image of eternity. The representation was, of course, imperfect, as was everything connected with the Mosaic economy, and rendered the more so by the failure of the people. Nevertheless, there was a real and discernible likeness furnished of the true, and it had been far more so had Israel's history approximated more closely to the ideal. Canaan was (as heaven is) the inheritance and home of God's redeemed. It was there Jehovah had His abode. It was the place of life and blessing (the land of "milk and honey"), and therefore death was regarded as abnormal and treated as a pollution. The inheritance was inalienable or untransferable; for if an Israelite sold his land, it reverted back to him at the jubilee.

"Canaan stood to the eye of faith the type of heaven; and the character and condition of its inhabitants *should have presented the image* of what theirs shall be who have entered on the kingdom prepared for them from the foundation of the world. The condition of such, we are well assured, shall be all blessedness and glory. The region of their inheritance shall be Immanuel's land, where the vicissitudes of evil and the pangs of suffering shall be alike unknown—where everything shall reflect the effulgent glory of its Divine Author, and streams of purest delight shall be ever flowing to satisfy the souls of the redeemed. But it is never to be forgotten that their condition shall be thus replenished with all that is attractive and good, because their character shall first have become *perfect in holiness.* No otherwise than as conformed to Christ's image can they share with Him in His inheritance" (P. Fairbairn). Hence, God's demand that Israel should be a holy and obedient people; and hence their banishment from Canaan when they apostatized.

In concluding this chapter let us pause and admire that wondrous comingling of justice and mercy, law and grace, holiness and leniency which was displayed throughout the Mosaic economy. This marvel of divine wisdom—for there is nothing that can be compared with it in all the productions of man—appears at almost every point. We see it in the "adding" of the Sinaitic covenant to the Abrahamic (Gal. 3:19); for whereas promises predominated in the one, precepts were more conspicuous in the other. We see it in God's delivering Israel from the bondage of Egypt and then taking them into His own service. We see it in the giving of the ceremonial law as a supplement to the moral. We see it in the fact that while the Levitical institutions were constantly emphasizing the purity which Jehovah required from His people, condemning all that was contrary thereto, yet means were provided for the promotion of the same and the removal of impurities. The whole is well summed up in "The law was given that grace might be sought; grace was given that the law might be fulfilled" (Augustine).

The entire ritual of the annual Day of Atonement (Lev. 16), which manifested the ground on which Jehovah dwelt in the midst of His people—the maintenance of *His* honor and the removal of *their* guilt—made it very evident that sin is a most solemn and serious matter, and that there was no hope for the guilty except on a footing of pure grace. Yet it just as clearly demonstrated the fact that sovereign mercy was exercised in a way that conserved the supremacy of the law. What else was the obvious meaning of Aaron's sprinkling the blood of atonement upon the very cover of the ark wherein were preserved the tables of stone (Lev. 16:14)? Each time Israel's high priest entered the holy of holies, the people were impressively taught that in the enjoyment of their national privileges their sinful condition was not lost sight of and that it was in no disregard of the law that they were so highly favored; for its just demands were satisfied by the blood of an innocent victim. Thus, the true object of all God's gracious conduct toward His people was to make them holy, delighting, after the inward man, in His law.

X

In bringing to a close these chapters on the Sinaitic covenant we propose to review the ground which has been covered, summarize the various aspects of truth which have been before us, and endeavor to further clarify one or two points which may not yet be quite clear to the interested reader. We began this study by asking a number of questions which we will now repeat and briefly answer.

"What was the precise nature of the covenant which God entered into with Israel at Sinai?" It was an arrangement or constitution which pertained to them as a nation, and was for the regulation of their religious, political, and social life. "Did it concern only their temporal welfare as a nation, or did it also set forth God's requirements for the individual's enjoyment of eternal blessings?" The latter; for the substance of the covenant was according to the unchanging principles on which God's throne is founded: none but those who are partakers of the divine holiness and are conformed to the divine righteousness can commune with God and dwell with Him forever. "Was a radical change now made in God's revelations to men and what He demanded of them?" No, for it had for its foundation the everlasting covenant of grace, while in substance it was a renewal of the Adamic covenant of works. Moreover, as we have shown, the Sinaitic transaction must not be considered as an isolated event, but as an appendage to the Abrahamic covenant, the ends of which it was designed to carry forward to their accomplishment.

In saying that the Mosaic economy was founded upon the everlasting covenant of grace, we mean that it was owing to the eternal compact which the three Persons of the Godhead had made with the Mediator, Christ Jesus, that the Lord dealt with Israel in pure grace when He delivered them from the bondage of Egypt and brought them unto Himself. When we say that in substance it was a renewal of the Adamic covenant of works, we mean that Israel was placed under the same law (in principle) as the federal head of the race was, and that as Adam's continued enjoyment of Eden was contingent upon his obedience. In saying that the Sinaitic constitution was an appendage to the Abrahamic covenant, we mean that it gathered up into itself the primordial and patriarchal institutions—the sabbath, sacrifices, circumcision—while it added a multitude of new ordinances which, though in themselves "weak and beggarly elements," were both instructive symbols and typical prefigurations of future spiritual blessings.

"Was an entirely different 'way of salvation' now introduced?" Most certainly not. Salvation has always been by grace through faith, never on the ground of works, but always producing good works. When Jude says that he proposed to write of "the common salvation" (v. 3), he signified that the saints of all ages have participated in the same salvation. The regenerate in Israel looked beyond the sign to the thing signified and saw in the shadow a figure of the substance, and obtained through Christ acceptance with God. Every aspect of the cardinal truth of justification is found in the Psalms just as it is set forth in the New Testament. First, the same confession of sin and depravity (Ps. 14:1). Second, the same acknowledgment of guilt and ill-desert (Ps. 40:12, 13). Third, the same fear of God's righteous judgment (Ps. 6:1). Fourth, the same sense of inevitable condemnation on the ground of God's law (Ps. 143:2). Fifth, the same cry for undeserved mercy (Ps. 51:1). Sixth, the same faith in God's revealed character as a just God and Savior (Ps. 25:8). Seventh, the same hope of mercy through redemption (Ps. 130:7). Eighth, the same pleading of God's name (Ps. 15:11). Ninth, the same trust in another righteousness than his own (Ps. 71:16; 84:9). Tenth, the same love for the Son (Ps. 2:12). Eleventh, the same joy and peace in believing (Ps. 89:15, 16). Twelfth, the same assurance in God's faithfulness to fulfill His promises (Ps. 89:1, 2). Let the reader carefully ponder these passages from the Psalms, and he will discover *the gospel itself in all its essential elements.*

"Wherein is the Sinaitic covenant related to the others, particularly to the everlasting covenant of grace and the Adamic covenant of works?—was it in harmony with the former or a renewal of the latter?" These questions raise an issue which presents the chief difficulty to be elucidated. In seeking its solution, several vital and basic considerations must needs be steadily borne in mind, otherwise a one-sided view of it is bound to lead to an erroneous conclusion. Those important considerations include the relation which the Sinaitic compact bore to the Abrahamic covenant; the distinction which must be drawn between the relation that existed between Jehovah and the nation at large, and between Jehovah and the spiritual remnant in it; and the contribution which God designed the Mosaic economy should make toward paving the way for the advent of Christ and the establishment of Christianity.

Now the Holy Spirit has Himself graciously made known to us in Galatians 3 the relation which the Sinaitic covenant sustained to the Abrahamic. The latter did not, "cannot disannul" the former (v. 17), it was "added" thereto (v. 19), it is "not against" it (v. 21), it had a gracious design (vv. 23, 24). It was "added" not by way of amendment or alteration, not to discredit it, nor to be blended with it as water may be mixed with wine; no, it still remained subservient to the promises made to Abraham concerning his seed. And yet it was not set up by itself alone, but was brought in as a necessary appendix, which clearly proves that God gave Israel the law with an *evangelical* design and purpose.

"It was added *because of transgressions,*" which probably has a double reference. First, because sin was then so rampant in the world, and Israel had acquired so many of the ways of the heathen during their long sojourn in Egypt, the law (both moral and ceremonial) was formally given at Sinai to serve as a restraint, and preserve a pure seed till the Messiah appeared. Second, in order to convict Israel of their guilt and convince them of the need of another righteousness than their own, thus preparing their hearts for Christ. If I preach the law to the unsaved, showing its spirituality and the breadth of its requirements, pressing upon them the justice of its demands, proving they are under its righteous condemnation, and all of this with the object of driving them out of themselves to Christ, then I make a right and legitimate service of the law. I "use it lawfully" (I Tim. 1:8) and do not pit it against the gospel.

In the historical order and dispensational relation between the Abrahamic and Sinaitic covenants we see again that marvel of divine wisdom which conjoins such opposites as law and grace, justice and mercy, requirement and provision. The fact that the latter was "added" to the former, shows that the one was not set aside or ignored by the other, but was acknowledged in its unimpaired validity. Now under the Abrahamic covenant, as we saw when examining the same, there was a striking conjunction of grace and law, yet the former more largely predominated—as is evident from the frequent references to the "promises" (Gal. 3:7, 8, 16, 18, 21) and from the "preached before *the gospel* to Abraham" (Gal. 3:8); so too under the Mosaic economy grace and law were both exhibited, yet the latter was far more conspicuous—as is clear from the contrast drawn in "for the law was given by Moses, but grace and truth came by Jesus Christ."

The Sinaitic covenant was supplementary and subsidiary to the Abrahamic, serving to promote both its natural and spiritual ends. Its object was not to convey, but to direct life. Its immediate design was to make clear to Abraham's seed how it behooved them to act toward God and toward each other, as a chosen generation, as the people of Jehovah. It made evident the character and conduct required from those who were partakers of the grace revealed in the promises. It made manifest the all-important principle that redemption carries in its bosom a conformity to the divine will, and that only when the soul really responds to the righteousness of heaven is the work of redemption completed. It trained the mind and stimulated the conscience of the regenerate unto a more enlightened apprehension of the mercy revealed, and which its instituted symbols served more fully to explain.

It was grace alone which delivered Israel from Egypt, but as God's acknowledged people they were going to occupy for their inheritance that land which the Lord claimed as more peculiarly His own. They must go there, then, as (typically, at least) partakers of His holiness, for thus alone could they either glorify His name or enjoy His blessings. Hence the holiness of Israel was the common end aimed at in all the Levitical institutions under which they were placed. Take, for example, the laver, at which the priests (under pain of death: Exodus 30:20, 21) were always required to wash their hands and feet before either serving at the altar or entering the tabernacle. That was symbolical of the inward purity which God required. The psalmist clearly intimates this, and shows he held it to be no less applicable to himself, when he says, "I will wash mine hands in innocency; so will I compass thine altar, O Lord" (26:6). That he spoke of no bodily ablution, but of the state of his heart and conduct, is evident from the whole tenor of the psalm.

By undeserved and sovereign goodness the Israelites were chosen to be the people of God, and their obedience to the law was never intended to purchase immunities or advantages not already theirs. Such an idea is preposterous. No, their obedience simply preserved to them the possession of what God had previously bestowed. The moral law made known the character and conduct which He required from His children (Deut. 14:1). That it revealed to them their shortcomings and convicted them of their depravity, only served to make the spiritually minded seek more earnestly fresh supplies of grace and be increasingly thankful for the provisions of mercy supplied for the removal of their sins and maintenance of fellowship with the Lord.

In requiring the guilty Israelite to lay his hand on the head of the sacrificial victim (Lev. 4:24), it was plainly taught that the worshiper could never approach God in any other character than that of a sinner, and by no other way than through the shedding of blood. On the annual Day of Atonement the people were required to "afflict their souls" (Lev. 16:29). The same principle is equally applicable under the new covenant era: the atonement of Christ becomes available to the sinner only as he approaches it with heartfelt convictions of sin, and with mingled sorrow and confidence disburdens himself of the whole accumulation of guilt at the foot of the cross. Repentance toward God and faith in the Lord Jesus Christ must grow and work together in the experience of the soul.

What has been said in the last eight paragraphs is all fairly obvious and simple, for it finds its exact counterpart in the New Testament. Everything connected with the earthly and temporal inheritance of Israel was so ordered as to plainly exhibit those principles by which God alone confers upon His people the tokens of His favor. God's ways with Israel on earth were designed to disclose the path to heaven. True obedience is possible only as the effect of sovereign grace in redemption. But grace reigns "through righteousness" (Rom. 5:21), and never at the expense of it; and therefore are the redeemed placed under the law as their rule of life. It is perfectly true that the gospel contains far higher examples of the morality enjoined in the law than any to be found in the Old Testament, and provides much more powerful motives for exercising the same; but that is a very different thing from maintaining that the morality itself is higher or essentially more perfect.

But the real problem confronts us when we consider the relation of the law to the great masses of the unregenerate in Israel. Manifestly it sustained an entirely different relation to them than it did to the spiritual remnant. They, as the fallen descendants of Adam, were born under the covenant of works (i.e., bound by its inexorable requirements), which they, in the person of their federal head, had broken; and therefore they lay under its curse. And the giving of the moral law at Sinai was well calculated to impress this solemn truth on them, showing that the only way of escape was by availing themselves of the provisions of mercy in the sacrifices—just as the only way for the sinner now to obtain deliverance from the law's condemnation is for him to flee to Christ. But the spiritual remnant, though under the law as a rule of life, participated in the mercy contained in the Abrahamic promises, for in all ages God has been administering the everlasting covenant of grace when dealing with His elect.

This twofold application of the law, as it related to the mass of the unregenerate and the remnant of the regenerate, was significantly intimated in the double giving of the law. The first time Moses received the tables of stone from the hands of the Lord (Exod. 32:15, 16), they were broken by him on the mount—symbolizing the fact that Israel lay under the condemnation of a broken law. But the second time Moses received the tables (Exod. 34:1), they were deposited in the ark and covered with the mercy-seat (Exod. 40:20), which was sprinkled by the atoning blood (Lev. 16:14)—adumbrating the truth that saints are sheltered (in Christ) from its accusations and penalty. "The Law at Sinai was a covenant of works to all the carnal descendants of Abraham, but a rule of life to the spiritual. Thus, like the pillar of cloud, the law had both a bright and a dark side to it" (Thomas Bell, 1814, *The Covenants*).

The predication made by Thomas Bell and others that the covenant of works was renewed at Sinai, requires to be carefully qualified. Certainly God did not promulgate the law at Sinai with the same end and use as in Eden, so that it was strictly and solely a covenant of works; for the law was most surely given to Israel with a gracious design. It was in order to impress them with a sense of the holiness and justice of Him with whom they had to do, with the spirituality and breadth of the obedience which they owed to Him, and this, for the purpose of convicting them of the multitude and heinousness of their sins, of the utter impossibility of becoming righteous by their own efforts, or escaping from the divine wrath, except by availing themselves of the provisions of His mercy; thus shutting them up to Christ.

The double bearing of the Mosaic law upon the carnal in Israel, and then upon the spiritual seed, was mystically anticipated and adumbrated in the history of Abraham—the progenitor of the one and the spiritual father (pattern) of the other. Promise was made to Abraham that he should have a son, yet at first it was not so clearly revealed by whom the patriarch was to have issue. Sarah, ten years after the promise, counseled Abraham to go in to Hagar, that by her she might have children (Gen. 16:3). Thus, though by office only a servant, Hagar was (wrongfully) taken into her mistress's place. This prefigured the carnal Jews' perversion of the Sinaitic covenant, putting their trust in the subordinate precept instead of the original promise. Israel followed after righteousness, but did not obtain it, because they sought it not by faith, but as it were by the works of the law (see Rom. 9:32, 33; 10:2, 3). They called Abraham their father (John 8:39), yet trusted in Moses (John 5:45). After all his efforts, the legalist can only bring forth an Ishmael—one rejected of God—and not as Isaac!

When Thomas Bell insisted that the Sinaitic covenant must be a renewal of the covenant of works (though subservient to the Abrahamic) because it was not the covenant of grace, and "there is no other," he failed to take into account the unique character of the Jewish theocracy. That it *was* unique is clear from this one fact alone, that all of Abraham's natural descendants were members of the theocracy, whereas only the regenerate belong to the body of Christ. The Sinaitic covenant formally and visibly manifested God's kingdom on earth, for His throne was so established over Israel that Jehovah became known as "*King* in Jeshurun" (Deut. 33:5), and in consequence thereof Israel became in a political sense "the people of God," and in that character He became "their God." We read of "the commonwealth [literally "polity"] of Israel" (Eph. 2:12), by which we are to understand its whole civil, religious, and national fabric.

That commonwealth was purely a temporal and external one, being an economy "after the law of a carnal commandment" (Heb. 7:16). There was nothing spiritual, strictly speaking, about it. It had a spiritual meaning when looked at in its typical character; but taken in itself, it was merely temporal and earthly. God did not, by the terms of the Sinaitic constitution, undertake to write the law on their hearts, as He does now under the new covenant. As a kingdom or commonwealth, Israel was a theocracy; that is, God Himself directly ruled over them. He gave them a complete body of laws by which they were to regulate all their affairs, laws accompanied with promises and threat-enings of a temporal kind. Under that constitution, Israel's continued occupation of Canaan and the enjoyment of their other privileges depended on obedience to their King.

Returning to the questions raised at the beginning of this section (p. 141), "Was the Sinaitic covenant a simple or mixed one: did it have only a letter significance pertaining to earthly things, or a 'spirit' as well, pertaining to heavenly things?" This has just been answered in the last two paragraphs; a "letter" only when viewed strictly in connection with Israel as a nation; but a "spirit" also when considered typically of God's people in general. "What specific contribution did it make unto the progressive unfolding of the divine plan and purpose?" In addition to all that has been said on this point in previous chapters, we will now, in closing, answer by pointing out how that further details of the everlasting covenant which God made with Christ were therein strikingly adumbrated.

1. By making the Sinaitic covenant with the nation of Israel, the Church of Christ was there prefigured in its *corporate* character.

2. By treating *through Moses* in all his dealings with Israel, God signified that we receive all His blessings through "*the mediator* of the better covenant" (Heb. 8:6).

3. By first redeeming Israel from Egypt and then placing them under the law, God intimated that His grace reigns "through righteous-ness" (Rom. 5:21).

4. By taking upon Himself the office of king (Deut. 33:5), God showed that He requires implicit submission (obedience) from His people.

5. By setting up the tabernacle in Israel's midst, God revealed that place of nearness to Himself into which He has brought us.

6. By the various institutions of the ceremonial law, we learn that "without holiness no man shall see the Lord."

7. By bringing Israel into the land of Canaan, God supplied an image of our heavenly inheritance.

PART SIX

The Davidic Covenant

I

In this chapter we shall attempt little more than to point out the connecting links between the Sinaitic and the Davidic covenants. The various covenants recorded in the Old Testament, as we have previously stated, mark the principal stages in the development of God's purpose of mercy toward our fallen race. Each one brought to light some further aspect of truth, and that, in keeping with particular incidents in the circumstances of God's people on earth. The covenants and the history are so intimately related that some knowledge of the one is indispensable to an understanding of the other, for each throws light upon the other. Only when the divine covenants and the sacred history connected with them are mutually studied, can we be in a position to trace the divine wisdom in those epoch-making transactions. But in order not to extend this study unto too great a length, our review of the history must necessarily be brief and incomplete.

The statutes and ordinances given for the regulation of Israel, the covenant people, assumed a definite form sometime before the death of Moses, who, on account of his sin, was not allowed to lead the people into the promised land. In view of his removal, he was divinely instructed to select Joshua as his successor, to whose leadership the nation was entrusted in the great enterprise which lay before them. The previous life of this eminent man had supplied a suitable training for the work which was assigned to him, and his future conduct manifested qualities which evidenced him to be equal to all the exigencies of his high service. Under his administration, the conquest of Canaan was, to a large extent, successfully accomplished, and the land was divided by lot to the several tribes. On the eve of his decease he was able to say, "Behold, this day I am going the way of all the earth: and ye know in all your hearts . . . that not one thing hath failed of all the good things which the Lord your God spake concerning you; all are come to pass unto you, not one thing hath failed thereof" (Josh. 23:14).

The above language (like much in Scripture) is not to be taken absolutely, as though the entire conquest of Canaan was now complete and the inheritance fully secured—the fact was otherwise. No, it is to be understood as affirming that up to this time no assistance had been withheld which their project required or that had been promised to them, and it was designed to strengthen their faith and encourage their hearts in regard to further success in its future prosecutions. Joshua had no successor, nor was any needed. Though Israel was a single nation, with common laws, under one King, yet each tribe had its own rulers, sufficient for orderly self-government and to take possession of that portion of the inheritance which had been allotted them. In some cases the land had yet to be acquired, and the tribes whose property it was were obligated to effect its conquest, whether by their own efforts or with the aid of their fellows. All of this is sufficiently apparent from the facts of the sacred history.

After the death of Joshua, Judah, assisted by the tribe of Simeon, was the first to go up, under divine direction, to fight against the Canaanites. For a time success attended their efforts, but soon they fell into the awful sin of idolatry (Judg. 2:11-13), and divine punishment quickly followed. Jehovah sold them into the hands of their enemies, until in pity for their affliction, He interposed for their relief. The historical account of their condition during a lengthy period is but fragmentary. The Book of Judges does not give us a continuous and connected narrative, but merely relates the principal disasters in which, at different times, their transgressions involved them, and of the various means which God graciously employed for their deliverance. If the reader will consult Judges 2:12-18 he will discover that the remainder of that book is but a series of illustrations of what is there stated.

The judges were extraordinary officers raised up by God, occasionally, by special designation, yet always acting with the free concurrence of the people. While their rule in most instances extended over the whole nation, in some it seems to have been confined to particular tribes only; but so far as their commission reached, they had under God supreme authority. Usually, they were the leaders in the military operations undertaken against the oppressors of Israel; though in some instances they were appointed for the suppression of disorders prevailing among the tribes themselves. Special circumstances alone determined their appointment. Their power was real; yet so far as the inspired record informs us, their habits continued simple. They had no external badge of distinction, received no emolument for their services, and enjoyed no exclusive privileges that were capable of being transmitted to the members of their several families.

The Book of Judges is mainly limited to giving us a summary statement of the official acts of these men. There are considerable intervals in respect to which we have no information—possibly because those particular periods were marked by comparative peace and prosperity, during which the worship of Jehovah was maintained and His blessing enjoyed. Of that state of things the Book of Ruth supplies a pleasing illustration. Throughout the whole of this period, the Levitical institutions supplied the people with all the instruction which was necessary for their direction in divine worship and the maintenance of that fellowship with God to which they had been admitted. Nothing in the form of addition was made to the truth which through the instrumentality of Moses had been disclosed and placed on permanent record. Some were raised up endowed with the gift of prophecy, but they appear to have been few in number, appearing only on rare occasions, their utterances being confined to what concerned the present duty of the people.

Though no new truth was given, nor even any amplification of what had been previously revealed, yet even so, Israel then supplied a striking type of the kingdom of God as it is now revealed under the gospel. They were a people under the immediate government of God, subject to His authority alone, bound together by ties which their relation to Him created, and enjoying the privilege of access to His mercy-seat (through their high priest) for counsel and aid in every emergency. Is it not thus, though in a truer and higher sense, with the saints of this dispensation? The Lord is enthroned in their hearts, His yoke they have freely taken upon them, and whatever distinctions in other respects may exist among them, they are one in fealty to Him and unite in the practical homage which He requires. But Israel understood not their position and appreciated not their advantages. They were discontented, distrustful, stiff-necked, ever forsaking their own mercies.

In one particular respect their outward condition remained defective: they had not yet acquired the full and peaceful possession of their inheritance. Their enemies were still powerful and involved them in perpetual trouble. This, however, was the effect of their own unfaithfulness. Had they resolutely obeyed the voice of the Lord and continued in the task to which He had called them, had they in humble dependence on His power and promised grace fulfilled their instructions, they would soon have realized a state of prosperity equal to all they were warranted to expect (Ps. 81:13-16). But their indolence and unbelief deprived them of blessings which were within their reach. They were unsettled. Their very worship was in a degree as yet provisional—indicated by the removal of the ark of the covenant from place to place. They were content that it should be so, being too carnal minded to really value the peculiar constitution which it was their privilege to enjoy.

Samuel was the last of the judges, and from his time the stream of history flows on in a more continuous course. Received in answer to prayer, he was from his birth consecrated to God. That consecration was graciously accepted, and while yet a child he became the subject of divine communications. Thus early did the Lord indicate the nature of that service in which his life was to be spent. Samuel, we are told, "grew, and the Lord was with him, and let none of his words fall to the ground. And all Israel from Dan even to Beersheba knew that Samuel was established to be a prophet of the Lord" (I Sam. 3:19, 20). At what time he publicly assumed the office of judge we are not directly informed: probably while yet a youth he was understood to be designed thereto, but only in mature life acknowledged in that capacity by the tribes assembled at Mizpeh (I Sam. 7:6).

Since Moses, no one exercised a more beneficial influence upon Israel, in every respect, than did Samuel. His administration was singularly able and prosperous. When the infirmities of age came upon him, he associated his sons with him in the office, doubtless with the concurrence of the people; but, as so often follows in such a case, the arrangement did not work well. The young men were very different in character from their aged parent, and they acted accordingly: "And his sons walked not in his ways, but turned aside after lucre, and took bribes, and perverted judgment" (I Sam. 8:3). The evil course they pursued seems to have been systematic and open, and was publicly felt to be all the more intolerable because of its marked contrast from the integrity which had uniformly marked the official conduct of Samuel himself.

Such scandalous conduct on the part of Samuel's sons caused the people to be loud in their expression of dissatisfaction, which was followed by a demand for which the aged servant of God was not prepared: "Then all the elders of Israel gathered themselves together, and came to Samuel unto Ramah. And said unto him, Behold, thou art old, and thy sons walk not in thy ways: now make us a king to judge us like all the nations" (I Sam. 8:4, 5). Various considerations incline us to form the conclusion that this proposal was far from being a sudden one on the part of the people. Although Samuel was neither slow nor unsuccessful in repelling the attacks of their enemies, yet his government was, on the whole, a pacific one, such as the condition of the people then called for. While much yet remained to be done for the complete conquest of their inheritance, they were enfeebled by unbelief and all its consequences, and therefore practically unfitted for the work assigned to them.

Time and training were required for their restoration to that state of efficiency on which, humanly speaking, their success depended. This was the result at which the administration of Samuel aimed. But there is reason to believe that his wise policy was anything but agreeable to them. However ill qualified for it, the passion for conquest had sprung up amongst the people. They had become dissatisfied with the occasional military efforts of the judges and, enamored with the regal pomp of the surrounding nations, they formed extravagant expectations of what a vast improvement in their condition the settled rule of a race of kings would produce. This, we take it, is what led up to and lies behind the demand which they made upon Samuel in the present instance.

But the demand involved a marked departure from the constitution which God had established amongst them. Jehovah Himself was their King, and He had given no outward intimation that things should not continue in the observance of those simple arrangements under which their political condition had been settled, with the assurance that the Lord was ever present with them, ready to afford them the counsel and aid which they needed. Their past history, notwithstanding their deep unworthiness, had abundantly proved how promptly and graciously that assurance had been made good. But this state of privilege the people were too earthly to value. In the intention of the mass of the people, the request made to Samuel was a practical renunciation of the theocracy. The demand itself, then, was wrong; and in spirit and purpose it was still more reprehensible.

The demand presented to Samuel indicated an unreasonable dissatisfaction with the divine goodness, and a rejection of the divine claims. In this light it was regarded by God Himself. The Lord said unto Samuel, "Hearken unto the voice of the people in all that they say unto thee: for they have not rejected thee, but they have rejected me, that I should not reign over them" (I Sam. 8:7). That the change now desired would be ultimately sought was foreseen from the first. An intimation to that effect was given through Moses and accompanied with instructions for the guidance of the people when that event occurred. "When thou art come unto the land which the Lord thy God giveth thee, and shalt possess it, and shalt dwell therein, and shalt say, I will set a king over me, like as all the nations that are about me; thou shalt in any wise set him king over thee, whom the Lord thy God shall choose: one from among thy brethren shalt thou set king over thee: thou mayest not set a stranger over thee, which is not thy brother. But he shall not multiply horses to himself, nor cause the people to return to Egypt," etc. (Deut. 17:14-20).

It is to be duly noted that the terms of the above passage simply anticipated what would assuredly happen: they neither ordered the change itself, nor expressed approval of it. The request made by Israel to Samuel was indeed granted, yet in such a way as to demonstrate the fallacy of the expectations which they had entertained, and to bring with it chastisement for their sin. God gave them their own desire, but mocked their vain hopes. The regal dignity was first conferred on Saul, one possessing the very qualifications which Israel desired: a man after their own heart. He was comely in person, commanding in appearance, just such a one as to suit their carnal tastes. To his appointment some dissatisfaction was at first shown, but this was speedily silenced by the success of his early actions, and subsequently his election was confirmed at Gilgal with the general concurrence of Israel (I Sam. 11:15).

But the reign of Saul was a disastrous one. He was grievously defective in those moral and spiritual qualities indispensable to the requirements of his high position. The defects of his character soon became apparent: he proved himself to be rash, self-willed, jealous, and disobedient to the divine command. His administration was marked by injustice and cruelty; disorder and feebleness increased toward the close of his reign, and, forsaken of God, he ultimately perished on the battlefield, where the armies of Israel suffered an ignominious defeat. Sorely wounded, he put an end to his miserable existence by taking his own life. Fearfully humiliating, then, was Israel's punishment for their presumptuous sin. To this sad episode the words of the prophet applied, when through him God said, "I gave thee a king in mine anger, and took him away in my wrath" (Hos. 13:11).

II

How mysterious and yet how perfect are the ways and works of "the Lord God omnipotent" (Rev. 19:6)! He makes all things subservient to His own glory, so directing the affairs of earth as to promote His own gracious designs. Though He be in no sense chargeable with the sins of the creature, yet He maketh "the wrath of man" to praise Him (Ps. 76:10). A striking, solemn, and yet blessed illustration of this appears in that incident of Israel's history which we are now considering—namely, their discontent at having Jehovah Himself for their King, and their demand for a human monarch, that they might be like the heathen nations surrounding them (I Sam. 8:5). This was most evil and wicked on their part, and as such, highly displeasing unto the Lord, who bade Samuel "protest solemnly unto them" (I Sam. 8:9). This was followed by God's chastening them by appointing Saul, whose reign was a most disastrous one for Israel.

So much for the human side; but what of the divine? The change now produced in the political constitution of Israel, though sinful in its origin and disastrous in its immediate effects, was in divine mercy overruled to disclose some new aspects of the divine purpose toward our fallen world. It became the means of unfolding by a fresh series of types the future exaltation of the Messiah, the nature and extent of His kingdom, and the beneficial effects of His administration. When the rejection of Saul was definitely intimated, steps were quickly taken under divine direction in the choice of his successor; and in this instance the carnal views of the people were in nowise consulted. God chose a man after His own heart: one whom His grace had prepared, and who in his official character, unlike Saul, would pay implicit deference to every intimation of the divine will.

But before we take a closer view of David himself, let us add a further word to the above upon what brought about the institution of the kingly office in the constitution of Israel. As we have seen, it was a sin for the people to seek a king, yet it was of the Lord that they sought one. This is a deep mystery; yet its underlying principle is being constantly exemplified. God accomplishes His holy counsels by the free actions of sinful men. According to God's sovereign purpose Saul must be made king of Israel; yet in bringing this to pass only the working of natural laws was employed. From the human side it was because the sons of Samuel were corrupt in judging, and in consequence the people had asked him for a king. Had those sons been of the same caliber as their father, the people would have been satisfied and no king would have been requested. It was by His ordinary providential control that God brought this to pass.

In nowise was the divine holiness compromised: the divine decree was accomplished, yet the people acted freely, and the guilt of their action was justly visited upon them. It may be asked, "Why did not Providence prevent this occasion of sin to His people? Why did His providence lay this stumblingblock before them? If God designed to give them a king, why did He not give them a king in a way that would have presented them with no occasion of rejecting Himself as King? God designed to show that rebellion was in them, and His providence manifests this, even in the way of fulfilling His own purposes, which coincided with theirs. Here is *sovereignty*" (Alexander Carson). Yes, and here is also infinite wisdom, that can bring to pass His own foreordinations without doing any violence to the responsibility of man, that can guide his evil inclinations, without any complicity therein. But to return to our more immediate inquiry.

At the time David was selected to be the successor of Saul, he was in the bloom of youth—the youngest son of his father's house. Although the intimation given of the high honor awaiting him was too distinct to be missed, it did not produce any injurious effects upon him. He continued to serve Saul as if he had been wholly ignorant of what God had designed. He was not puffed up with his prospects, nor did he give any intimation of a selfish ambition. He never presumed to anticipate by any effort of his own the fulfillment of the divine purpose, but left it entirely with God to effect the same in His own time and way. From Saul himself he received sufficient provocation to have tempted him to pursue an opposite course, but he quietly submitted to God's sovereignty and waited for Him to make good His promise. Well may we seek grace to emulate such becoming meekness and patience.

In due time God fulfilled His word. On the death of Saul, the tribe of Judah annointed David king at Hebron (II Sam. 2:4), and seven years later, every hindrance having been providentially removed, all the other tribes concurred in his election (II Sam. 5:3). During the early part of his reign, the attention of David was directed to suppressing the assaults of the Philistines and other enemies. His military operations were most successful, and the foes of Israel were humbled and subdued. On the establishment of peace throughout his kingdom, David's thoughts were directed to the removal of the ark, which had hitherto been migratory, to a settled place in Jerusalem. That city, in its entire extent, had recently come into his possession and had been chosen as the royal residence and the seat of divine worship. The conquering of the promised land, through the divine blessing on his administration, was now in a great measure completed; and David concluded that the time was ripe for him to erect a fixed and permanent habitation for the worship of Jehovah.

He formed the resolution to build a house for the Lord, and made known the same unto the prophet Nathan, by whom he was at first encouraged. But though God approved the thought of David's heart, He would not permit him to give effect to his intentions. That particular honor was reserved for his son and successor, Solomon, although he was not then born. The reason for this is expressly stated: God said to him, "Thou hast shed blood abundantly, and hast made great wars; thou shalt not build a house unto my name, because thou hast shed much blood upon the earth in my sight" (I Chron. 22:8). This statement does not mean that the wars in which David had engaged were unauthorized and sinful; on the contrary, they were undertaken by divine orders, and their success was often secured by signal manifestations of God's interposition. But that aspect of the divine character revealed in those events was different from that which worship mainly disclosed; therefore, there had been an evident incongruity in one who had shed so much blood erecting a house for the God of mercy and grace.

By the intended house of prayer, symbolic instruction was designed to be conveyed, and in order for that to be accomplished, peaceful conditions were required in association with its erection. Accordingly Nathan was sent to David to prohibit the accomplishment of his design. The divine message, however, was accompanied with the most striking assurances of the favor of God toward himself. After reminding David of the humble condition from which he had been taken to be ruler over Israel, and of the invariable proofs of the divine presence and blessing which had attended all his enterprises, the prophet declared, "The Lord telleth thee that he will make thee a house. And when thy days be fulfilled, and thou shalt sleep with thy fathers, I will set up thy seed after thee, which shall proceed out of thy bowels, and I will establish his kingdom. He shall build a house for my name, and I will establish the throne of his kingdom forever. I will be his Father, and he shall be my son. If he commit iniquity, I will chasten him with the rod of men, and with the stripes of the children of men. But my mercy shall not depart away from him, as I took it from Saul, whom I put away before thee. And thine house and thy kingdom shall be established forever before thee: thy throne shall be established forever" (II Sam. 7:11-16).

It is pitiable that any should raise a quibble that because there is no express mention here of any "covenant" being made, therefore we are not warranted in so regarding this event. It is true we have no formal account of any sacrifices being offered in connection with it, no express figurative ratification of it, such as we find attending every similar transaction of which mention is made in Scripture. But the silence observed on this point is no proof that no such formality took place. The legitimate inference rather is that those observances were so customary on such occasions, and were so well understood, as to make any specific allusion to them here quite unnecessary. However, that it was a true covenant is evident from the distinct and frequent mention of it under this very designation in other passages.

That the great transaction narrated in II Samuel 7 was thus regarded

by David himself as a covenant is clear from his own declaration:
• "Although my house be not so with God, yet he hath made with me
an everlasting *covenant,* ordered in all things, and sure; for this is all
my salvation, and all my desire" (II Sam. 23:5). When was it that God
made this everlasting covenant with David, if not in the place which
we are now considering? But what is still more to the point, the Lord
Himself refers to the same as a covenant, as we may see from His
response to Solomon's prayer: "If thou wilt walk before me, as David
thy father walked, and do according to all that I have commanded
thee, and shalt observe my statutes and my judgments; then will I
establish the throne of thy kingdom according as I have *covenanted*
• *with David* thy father, saying, There shall not fail thee a man to be
ruler in Israel" (II Chron. 7:17, 18). With these statements before us,
we cannot doubt that this divine transaction with David was a true
covenant, even though there is no formal record of its ratification.

That the Davidic covenant constituted another of those remarkable
revelations which at different times distinguished the history of the
Jewish people, a cursory examination of its contents is sufficient to
show. Like every similar transaction which occurred during the Old
Testament era, it has certain typical aspects which were the figures of
higher spiritual blessings. Those had special reference to David and his
family. He was, for instance, assured that the temple should be built
by his immediate successor, and that his family was destined to
occupy a prominent place in the future history of Israel, and that the
regal dignity conferred upon him should be perpetuated in his descendants so long, at least, as they did not by their sins forfeit the earthly
advantages those secured to them. Those temporal promises were the
ground on which the covenant rested, and were the elements which
expanded into richer spiritual blessings in the distant future.

Viewed in relationship to the more spiritual results, David affirmed
that the covenant was "ordered in all things, and sure" (II Sam. 23:5).
Against every possible contingency provision was made; nothing
should ever prevail to defeat the fulfillment of those promises. Even
the sins of the individuals of his race, though they would certainly
meet with righteous punishment and might terminate in the ruin of
those who committed them and in the permanent depression of the
family, (as in fact they did), would not annul them. It is with these
higher aspects of the Davidic covenant we shall be chiefly concerned.
From them we may gather the true nature of the solemn engagements
it contained, and estimate the addition made by it to the sum of
revealed truth—the increased light which it shed on the scheme of
divine mercy, then in the course of disclosure.

The substance of the information conveyed by this covenant had reference to the exaltation, kingdom, and glory *of the Messiah.* I of a similar kind, though few, obscure, and isolated, are certainly to be found in the previous portions of Scripture, the most striking of which is the intimation given through Jacob, that "the sceptre shall not depart from Judah, nor a lawgiver from between his feet, until Shiloh come; and unto him shall the gathering of the people be" (Gen. 49:10). But those hints were then, and up to the time of David, very imperfectly, if at all, understood, even by the most spiritually minded of the people. They do not seem to have attracted notice; now, however, they were concentrated in and amplified with far greater distinctness through the promises of the Davidic covenant. For the first time the regal dignity of the Messiah was exhibited, which, especially when enlarged by the later prophetic representations, the Jews were not slow to interpret in accord with their carnal ideas.

Thus far all has been, comparatively, plain sailing; but when we come to the actual interpretation of the promises made to David in II Samuel 7, real difficulty is encountered. Those which relate particularly to the ultimate design of the covenant require a much closer examination, and when attempting it a reference to other passages treating of the same subject will be essential. But before entering these deeper waters, let it be pointed out that, by the terms of this covenant a further and distinct limitation was given as to the actual line from which the promised Seed should spring. In the progress of divine revelation, the channel through which the future Deliverer should issue was, at successive periods, considerably narrowed. Though this has often been traced out by others, it is too important and interesting for us to ignore.

The first prediction, recorded in Genesis 3:15, was couched in the most general form, simply intimating that the Vanquisher of the serpent would assume humanity, though supernaturally. On the destruction of the old world, the promise was renewed to Noah, together with an intimation that it would be through Seth its fulfillment should take place (Gen. 9:27). A further step forward was taken when Abraham was chosen as the progenitor of Him in whom all the families of the earth should be blessed. His descendants, in the line of Isaac, on whom the promise was entailed, were, however, so numerous that no definite view could be taken as to the precise quarter from which its fulfillment might be looked for. Subsequently, the tribe of Judah was indicated, but this being one of the most numerous of the tribes, the same indefiniteness, though in a less degree, would exist as to the particular family on whom this honor was to be conferred.

Time rolled on, and now the family of David was selected as the medium through which the promise was to take effect. To that family the longings of all who looked for the Hope of Israel was henceforth restricted, and greater facility was thereby afforded for obtaining the requisite proof of the claims of the Messiah when He should appear. Thus, by a succession of steps God defined the course through which His gracious purpose would be wrought out, and with increasing distinctness concentrated the attention of the faithful toward the true direction in which the divine promise would be realized; the last limitation possessing a definiteness to which none of the others could lay claim.

(In these two chapters we have followed closely John Kelly in his work [1861] on *The Divine Covenants.*)

III

We closed the previous chapter by pointing out the successive steps by which God gradually made known the counsels of His will which were to eventuate in the advent and incarnation of His Son. Under the Davidic covenant, the royal dignity of the Messiah was for the first time definitely revealed. It should however be pointed out that a remarkable anticipation of this was given through the inspired song of Hannah, recorded in I Samuel 2:1-10. Therein we find a blessed blending of the typical with the prophetical, whereby the former pointed forward to things of a similar nature but of higher and wider importance. In other words, typical transactions supplied the material for a prediction of something analogous yet much loftier and grander in kind. The future was anticipated by present incidents, so ordered by God as to foreshadow gospel verities, the historical thus serving as a mold to give prophetic shape to the future things of God's kingdom.

Hannah's song was evoked, under the moving of the Holy Spirit, by the birth of Samuel. The spiritual life of Israel was then at a very low ebb. The natural barrenness which had previously characterized Hannah adumbrated the sterility of the nation Godward. The provocation which she received from "her adversary" and which provoked her sorely (I Sam. 1:5) was a figure of the contempt in which Israel was held by her foes, the surrounding nations. The feebleness of Eli and his lack of discernment imaged the decrepitude of the religious leaders in general: "in those days there was no open vision" (I Sam. 3:1). The corruptness of Eli's sons and the readiness of the people to offer them bribes indicates clearly the sad level to which conditions had sunk.

Such, in brief, is a historical outline of the situation at that time, typically featured in the items we have mentioned.

The gratitude and joy of Hannah when the Lord opened her womb served as a suitable occasion for the Spirit to utter through her the prophetic song alluded to above. Deeply moved at having received the child of her hopes and prayers, which she had devoted from his birth as a Nazarite to the Lord's service, her soul was stirred by a prophetic impulse and her vision enlarged to perceive that her experience in becoming a mother was a sign of the spiritual fruitfulness of the true Israel of God in the distant future. Under that prophetic impulse she took a comprehensive survey of the general scheme of God, observing that gracious sovereignty which delights to exalt a humble piety, but which pours contempt on the proud and rebellious, until in the final crescendo she exclaimed, "The adversaries of the Lord shall be broken in pieces; out of heaven shall he thunder upon them; the Lord shall judge the ends of the earth; and he shall give strength unto his king, and exalt the horn of his anointed" (I Sam. 2:10).

Remarkable indeed is that language. The final words "his anointed" are literally "his Messiah" or "Christ." This is the first time in Holy Writ that that blessed title is found in its most distinctive sense, though as we all know it occurs hundreds of times afterward as the synonym for the consecrated King, or Head of the divine kingdom. The other expressions in the same verse "The adversaries of the Lord shall be broken in pieces" and "the Lord shall judge the ends of the earth" show that it was of the Messiah's kingdom that Hannah was moved by the Holy Spirit to speak. How striking, then, is it to see that the historical features of Hannah's day possessed an undoubted typical significance, and that they formed the basis of a prophecy which was to receive its fulfillment in the distant future! This supplies a valuable key to many of the later Messianic predictions.

Any possible doubt as to the prophetic purport of Hannah's song is at once removed by a comparison of the "Magnificat" uttered by Mary at the announcement of the Messiah's birth (see Luke 1:46-55). It is indeed striking to find how the Virgin reechoed the same sentiments and in some instances repeated the very words used by the mother of Samuel a thousand years previously. "Why should the Spirit, breathing at such a time in the soul of Mary, have turned her thoughts so nearly into the channel that had been struck out ages before by the pious Hannah? Or why should the circumstances connected with the birth of Hannah's Nazarite offspring have proved the occasion of strains which so distinctly pointed to the manifestation of the King of Glory, and so closely harmonize with those actually sung in celebration of the event? Doubtless to mark the *connection* really subsisting between the two. It is the Spirit's own *intimation* of His ultimate design in transactions long since past, and testimonies delivered centuries before—namely, to herald the advent of Messiah, and familiarize the children of the kingdom with the essential character of the coming dispensation" (P. Fairbairn).

The combination of typical history with prophetic utterance which we observe in Hannah's song is seen again and again in the later Scripture, where the predictive feature is more extended and the typical element in the transactions which gave rise to it more definite. Such is especially the case with the Messianic psalms, which being of a lyrical character afforded a freer play of the emotions than could be suitably introduced into more formal prophecy. But this, in turn, had its basis in the intimate connection there was between the present and the future, so that the feelings awakened by the one naturally incorporated themselves into the delineations of the other. It was the very institutions of the temporal kingdom in the person and family of David which constituted both the ground and occasion of the predictions concerning Christ's future kingdom, and how beautifully the type prefigured the antitype it will be our delight yet to notice.

The introduction of the royal scepter into the hands of an Israelitish family produced a radical change in the theocracy, one that was calculated to draw the attention of the people more to the earthly and visible, and remove their minds from the heavenly and eternal. The constitution under which Jehovah, through Moses, had placed them, though it did not absolutely prohibit the appointing of a king, yet was of such a character that it seemed far more likely to suffer than be aided by the allowing of what would consist so largely of the human element. Till the time of Samuel it was strictly a theocracy: a commonwealth that had no recognized head but the Lord Himself, and which placed everything that concerned life and well-being under His immediate government. It was the distinguishing glory of Israel as a nation that they stood in this near relation to God, evoking that outburst of praise from Moses: "The eternal God is thy refuge, and underneath are the everlasting arms. . . . Happy art thou, O Israel: *who like thee,* O people saved by the Lord: the shield of thy help" (Deut. 33:27, 29).

But alas! Israel were far too carnal to appreciate the peculiar favor God had shown them, as was made evident when they sought to be like the Gentiles by having a human king of their own. That was tantamount to saying they no longer desired that Jehovah should be their immediate sovereign, that they lusted after a larger measure of self-government. But this was not the only evil likely to result from the proposed change. "Everything under the Old Covenant bore reference to *the future* and more perfect dispensation of the Gospel; and the ultimate reason of any important feature or material change in respect to the former, can never be understood without taking into account the bearing it might have on the future state and prospects of men under the Gospel. But how could any change in the constitution of ancient Israel, and especially such a change as the people contemplated, when they desired a king after the manner of the Gentiles, be adopted without altering matters in this respect to the worst.

"The dispensation of the Gospel was to be, in a peculiar sense, the 'kingdom of heaven' or of God, having for its high end and aim the establishment of a near and blessed intercourse between God and man. It attains to its consummation when the vision seen by St. John, and described after the pattern of the constitution actually set up in the wilderness, comes into fulfillment—when 'the tabernacle of God is with men, and He dwells with them.' Of this consummation it was a striking and impressive image that was presented in the original structure of the Israelitish commonwealth, wherein God Himself sustained the office of *king,* and had His peculiar residence and appropriate manifestations of glory in the midst of His people. And when they, in their carnal affection for a worldly institute, clamoured for an earthly sovereign, they not only discovered a lamentable indifference toward what constituted their highest honor, but betrayed also a want of discernment and faith in regard to God's prospective and ultimate design in connection with their provisional economy" (P. Fairbairn).

In view of what has been before us, it is not to be wondered at that God manifested His displeasure at the fleshly demand for a human king, and that He declared to Samuel that the nation had thereby virtually rejected Himself (I Sam. 8:7). It is but natural that we should inquire why, then, did the Lord yield to their evil desire? Ah, wondrous indeed are the ways of Him with whom we have to do: the very thing which the people, in their sin, lusted after, served to supply on a lower plain a striking adumbration of the nature and glory which Christ's kingdom should yet assume on a higher plane. It was the eternal purpose of God that He would ultimately entrust the rule of the universe unto the Man of His own right hand! Thus the divine procedure on this occasion supplies one of the most striking instances found in all the Old Testament of the overruling providence of God, whereby He is able to bring a clean thing out of an unclean.

God not only averted the serious damage which Israel's demands threatened to do unto the theocracy, but He turned it to good account, in familiarizing the minds of future generations with what was designed to constitute the grand feature of the Messianic kingdom, namely, the Son of God assuming *human* nature. After the people had been solemnly admonished for their guilt in the appointing of a king after *their* worldly principles, they were permitted to raise one of their number to the throne, though not as an absolute and independent sovereign, but as the deputy of Jehovah, ruling in the name and in subordination to the will of God; and for this reason his throne was called "the throne of the Lord" (I Chron. 29:23). But to render His purpose the more evident to those who had eyes to see, the Lord allowed the earthly throne to be first occupied by one who was little disposed to submit to the authority of heaven, and was therefore supplanted by another who, as God's representative, is over thirty times called His "servant."

It was in this second person, David, that the kingly administration of Israel properly began. He was the root and foundation of the earthly kingdom—*as* a "kingdom"—in which the divine and the human were officially united, as they were ultimately to be in a hypostatic or personal union. Most remarkably did the shaping providence of God cause the preparatory and typical to shadow forth the ultimate and antitypical, making the various trials through which David passed ere he reached the throne, and the conflicts in which he engaged subsequently, to prefigure throughout the sufferings, work, and kingdom of the Messiah. A whole volume might well be devoted to a full amplification of that statement, showing how, in the broad outlines, the entire history of David possessed a typical significance, so that it was really a prophetic panorama. The same principle applies with equal force to many of his psalms, where we find historical events turned into sacred songs in such a way that they became predictions of what was to be realized by Christ on a grander scale.

It was in this way that what had otherwise tended to veil the purpose of God, and obstruct the principal design of His preparations under the old covenant, was made to be one of the most effective means for revealing and promoting it. "The earthly head, that now under God stood over the members of the commonwealth, instead of overshadowing His authority, only presented this more distinctly to their view, and served as a stepping-stone to faith, in enabling it to rise nearer to the apprehension of that personal indwelling of Godhead, which was to constitute the foundation and the glory of the Gospel dispensation. For occasion was taken to unfold the more glorious future in its practical features with an air of individuality and distinctness, with a variety of detail and vividness of colouring, not to be met with in any other portions of prophetic Scripture" (P. Fairbairn).

As an illustration of this combination of typical history with prophecy, we refer to Psalm 2—which we hope to consult again in a later chapter. It has been termed "an inaugural hymn" designed to

celebrate the appointment and triumph of Jehovah's King. The heathen nations are pictured as opposing (vv. 1, 2), as vowing together
that if such an appointment was consummated, they would defy it (v.
3). Notwithstanding, the Most High, disdaining the threats of such
puny adversaries (v. 4), accomplishes His counsel. The everlasting
decree goes forth that the anointed King is established on Zion; and,
because He is God's own Son, He is made the heir of all things, even to
the uttermost limits of the earth (vv. 5-9). The psalm therefore closes
with a call to earth's rulers to submit to the scepter of the King of
kings, warning them of the sure doom that would follow defiance.

Before pointing out the obvious connection of this psalm with the
life and history of David, let us carefully note the entire absence of
any slavish literality. In his elevation to the throne of Israel, David was
not opposed by heathen nations and their rulers, for they probably
knew little and certainly cared less about it. Again, his being anointed
king certainly did not synchronize with his being set on the holy hill
of Zion, for there was an interval of some years between them.
Moreover, when he was established in the kingdom, there is no record
of his pressing the claims of his dominion on other monarchs, demanding that they pay allegiance to him. We emphasize these points,
not to suggest there is any failure in the type, but as a warning against
that modern species of literalism which so often reduces Scripture to
an absurdity.

Shall we, then, go to an opposite extreme, and say there is no real
relation between this Messianic psalm and the life and kingdom of
David? Surely not. Certainly it *has,* and a relation so close that his
experiences were the beginning of what, on a higher plane and on a
larger scale, was to be accomplished in his Son and Lord. While the
language there employed for celebrating the Messianic King and His
kingdom rises high above the experiences which pertain to His prototype, yet it bears the impress of them. In both alike we see the
sovereign determination on the part of God to the regal office. In each
case there is opposition of the most violent and heathenish kind to
withstand that appointment—in David's case, first on the part of Saul,
and then of Abner and Ishbosheth. In each case we behold the slow
but sure removal of all the obstacles raised against the purpose of God,
and the extension of the sphere of empire till it reaches the limits of
the divine grant. The lines of history are parallel, the agreement
between type and antitype unmistakable.

IV

We recently saw an article which was headed "Humility and the Second Advent"; but after reading through the same, we laid it down with a feeling of disappointment. We had hoped from its title that the writer of it (quite unknown to us) would emphasize the deep need for lowliness of heart when taking up the prophetic Scriptures. God's holy Word ought ever to be approached with great reverence and sobriety, but particularly is this the case with prophecy, for on no other subject (except it be the vexed question of church government) have God's servants differed more widely than in their views of things to come. It seems as though God has put not a little into His Word for the express purpose of staining human pride. Certainly, dogmatism ill becomes any of us where so many have erred.

We dare not say it is in a spirit of true humility that we now take up our pen, for the heart is very deceitful, and it generally follows that when we deem ourselves most humble, pride is at work in its subtlest form. It is, however, with considerable diffidence that we continue these chapters on the Davidic covenant, for it presents to me the most difficult aspect of the whole subject. Possibly this is because of my early training, for it is never an easy matter to get quite away from our first thoughts and impressions on a subject. During the years of our spiritual infancy we heard and read nothing but the premillennial interpretation of prophecy, and, of course (as a spiritual child), we readily accepted all that our teachers said. But for the last decade, we have sought to carefully examine what was taught us, and we have discovered that, some of it at least, was but "fairy tales."

Common fairness compelled us to weigh the postmillennial view. In doing so, we recognized a very real danger of allowing our mind to run to an opposite extreme. We are free to admit that, upon a number of important points this system of prophetic interpretation is no more satisfying to us than the "pre"; and therefore at the present time we are not prepared to commit ourselves to the entire position of either the one or the other. Nor does that which is known as amillennialism completely solve the problems. In other words, we now have no definite ideas concerning coming events, applying to ourselves those words of the Lord, "It is not for you to know the times or the seasons, which the Father hath put in his own power" (Acts 1:7). But this makes it the more difficult to write on our subject, and we can do so only according to that measure of light which God has vouchsafed us, urging our readers to "prove all things; hold fast that which is good" (I Thess. 5:21).

We seem to be fully warranted in saying that what serves to divide interpreters of prophecy more than anything else is whether its language is to be taken literally or figuratively. This, of course, opens a wide and most important field of study, into which we must not now enter. Yet we cannot forbear from pointing out that—it certainly seems to me—we have a most solemn warning in the papist perversion of the Lord's Supper, of the real danger there is of wresting Scripture at the very time we appear to honor it (by "childlike" faith and simplicity) in taking it at its face value. If Rome's insistence that "this is my body" means just what it says, shows us what serious results follow when mistaking the emblem for the reality which it represents, ought not this to serve as a very real check against the gross carnalizings of chiliasm which literalizes what is spiritual and makes earthly what is heavenly?

The above remarks have been prompted by the promises contained in the Davidic covenant, recorded in II Samuel 7:11-16. In view of all that has been before us in connection with the preceding covenants, it is but reasonable to expect that this one too has both a "letter" and a "spirit" significance. This expectation is, we believe, capable of clear demonstration: in their primary and inferior aspects those promises respected Solomon and his immediate successors, but in their ultimate and higher meaning they looked forward to Christ and His kingdom. In the account which David gave to the princes of Israel of the divine communications he had received concerning the throne, he affirmed that God said unto him, "Solomon thy son, he shall build my house and my courts: for I have chosen him to be my son, and I will be his Father" (I Chron. 28:6). Yet the application of the same words to Christ Himself—"I will be to him a Father, and he shall be to me a Son" (Heb. 1:5)—leaves us in no doubt as to their deeper spiritual import.

The thrice occurrence of "for ever" in II Samuel 7:13, 16 obliges us to look beyond the natural posterity of David for the ultimate accomplishment of those promises. God did indeed set the carnal seed of David upon the throne of Israel and establish his kingdom, though certainly not unto all generations. Those who have contended that this covenant of royalty guaranteed to David the occupancy of his throne by one of his own descendants until the coming of the Messiah, take a position which it is impossible to defend—the facts of history flatly contradict them. David transmitted the kingdom of Israel to Solomon, and he in turn to Rehoboam, but there the reign of the family of David over all Israel actually (and so far as I perceive, *forever*) ceased. Let us enlarge upon this a little.

Rehoboam, by the haughtiness of his bearing and the cruelty of his measures, forfeited the attachment of his subjects. Ten of the tribes

revolted unto Jeroboam, being completely dissevered from their brethren, and were never after recovered to their government. Thus, the
reign of David's family *over all Israel* lasted, from beginning to end, at
most but three generations, or about a century. Over Judah alone, his
descendants continued to reign for several centuries more, until, at
length Nebuchadnezzar invaded and conquered the nation, destroyed
Jerusalem, burned the temple, carried the people into captivity, and
desolated the whole land. With this overthrow, which occurred some
six centuries before the birth of Christ, ended the reign of David even
over the tribe of Judah. His literal throne exists no more!

It is true that after the Babylonian captivity, which continued
seventy years, a remnant of the people returned, and for another
century Judah was ruled by Zerubbabel, Ezra, and Nehemiah. The
first of these was of the house of David, but both the others belonged
to the tribe of Levi! None of them, however, were kings in any sense,
but merely governed under foreign authority. During the next two
centuries Judah was governed by their high priests, all of whom
pertained to the house of Aaron! Meanwhile, the nation was tributary
successively to the Persians, Greeks, Egyptians, and Syrians. From the
close of this period, until Judea became a Roman province under
Herod, when Christ was born, the Jews were under the government of
the Asmonian family, known as the Maccabees, all of whom belonged
to the priestly tribe. History, then, manifestly refutes that interpretation of the Davidic covenant which asserts that it promised David that
his natural seed should reign upon his literal throne until Christ
appeared. We are therefore forced to seek another interpretation.

Before considering the spiritual and higher import of the divine
promises in the Davidic covenant, further attention must be given to
their application unto David's natural descendants, and particularly in
connection with their failures; and here we cannot do better than
quote from P. Fairbairn. "On that prophecy (II Sam. 7:5-17), as on a
sure foundation, a whole series of predictions began to be announced,
in which the eye of faith was pointed to the bright visions in prospect,
and, in particular, to that Child of promise, in whom the succession
from David's loins was to terminate, and who was to reign forever over
the heritage of God. But while the appointment itself was absolute,
and the original prophecy was so far of the same character, that it
indicated no suspension in the sovereignty of David's house, or actual
break in the succession to his throne, David himself knew perfectly
that there was an implied condition, which might render such a thing
possible, and that the prophecy behooved to be read in the light of
those great principles which pervade the whole of the Divine
economy.

"Hence, in addition to all he had penned in his Psalms, he gave forth in his dying testimony, for the special benefit of his seed, a description of the ruler, such as the Word of promise contemplated, and such as ought to have been, at least, generally realized in those who occupied the throne of his kingdom: 'he that ruleth over men must be just, ruling in the fear of God' (II Sam. 23:3). Not only so, but in his last and still more specific charge, delivered to his immediate successor on the throne, he expressly rested his expectation of the fulfillment of the covenant made with him, on the faithful adherence of those who should follow him to the law and testimony of God. For after enjoining Solomon to walk in the ways and keep the statutes of God, he adds as a reason for persuading to such a course, 'that the Lord may continue His word, which He spake concerning me, saying, *If* thy children take heed to their way to walk before Me in truth, with all their heart and with all their soul, there shall not fail thee a man on the throne of Israel' (I Kings 2:4).

"But when this fundamental condition was violated, as it began to be in the time of Solomon himself, the prophetic word became, in a manner, responsive to the change; so that now it spoke almost in the same language respecting the house of David, which had formerly been addressed to that of Saul—'I will rend the kingdom from thee, and give it to thy servant:' I Kings 11:11 compared with I Samuel 15:28; coupled only with the reservation that so much was still to be left to the house of David as was needed for maintaining the essential provisions of the covenant. Even this, however, appeared for a time to give way; the inveterate folly and wickedness of the royal line called forth such visitations of judgment, that the stately and glorious house of David, as it appears in the original prophecy, came afterwards to look like a frail tabernacle, and even this at a still future stage, as fallen prostrate to the ground—according to the figure in Amos 9:11.

"In consequence of these changes, darkness settled down on the hearts of God's people, and fearful misgivings arose in their minds concerning the faithfulness of God to His covenant engagements. The painful question was stirred in their bosoms, 'Has His promise failed for evermore?' The thought even escaped from their lips, 'He has made void the covenant of His servant.' The whole Psalm from which these words are taken (the 89th), is a striking record of the manner in which *faith had to struggle* with such doubts and perplexities, when the house of David was (for a time) cast down from its excellency, and God's plighted word, like the ark of His covenant, seemed to be given up into the hands of His enemies.

"God, however, vindicated in due time the truthfulness of His word, and the certainty of the result which it contemplated. The prophecy *stood fast* as regarded the grand article of its provisions—only in travelling on to its accomplishment, it had to pass through apparent defections and protracted delays, which could scarcely have been anticipated from the terms of its original announcement, and which were, in a sense, forced on it by human unbelief and waywardness. And so, within certain definite limits—those, namely, which connected the Divine promise with the sphere of man's responsibility, and bore on the time and mode of its fulfilment—it might justly be said to carry a *conditional* element in its bosom, in respect to those whom it more immediately concerned; while still, from first to last, the great purpose which it enshrined, *varied not* and continued to be, as a determinate counsel of Heaven, without shadow of turning."

We must not here anticipate too much what we hope to yet take up in detail, but in bringing this chapter to a close it is pertinent to point out that, in view of what was before us in the previous chapter—on the terms of Messianic prophecy being cast, more or less, in the mold of the typical history of Israel—we surely should not repeat the mistake of the carnal Jews, who expected Christ to sit on an earthly throne. When Old Testament prediction announced that the Messiah was to occupy the throne and kingdom of David, was it not intimated that He was *to rule over God's heritage,* and accomplish spiritually and perfectly what His prototype did but temporally and partially— namely, bring deliverance, security, and everlasting blessing to the people of God? In view of *the divine personality* of the Messianic King and the worldwide extent of His kingdom, all of necessity rises to a higher plane, Immanuel's reign must be of another order than that of the son of Jesse—spiritual, heavenly, eternal.

It should be quite obvious to those who are really acquainted with the earlier Scriptures that, in keeping with the character and times of the old covenant, any representation then made of Christ's throne and kingdom would, in the main at least, be of a figurative and symbolic nature, exhibited under the veil of the typical images supplied by Israel's commonwealth and history. It was thus that all the "better" things of the new covenant were shadowed forth. The immeasurable superiority of Christ's person over all who were His types compels us to look for a far grander and nobler discharge of His offices than which pertained unto them. It is true there is a resemblance between Christ as prophet and Moses (Deut. 18:18); nevertheless the contrast is far more evident (Heb. 3:3, 5). It is true that there is an agreement between Christ as priest and Melchizedek and Aaron (Heb. 5:1-5; 7:21); nevertheless the antitype far excels them (Rev. 5:6, etc.). So the throne He sits on and the kingdom He administers is infinitely higher than any that David or Solomon ever occupied (Heb. 2:9; 1:3). Beware of degrading the divine King to the level of human ones!

The Lord of glory no more stood (or stands) in need of any outward enthronement or local seat of government on earth, in order to prove His title to David's kingdom, than He required any physical "anointing" to constitute Him priest forever, or a material altar for the due presentation of His sacrifice to God. As another has well said, "Being the Son of the living God, and as such, the Heir of all things, He possessed from the first all the powers of the kingdom, and proved that He possessed them by every word He uttered, every work of deliverance He performed, every judgment He pronounced, every act of mercy and forgiveness He dispensed, and the resistless control He wielded over the elements of nature and the realms of the dead. *These were the signs of royalty He bore about with Him upon earth; and wonderful though they were, eclipsing in real grandeur all the glory of David and Solomon, they were still but the earlier preludes of that peerless majesty which David described from afar when he saw Him, as the Lord, seated in royal state at His Father's right hand.*"

V

In the preceding chapter we pointed out that in view of all which has been before us in connection with the earlier covenants, it is but reasonable to expect that the Davidic one also has both a "letter" and "spirit" significance. This expectation is, we believe, capable of clear demonstration: in their primary and inferior aspects the promises in II Samuel 7:11-16 respected Solomon and his immediate successors, but in their higher and ultimate meaning, they looked forward to Christ and His kingdom. And is not this fact evident from the immediate sequel? Does not that which is recorded in II Samuel 7:18-25 plainly intimate that David himself was enabled to perceive the spiritual purport of those promises, that they had to do with Christ Himself? There is not a doubt in my mind that such was the case, and we shall now endeavor to make this clear to the reader.

"Then went king David in, and sat before the Lord" (II Sam. 7:18). His posture was, we think, indicative of the earnest consideration which David was giving to the message he had just received. As he pondered the divine promises and surveyed the wondrous riches of divine grace toward him, he burst forth in self-effacing and God-honoring language: "And he said, Who am I, O Lord God? and what is my house, that thou hast brought me hitherto?" (v. 18). Why, his "house" pertained to the royal tribe: he was the direct descendant of the prince of Judah, so that he was connected with one of the most honorable families in all Israel. Yes, but such fleshly distinctions were now held very lightly by him. "Brought me hitherto": why, he had been brought to the throne itself, and given rest from all his enemies (7:1). Yes, but these faded into utter insignificance before the far greater things of which Nathan had prophesied.

"And this was yet a small thing in thy sight, O Lord God; but thou hast spoken also of thy servant's house for a great while to come. And is this the manner of men, O Lord God? And what can David say more unto thee? for thou, Lord God, knowest thy servant" (vv. 19, 20). Here again we see the effect which the Lord's message had wrought upon the mind of David. "He beheld in spirit another Son than Solomon, another Temple than one built of stones and cedar, another Kingdom than the earthly one, on whose throne he sat. He perceived a sceptre and a crown of which his own on mount Zion were only feeble types—dim and shadowy manifestations" (Krummacher's *David and the Godman*). That the patriarch David understood the whole of those promises to receive their fulfillment in the Lord Jesus Christ, is evident from his next utterance.

"For thy Word's sake, and according to thine own heart, hast thou done all these great things, to make thy servant to know them" (v. 21). The reference was to the *personal* Word, Him of whom it is declared, "In the beginning was the Word, and the Word was with God, and the Word was God" (John 1:1); and "according to thine own heart" meant according to God's gracious counsels. That David was not referring to God's spoken or written Word is evident from the fact that nothing of the kind had been uttered to him before, while of the written Word there was no Scripture then extant which predicted Christ, either personal or mystical, under the similitude of a "house." Let it be duly noted that all later references in Scripture to Christ under this figure are borrowed from and based upon this very passage. Unto David in vision was then given the first revelation, and hence it is that in that wondrous 89th Psalm we have other great features of it more particularly marked.

"I will sing of the mercies of the Lord forever: with my mouth will I make known thy faithfulness to all generations. For I have said, Mercy shall be built up forever: thy faithfulness shalt thou establish in the very heavens. I have made a covenant with my chosen, I have sworn unto David my servant, Thy seed will I establish forever, and build up thy throne to all generations. Selah" (Ps. 89:1-4). Of that oath, God the Holy Spirit was graciously pleased to tell the church by the mouth of Peter on the day of Pentecost: "Therefore being a prophet, and knowing that God had sworn with an oath to him, that of the fruit of his loins, according to the flesh, he would raise up *Christ* to sit on his throne" (Acts 2:30). Here, then, is the most decided and express proof that not David's son Solomon, nor any of the seed of Adam after the flesh, but to Christ Himself II Samuel 7:11-16 definitely alluded. David fully understood it so, that it was of Christ and Him alone the promises referred, and it was this which so overwhelmed his mind and moved him to burst forth with such expressions of humility.

What has just been before us supplies an illustration of the fact that all the patriarchs and saints of Old Testament times lived and died *in the faith of Christ:* "not having received the promises, but having seen them afar off, and were persuaded of them, and embraced them" (Heb. 11:13). Hence it was that by faith, with an eye to Christ, Abel offered unto God an acceptable sacrifice. Hence by faith, Noah prepared an ark, as beholding Christ set forth therein as a hiding place from the wind and a covert from the tempest. Hence too, by faith Abraham offered up his only-begotten son, expressly with an eye to the offering of God's only-begotten Son in the fulness of time. Therefore it was that David eyed Christ in the promises of God to build him a house, in the confidence whereof he took comfort amidst all the sad circumstances of himself and his children (II Sam. 23:5).

These holy men of old, and all the faithful in each generation of the church before the coming of Christ, lived in the blessed assurance of that faith. They beheld the promises afar off, yet that did not have the slightest effect in lessening their conviction in the veracity of them. Their faith gave to them a present subsistence: it substantiated and realized them, as if those saints had the fulfillment in actual possession, just as a powerful telescope will bring near to the eye objects far remote. Their faith gave as great an assurance of the reality of what God promised as though they had lived in the days when the Son of God became incarnate and tabernacled among men. In like manner, it is only by the exercise of a similar faith that we can now have a real knowledge of Christ by union and communion with Him.

Before we give further consideration to the contents of Psalm 89—which supplies a divine exposition of the promises made to David in I Samuel 7—we must first turn again to Psalm 2. As C. H. Spurgeon said in his introductory remarks thereon, "We shall not greatly err in our summary of this sublime Psalm if we call it 'The Psalm of Messiah the Prince, for it sets forth, as in a wondrous vision, the tumult of the people against the Lord's Anointed, the determinate purpose of God to exalt His own Son, and the ultimate reign of that Son over all His enemies. Let us read it with the eye of faith, beholding, as in a glass, the final triumph of our Lord Jesus Christ over all His enemies."

This second psalm is divided into four sections of three verses each. The first tells of the widespread opposition to the kingdom and government of Christ: His enemies cannot endure His yoke and they rebel against His commandments; these verses (1-3) were applied by Peter under the immediate inspiration of the Holy Spirit, to the opposition which Christ met with and the indignities that He suffered at the hands of the Jews and Gentiles (see Acts 4:24-27). The second section of it reveals God's utter contempt of those who sought to thwart His purpose: He derides their foolish counsels and puny efforts, and makes known the accomplishment of His will. He does not smite them, but gallingly announces that He has performed what they sought to prevent. "While they are proposing, He has disposed the matter. Jehovah's will is done, and so man's will frets and fumes in vain. God's Anointed is appointed, and shall not be disappointed" (C. H. Spurgeon).

"Yet have I set my king upon my holy hill of Zion" (Ps. 2:6). It is the investiture of Christ in His kingly office which is here in view. Just as Jehovah defeated the efforts of all his enemies and set the son of Jesse on the throne, making him king in Jerusalem over all Israel, so He raised His own Son from the dead, exalted Him as head of the church, and seated Him as victorious King upon His mediatorial throne, and therefore did the risen Redeemer declare, "All power is given unto me in heaven and in earth" (Matt. 28:18). Scholars tell us that "Zion" is derived from *tzun*, which means "a monument raised up." Such indeed is the church of God: a monument of *grace* now, and of *glory* hereafter; raised up to all eternity. It was there that David built his city, a type of the City of God in Christ. It was there that Solomon built the temple, a type also of Christ's mystical body. Hence, when we read, "The Lord hath founded Zion, and the poor of his people shall trust in it" (Isa. 14:32), when we hear Him saying, "Behold, I lay in Zion for a foundation a stone, a tried stone, a precious corner stone, a sure foundation" (Isa. 28:16—the Holy Spirit moving an apostle to tell the church that this is Christ: I Peter 2:6-8), and when with the eye of faith we behold "a Lamb stood on mount Zion, and with him a hundred forty and four thousand, having his Father's name written in their foreheads" (Rev. 14:1), who can refrain from exclaiming, "Praise waiteth for thee, O God, in Zion" (Ps. 65:1).

It seems strange that any should question the fact, or, shall we say, challenge the statement, that even now the Lord Jesus is King and discharging His royal office. The whole burden of the Epistle to the Hebrews is the proffering of proof that He is Priest "after the order of Melchizedek": that is, Priest-King. Collateral confirmation of this is found in the statement that believers are "a *royal* priesthood" (I Peter

2:9), and they are so only because of their union with the antitypical
Melchizedek. Christ has already been "crowned," not with an earthly
or material diadem, but "with glory and with honour" (Heb. 2:9). He
has "sat down on the right hand of the Majesty on high," and
therefore is He "upholding all things by the word of his power" (Heb.
1:3). The "sceptre of righteousness" is wielded by Him (Heb. 1:8),
"ambassadors" have been sent forth by Him (II Cor. 5:20), and both
men and angels are subject to Him.

Christ is the King of His *enemies,* and He shall reign till He has
placed the last of them beneath His feet. "Who would not fear thee, O
king of nations" (Jer. 10:7). True, many of them do not own His
scepter, yea, some deny His very being; nevertheless He is their
sovereign, "the prince of the kings of the earth" (Rev. 1:5), and this
because God has already "highly exalted him and given him a name
which is above every name" (Phil. 2:9). This was the reward for His
sufferings: the head that once was crowned with thorns is crowned
with glory now: a royal diadem adorns the mighty victor's brow. "He
hath on his vesture and on his thigh a name written, King of kings, and
Lord of lords" (Rev. 19:16). Ah, my reader, what are all the great, the
mighty, and honorable men of the earth in comparison with Him who
is "the *only* Potentate" (I Tim. 6:15).

Again: Christ is King *of the church:* "The King of saints" (Rev.
15:3). He is King of the evil and King of the good: He is King *over* the
former, He is King *in* the latter. Christ rules over the wicked by His
might and power; He rules in the righteous by His Spirit and grace.
This latter is His spiritual kingdom, where He reigns in the hearts of
His own, where His sovereignty is acknowledged, His scepter kissed,
His laws heeded. This is brought about by the miracle of regeneration,
whereby lawless rebels are transformed into loyal subjects. As the
King of Zion Christ exercises His royal authority by appointing
officers, both ordinary and extraordinary, for His church (see Eph.
4:11, 12). It is the prerogative of the king to nominate and call those
who serve him in the government of his kingdom: this Christ does. He
also exerts His royal authority by ordering His officers in their
governing of His subjects to teach no other things than those He has
commanded (Matt. 28:19). Oh, that both writer and reader may
render to Him that allegiance and fealty which are His due!

Finally, be it noted that Christ is *the Father's* King, and this in at
least three respects. First, by the Father's *appointing:* "I appoint unto
you a kingdom, as my Father hath appointed unto me" (Luke 22:29).
Christ is eminently qualified to bear the government upon His shoulder; and being infinitely dear to the Father this honor He delighted to
confer upon Him. Second, by the Father's *investiture:* "I have set my

King upon my holy hill of Zion." God has entrusted Christ with the sole administration of government and judgment: "And hath given him authority to execute judgment also, because he is the Son of man" (John 5:27). Third, because Christ rules *for* His Father: to fulfill His purpose, to glorify His name. That Christ rules for His Father is clear from, "Then cometh the end, when he shall have delivered up the kingdom to God, even the Father" (I Cor. 15:24). It is the Father's kingdom; and therefore do we pray, "Thy kingdom come"— that is, in its fuller open manifestation. Yet it is the Son's kingdom (Col. 1:14) because administered by Him.

Christ's power as the King of Zion is absolute and universal. Alas that this is now so dimly perceived and so feebly apprehended by many of those bearing His name. Dispensationalists will have much to answer for in the coming Day, for by denying His present kingship, postponing His rule unto "the millennium," they both rob Him of His personal honors and deprive us of precious comfort. Christ is sovereign, supreme over all creatures. He bridles both man and demons, saying to them, as He does to the proud waves of the sea, "Hitherto shalt thou come, but no further." As the King of Zion, Christ has His chain about the necks of Satan and all his wicked instruments; and when they have gone their appointed lengths, they are obliged to stop. We see this in the case of Job: when the devil was permitted to harass him, he went only so far as his chain allowed. So it is now.

This royal and absolute power of Christ He is exercising in protecting His church in the midst of grave and imminent dangers. A vivid portrayal of this was made unto Moses when Christ appeared to him in the burning bush. He saw the bush burning in the midst of the fire; yet it was not consumed. That represented the situation of the church in Egypt at that time: under the tyranny of most cruel taskmasters, lorded over by Pharaoh who hated them and thirsted for their annihilation. Yet under the care of Christ, He delivered them from being swallowed up by their enemies. This He has done in all ages, shielding His people when their foes threatened to swallow them up.

In the third section of Psalm 2 Christ is heard declaring His sovereign rights, with the Father's response thereto. We would recommend those who have access to the works of John Newton to read his sermon on Psalm 2:9. Therein he has shown how that, since Christ's enemies will not submit to the golden scepter of His grace, they are under His iron rod. This iron rule over them consists, first, in the certain and inseparable connection He has established between sin and misery: where the Lord does not dwell, peace will not inhabit. Second, in His power over conscience: what awful thoughts and fears sometimes awaken them in the silent hours of the night! Third, in that terrible blindness and hardness of heart to which some sinners are given up.

VI

In the opening chapter of this study it was pointed out that the various covenants which God entered into with men, from time to time, adumbrated different features of the everlasting covenant which He made with the Mediator ere time began. As we have followed the historical stream it has been shown wherein the Adamic, the Noahic, and the Sinaitic covenants shadowed forth the essential features of that eternal compact which constituted the basis of the salvation of God's elect. In connection with the Davidic it is observable there is an absence of those details which marked the earlier ones, that renders it less easy to determine the exact purpose and purport of it so far as the "letter" of it was concerned. Yet the reason for this is not far to seek: as the last of the Old Testament covenants, the type merged more definitely with the antitype. This becomes the more patent when we examine carefully those Scriptures bearing directly thereon, for in some of them it is almost impossible to say whether the type or the antitype be before us.

A notable instance of this is furnished by Psalm 89. Though we cannot be sure of the precise time when it was first penned, there seems good reason to conclude that it is to be dated from the reign of Rehoboam. Its closing verses make it quite plain that it was written at a period when the honor and power of David's royal line had been reduced to a very low ebb; yet before the destruction of Jerusalem and its temple—for no hint of that calamity is here given. It was in the days of Rehoboam ten of the tribes revolted from him; and that the one placed over them because his powerful adversary, while the king of Egypt so weakened and humbled him that it appears he only retained his kingdom at all by the clemency of Shishak. A sad condition had arrived, for the fortunes of David's family had sunk to a deplorable degree.

It was under such circumstances Psalm 89 was composed. That its writer was fearfully agitated appears from its last fourteen verses, though perhaps he was there voicing the general sentiment which then obtained. Everything looked as though the divine promises to David had failed and were on the eve of being made completely void. It was then that faith had its opportunity, and ignoring the black clouds which covered the firmament, took refuge in Him who dwelleth above it. It was in the covenant faithfulness of the Father of mercies that the psalmist now found comfort. "I will sing of the mercies of the Lord forever: with my mouth will I make known of thy faithfulness to all generations. For I have said, Mercy shall be built up forever: thy faithfulness shalt thou establish in the very heavens. I have made a covenant with my chosen, I have sworn unto David my servant: thy seed will I establish forever, and build up thy throne to all generations. Selah" (Ps. 89:1-4).

One view only has obtained among the spiritually minded. Said the Puritan Brooks, "There are many passages in the Psalm which do clearly evidence it is to be interpreted of *Christ,* yea there are many things in this Psalm which cannot be clearly and pertinently applied to any but Christ." Toplady (author of the hymn "Rock of Ages") asked, "Do you suppose this was spoken of David in his own person only? No indeed, but to David as type and forerunner of Christ." "The whole contexture of the Psalm discovers the design of it to be to set forth some higher Person than David, for it seems to be too magnificent and lofty for an earthly prince" (S. Charnock). "The whole of the 89th Psalm, which is altogether devoted to the covenant, is expressly said to be a vision in which Jehovah spake to His Holy One (v. 19), and all the purport of it is to show how Jehovah had entered into covenant engagement with Christ for the redemption of His people" (Robert Hawker).

Psalm 89, then, is the key to II Samuel 7:4-17. Not only does it unlock for us the meaning of the Davidic covenant, but it also fixes the interpretation of those passages in the prophets which obviously look back to and are based upon the same. "The covenant is made with David, the covenant of royalty is made with him, as the father of his family, and all his seed through him, and for his sake, representing the Covenant of Grace made with Christ as Head of the Church, and with all believers in Him. . . . The blessings of the covenant were not only secured to David himself, but were entailed on his family. It was promised that his family should continue—'thy seed will I establish forever,' so that 'David shall not want a son to reign' (Jer. 33:17). And that it should continue a royal family: 'I will build up his throne to all generations.' This has its accomplishment *only in Christ"* (Matthew Henry).

"I have made a covenant with my chosen, I have sworn unto David my servant" (v. 3). "David was the Lord's elect, and with him a covenant was made, which ran along in the line of his seed until it received a final and never-ending fulfillment in 'the Son of David.'

David's house must be royal: as long as there was a sceptre in Judah, David's seed must be the only rightful dynasty; the great 'King of the Jews' died with that title above His head in the three current languages of the then known world, and at this day He is owned as King by men of every tongue. The oath sworn to David has not been broken, though the temporal crown is no longer worn, for in the covenant itself his kingdom was spoken of as enduring forever. In Christ Jesus there is a covenant established with all the Lord's *chosen,* and they are by grace led to be the Lord's *servants,* and then are ordained kings and priests by Jesus Christ. . . . After reading this (II Sam. 7:12-16), let us remember that the Lord has said *to us* by His servant Isaiah, 'I will make an everlasting covenant with you, even the sure mercies of David' " (C. H. Spurgeon).

"Thy seed will I establish forever, and build up thy throne to all generations" (v. 4). "David must always have a seed, and truly in Jesus this is fulfilled beyond his hopes. What a seed David has in the multitude which have sprung from Him who was both his Son and his Lord. The Son of David is the great Progenitor, the last Adam, the everlasting Father, He sees His seed, and in them beholds of the travail of His soul. David's dynasty never decays, but on the contrary, is evermore consolidated by the great Architect of heaven and earth. Jesus is a king as well as a progenitor, and His throne is ever being built up—His kingdom comes—His power extends. Thus runs the covenant: and when the Church declines, it is ours to *plead it* before the ever-faithful God, as the Psalmist does in the latter verses of this sacred song. Christ must reign, but why is His name blasphemed and His Gospel so despised? The more gracious Christians are, the more will they be moved to jealousy by the sad estate of the Redeemer's cause, and the more will they argue the case with the great Covenant-maker, crying day and night before Him, 'Thy kingdom come' " (C. H. Spurgeon).

We shall not proceed any further with a verse by verse comment of this psalm, but rather seek to call attention to its more essential features, as they serve to elucidate the Davidic covenant. The first section of the psalm closes with the declaration, "Justice and judgment are the habitation of thy throne." This has reference to the mediatorial throne of God in Christ, as is clear from the remainder of the verse and what follows: justice and judgment are the establishment (margin) of His throne—the firmest foundations on which any throne can be settled. The Son of God, as the surety of His elect, undertook to satisfy divine justice, by rendering perfect obedience to the precepts of the law and by suffering its penalty, whereby He brought in everlasting righteousness. God's administration of grace, then, is founded upon the complete satisfaction of His justice by Christ as the sponsor of His people (Rom. 3:24-26; 5:21).

Having at some length praised the God of Israel by celebrating His perfections, the psalmist next declared the happiness of the true Israel of God, closing with the blessed affirmation, "For the Lord is our defense, and the Holy One of Israel is our king" (v. 18). The people that "know the joyful sound" (v. 15) are they whose ears have been opened by the Spirit to take in the glad tidings of the gospel, so that they understand the covenant promises and perceive their own personal interest therein. They walk in the light of Jehovah's countenance, for they are accepted in the Beloved. In God's righteousness they shall continue to be exalted, for divine justice is on their side and not against them. In God's favor their horn or spirit shall be elevated, for nothing so exhilarates the heart as a realization of God's free grace. As their King, the Holy One of Israel will both rule and protect them.

At verse 19 the psalmist returns to a consideration of the covenant which God made with David, enlarging upon his previous reference thereto; and pleading it before God for His favor unto the royal family, now almost ruined. Yet one has only to weigh the things here said to perceive that they go far beyond the typical David; yea, some of them could scarcely apply to him at all, but receive their fulfillment in Christ and His spiritual seed. The covenant which God made with the son of Jesse was an outward adumbration of that eternal compact He had entered into with the Mediator on behalf of His people: it was a publishing on earth something of what transpired in the secret councils of heaven. The ultimate reference in "Then thou spakest in vision to thy holy one" is unto the Father's intercourse with the Son before time began (see Prov. 8:22, 23, 30; Matt. 11:27; John 5:20).

"I have laid help upon one that is mighty" (v. 19). How fully was that demonstrated in Christ's life, death, and resurrection! He was mighty because He is the Almighty (Rev. 1:8). As God the Son in personal union with the Son of Man, He was in every way qualified for His stupendous undertaking. None but He could magnify the law and make it honorable, make atonement for sin, vanquish death, bruise the serpent's head, and so preserve His church on earth that the gates of Hades should not prevail against it. As this mighty one, "the Lion of the tribe of Judah," the apostle John beheld Him in the Patmos visions (Rev. 5:5). Because He is such, therefore "he is able to save unto the uttermost them that come unto God by him" (Heb. 7:25).

"I have exalted one chosen out of the people" (v. 19). It is this, essentially, which qualifies Christ to occupy the mediatorial throne, for not only is He "the mighty God" (Isa 9:6), but as the woman's seed (Gen. 3:15) He has taken unto Himself our very nature: "In all things it behoved him to be made like unto his brethren, that he might be a merciful and faithful high priest" (Heb. 2:17). One of the titles by which God addresses the redeemer is, "Behold my servant, whom I uphold; mine *elect* [or chosen] in whom my soul delighteth" (Isa. 42:1). And this blessed one God has exalted to His own right hand.

"I have found David my servant: with my holy oil I anointed him" (v. 20). "This must also be expounded of the Prince Emmanuel: He became the Servant of the Lord for our sakes, the Father having found for us in His person a mighty Deliverer, therefore upon Him rested the Spirit without measure, to qualify Him for all the offices of love to which He was set apart. We have not a Savior self-appointed and unqualified, but one sent of God and Divinely endowed for His work. Our Savior Jesus is also the Lord's Christ, or anointed. The oil with which He is anointed is God's own oil, and holy oil; He is Divinely endowed with the Spirit of holiness—cf. Luke 4:18" (Spurgeon). In the prophets Christ is called "David" again and again, the name meaning "the Beloved," for He is most dearly beloved of the Father. "He shall cry unto me, Thou art my father, my God" (v. 26). Where is there any record that David ever addressed God by this endearing term? Obviously the reference is to Him who, on the morning of His resurrection, declared, "I ascend unto my Father, and your Father; and to my God, and your God" (John 20:17). "Also I will make him my firstborn, higher than the kings of the earth" (v. 27). This too is intelligible only of the true David, who must have the preeminence in all things. Christ was made higher than the kings of the earth when God seated Him at His own right hand in the heavens, "far above all principality, and power, and might, and dominion, and every name that is named" (Eph. 1:20, 21).

"His seed also will I make to endure forever" (v. 29). Here again, the type loses itself in the antitype. Literally, David's seed lives on forever in the person of Christ, who was made of David according to the flesh (Rom. 1:3). But spiritually, it is the seed of the true David, namely, *believers;* for they alone own His scepter and are His subjects. "Saints are a race that neither death nor hell can kill" (Spurgeon). Of old it was declared of Christ, "He shall see his seed. . . . He shall see of the travail of his soul and be satisfied" (Isa. 53:10, 11). In a coming Day, Christ shall exclaim, "Behold I and the children which God hath given me" (Heb. 2:13). "And his throne as the days of heaven" (v. 29). Let it be duly noted that both here and in verse 36 Christ's "seed" and His "throne" are coupled together, as though His throne could not stand if His seed should fail. Well did Charnock ask: "If His subjects should perish, what would He be King of? If His members should consume, what would He be head of?" It is His mediatorial throne and its perpetuity which are here in view: on the new earth there will be "the throne of God *and of the Lamb*" (Rev. 22:1).

If any doubt remains in the reader's mind as to the accuracy or truth of our interpretation above, that which is recorded in verses 30-37 should at once completely remove it. Nothing could be plainer than that the believing children of the antitypical David are there in view. In this most previous passage God makes known His ways—the principles according to which He deals with the redeemed: operative in all dispensations. Christ's children still have a sinful nature, and thus are ever prone to forsake God's law, yet even though they do so this will not annul the promises which God made to them in Christ. True, God is holy, and therefore will not wink at their sins; He is righteous, and so chastises them for their iniquities; but He is also both faithful and gracious, and so will not break His word to Christ, nor take away His loving-kindness from those for whom His Son died.

God had declared, "I have made a covenant with my chosen, I have sworn unto David my servant: Thy seed will I establish forever" (vv. 3, 4). Yes; but suppose David's seed should prove thoroughly unworthy and unfaithful—what then? Will God cast them out of His covenant? No indeed: this is why verses 30, 31 began with "If": an objection is anticipated, the Arminian bogie of falling from grace and being lost is here laid by the heels. If the seed of the antitypical David break God's statutes and keep not His commandments, will divine rejection and eternal destruction be their inevitable portion? No; God will make them smart severely for their perverseness, yet it is the disciplinary *rod* He uses, and not the sword or axe of the executioner. God is not fickle: whom He loves, He loves forever; and therefore neither man nor Satan shall ever destroy any of the seed of the true David.

VII

In the preceding chapter it was pointed out how that the historical account of the Davidic covenant lacks that fulness of detail which marked the earlier ones: the reason for this being, the nearer the approach unto the advent of Christ the more the type merged into the antitype. It was also shown how that Psalm 89 supplies us with the divine interpretation of the promises given through the prophet Nathan to the son of Jesse. The superlative importance of this fact cannot be too strongly insisted upon, for it settles the vexing question as to the character and location of Christ's throne and kingdom. It is here that we are furnished with clear and conclusive answers to the questions and disputes which have been raised concerning the terms found in II Samuel 7:11-16.

What we are most anxious to make clear to the reader is this: is the seed promised to David in II Samuel 7:12 a carnal or a mystical one? Is His kingdom (v. 12) an earthly or a heavenly one? Is His house and throne a material or spiritual one? If one of these questions can be definitely and finally settled, then the others will be, for it is obvious that the passage must be dealt with consistently throughout. All is to be understood literally or all mystically, carnally or spiritually. Now all doubt is removed as to the answer to the first question: the seed promised to David, like the seed promised to Abraham (Gal. 3:7, 16) is a mystical one; that is to say, it finds its accomplishment not in Christ personally, but in Christ mystically, that is, Christ together with the members of His body—the church of which He is the head. The proof of this is found in Psalm 89.

In II Samuel 7 God promised David, "I will set up thy seed after thee. . . . I will be his father, and he shall be my son. If he commit iniquity, I will chasten him with the rod of men, and with the stripes of the children of men" (vv. 12-14). In Psalm 89 God declared, "I have found David my servant . . . He shall cry unto me, Thou art my father . . . my covenant shall stand fast with him. . . . If his children forsake my law then will I visit their transgression with the rod, and their iniquity with stripes" (vv. 20, 26, 28, 29, 31). Nothing could be plainer than this: the "if *he* commit iniquity, I will chasten *him* with the rod" of II Samuel 7:14 is here changed to "I will visit *their* transgressions with the rod." Thus the seed of David is Christ and His children. Their absolute identification is further emphasized in "I will visit *their* transgressions with the rod, nevertheless my loving-kindness will I not take from *him*" (vv. 32, 33). Thus, the Redeemer and the redeemed are inseparably linked, for together they form one (mystical) body.

The grand promise made to David in II Samuel 7 was that though his seed should commit iniquity God's mercy would "not depart away from him," but that his house and kingdom should be "established forever" (vv. 14-16). It was no fleshly or earthly blessing, but a spiritual and eternal one. Therein it differs radically from what had gone before. Both Adam in Eden and Israel in Canaan had forfeited their heritage, but the inheritance Christ secured for His people is an inalienable one. This is made so prominent in Psalm 89: of Christ God declared, "His seed also will I make to endure *forever*" (v. 29). This is God's covenant engagement with the Mediator, and no failure or sin on the part of His people shall cause God to cancel it. True, He will severely chastise them for their transgressions—for in God's family the rod is not spared nor the children spoiled—but He will not cast them off as incorrigible rebels. The atonement of Christ fully met all their liabilities; and as He enjoys God's favor forever, so must those vitally united to Him.

The same grand feature marks the throne and kingdom of Christ, distinguishing it from all that pertains to the earth: "I will establish the throne of his kingdom *forever*" (II Sam. 7:13). That there should be no uncertainty on this point, God repeats: "Thy throne shall be established *forever*" (v. 16). It is no temporal and temporary throne which the true David occupies, enduring only for a thousand years; as the New Testament expressly declares, "Of his kingdom there shall be *no end*" (Luke 1:33). The same grand truth is emphasized in Psalm 89; "And his throne as the days of *heaven*" (v. 29)—not "as the days of earth." "His seed shall endure forever, and his throne as the *sun* before me; it shall be established forever as the *moon*" (vv. 36, 37): the most enduring objects in nature are selected as the figure and proof of the absoluteness of the perpetuity affirmed. That Christ's kingdom is celestial and not earthly is seen in "and as a faithful witness *in heaven*" (v. 37).

Another psalm which casts its light upon the character and contents of the Davidic covenant is the 132nd, upon which we must offer a few remarks. It has two divisions. In the first (vv. 1-10) there is a pleading with Jehovah to be merciful unto His people "for David's sake" (v. 10); in the second section (vv. 11-18) we have His response, promising, "I will make the horn of David to bud, upon himself shall his crown flourish" (vv. 17, 18). In the first, God is reminded of David's deep concern to supply a permanent house for the holy ark; in the second, the Lord declares that He has found a satisfying and eternal resting place in Zion. In the first, prayer is made that God's priests might be "clothed with righteousness"; in the second, God affirms that He will clothe His priests "with salvation." The second half strictly balances the first throughout.

Now that which invests this 132nd Psalm with particular interest for us is what is found therein concerning God's resting place and the relation of this to the Davidic covenant. It will be remembered that II Samuel 7 opens with an account of David's anxiety to provide a suitable residence for the ark, and that it was in response thereto Nathan made such a wondrous and gracious revelation to him. Let it be duly noted that among the covenant promises which God then made to David concerning the blessed one who (according to the flesh) should descend from him, was this declaration: "He shall build *a house* for my name"; and to Him God says, "Thine *house* and thy kingdom shall be established forever" (vv. 13, 16). Like the throne and kingdom mentioned in the same passage, this house is not material, earthly, and temporal, but a spiritual, heavenly, and eternal one; it is no mere Jewish temple for "the millennium," but a divine dwelling place for the ages of the ages.

The tabernacle, as is well known, was the symbol of God's residing among the covenant people and of the divine fellowship to which He had graciously admitted them. This symbolical significance was transferred to the temple, with the additional idea—suggested by its very structure—of durability and permanency. With this place of worship the throne of David was indissolubly bound up. The destruction of the temple only became possible as the effect of the confirmed apostasy of the occupants of David's throne, and its restoration was only to be expected as the work of someone of the royal race being brought into renewed fellowship with God. This is verified in the reconstruction of the second temple by Zerubbabel. The symbol, however, was the type of something higher: the true temple of God is the sanctified hearts of His saints. It is with His spiritual church that the throne of David, as occupied by the Redeemer, is permanently and inseparably united.

The kingdom of Christ and the house of God are one and the same, viewed from different angles. It is the redeemed who constitute the true subjects of Christ's kingdom, for they alone own His scepter: where there are no subjects, there can be no kingdom. And it is the redeemed who provide God with a satisfying resting place. In the later prophets it was expressly foretold, "Thus speaketh the Lord of hosts, saying, Behold the man whose name is The Branch: and he shall grow up out of his place, and he shall build the temple of the Lord: even he shall build the temple of the Lord, and he shall bear the glory" (Zech. 6:12, 13). Now the true house in which God dwells is a spiritual one, composed of living stones, converted souls, which is "built upon the foundation of the apostles and prophets, Jesus Christ himself being the chief cornerstone; in whom all the building fitly framed together groweth unto a holy temple in the Lord" (Eph. 1:20, 21).

Returning to Psalm 132. "The Lord hath sworn in truth unto David: He will not turn from it; Of the fruit of thy body will I set upon thy throne. If thy children will keep my covenant and my testimony that I shall teach them, their children shall also sit upon thy throne for evermore" (vv. 11, 12). These verses make it clear beyond all doubt that our psalm has to do directly with the Davidic covenant. In their "letter" significance, they respected David's throne upon earth and the condition which determined its continuance—a condition which was not met by his descendants. In their spiritual purport

they concern the antitypical David and His children, His infinite
merits assuring that God would grant the needed grace for them to
render to Him that obedience which the new covenant required—
namely, a real and sincere one, though not flawless and perfect. (This
will be carefully considered by us when we take up the new covenant.)
Such Scriptures as the following are to be pondered for the fulfillment
of this promise of Christ's children occupying His throne: Luke 22:29,
30; I Corinthians 6:2, 3; I Peter 2:9 ("a royal priesthood"); Revelation
3:21.

"For the Lord hath chosen Zion: he hath desired it for his habitation" (v. 13). "It was no more than any other Canaanite town till God
chose it, David captured it, Solomon built it, and the Lord dwelt in it.
So was the Church a mere Jebusite stronghold till grace chose it,
conquered it, rebuilt it, and dwelt in it. Jehovah has chosen His
people, and hence they are His people; He has chosen the Church, and
hence it is what it is. Thus in the covenant David and Zion, Christ and
His people, go together. David is for Zion, and Zion for David; the
interests of Christ and His people are mutual" (C. H. Spurgeon). In
Hebrews 12:22 the kingdom of Christ is expressly denominated
"Mount Zion."

"This is my rest forever. Here will I dwell; for I have desired it" (v.
14). "Again are we filled with wonder that He who fills all things
should dwell in *Zion*—should dwell in His *Church*. God does not
unwillingly visit His chosen; He desires to dwell with them; He desires
them. He is already in Zion, for He says *here*, as one upon the spot.
Not only will He occasionally come to His Church, but He will dwell
in it, as His fixed abode. He cared not for the magnificence of
Solomon's temple, but He determined that at the mercy-seat He
would be found by suppliants, and from thence He would shine forth
in brightness of grace among the favoured nation. All this, however,
was but a type of the spiritual house, of which Jesus is foundation and
cornerstone, upon which all the living stones are builded together for
an habitation of God through the Spirit. O the sweetness of the
thought that God *desires* to dwell in His people and rest among
them!" (C. H. Spurgeon).

If further proof be required that the church is the dwelling place of
God, it is forthcoming in "that thou mayest know how thou oughtest
to behave thyself in the house of God, which is the church of the
living God, the pillar and ground of the truth" (I Tim. 3:15). Here,
then, is the ultimate accomplishment of those promises God made
through Nathan. The antitypical David *has built* the house for God's
name (II Sam. 7:13; cf. his use of the word "build" in Matt. 16:18).
Unto Him God said, "Thine house and thy kingdom shall be estab-

lished forever" (II Sam. 7:16); for the Father and the Son are *one*. In this House the Lord Jesus presides, for we read, "But Christ as a son over his own house: whose house are we, if we hold fast the confidence and the rejoicing of the hope firm unto the end" (Heb. 3:6). When the first heaven and the first earth are passed away, it shall be said, "Behold, the tabernacle of God is with men, and he will dwell with them, and they shall be his people, and God himself shall be with them, and be their God" (Rev. 21:3). The Lord God will then "rest in his love" (Zeph. 3:17).

Nor was David himself left in ignorance as to the higher and spiritual purport of the covenant promises which the Lord had made to him. This appears first in the expressions of his deep wonderment and overwhelming gratitude at the time they were first made to him (II Sam. 7:18-29): "Thou hast also spoken of thy servant's house for a great while to come," he declared, language which connotes a period of vast extent, far in excess of that covered by the lengthiest human dynasties. Then he added, "Is this the manner [or "law," margin] of man, O Lord God?" Christ's kingdom shall be ordered by a principle securing for it a perpetuity which was wholly inapplicable to any human rule, and therefore all pertaining to His kingdom obviously stands in marked contrast from the established order of things which belongs to all merely human dynasties.

David's own understanding of the deeper import of the contents of the covenant also appears in those Messianic psalms of which he was the author. As we have already seen, in Psalm 2 David declares of that one whom God was to establish King in Zion, that He would possess the dominion of the whole earth, kings being commanded to acknowledge Him on pain of incurring His ruinous disfavor—something which plainly denoted that a greater than Solomon was in view. From the many things he predicated in Psalm 89 of his seed, it is evident David must have known that in no proper sense could they be applied to his immediate successors on the throne. While in Psalm 110 David himself calls his promised descendant his *Lord:* "The Lord said unto my Lord, sit thou at my right hand until I make thine enemies thy footstool" (v. 1).

Not only does it appear from the psalms that David's mind was freely occupied with the covenant promises and that God granted him much light thereon, but we also learn from Scripture that they formed the principal solace and joy in the prospect of his dissolution, for when the world was fast receding from his view, he clung to them as "all his salvation and all his desire." As he contemplated death, the future of his family seriously engaged his thoughts. Sorely had he suffered from and by his children, and few if any appeared to have the fear of God upon them. He was probably exercised as to who should succeed him in the kingdom. Then it was he exclaimed, "Although my house be not so with God; yet he hath made with me an everlasting covenant, ordered in all things and sure: for this is all my salvation and all my desire, although he make it not to grow" (II Sam. 23:5).

"Although my house be not so [i.e., as described in vv. 3, 4] with God, *yet* . . . although he make it not to grow," that is, it declines and diminishes naturally. Absalom was dead; Adonijah, another of his sons, would be slain (I Kings 2:24, 25); yet God would preserve him a seed from which Christ would come. The dying king was convinced that nothing could prevail to prevent the fulfillment of the divine promises, that full provision was made for every possible contingency.

VIII

From the Psalms we turn now to the Prophets, in which we find a series of divine predictions based upon the promises made to David in II Samuel 7. Before turning to some of the more important of these, let it be again pointed out that the *new* things of Christ's kingdom were portrayed under the veil of the *old*, that when the Holy Spirit made mention of gospel times they necessarily partook of a Jewish coloring. In other words, existing things and institutions were employed to represent other things of a higher order and nobler nature, so that the fulfillment of those ancient predictions are to be looked for in the spirit and not in the letter, in substance and not in regards to actual form. Only as this clearly established principle is held fast shall we be delivered from the carnalizing of the Jews of old, and the gross literalizing of dispensationalists of today.

Many pages might be written in amplification of what has just been said and in supplying proof that it is "a clearly established principle." The person, the office, and the work of Christ, as well as the blessings which He purchased and procured for His people, were very largely foretold in the language of Judaism. But the fact that the antitype is spoken of in the terms of the type should not cause us to confuse the one with the other. The Old Testament is to be interpreted in the light of the New—not only its types, but its prophecies also. When we read that "Christ our Passover is sacrificed for us" (I Cor. 5:7) we understand what is meant thereby. When we are told that Christians are the seed and children of Abraham (Gal. 3 and 4) we perceive the fulfillment of God's promise to the patriarch that he should have a numerous seed. In the light of the Epistles we have no difficulty in recognizing that a spiritual cleansing was denoted by "then will I sprinkle clean water upon you, and ye shall be clean" (Ezek. 36:25).

Take again the wondrous events of the day of Pentecost. Peter explained them by declaring, "This is that which was spoken by the prophet Joel: And it shall come to pass in the last days, saith God, I will pour out of my Spirit upon all flesh: and your sons and your daughters shall prophesy, and your young men shall see visions, and your old men shall dream dreams" (Acts 2:16). The apostle did not mean that Joel's prophecy had received an exhaustive accomplishment in the phenomena of that particular day, for they were, in measure, repeated in both Acts 8 and 10; nevertheless, there was an actual fulfillment in the larger spiritual endowments then granted the Twelve. But let it be carefully noted it was not a literal fulfillment. The freer communications of the Spirit were foretold under the peculiar form of visions and dreams, because such was the mode when Joel lived in which the more especial gifts of the Spirit were manifested. The promised gift of the Spirit was conferred, yet with a new mode of operation far higher than that of which the Old Testament prophet was cognizant.

Let what has been said above be carefully borne in mind in connection with all that follows. "For unto us a child is born, unto us a son is given; and the government shall be upon his shoulder: and his name shall be called Wonderful, Counsellor, The mighty God, The everlasting Father, The Prince of Peace. Of the increase of his government and peace there shall be no end, upon the throne of David, and upon his kingdom, to order it, and to establish it with judgment and with justice from henceforth even for ever." (Isa. 9:6, 7). The relation between this illustrious passage and its context shows that the scope of the Holy Spirit in the whole was to intimate the character of Christ's kingdom. In the previous chapter the prophet had spoken of dark and dismal days of trouble and distress, and then he comforted and encouraged the hearts of true believers by announcing the good and grand things which the Messiah would provide. Three New Testament blessings are spoken of in Old Testament terms.

The first was that great light should spring up in a lost world: "The people that walk in darkness [without a written revelation from God] have seen a great light: they that dwell in the land of the shadow of death, upon them hath the light shined" (v. 2). We are not left in any doubt as to the meaning of this, for the Holy Spirit has explained it at the beginning of the New Testament. In Matthew 4 we read that the Lord Jesus came and dwelt in Capernaum "that it might be fulfilled which was spoken by Isaiah," quoting this very verse. The following facts were thereby unequivocally established: that the prophecy of Isaiah 9 referred to no far distant "millennium," but to this Christian dispensation; that its accomplishment lies not in some remote era, but in the present; that it concerned not Jews as such, but "the Gentiles"; that the blessing foretold was not a carnal or material one, but a spiritual.

The second blessing here announced was an enlargement, and rejoicing in the Lord: "Thou hast multiplied the nation, and not increased the joy: they joy before thee according to the joy in harvest, and as men rejoice when they divide the spoil" (v. 3). The "nation" is that "holy nation" of I Peter 2:9—compare Matthew 21:43. By means of the promulgation of the gospel light (spoken of in the previous verse), the holy nation of the New Testament church would be multiplied, as the Book of Acts records. Those who are supernaturally enlightened by the Spirit become partakers of a spiritual joy, so that they "rejoice with joy unspeakable and full of glory." The clause "not increased the joy" signifies it is not a carnal happiness which is in view (such as the Jews dreamed of), but "they joy *before thee.*" Their lot in this world is "as sorrowful, yet alway rejoicing" (II Cor. 6:10).

The third blessing is spiritual liberty and freedom: "For thou hast broken the yoke of his burden, and the staff of his shoulder, the rod of his oppressor, as in the day of Midian. For every battle of the warrior is with confused noise, and garments rolled in blood; but this shall be with burning and fuel of fire" (vv. 4, 5). As Gideon was an instrument in the hand of God for breaking the heavy yoke of oppression that Midian had placed on the neck of Israel, so Christ, upon His coming, would deliver poor sinners from the hands of all their enemies—sin, Satan, the world, and the curse of a broken law, unto which they were in bondage (cf. Luke 1:74, 75; 4:18).

"For unto us a child is born, unto us a son is given." The opening "For" shows the definite connection with the context, and announces who it is that would secure those grand blessings for His people. "For unto *us* a child is born" refers not to the fleshly descendants of Abraham, but to the entire election of grace. The "government" upon His shoulder is no mere rule over Palestine, but is over the entire universe; for all power is given unto Christ in heaven and in earth (Matt. 28:18). Nor is His a temporary reign for a thousand years only, but "even forever" (v. 7). That which the throne and kingdom of the natural David dimly foreshadowed is now being cumulatively, and shall be increasingly, accomplished by the spiritual David on an infinitely higher plane and in a far grander way.

"And in that day there shall be a root of Jesse, which shall stand for an ensign of the people; to it shall the Gentiles seek, and his rest shall be glorious" (Isa. 11:10). The theme of this blessed chapter is the ministry of the Lord Jesus, and the infinitely and eternally glorious and delightful effects thereof. Its details are to be understood in accord with its main drift, so that its metaphors and similes are to be taken in their proper and figurative sense. To take them literally would be like taking the Levitical priesthood for the priesthood of Christ, whereas the former was only intended to represent the latter. It would be like taking the earthly Canaan for that inheritance which is incorruptible, undefiled, and that fadeth not away. As its contents have been so grievously corrupted, we offer a few remarks thereon.

"And there shall come forth a rod out of the stem of Jesse, and a Branch shall grow out of his roots" (v. 1). Thus the opening words of the chapter indicate clearly enough that its language is not to be taken literally. The rod is the symbol of the rule and governing power of Christ, as in "The Lord shall send the rod of thy strength out of Zion: rule thou in the midst of thine enemies" (Ps. 110:2). "And a Branch shall grow out of his roots" signifies Christ's fruitfulness (cf. John 15:2), which fruitfulness is the result of the Spirit's being given to Him without measure (vv. 2, 3). Next follows in verses 4, 5 a description of Christ's ministry and the principles which regulated it—righteousness, equity, and faithfulness. Then we have a figurative description of the effects of His ministry in the conversion of sinners. They to whom the ministry of Christ is sent—that is, those to whom the gospel comes in its saving power—are here likened to the beasts of the field.

We are so distorted and degraded by the Fall that we are fitly compared to wild beasts and creeping things (vv. 6-8). Yet these were to undergo such a transformation that God declares, "They shall not hurt nor destroy in all my holy mountain" (v. 9). The whole of this is to be understood spiritually. A mountain is a local elevation of the land, and to be on a mountain is to be raised and exalted. So conversion brings us to a state of elevation before God, conducting us from our low and depraved state by nature and elevating us into the holiness we have in Christ. Observe that this mountain is called "my holy mountain," being the same as that described in "the Lord bless thee, O habitation of justice, and mountain of holiness" (Jer. 31:23): called the "habitation of justice" because the Mediator is there, a "mountain of holiness" because He has made an end of all our sins.

But let it not be supposed that believers only reach this "holy mountain" when they arrive at heaven. No, they are brought there experimentally in this life, or they will never reach heaven in the next; for it is written "Ye *are* come unto mount Zion" (Heb. 12:22). And who is it that are come thither? Those who by nature are likened by the prophet to wolves and lambs, leopards and kids. In Acts 10 they are likened to "all manner of fourfooted beasts of the earth, and wild beasts, and creeping things, and fowls of the air" (v. 12), which makes it unmistakably clear that the language used by Isaiah is to be understood spiritually and not literally, as the dispensationalists vainly dream. Let us use the terms of Peter's vision to interpret the figures of Isaiah 11, noting the fourfold classification.

The "fourfooted beasts of the earth," that is, sheep and oxen, are distinguished from the "wild beasts." There is a difference between men, not in nature but in outward conduct—the consequence of disposition, civilization, or religious upbringing: some being more refined, moral, and conscientious than others. "That our sheep may bring forth thousands and ten thousands in our streets" (Ps. 144:13) refers to this first class; and was it not actually the case in the time of the apostles when thousands were converted (Acts 4:4). A solemn portrayal of the "wild beasts" is found in Psalm 22, where the suffering Savior exclaims, "Many bulls have compassed me: strong bulls of Bashan have beset me round. They gaped upon me with their mouths, as a ravening and roaring lion" (vv. 12, 13). Was not Saul of Tarsus one of these wild bulls and ravening lions (see Acts 9:1; 22:4); and yet *grace tamed him.*

In Micah 7 we have a beautiful description of the third class, or "creeping things." "The nations [Gentiles] shall see and be confounded at all their might" (v. 16). Yes, when grace works it humbles, so that we are ashamed at what we once boasted of as our righteousness, and confounded at our former self-sufficiency. "They shall lay their hand upon their mouth," having no longer anything to say in self-vindication. "Their ears shall be deaf" to anything Satan says against the gospel. "They shall lick the dust like a serpent," humbling themselves beneath the mighty hand of God. "They shall move out of their holes like worms of the earth"—margin, like "creeping things"! Yes, the gospel unearths us, making us to set our affection on things above. "They shall be afraid of the Lord our God, and shall fear because of thee"—when His holy law is applied to their hearts. And what is the effect produced? Hear their blessed testimony: "Who is a God like unto thee, that pardoneth iniquity, and passeth by the transgression of the remnant of his heritage" (Micah 7:18).

And what of the fourth class, the "fowls of the air"? Do we not see them beautifully portrayed in Ezekiel 17? The "cedar" was the tribe of Judah, and "the highest branch of it" (v. 2) was the royal house of David. The "tender branch" in verse 22 is Christ (cf. Isa. 53:2), of whom it was promised, "In the mountain of the height of Israel will I plant it: and it shall bring forth boughs and bear fruit, and be a goodly cedar; and under it shall dwell all fowl of every wing; in the shadow of the branches thereof shall they dwell" (v. 23). But let us now notice, though it must be very briefly, the blessed transformation which is wrought when these creatures, so intractable by nature, are converted unto God.

"The wolf also shall dwell with the lamb, and the leopard shall lie down with the kid, and the calf and the young lion and the fatling together; and a little child shall lead them" (Isa. 11:6). How wondrous the grace which brings the wolfish rebel into the mildness and meekness of the lamb! How mighty the power that changes the ferocity of the lion so that a child may lead it! Their enmity against God and His truth is subdued, and they are brought down to the feet of Christ. The more they grow in grace, the lower estimation they have of themselves. "And the cow and the bear shall feed; their young ones shall lie down together; and the lion shall eat straw like the ox" (v. 7). The lion passes from the carnivorous to the graminivorous: take that literally and it amounts to little, understand it spiritually and it signifies a great deal—when born again we can no longer find satisfaction in creature things, but long for heavenly food. "And the sucking child shall play on the hole of the asp, and the weaned child shall put his hand on the cockatrice's den" (v. 8); this is victory over the enemy (cf. Ps. 91:13, 14; Luke 10:19).

"They shall not hurt nor destroy in all my holy mountain" (v. 9). Here is the perfect safety of the Lord's people. Comparing again Psalm 144, the 13th verse of which we quoted above, what immediately follows? This, "that our oxen may be strong to labour: that there be no breaking in, nor going out" (v. 14). They are absolutely safe in this mystic fold: none of Christ's sheep shall perish. And what is it that ensures their safety in God's holy mountain? This, "for the earth shall be full of the knowledge of the Lord, as the waters cover the sea" (v. 9)—not the material globe, but the spiritual "earth," the church. "All thy children shall be taught of the Lord" (Isa. 54:13). It is the new covenant "earth" or family: "For all shall know me, from the least to the greatest" (Heb. 8:11). "And in that day there shall be a root of Jesse, which shall stand for an ensign of the people; to it shall the Gentiles seek: and his rest shall be glorious" (v. 10). And thus we have completed the circle—it is the antitypical David whose banner waves over the whole election of grace.

IX

"And I will make an everlasting covenant with you, even the sure mercies of David" (Isa. 55:3). "As we had much of Christ in the 53rd chapter and much of the Church of Christ in the 54th, so in this chapter we have much of the covenant of grace made with us in Christ" (Matthew Henry). The chapter opens with a gracious invitation, for those who felt their need of them, to partake of spiritual blessings. The prophet seems to personate the apostles as they went forth in the name of the Lord calling His elect unto the marriage supper. Then he expostulates with those who were laboring for that which satisfied not, bidding them hearken unto God, and assuring them that He would then place Himself under covenant bonds and bestow upon them rich blessings.

The "sure mercies of David" were the things promised to the antitypical David in Psalm 89:28, 29, and so forth. That it is not the typical David or son of Jesse who is here intended is clear from various considerations. First, the natural David had died centuries before. Second, *this* David whose mercies are sure was yet to come when the prophet wrote, as is plain from verses 4, 5. Third, none but the Messiah, the Lord Jesus, answers to what is here predicated. Finally, all room for uncertainty is completely removed by the apostle's quotation of these very words in "And as concerning that he raised him up from the dead, now no more to return to corruption, he said on this wise, I will give you the sure mercies of David" (Acts 13:34). Thus "the sure mercies" of the true David signified God would raise Him from the dead unto everlasting life.

These "sure mercies" are extended by Isaiah unto all the faithful as the blessings of the covenant, and therefore may be understood to denote all saving benefits bestowed on believers in this life or that to come. This need occasion no difficulty whatever. Those "mercies" were Christ's by the Father's promise and by His own purchase, and at His resurrection they became His in actual possession, being all laid up in Him (II Cor. 1:20); and from Him we receive them (John 1:16; 16:14-16). The promises descend through Christ to those who believe, and thus are "sure" to all the seed (Rom. 4:16). It was the covenant which provided a firm foundation of mercy unto the Redeemer's family, and none of its blessings can be recalled (Rom. 11:32).

Those "sure mercies" God swore to bestow upon the spiritual seed or family of David (II Sam. 7:15, 16; Ps. 89:2, 29, 30), and they were made good in the appearing of Christ and the establishing of His kingdom on His resurrection, as Acts 13:34 so clearly shows, for His coming forth from the grave was the necessary step unto His assump-

The Davidic Covenant 251

tion of sovereign power. God not only said, "Behold, I have given him for a witness to the people," but also a "leader and commander to the people" (v. 4). As the "witness" Christ is seen in Revelation 1:5 and 3:14, and again in John 18 where He declared to Pilate, "My kingdom is not of this world, else would my servants fight" (v. 36). It is not based on the use of arms as was David's, but on the force of truth (see v. 37).

Christ became "commander" at His resurrection (Matt. 28:19); as the apostles expressly announced, "Him hath God exalted with his right hand to be a Prince and a Saviour" (Acts 5:31). It is the wielding of His royal scepter which guarantees unto His people the good of all the promises God made unto Him—"the sure mercies of David." "Behold, thou [it is God speaking to the antitypical David, designated in verse 4 "witness" and "commander"] shalt [showing this was yet future in Isaiah's time] call a nation whom thou knowest not," which is referred to in "The kingdom of God shall be taken from you, and given to a nation bringing forth the fruits thereof" (Matt. 21:43)—the "holy nation" of I Peter 2:9. "And nations that know not thee shall run unto thee" (v. 5), which manifestly has reference to the present calling of the Gentiles.

"I will set up one shepherd over them, and he shall feed them, even my servant David: he shall feed them, and he shall be their shepherd" (Ezek. 34:23). This is Jewish language with a Christian meaning. The reference here, as also in Psalm 89:3, Jeremiah 30:9, and Hosea 3:5, is to the antitypical David. "David is in the prophets often put for Christ in whom all the promises made unto David are fulfilled" (Lowth). A threefold reason may be suggested why Christ is thus called David. First, because He is the man after God's own heart—His "Beloved" which is what "David" signifies. Second, because David, particularly in his kingship, so manifestly foreshadowed Him. Third, because Christ is the root and offspring of David, the one in whom David's horn and throne is perpetuated forever.

"The book of the generation of Jesus Christ, the son of David, the son of Abraham" (Matt. 1:1). These words are to be understood not only as an introduction to the Gospel of Matthew, but rather as the divine summary of the whole of the New Testament. The Redeemer is here presented in His official and sacrificial characters: the true Solomon, the true Isaac. Inasmuch as the beloved Son of God willingly submitted to the altar, and being now risen from the dead, He is seated upon the throne. It was to Him as the Son of David that the poor Canaanitish woman appealed. Dispensationalists tell us she was not answered at first because she, being a Gentile, had no claim upon Him in *that* character—as though our compassionate Lord would be (as another has expressed it) "a stickler for ceremonial, for court etiquette!" The fact is that she evidenced a faith in the grace associated with that title which was sadly lacking in the Jews, for one of the things specially connected with Solomon was *his grace to the Gentiles.*

"Behold, thou shalt conceive in thy womb, and bring forth a son, and shalt call his name Jesus. He shall be great, and shall be called the Son of the Highest; and the Lord God shall give unto him the throne of his father David: and he shall reign over the house of Jacob forever, and of his kingdom there shall be no end" (Luke 1:31-33). First, let it be duly noted that this is recorded by Luke, the essentially *Gentile* Gospel. Second, herein it was expressly announced that Christ should reign "forever," and not merely for a thousand years; and that of His kingdom "there should be no end," instead of terminating at the close of "the millennium." Third, the prophecy of verse 32 has already been fulfilled, and that of verse 33 is now in course of fulfillment. Christ is already upon the throne of David and is now reigning over the spiritual house of Jacob. Clear proof of this is furnished in Acts 2, to which we now turn.

The argument used by Peter in his Pentecostal sermon is easily followed, and its conclusions are decisive. The central purpose of that sermon was to furnish proof that Jesus of Nazareth, whom the Jews had wickedly crucified, was the promised Messiah and Savior. We cannot now analyze the whole of Peter's inspired address, but confine ourselves to that portion which is pertinent to our present subject. In verse 24 declaration is made that God had loosed Jesus from the pains of death. Then follows a quotation from Psalm 16. Upon that quotation the apostle made some comments. First, David was not there referring to himself (v. 29). Second, it was a Messianic prediction, for God having made known that his seed should sit upon his throne, David wrote his psalms accordingly (i.e., with an eye to the Messiah); and therefore Psalm 16 must be understood as referring to Christ Himself (vv. 30, 31); the apostles themselves being eyewitnesses of the fact that God had raised up Christ (v. 32).

In Acts 2:33-36 the apostle made application of his discourse. First, he showed that what he had just set forth explained the wondrous effusion of the Holy Spirit in the extraordinary gifts He had bestowed upon the Twelve. In verse 12 the people had asked "What meaneth this?"—the apostles speaking in tongues. Peter answers that this Jesus having been exalted to the right hand of the Majesty on high, and having received the promised Spirit from the Father, had now "shed forth" that which they both saw and heard (v. 33). Second, this was self-evident, for David had not ascended into heaven, but his Son and

Lord had, as he himself foretold in Psalm 110:1 (vv. 34, 35). Third, therefore this proved what we are all bound to believe, namely, that Jesus of Nazareth is the true Messiah and Savior of sinners, for God hath made Him "both Lord and Christ" (v. 36).

It is with verse 30 of Acts 2 we are here more especially concerned: that God swore to David that Christ should sit on *his* throne. Let us consider the negative side first: there is not a hint or a word in Peter's comments that Christ would ascend David's throne in the future, and when in verse 34 he quoted Psalm 110:1 in fulfillment of Christ's ascension—"The Lord said unto my Lord, sit thou at my right hand"— he did not add "until thou assume the throne of David," but "until I make thy foes thy footstool"! Coming now to the positive side, we have seen that the scope of the apostle's argument was to show that Jesus of Nazareth was the promised Messiah, and that He was risen from the dead, had ascended to heaven, and we now add, was seated upon David's throne.

That which clinches the last-made statement is the "therefore" of verse 36. The apostle there draws a conclusion, and unless his logic was faulty (which it would be blasphemy to affirm), then it must cohere with his premise, namely, Christ's present possession of the throne of David in fulfillment of the oath God had sworn to the patriarch. For the purpose of clarity we paraphrase: the premise was that Christ should sit on David's throne (v. 30): the conclusion is that God hath made Jesus "both Lord and Christ" (v. 36). None but those whose eyes are closed by prejudice can fail to see that in such a connection, being "made Lord and Christ" can mean nothing else than that He is now seated on David's throne. Peter's hearers could come to no other possible conclusion than that God's promise to the patriarch, re the occupancy of his throne, had now received its fulfillment.

Nor does the above passage stand alone. If the reader will carefully consult Acts 4:26, 27 it will be found that the apostles were addressing God, and that they quoted the opening verses of Psalm 2, which spoke of those who were in governmental authority combining together against Jehovah and His Christ, which the apostles (by inspiration) applied to what had recently been done to the Redeemer (v. 27). They referred to the Savior thus: "For of a truth against thy holy child [or "servant"] Jesus, whom thou hast anointed" (v. 27). Now in such a connection the mention of Jesus as the one whom God had anointed could only mean what is more fully expressed in Psalm 2, "my anointed *king*"—"yet have I anointed [see margin] my king upon my holy hill of Zion" (Ps. 2:6). Otherwise the application of Psalm 2 to the crucifixion had been fitted only to mislead.

"In that day will I raise up the tabernacle of David that is fallen"

(Amos 9:11). This is another old covenant promise possessing a new covenant significance, as will appear by the inspired interpretation of it in Acts 15. Let us first notice its time-mark: "in that day." The immediate context explains this: it was to be the day when "the sinful kingdom" of Israel would be destroyed by God "from off the face of the earth" (v. 8, saving that He would not utterly destroy the house of Jacob—the godly remnant), when He would "sift the house of Israel among all nations" (v. 9), when "all the sinners of his people should die by the sword" (v. 10). What follows in verses 11, 12 predicted the establishment of Messiah's kingdom. Second, let us now observe its citation in Acts 15.

In verses 7-11 Peter spoke of the grace of God having been extended to the Gentiles, and in verse 12 Paul and Barnabas bore witness to the same fact. Then in verses 13:21 James confirmed what they said by a reference to the Old Testament. "And to this [i.e., the saving of a people from the Gentiles and adding them to the saved of Israel: see vv. 8, 9, 11] agree the word of the prophets" (Acts 15:14). Yes, for the promised kingdom of the Messiah, in the Old Testament, was not placed in opposition to the theocracy, but as a continuation and enlargement of it. See II Samuel 7:12 and Isaiah 9:6, where it was said that the Prince of peace should sit on David's throne and prolong His kingdom forever; while in Genesis 49:10 it was announced that the Redeemer should spring from Judah and be the enlarger of his dominion.

Then James quoted Amos: "After this I will return, and will build again the tabernacle of David, which is fallen down; and I will build again the ruins thereof, and I will set it up: that the residue of men might seek after the Lord, and all the Gentiles upon whom my name is called" (Acts 17). The "tabernacle of David" was but another name for God's earthly kingdom (note how in I Kings 2:12 we read, "Then sat Solomon upon the throne of David his father," while in I Chronicles 29:23 it is said, "Then Solomon sat on the throne of the Lord"), for during the last thousand years of Old Testament history His kingdom on earth was inseparably identified with David's throne. But now the shadow has been displaced by the substance, and it is the "tabernacle" of the antitypical David. The church militant is aptly designated a "tabernacle" in allusion to the tabernacle in the wilderness, for it is (as that was) God's habitation, the place where the divine testimony is preserved, and where He is worshipped.

The setting up of the kingdom of Christ was designated a raising of the fallen tabernacle of David, first, because Christ Himself was the Seed of David, the one through whom the promises of II Samuel 7 were to be made good. Second, because He is the antitypical and true

David: as the natural David restored the theocracy by delivering it from its enemies (the Philistines, etc.) and established it on a firm and successful basis, so Christ delivers the kingdom of God from its enemies and establishes it on a sure and abiding foundation. Third, because Christ's kingdom and church is the continuance and consummation of the Old Testament theocracy—New Testament saints are added to the Old (Eph. 2:11-15; 3:6; Heb. 11:40). Thus the prophecy of Amos received its fulfillment, first, in the raising up of Christ (at His incarnation) out of the ruins of Judah's royal house; second, when (at His ascension) God gave unto Christ the antitypical throne of David—the mediatorial throne; third, when (under the preaching of the gospel) the kingdom of Christ was greatly enlarged by the calling of the Gentiles. Thus Acts 15:14-17 furnished us with a sure key to the interpretation of Old Testament prophecy, showing us it is to be understood in its spiritual and mystical sense.

"And again Isaiah saith, There shall be the Root of Jesse, and he that ariseth [Greek in the present tense] to rule [reign] over the Gentiles: on him shall the Gentiles hope" (Rom. 15:12, RV). This was quoted here by the apostle for the express purpose of demonstrating that the true David was the Savior of and King over the Gentiles. If the Davidic reign or kingdom of Christ were yet future, this quotation would be quite irrelevant and no proof at all. In verse 7 the apostle had exhorted unto unity between the Hebrew and Gentile saints at Rome. In verse 8 and 9 he declared that Christ became incarnate in order to unite both believing Jews and Gentiles into one body. Then in verses 9-12 he quotes four Old Testament passages in proof— multiplying texts because this was a point on which the Jews were so prejudiced.

"These things saith he that is holy, he that is true, he that hath the key of David, he that openeth and no man shutteth, and shutteth and no man openeth" (Rev. 3:7). This need not detain us long, for the meaning of these words is obvious. In Scripture the key is the well-known symbol of authority, and the key of David signifies that Christ is vested with royal dignity and power. To one of those who foreshadowed Christ, God said, "I will commit thy *government* into his hand, and he shall be a father to the inhabitants of Jerusalem, and to the house of Judah. And the *key* of the house of David will I lay upon his shoulder; he shall open, and none shall shut; and he shall shut, and none shall open" (Isa. 22:21, 22). Note well, dear reader, that Revelation 3:7 was spoken by Christ to a Christian church, and not to the Jews! The use of the present tense utterly repudiates the ideas of those who insist that Christ's entering upon His Davidic or royal rights is yet future.

"Behold, the Lion of the tribe of Judah, the Root of David, hath prevailed to open the book" (Rev. 5:5). We cannot now enter into a detailed examination of the blessed scene presented in Revelation 5, but must content ourselves with the briefest possible summary. First, we take it that the sealed book is the title deeds to the earth, lost by the first Adam (cf. Jer. 36:6-15). Second, Christ as the Lion of Judah "prevailed" to open it: He secured the right to do so by His conquering of sin, Satan, and death. Third, it is as the "Lamb" He takes the book (vv. 6, 7), for as such He redeemed the purchased possession. Fourth, He is here seen "in the midst of the throne," showing He is now endowed with royal authority. There is no hint in the chapter that its contents respect the future, and therefore we regard the vision as a portrayal of God's placing His King upon the hill (mountain) of His holiness, and giving to Him the uttermost parts of the earth for His possession. Christ's throne is a heavenly and spiritual one: "Even so might grace reign through righteousness unto eternal life by Jesus Christ our Lord" (Rom. 5:21).

PART SEVEN

The Messianic Covenant

I

We have designated this final covenant "the Messianic" rather than "the Christian" or "the New" covenant, partly for the sake of alliteration and partly for the sake of emphasis. Before we consider its special nature and contents, we must first bridge the interval that elapsed between the making of the Davidic covenant and the commencement of the Christian era—an interval of approximately one thousand years. From the times of David a special feature gradually became more prominent in the history of the covenant people. The gift of prophecy, enjoyed by the psalmist, was now more widely diffused than it had been previously, and was conferred in greater fullness and upon a larger number of individuals, who in succession were raised up and in different degrees exercised a most important influence upon the nation of Israel.

This gift of prophecy was by no means a new one. Moses possessed it in a large measure, yet under conditions which separated him from all who followed up to the coming of Christ. With him God spake "mouth to mouth, even apparently, and not in dark speeches, and the similitude of the Lord did he behold" (Num. 12:8). In this respect he was an eminent type of Him that was to come, on whom the prophetic influence rested in unlimited measure: of this God, through Moses, gave intimation when He said, "I will raise them up a prophet from among their brethren, like unto thee, and will put my words in his mouth; and he shall speak unto them all that I shall command him. And it shall come to pass, that whosoever will not hearken unto my words, which he shall speak in my name, I will require it of him" (Deut. 18:18, 19). To others, during the life of Moses, the gift was communicated, if only for a season. The most striking case was that of

259

Balaam, a worthless character, who, against his own intentions, was constrained to pronounce blessings on Israel.

In the period that followed we find traces of its bestowment, though only occasionally, and after considerable intervals, until the last of the judges. That eminent person, Samuel, was not only a prophet himself, but on him was conferred the honor of founding schools for young men for the prophetic office. The object of those institutions, so far as we can gather, seems to have been to impart a knowledge of the law to men suitably endowed, fitting them to teach and influence the nation. From what little is recorded of them, we may conclude that those sons of the prophets enjoyed, as circumstances required, special assistance from God in the work to which they were devoted. On David, however, the gift was conferred in unusual measure, the fruit of which appears in his inspired psalms. Several of his contemporaries were similarly endowed. From this period the prophetic element, with some brief intervals, became more prominent and influential in Israel, increasing in the copiousness of its communications till the depression of the house of David during the captivity.

The peculiar work of the prophet has not always been correctly understood. That element in some of them which had respect to the foretelling of future events has attracted undue attention and been magnified out of all proper proportions. This may be accounted for from its striking uniqueness, and the use to which it has been put as an important department of Christian evidence—drawing from it an invincible argument for the divine inspiration of Scripture. Yet this concentration upon the predictive aspect of prophecy has served to create a widespread misconception concerning the nature of the gift itself and the chief design in its exercise. The main purpose of the prophetic office has almost been lost sight of. By many today it is unknown that its leading object contemplated the practical spiritual interests of the people: that the prophets were principally employed in imparting instruction to them, exposing their sins, calling them to repent, setting before them the paths of duty, and in various ways seeking to promote their religious improvement.

Prediction, in the strict sense of the term, occupies a very inconspicuous place in the ministry of Moses, the chief of all the prophets. Some of the more prominent among them—as Samuel, Elijah, and Elisha—seem hardly to have uttered any predictions at all. Their business consisted mainly in denouncing the idolatrous practices of the people and in vindicating the claims of God to their homage and service. It is true that in the writings of two or three, predictions largely abound; nevertheless, if they are examined with care it will quickly be seen that their ministry had largely to do with the existing spiritual conditions of those among whom they labored. Take for example Isaiah, who of all the prophets was perhaps most honored with revelations of the future. A cursory investigation will show that foretelling constituted only one portion of the message he delivered. The true idea of the prophet is that of a man raised up to witness for God, His mouthpiece to the people—to rebuke sin, counsel in perplexity, and instruct them in the ways of the Lord.

Even the positive predictions delivered by the prophets, while contemplating the benefit of future generations (by which alone, on their fulfillment they could be fully understood), were subservient to the immediate purposes of their ministry, by affording encouragement and hope unto those who feared God amidst the general disorders and declension of the times in which they lived. This plain view of the case, which numerous and obvious facts support, must be understood in order to gain a correct conception of the prophetical Scriptures in their general structure. On the subject of the covenants, the predictive portions of their writings, as would naturally be expected, have the more direct bearing; yet the practical parts, which deal with the sins and duties of the people, make their own contribution—the practical sections furnishing many striking illustrations of the previous revelations and giving definiteness to the meaning of many particulars embraced in the covenants.

The didactic and the practical are often strangely mingled. Statements which at first bear on present duty, sometimes insensibly, and at other times more abruptly, pass into representations of the future which startle us, not less by the suddenness of their introduction, than by the vividness of their coloring. All, however, is made strictly subservient to the immediate purpose which the prophets had in view. The intimate blending of these different elements makes it far from easy to separate them in all instances, nor is is necessary to attempt it. As they now stand, they more effectually promoted the end in view in the spiritual improvement of the people. The glowing prospects of the future either supplied an incentive to the discharge of present duty, or ministered to their support under present trial. Still, to the predictions, strictly so called, we must look as the chief means of furnishing the fullest light on the prospective covenant transactions of God with His people.

The nature and extent of the help we shall derive from these intimations of the future will turn, to a large extent, on the mode in which we deal with them. The interpretation of prophecy, in all its principles and results, is a large subject, but a few words are called for here so as to prevent misconception. A slight examination of the

The Divine Covenants

prophetical Scriptures is enough to show that their language is not unfrequently taken—leaving out of consideration the figures which natural scenery supply—either from past events in the history of Israel or from the sacred institutions and arrangements with which they had long been familiar. And of course this is quite natural when we bear in mind the typical character impressed on the Old Testament dispensation throughout; yea, probably it was necessary as the best means of imparting to the Jewish people an intelligible representation of the future.

The creation of an entirely new nomenclature in literal adaptation to the better things to come, instead of being understood, would only have occasioned perplexity and defeated the object for which the revelation was given. Be this as it may, the fact is certain that in terms peculiar to the theocracy, or descriptive of theocratic events, the revelation of future things was made. In other words, the language of the type is familiarly employed in delineation of the antitype. Thus, for example, "Israel" is the term used in reference to the spiritual seed; "visions and dreams" (the current mode of the divine communications in those times) describe the future operations of the Holy Spirit under the gospel dispensation; "David," in like manner, is the name applied again and again to the Messiah, the true Shepherd of Israel; and the events of the future are represented in terms derived from the dispensation then existing. Occasionally express statements are made affirming that the order of things then in being was destined to pass away—as in Jeremiah 3:16; at other times the change impending was as plainly implied.

On this principle, then, these predictions are constructed almost throughout, and on no other can they be correctly interpreted. It was thus that the apostles dealt with them, yet it is sadly overlooked by many of our moderns. A slavish adherence to a literal interpretation—which is the survival of a Jewish error—if consistently carried out, necessarily leads to consequences which few are prepared to face, opposed as they are to both the letter and the spirit of the gospel. It is certainly a humiliating proof of human infirmity, even in good men, that at this late date, the principle on which so large a part of the Word is to be interpreted has yet to be settled, and that from the same prophetical statements the most diverse conclusions are derived. Surely it should be apparent that since the literal cannot be fairly applied without eliciting conclusions contradicting apostolic testimony, we are bound to abide by the typical and figurative as the only safe principle.

There is one other misconception against which we must guard. It must not be concluded that because the Messianic predictions are for the most part plain to us, acquainted as we are with the events in which they found their fulfillment, that therefore they must have been equally plain unto those to whom they were first delivered, but from whose times these events were far distant. In dealing with those Scriptures for our own edification, it is our privilege to take advantage of all the light furnished by the New Testament, but in so doing we must not forget that our position is vastly different from that of those amongst whom the prophets exercised their ministry. Take, for instance, the predictions respecting the Messiah—the great subject of the covenant promises. Consider the many references to His lowly condition, His sufferings and death, and then to the triumphant strain in which His exaltation and glory are so largely· set forth. Some passages represent Him as a man amongst His fellowmen; others as the mighty God. How perplexing must those representations—apparently so much at variance with each other—have been to the Jews!

Keeping these things in mind, we may now observe that the ministry of the prophets, commencing with David, and, after a break, continuing from Joel onwards, was of considerable value in filling up the truth which, in brief outline, the covenants exhibited, yet leaving much to be still supplied by the actual fulfillment of the promises they contained. No one contributed more to this result than Isaiah. On the one hand, he furnishes the most vivid portrayals of the treatment which the Messiah would receive from His countrymen, and of the nature and severity of the sufferings He was to endure, both at the hands of God and of men, in the accomplishment of His work. On the other hand, he supplies the most blessed testimony to the essential dignity of His person, and the most animating assurances of the extent and glory of His kingdom; and, under highly figurative language, describes the beneficent and peaceful effects of His government and the spiritual results of His reign.

With few exceptions, the rest of the prophets corroborated and supplemented the testimony of Isaiah. The person and work of the Messiah are represented from various angles, the stupenduous results of His undertaking depicted under striking imagery, and divine wisdom is clearly evidenced in the phraseology—derived from the religious institutions of the Jews or from events of their history—which is employed to give vividness to their representations. The effects of this must have been to impart to the mass of the people a new and deeper realization of the magnitude of the results involved in the covenants under which they were placed, however perverted their views of the nature of these results may have been; and to awaken in the godly remnant of them expectations of a future immensely surpassing anything yet realized in their history—a future with which, in some mysterious way, their own spiritual life was bound up.

As the earthly prospects of Israel became darker, through the growing corruption of the nation, hastening toward that catastrophe which destroyed their temple, and for a time removed them as captives into a strange land, those prophets who then exercised their ministry were far more explicit in regard to the nature of the great alteration which the appearing of the Messiah would produce and of the blessings which He would dispense. In their hands the future assumed a more precise shape, and the expectations warranted by their language exhibited an expansion far in advance of anything to be found in Scripture. This was just what the circumstances of the time required. One can readily conceive the despondency with which the pious Jews must have looked on the course which events were taking. The idolatrous propensities of the masses, the general immorality which was encouraged by idol worship, the common contempt with which God's servants were treated, the wickedness of their kings, and the frequent invasion of their land by hostile forces, all presaged the dissolution of their state.

When assured that the divine patience was at last exhausted, that the infliction of the oft-threatened punishment was nigh at hand, and that the triumph of their enemies was certain, at what conclusion could they arrive than that for their sins they were forsaken of God, that the covenant was about to be made void, and that all their hopes would soon be buried in the ruin of their country? They might not unreasonably have supposed that the stability of the covenant was dependent upon their obedience, and since that obedience had been withheld, and all the gracious measures taken to reclaim them had failed—since, in the review of their past history, no lesson was so impressively taught as their incurable tendency to sin—they might have concluded that God was absolved from His promise, and that even His righteousness demanded the people should be cut off and left to the ruin which they had so persistently courted, the near approach of which everything seemed to indicate.

Such a despondent condition required special encouragement, and the form which that encouragement assumed deserves particular attention. It consisted in the assurance of a thorough change in the dispensation under which Israel had hitherto been placed, and of the establishment of a new covenant under the immediate administration of the Messiah, the purely spiritual character of which is described in language far more explicit than had hitherto been given. This more glorious constitution of things they were taught was the designed issue of all God's dealings toward them, and to it their hopes were henceforth to be confined. Notwithstanding their present calamities, the continuance of their national existence was assured to them until in due time the new order of things was inaugurated. Could anything be conceived better fitted to kindle the hopes and communicate the richest consolation to the devout portion of the Jews than such an assurance?

II

In the preceding chapter it was pointed out that, following the times of David, the prophets occupied a more and more prominent place in Israel, and that the primary purpose of their office was a practical one, designed for the good of those to whom they immediately ministered. As the spiritual life of the nation degenerated, the voice of the prophets was heard more frequently—pressing the claims of God, rebuking the people for their sins, and affording comfort to the faithful. It was this third item that we enlarged upon in the closing paragraphs of our last chapter, calling particular attention to the large place given in the communications of the "major" prophets unto things to come. Where sin abounded, grace did much more abound; for as things went from bad to worse in the earthly kingdom of Israel, God was pleased to grant much fuller revelations concerning the heavenly kingdom of the Messiah.

What has just been pointed out reveals a principle which is of great practical value for our own souls today. The further Israel's religious apostasy advanced and wickedness increased, the more were the godly handful among them taught to look away from the present to the future, to walk by faith and not by sight, to regale their desponding hearts with those covenant blessings which the Messiah would obtain for all His people. It is not necessary to suppose that they fully understood the import of what the prophets set before them; yea, they were far from comprehending the entire truth which they contained. Nevertheless, they must have gathered sufficient from them to relieve their minds from that distressing anxiety which their present circumstances had awakened. Those predictions which more particularly dealt with the new order of things which God promised should yet be ushered in, supply the real key to the interpretation of the numerous predictions regarding the Messiah's work with which they had long been familiar.

Here, then, is the grand lesson for us to heed. Though the present state of Christendom be so deplorable and saddening; though the enemy has come in like a flood, threatening to carry everything before him; though the voice of the true servant of God be no more heeded today than was the prophets' before the captivity, yet God still has a remnant of His people upon the earth. Heavy indeed are their hearts at the dishonor done to the name of their Lord, at the low state of His cause on earth, at their own spiritual leanness. Yet, while it is meet they should sigh and cry for the abominations in the churches, deplore the wickedness abounding in the world, and penitently confess their own sad failures, nevertheless it is their privilege to look forward unto the grand future which lies before them, to the sure accomplishment of all God's covenant promises. Nor is it necessary that they should understand the order of coming events, or the details of unfulfilled prophecy: sufficient for them that Christ will yet see of the travail of His soul and be satisfied, reign till every enemy be placed under His feet, and come again to receive His people unto Himself.

Both the prophets Jeremiah and Ezekiel, who exercised their ministry about the same time among different portions of the covenant people, spoke the same language and gave the same assurances, in close connection with the promise of their future reestablishment in their own land. That particular promise was partly accomplished in their return from Babylon, but is fully understood only when viewed in the light of the *typical* import of the language used. The grand statement found in Jeremiah 31:31-34 is repeated with equal definiteness in chapter 32: "Behold, I will gather them out of all countries, whither I have driven them in mine anger, and in my fury, and in great wrath: and I will bring them again unto this place, and I will cause them to dwell safely, And they shall be my people, and I will be their God. And I will give them one heart, and one way, that they may fear me forever, for the good of them, and of their children after them. And I will make an everlasting covenant with them, that I will not turn away from them, to do them good; but I will put my fear in their hearts, that they shall not depart from me." So again in 33:14-16.

In a similar strain and in terms equally explicit, Ezekiel addresses that portion of the Jews amongst whom he exercised his ministry. "I will set up one shepherd over them, and he shall feed them, even my servant David: he shall feed them, and he shall be their shepherd. And I the Lord will be their God, and my servant David a prince amongst them: I the Lord have spoken it. And I will make with them a covenant of peace, and will cause the wild beasts to cease out of the land: and they shall dwell safely in the wilderness, and sleep in the woods. And I will make them and the places round about my hill a blessing; and I will cause the shower to come down in his season; there shall be showers of blessing" (34:23-26). And again: "Then will I sprinkle clean water upon you, and ye shall be clean: from all your filthiness and from all your idols will I cleanse you. A new heart also will I give you and a new spirit will I put within you . . . and cause you to walk in my statutes" (36:25-27).

But the clearest of all of these later communications by the prophets is that furnished in Jeremiah 31:31-34: "Behold, the days come, saith the Lord, that I will make a new covenant with the house of Israel, and with the house of Judah: Not according to the covenant that I made with their fathers, in the day that I took them by the hand to bring them out of the land of Egypt: which my covenant they brake, although I was a husband unto them, saith the Lord. But this shall be the covenant that I will make with the house of Israel: after those days, saith the Lord, I will put my law in their inward parts, and write it in their hearts; and will be their God, and they shall be my people. And they shall teach no more every man his neighbour, and every man his brother, saying, Know the Lord: for they shall all know me, from the least of them unto the greatest of them, saith the Lord: for I will forgive their iniquity, and I will remember their sin no more." On the two main points adverted to by us, namely, the *change* of the then existing dispensation, and the *spiritual* nature of that which was to succeed, its testimony is most decisive.

First, we must seek to remove a radical misconception which obtains in certain quarters as to the ones with whom God here promised to make this "new covenant," namely, "with the house of Israel and with the house of Judah." Modern dispensationalists insist that this says just what it means, and means just what it says; and with this I am in hearty accord. Nevertheless, we would point out that it is entirely a matter of *interpretation* if we are to rightly understand what *is* said; and this can only be accomplished as the Spirit Himself enlightens our minds. Any method of Bible study, or any system of interpretation (if such it could be called) that renders us self-sufficient, independent of the Holy Spirit, is self-condemned. An unregenerate man, by diligent application and the use of a good concordance, may soon familiarize himself with the letter of Scripture, and persuade himself that because he takes its letter at its face value, he has a good understanding of it; but that is a vastly different thing from a spiritual insight into spiritual things.

The first time the name "Israel" occurs upon the sacred page is in Genesis 32:28, where it was given to Jacob: "And he said, Thy name shall be called no more Jacob, but Israel: for as a prince hast thou power with God and with men, and hast prevailed." This is most suggestive and significant: it was not his name by nature, but by grace! In other words, "Israel" stamped Jacob as a regenerate man, thereby intimating that this name primarily pertains to the spiritual seed of

Abraham and not to his natural descendants. That this term "Israel" would henceforth possess this double significance (primary and secondary) was more than hinted at here in Genesis 32, for from this point onward the one to whom it was orginally given became the man with the double name: sometimes he is referred to as "Jacob," at other times he is designated "Israel," and this according as the flesh or the spirit was uppermost in him.

In what has just been before us there was most accurately anticipated the subsequent usage of the term, for while in many passages "Israel" has reference to the natural descendants through Jacob, in many others it is applied to his mystical seed. Take for example: "Truly God is good to Israel, even to such as are of a clean heart" (Ps. 73:1). Who are the ones referred to under the name "Israel" in this verse? Obviously it does not refer to the nation of Israel, to all the fleshly descendants of Jacob who were alive at the time Asaph wrote this psalm, for most certainly it could not be said of by far the greater part of them that they were "of a clean heart" (cf. Ps. 12:1). A clean heart is one which has been cleansed by the sanctifying operations of divine grace (Titus 3:5), by the sprinkling of the blood of Jesus on the conscience (Heb. 10:22), and by a God-communicated faith (Acts 15:9). Thus, the second clause of Psalm 73:1 obliges us to understand the Israel of the first clause as the spiritual Israel—God's chosen, redeemed, and regenerated people.

Again: when the Lord Jesus exclaimed concerning Nathanael, "Behold an Israelite indeed, in whom is no guile" (John 1:47), exactly what did He mean? Was nothing more signified than, "Behold a fleshly descendant of Jacob"? Assuredly it was this: Christ's language here was discriminating, as discriminating as when He said, "If ye continue in my word, then are ye my disciples indeed" (John 8:31). When the Savior declared that they were "disciples indeed," He intimated they were such not only in name, but in fact; not only by profession, but in reality. And in like manner, when He affirmed that Nathanael was "an Israelite indeed," He meant that he was a genuine son of Israel, a man of faith and prayer, honest and upright. The added description "in whom is no guile" supplies still further confirmation that a spiritual and saved character is there in view: compare "Blessed is the man unto whom the Lord imputeth not iniquity and in whose spirit there is no guile" (Ps. 32:2).

"Behold Israel after the flesh" (I Cor. 10:18). Here again discriminating language is used; why speak of "Israel after the flesh" unless it be for the express purpose of distinguishing them from Israel after the Spirit—that is, the regenerated and spiritual Israel. Israel "after the flesh" were the natural descendants of Abraham, but spiritual Israel, whether Jews or Gentiles, are those who are born again and who worship God in spirit and in truth. Surely it must now be plain to every unbiased reader that the term Israel is used in Scripture in more senses than one, and that it is only by noting the qualifying terms which are added, that we are able to identify which Israel is in view in any given passage. Equally clear should it be that to talk of Israel being an "earthly people" is very loose and misleading language, and badly needs modifying and defining.

Admittedly it is easier to determine which Israel is in view in some passages than in others—the natural or the spiritual; yet in the great majority of instances, the context furnishes a definite guide. When Christ said, "I am not sent but unto the lost sheep of the house of Israel" (Matt. 15:24), He certainly could not intend the fleshly descendants of Jacob; for, as many Scriptures plainly state, He was equally sent unto the Gentiles. No, "the lost sheep of the house of Israel" there means the whole election of grace. "Of this man's seed hath God, according to his promise, raised unto Israel a Saviour, Jesus" (Acts 13:23). Here too it is the spiritual Israel which is meant, for He did not save the nation at large. So too when the apostle declared, "For the hope of Israel I am bound with this chain" (Acts 28:20), he must have had in view the antitypical Israel. "And as many as walk according to this rule, peace be on them, and mercy, and upon the Israel of God" (Gal. 6:16). This could not possibly refer to the nation, for God's curse was on that. It is the Israel chosen by the Father, redeemed by the Son, regenerated by the Spirit.

"Not as though the word of God hath taken none effect. For they are not all Israel, which are of Israel" (Rom. 9:6). In this verse the apostle begins his discussion of the rejection of the Jews and the calling of the Gentiles, and shows that God had predetermined to cast off the nation as such and extend the gospel call to all men indiscriminately. He does this by showing God was free to act thus (vv. 6-24), that He had announced through His prophets He would do so (vv. 25-33). This was a particularly sore point with the Jew, who erroneously imagined that the promises which God had made to Abraham and his seed included all his natural descendants, that those promises were sealed unto all such by the rite of circumcision, and that those inherited all the patriarchal blessings: hence their claim, "*We* have Abraham to our father" (Matt. 3:9). It was to refute this error, common among the Jews (and now revived by the dispensationalists), that the apostle here writes.

First, he affirms that God's Word was not being annulled by his teaching (v. 6, first clause), no indeed; his doctrine did not contravene the divine promises, for they had never been given to men in the flesh, but rather to men in the spirit—regenerate. Second, he insisted upon an important distinction (v. 6, second clause), which we are now seeking to explain and press upon our readers. He points out there are two kinds of Israelites: those who are such only by carnal descent from Jacob, and others who are so spiritually, these latter being alone the "children of the promise" (v. 8) (cf. Galatians 4:23, where "born after the flesh" is opposed to born "by promise"). God's promises were made to Abraham, Isaac, and Jacob, as believers; and they are the spiritual food and property of none but believers (Rom. 4:13, 16). Until this fact be clearly grasped, we shall be all at sea in under-standing scores of the Old Testament promises.

When the apostle here affirms that "they are not all Israel, which are of Israel" (Rom. 9:6), he means that not all the lineal descendants of Jacob belonged unto "the Israel of God" (Gal. 6:16)—those who were God's people in the highest sense. So far from that being the case, many of the Jews were not God's children at all (see John 8:42, 44), while many who were Gentiles by nature, have (by grace) been made "fellow-citizens with the [Old Testament] saints" (Eph. 2:19) and "blessed *with* faithful Abraham" (Gal. 3:9). Thus the apostle's language in the second clause of Romans 9:6 has the force of: Not all who are members of the (ancient) visible church are members of the true church. The same thought is repeated in Romans 9:7, "Neither because they are the [natural] seed of Abraham, are they all children"—that is, the "children [or inheritors] of the promise," as verse 8 explains—but "in Isaac [the line of God's election and sovereign grace] shall thy [true and spiritual] seed be called." God's promises were made to the spiritual seed of Abraham, and not to his natural descendants as such.

This same principle of double application holds equally good of many other terms used of the covenant people. For example, Christ said to His spouse, "Thou art beautiful, O my love, as Tirzah, comely as Jerusalem, terrible as an army with banners" (Song of Sol. 6:4). Now the church goes under this name of "Jerusalem" in both the Old Testament and the New. "Speak ye comfortably to Jerusalem" (Isa. 40:2). Obviously this did not mean the literal city, nor even its inhabitants in general, for the great majority of them were unregener-ate idolaters, and God sends no message of comfort to those who despise and oppose Him. No, it was the godly remnant. "For this Agar is mount Sinai in Arabia, and answereth to Jerusalem which now is, and is in bondage with her children. But Jerusalem which is above is free, which is the mother of us all" (Gal. 4:25, 26). One of Christ's promises to the overcomer is "I will write upon him the name of my

God, and the name of the city of my God—new Jerusalem" (Rev. 3:12)!

III

In the second half of the last chapter it was shown that the name Israel has a twofold application, both in the Old Testament and in the New, being given to the natural descendants of Jacob and also to all believers. Nor should this in anywise surprise or stumble us, seeing that the one whom God first denominated "Israel" was henceforth the man with the double name, according as he was viewed naturally or spiritually. It should also be duly noted that God's giving this name unto Jacob is recorded twice in Genesis: "And he said, Thy name shall be called no more Jacob, but Israel: for as a prince hast thou power with God and with men, and hast prevailed" (32:28); "And God said unto him, Thy name is Jacob. thy name shall not be called any more Jacob, but Israel shall be thy name" (35:10). Is there not here something more than bare emphasis—namely, a divine intimation to us of the dual application or usage of the name?

This double significance of the word Israel holds good for other similar terms. For example, to the "seed of Abraham": "Know ye therefore that they which are of faith, the same are the children of Abraham" (Gal. 3:7). The "children of Abraham" are of two kinds, physical and spiritual, those who are his by nature and those who are connected with him by grace. "To be the children of a person in a figurative sense, is equivalent to 'resemble him, and to be involved in his fate, good or bad.' The idea is of similarity both in character and in circumstances. To be 'the children of God,' is to be like God; and also, as the apostle states, it is to be 'heirs of God.' To be 'the children of Abraham' is to resemble Abraham, to imitate his conduct, and to share his blessedness" (John Brown). To which we may add, to be "the children of the wicked one" (Matt. 13:38) is to be conformed to his vile image, both in character and in conduct (John 8:44), and to share his dreadful portion (Matt. 25:41).

The carnal Jews of Christ's day boasted that "Abraham is our father," to which He made answer, "If ye were Abraham's children, ye would do the works of Abraham" (John 8:39). Ah, the spiritual children of Abraham "walk in the steps of that faith" which he had

(Rom. 4:12). Those who are his spiritual children are "blessed with faithful Abraham" (Gal. 3:9). The apostle was there combating the error which the Judaizers were seeking to foist upon the Gentiles—namely, that none but Jews, or Gentiles proselyted by circumcision, were the "children of Abraham," and that none but those could be partakers of his blessing. But so far from that being the case, all unbelieving Jews shut heaven against themselves, while all who believed from the heart, being united to Christ—who is *the* son of Abraham" (Matt. 1:1)—enter into all the blessings which God covenanted unto Abraham.

The double significance pertaining to the expression "children" or "seed" of Abraham was very plainly intimated at the beginning, when Jehovah said unto the patriarch, "In blessing I will bless thee, and in multiplying I will multiply thy seed as the stars of the heavens, and as the sand which is upon the seashore" (Gen. 22:17). What anointed eye can fail to see in the likening of Abraham's seed unto the stars of heaven a reference to his spiritual children, who are partakers of the heavenly calling (Heb. 3:1); and in the likening of his seed unto the sand which is upon the seashore a reference to his natural descendants, who occupied the land of Palestine.

Again, the same is true of the word "Jew." "For he is not a Jew, which is one outwardly; neither is that circumcision which is outward in the flesh: But he is a Jew, which is one inwardly; and circumcision is that of the heart, in the spirit, and not in the letter; whose praise is not of men, but of God" (Rom. 2:28, 29). What could be plainer than that? In the light of such a Scripture, is it not passing strange that there are today those—boasting loudly of their orthodoxy and bitterly condemning all who differ—who insist that the name "Jew" belongs only to the natural descendants of Jacob, and ridicule the idea that there is any such thing as spiritual Jews. When the Holy Spirit here tells us "he is a Jew, who is one inwardly," He manifestly signifies that the true Jew, the antitypical Jew is a regenerate person, who enjoys the "praise" or approbation of God Himself.

Here, then, is the reply to the childish prattle of those who declare that "Israel" means *Israel,* and "Jew" means *Jew,* and that when Scripture speaks of "Jerusalem" or "Zion" nothing else is referred to than those actual places. But this is nothing more than a deceiving of ourselves by the mere sound of words: as well argue that "flesh" signifies nothing more than the physical body, that "water" (John 4:14) refers only to that material element, and that "death" (John 5:24) means naught but physical dissolution. There is an end to all interpretation when such a foolish attitude is adopted. Each passage calls for careful and prayerful study, and it has to be fairly ascertained *which* the Spirit has in view; whether the carnal Israel or the spiritual, the literal seed of Abraham or the mystical, the natural Jew or the regenerate, the earthly Jerusalem or the heavenly, the typical Zion or the antitypical. God has not written His Word so that the ordinary reader is made independent of that help which He deigns to give through His accredited teachers.

It may seem to some of our readers that we have wandered a considerable distance away from the subject of the Messianic covenant. Not so: that covenant is made with "the house of Israel and with the house of Judah"; and it is impossible to understand those terms aright until we can determine which Israel is meant. So many, assuming that there is but one Israel in Scripture, namely, the Hebrew nation, have insisted that the promise of Jeremiah 31:31 is entirely future, receiving its accomplishment in "the millennium." To make good their contention, they must show: first, that it does not and cannot refer to the mystical Israel; second, that it has not already been made good; third, that it will be accomplished in connection with the literal nation in a day to come—concerning which we ask, Where is there one word in the *New* Testament which declares God will yet make a new covenant with national Israel?

What, then, does Jeremiah 31:31 signify? Has that divine promise already received its fulfillment, or is it now in course of receiving its fulfillment, or does it yet await fulfillment? This is far more than a technical question devoid of practical interest. It raises the issue, Has the Christian a personal interest therein? If the older commentators be consulted—the ablest teachers God has granted to His people since the Reformation—it will be found that they unanimously taught that Jeremiah 31:31 receives its accomplishment in this present dispensation. While we freely grant this is not conclusive proof that they were right, and while we must call no man (or set of men) "father," yet the writer for one is today very slow in allowing that the godly Puritans were all wrong on this matter, and slower still to turn away from those luminaries which God granted in the brightest period of the church's history since the time of the apostles, in order to espouse the theories of our moderns. Then let us seek to "Prove all things: hold fast that which is good" (I Thess. 5:21).

In his comments on Jeremiah 31:31-33 Matthew Henry said, "This refers to Gospel times . . . for of Gospel times the apostle understands it (Heb. 8:8, 9), where the whole passage is quoted, as a summary of the covenant of grace made with believers in Jesus Christ." "The first solemn promulgation of this new covenant, made, ratified and established, was on the day of Pentecost, seven weeks after the resurrection of Christ. It answered to the promulgation of the Law on mount Sinai, the same space of time after the deliverance of the people out of Egypt. From this day forward the ordinances of worship and the institutions of the new covenant became obligatory upon all believers" (John Owen). To which we may also add that C. H. Spurgeon throughout his sermon on Jeremiah 31:32 speaks of that covenant as the Messianic one: "In the covenant of grace God conveys Himself to you and becomes yours."

But we are not dependent upon human authorities. Each one may see for himself that the New Testament makes it unmistakably plain that the promises contained in Jeremiah 31:31-33 are made good in the Christian economy. In the Epistle to the Hebrews—which supplies an infallible key to the interpretation of Old Testament Scripture—Paul quotes this very passage for the express purpose of showing that its terms provided an accurate description of gospel blessings. The apostle's argument in Hebrews 8 would be entirely meaningless did not Jeremiah's prediction supply a vivid portrayal of that order of things which Christ has established. First, he declares, "But *now* [and not in some future "millennium!"] hath he obtained a more excellent ministry, by how much also He *is* [not "will be!"] the mediator of a better covenant, which was established upon better promises" (v. 6); and what is added is in confirmation of this statement.

Before turning to the light which the New Testament casts upon Jeremiah 31, it should be noted that at the time God announced His purpose and promise through the prophet, the fleshly descendants of Abraham were divided into two hostile groups. They had separate kings and separate centers of worship, and were at enmity one with another. As such they fitly adumbrated the great division between God's elect among the Jews and the Gentiles in their natural and dispensational state. There was between these a "middle wall of partition" (Eph. 2:14); yea, there was actual "enmity" between them (Eph. 2:16). But just as God announced through Ezekiel that Judah and the Gentiles are now one in Christ (Gal. 3:28; Eph. 2:14-18); and therefore all born-again believers are designated the "children" and "seed" of Abraham, and blessed with him (Gal. 3:7, 9, 29).

It is pertinent to raise the point, if the principal reference in Jeremiah's prophecy was unto the gospel church of this era, wherein Gentiles so largely predominate, why is the covenant there said to be made with "the house of Israel and the house of Judah"? Several answers may be given to this question. First, to make it clear that this covenant is not made with all the fallen descendants of Adam, but only with God's chosen people. Second, because during Old Testament times the great majority of God's elect were taken out of the Hebrew nation. Third, to signify that the Jewish theocracy has given place to the Christian church: "He taketh away the first [covenant] that he may establish the second" (Heb. 10:9; cf. Matt. 21:43). Fourth, to intimate that the Old Testament saints and the New Testament saints form one body, being the same church of God in different dispensations. Fifth, because it is a common thing to call the antitype by that designation which belongs to its type.

Returning now to Hebrews 8. The grand design of the apostle in this epistle was to demonstrate that the Lord Christ is the mediator and surety of a vastly superior covenant (or economy) than that wherein the worship and service of God obtained under the old covenant or economy of the law. From which it necessarily followed that His priesthood was far more excellent than the Aaronic, and to this end he not only gives Scriptural proof that God had promised to make a new covenant, but he declares the very nature and properties of it in the words of the prophet. In particular, from this Old Testament citation, the imperfections of the old covenant (the Sinaitic) is evident by its issues: it did not effectually secure peace and fellowship between God and the people, for being broken by them, they were cast off by Him, and this rendered all its other benefits and advantages useless. This demonstrated the need for a new and better covenant, which would infallibly secure the obedience of the people forever.

"For if that first covenant had been faultless, then should no place have been sought for the second" (Heb. 8:7). The reference is to that solemn transaction which took place at Sinai. That was not the "first" covenant absolutely, but the first entered into with Israel nationally. Previously, God made a covenant with Adam (Hos. 6:6), which in some respects the Sinaitic adumbrated, for it was chiefly one of works. So too He had made a covenant with Abraham, which shadowed out the everlasting covenant, inasmuch as grace predominated in it. The "faultiness" of the Sinaitic covenant was due to the fact that it was wholly external, being accompanied by no internal efficacy: it set before Israel an objective standard, but it communicated no power for them to measure up to it. It treated with *natural* Israel, and therefore the law was impotent "through the weakness of the flesh" (Rom. 8:3). It provided sacrifices for sin; yet their value was only ceremonial and transient. Because of its inadequacy a new and better covenant was needed.

"For finding fault with them, He said, Behold, the days come, saith the Lord, when I will make a new covenant with the house of Israel and with the house of Judah" (Heb. 8:8). The opening "For" intimates that the apostle was now confirming what he had declared in verses 6, 7. The "finding fault" may refer either to the covenant or the covenantees—"with it" or "with them." In view of what is said in verse 9, the translation of the Authorized Version is to be preferred: it was against the people God complained, for their having broken His covenant. The word "Behold" announces the deep importance of what follows, calling our diligent and admiring attention to the same. The time fixed for the making of this new covenant is defined in "the days [to] come." In the Old Testament the season of Christ's appearing was called "the world to come" (Heb. 2:5), and it was a periphrasis of Him that He was "he that should come" (Matt. 11:3). The faith of the Old Testament church was principally exercised in the expectation of His advent.

The subject matter of what Jeremiah specially announced was a "covenant." "The new covenant, as collecting into one all the promises of grace given from the foundation of the world, accomplished in the actual exhibiting of Christ, and confirmed in His death, and by the sacrifice of His blood, thereby became the sole rule of new spiritual ordinances of worship suited thereunto, being the great object of the faith of the saints of the O.T., and is the great foundation of all our present mercies. ['Whereof the Holy Spirit also is witness *to us:* for after that He had said before, this is the covenant that I will make with them after those days, saith the Lord:' Heb. 10:15, 16—yes, 'is witness to *us,'* and not to those who live in some future 'millennium.' A.W.P.]

"There was in it a recapitulation of all promises of grace. God had not made any promise, any intimation of His love or grace unto the Church in general, nor unto any particular believer, but He brought it all into *this* covenant, so as that they should be esteemed, all and every one of them, to be given and spoken unto every individual person that hath an interest in this covenant. Hence all the promises made unto Abraham, Isaac and Jacob, with all the other patriarchs, and the oath of God whereby they were confirmed, are *all* of them made *unto us,* and do belong unto us, no less than they did unto them to whom they were first given, if we are made partakers of this covenant. The apostle gives an instance of this in the singular promise made unto Joshua, which he applies unto Christians: 13:5" (John Owen).

IV

The apostle's design in Hebrews 8 is to evidence the immeasurable superiority of Christ's priesthood above the Aaronic, and he does so by showing the far greater excellency of that covenant or dispensation of grace of which the Lord Jesus is the mediator. When mentioning the "first covenant," he refers to that economy or order of things under which the Hebrew people were placed at Sinai, and of which the Levitical priests were the mediators, interposing between God and the people. The "second" or "new covenant" is that grand economy or order of things which has been introduced and established by Christ, of which He is the sole mediator. In proof of this Paul quoted Jeremiah 31:31-33, and it is quite obvious that the passage would have no relevancy whatever to his argument, if the prophet was there referring to God's dealings with carnal Israel in a period which is yet future. That covenant is made with the gospel church, the "Israel of God" (Gal. 6:14), on which peace rests forever.

Let us next point out that this "new covenant," the Messianic, has assumed a form which no other covenant ever did or could, due to the death of its covenanter, namely, a "testament." The same Greek term does duty for both English words, being rendered "covenant" in Hebrews 8:6, 8, 9, and "testament" in 9:15-17. No word is more familiar to the reader of Scripture, for the second main division is rightly termed "The New Testament," yet it had been just as accurate to designate it "The New Covenant." But let it be clearly understood that it is called "New" not because its contents differ from the Old, for it is simply a fulfillment and confirmation of all that went before, everything in the Old Testament containing the shadow and type of the substance of the New Testament. The peculiar reason for naming it the New Testament is because it was newly accomplished and sealed by the precious blood of Christ just before it was written.

The second grand division of God's Word sets forth the gospel in all its unveiled fullness, and the gospel (in contrast to the law, the predominant revelation of the Old Testament) was called "the New Testament" because it contains those legacies and testamentary effects which Christ has bequeathed His people. How inexpressibly blessed, then, should be the very name of the New Testament unto every one of the Lord's people, who by the regenerating operations of the Holy Spirit can establish his own personal interest in the contents of it. "This is my blood of the new testament" (Matt. 26:28). By His death Christ has ratified the new covenant and turned it into a "testament," making all its riches and legacies secure and payable to His people: "For a testament is of force after men are dead: otherwise it is of no

strength at all while the testator liveth" (Heb. 9:17). What has Christ
left? to whom has He bequeathed His vast property? The answer is,
every conceivable blessing: temporal, spiritual, eternal—the most dura-
ble treasure of all; unto "His own," whom He loved with an un-
quenchable love.

Before His departure, Christ expressed Himself to His disciples on
this blessed subject when He said, "Peace I leave with you, my peace I
give unto you: not as the world giveth, give I unto you" (John 14:27).
Thus we see that the Savior's legacies are to His dear people, His
beloved spouse. As men before they die make their wills, and give
their property to their relatives and friends, so did the Redeemer:
"Father, *I will,* that they also whom thou hast given me, be with me
where I am" (John 17:24). Oh, for grace to "prove" the Savior's will,
to personally lay claim to all the rich legacies it contains! Have I been
brought out of nature's darkness and become a new creature in Christ?
Has the Lord given me a new heart and mind? Then I have an interest
in Christ's will, and He died to make His testament valid, and ever
liveth to be the executor and administrator of it.

The covenant (the "new," the "second," the Messianic) to which
the apostle alludes so often in his writings, particularly in the Hebrews
Epistle, is ratified by the death of Him who makes it, and therefore it
is a testament as well. This covenant was confirmed by Christ, both as
that His death was the death of the testator and as was accompanied
by the blood of sacrifice. Hence it is such a covenant as that in it the
Covenanter bequeaths His goods in the way of a legacy, and thus we
find Him calling this very covenant "the new testament in my blood."
It is in full accord with this that the believer's portion is designed an
"inheritance" (Rom. 8:16, 17; Eph. 1:18; I Peter 1:4), for in a will or
testament there is an absolute grant made of what is bequeathed. The
title which the believer has to his portion is not in himself: it has been
made over to him by the death of Christ, and nothing can possibly rob
him of it.

We must next consider the substance or contents of the Messianic
covenant. Broadly speaking, it is distinctly a covenant of promise,
which gives security by pure grace for the sanctification of God's
people and their preservation in a state and course of holiness, to their
final salvation. In other words, their right of inheritance is not by the
law or their own works: "For if they which are of the law be heirs,
faith is made void, and the promise made of none effect . . . therefore
it is of faith, that it might be *by grace;* to the end the promise might
be sure to all the seed" (Rom. 4:14, 16). But is it not true that if the
Christian should wholly and finally depart from God, that this would
deprive him of all the benefits of grace? This hypothetical supposition

is undoubted truth, yea, it is presupposed in the promise itself, which is likewise of certain and infallible truth: "I will make an everlasting covenant with them, that I will not turn away from them to do them good: but I will put my fear in their hearts, that they shall *not* depart from me" (Jer. 32:40).

Considering the contents of this covenant, we are fully in accord with John Owen that there is in it "a recapitulation and confirmation of all the promises of grace that have been given unto the Church from the beginning, even all that was spoken by the mouth of the holy prophets that had been since the world began (Luke 1:70)." The original promise (Gen. 3:15) contained in germ form the whole essence and substance of the new covenant: all promises given unto the church afterward being but expositions and confirmations of it. In the whole of them there was a full declaration of the wisdom and love of God in the sending of His Son, and of His grace unto men thereby. God solemnly confirmed those promises with an oath that they should be accomplished in their season. Thus the covenant promised by Jeremiah included the sending of Christ for the accomplishment thereof, all promises being there gathered together in one glorious constellation.

"For this is the covenant that I will make with the house of Israel after those days, saith the Lord; I will put my laws into their mind, and write them in their hearts: and I will be to them a God, and they shall be to me a people" (Heb. 8:10). In passing, be it duly noted that God did not here promise He would establish the nation in any earthly land, or bestow upon them any material inheritance. No, indeed; the blessings of this covenant immeasurably transcend any mundane or fleshly portion. Briefly, its contents may be summed up in four words: regeneration, reconciliation, sanctification, and justification. We will explain and amplify in what follows.

"I will put my laws into their mind, and write them in their hearts." The "law" here signifies that which enjoins supreme love to God, and, flowing out of it, love to our neighbor. Of this grand principle the whole round of duty is to be the fruit and expression, and from it each duty it to take its character. If love be not the animating spring, then our obedience is little worth. When it is said God will put His law in our inmost parts and write it in our hearts, it signifies that preparation of soul which is effected by divine power so that the law is cordially received into our affections. Elsewhere this miracle of grace is spoken of as "I will take away the stony heart out of your flesh, and I will give you a heart of flesh" (Ezek. 36:26). It implies an inward spiritual appreciation of its goodness and equity—the result of divine illumination; an assimilation of the tastes or inclinations of the heart to it, and the conformity of the will to its righteous requirements.

There must be a true delight in the purity which the law inculcates, for this is the only effectual preparation for obedience. So long as the law of God utters its voice to us from without only, so long as there is no sympathy in the soul with its demands, so long as the heart is alienated from its spirituality, there can be no obedience worthy of the name. We may be awed by its peremptory utterances, alarmed at the consequences of its transgression, and driven to attempt what it requires, but the effort will be cold, partial, and insincere. We shall feel it a hard bondage, the pressure of which will certainly irritate, and against the restraints of which we shall inwardly rebel. Such is the real character of all graceless obedience, however it may be disguised. How can it be otherwise when "the carnal mind is enmity against God: for it is not subject to the law of God, neither indeed can be" (Rom. 8:7)—as true today as nineteen centuries ago, as the modern hatred of and outcry against the law clearly manifests.

Concerning the Hebrew nation at Sinai, who had stoutly affirmed, "All that the Lord hath said, will we do," God declared, "Oh, that there were such a heart in them, that they would fear me, and keep all my commandments always" (Deut. 5:29). Ah, that explains their wilderness perverseness, and the whole of their subsequent history: they had *no heart* to serve God, their affections were divorced from Him. And it is just at this point that the new covenant differs so radically from the old. God has given no new law, but He has bestowed upon His people a heart—a heart in harmony with its holiness and righteousness requirements. This enables them to render unto Him that obedience, which, through the mediation of Christ, is accepted by Him. Each of them can say with the apostle, "I delight in the law of God after the inward man" (Rom. 7:22).

Once the law in all its spirituality and extent is not only intellectually apprehended but wrought into the affections, once our inmost inclinations and tendencies are molded by it and brought into unison with it, genuine obedience will be the natural and necessary result. This is the import of the first great blessing here enumerated in the Messianic covenant. It necessarily comes first; for the miracle of regeneration is the foundation of reconciliation, justification, and sanctification. The one in whom this divine work of grace is wrought finds enlargement of heart to run in the way of God's commandments. He now serves in "newness of spirit." What was before regarded as bondage is now found to be the truest liberty. What was before an irksome task is now a delight. Love for God inspires a desire to please Him: love for its Author produces a love for His law.

"I will put my laws into their mind, and write them in their hearts." The terms in which this blessing is expressed indicate a designed contrast between the old and new covenants. Under the former, the law was written upon tables of stone—not only to denote its abiding character, but also to symbolize the hardheartedness of those to whom it was then given; and publicly exhibited as a rule which they were under solemn obligations to observe. But it contained no provision to secure obedience. By the vast majority of the people its design was misunderstood and its requirements practically disregarded, proving to them the ministration of condemnation and death. Under the Messianic covenant, the law is written on the heart—incorporated with the living springs of action in the inward parts, thus bringing the whole man into harmony with the will of God.

A further contrast is implied in the second blessing here specified: "I will be to them a God, and they shall be to me a people" (Heb. 8:10). While the Hebrews were yet in Egypt the Lord announced, "I will take you to me for a people and I will be to you a God" (Exod. 6:7). Later He declared, "I will set my tabernacle among you, and my soul shall not abhor you; and I will walk among you, and will be your God, and ye shall be my people" (Lev. 26:11, 12). But that was a vastly different thing from what now obtains under the new covenant: that was a natural relationship, this a spiritual; that was external, this internal; that was national, this is individual; that was temporal, this is eternal. Under the theocracy all of Abraham's natural descendants were true subjects and properly qualified members of the Jewish church—such only excepted as had not been circumcised according to the order of God, or were guilty of some capital crime. To be an obedient subject of the civil government and a full member of the ecclesiastical state was manifestly the same thing; because by treating Jehovah as their political Sovereign, they owned Him as the true God and were entitled to all the blessings of the national covenant.

Under the Sinaitic economy Jehovah acknowledged all those to be "His people" and Himself to be "their God" who performed an external obedience to His commands, even though their hearts were disaffected to Himself (Judg. 8:23; I Sam. 8:6, 7; etc.). Those prerogatives were enjoyed irrespective of sanctifying grace, or of any pretension to it. But the state of things under the Christian economy is entirely different. God will not now acknowledge any as "His people" who do not know and revere Him, love and obey Him, worship Him in spirit and in truth. Only those are now owned as His people who have His law written on their hearts, and He is their God in a far higher and grander sense than ever He was of the nation of Israel: He is their enduring and satisfying portion. They are His people not by outward designation only, but by actual surrender of their hearts to Him. To be "their God" necessarily denotes they have been reconciled to Him, and have voluntarily accepted Him as such.

"I will be to them a God, and they shall be to me a people." This is a distinct promise which comprises and comprehends all the blessings and privileges of the covenant. It is placed in the center of the whole as that from whence all the grace of it doth issue, wherein all the blessedness of it doth consist, and whereby it is secured. This relationship necessarily implies mutual acquiescence in each other, for it could not exist if the hearts and minds of those who are taken into it were not renewed. God could not approve of, still less rest in His love toward them,-while they were at enmity against Him; nor could they find satisfaction in Himself so long as they neither knew nor loved Him. Because they still have sin in them, this relationship is made possible through the infinite merits of the Mediator.

V

The substance of the Christian covenant is, broadly speaking, divine *promises* which pledged the sanctification of God's people and their effectual preservation in a state and course of holiness to their final salvation. Those promises are summarized in Hebrews 8:10-12, and are four in number. First, is the declaration that the Lord would write His laws in the hearts of those for whom Christ died, which signifies such a change being wrought in them that the divine statutes are cordially received in their affections. Second, is the assurance that the Lord will be the God of His people, giving Himself to them in all His perfections and relationships, so that the supply of their every need is absolutely guaranteed: "They shall call on my name, and I will hear them: I will say, It is my people; and they shall say, The Lord is my God" (Zech. 13:9). He is the God of His people in a spiritual and everlasting sense, through the meritorious mediation of Christ.

"And they shall not teach every man his neighbour and every man his brother, saying, Know the Lord: for all shall know me, from the least to the greatest" (Heb. 8:11). This is the third promise, and like the two preceding it points a marked and blessed contrast from that which obtained under the regime of the old covenant, and that in connection with the knowledge of God. During the Mosaic dispensation, God granted many revelations of Himself, discovering various aspects of His character, and these were augmented by frequent descriptions of His perfections and dealings through the prophets, all of which placed the Jews in a condition of privilege immeasurably superior to the rest of the nations. Nevertheless, there were difficulties connected with those divine discoveries which even the most spiritual of Israel could not remove, while the great majority of them knew not God in the real sense of the word. The truth about God was apprehended but dimly and feebly by most, and by the great mass of them it was not rightly apprehended at all.

So far as the nation at large was concerned, the revelation God granted them of Himself was wholly external, and for the most part given through symbols and shadows. Many of them trusted in the letter of Scripture, and rested in human teaching—often partial and imperfect at the best. They had no idea of their need of anything higher. Complaints of their ignorance are common throughout the Old Testament: "The ox knoweth his owner, and the ass his master's crib; but Israel doth not know"(Isa. 1:2); "They know not the way of the Lord nor the judgment of their God. . . . They proceed from evil to evil, and they know not me, saith the Lord" (Jer. 5:4; 9:3). Ignorance of God, notwithstanding all their advantages, was their sin and their ruin. Ultimately, their teachers became divided into schools and sects: Pharisees, Sadducees, Essenes, and so forth, until the last of their prophets declared: "The Lord will cut off the man that doeth this: the master and the scholar out of the tabernacles of Jacob" (Mal. 2:12).

"For all shall know me, from the least to the greatest"—that is, all who belong to the true Israel of God. God has now given not only a fuller, yea, a perfect revelation of Himself, in the person of His incarnate Son (John 1:18; Heb. 1:2), but the Holy Spirit is given to guide us into all truth; and it is at this point the vast superiority of the new covenant again appears. Those for whom Christ is the mediator receive something more than an external revelation from God, namely, an internal: "For God, who commanded the light to shine out of darkness, hath shined in our hearts, to give the light of the knowledge of the glory of God in the face of Jesus Christ" (II Cor. 4:6). They have something far better than human teachers to explain the law to them, even the Holy Spirit to effectually apply it unto their consciences and wills. It was to this Christ referred when He said, "They shall all be taught of God" (John 6:45): "taught" so that they know Him truly and savingly.

It is to this individual, inward, and saving knowledge of God that the apostle referred: "Ye have an unction from the Holy One and ye shall know all things . . . the anointing which ye have received of him abideth in you, and ye need not that any man teach you: but as the same anointing teacheth you of all things, and is truth, and is no lie, and even as it hath taught you, ye shall abide in him" (I John 2:20, 27). That unction operates on their souls with an ever quickening power. Nor is this some special blessing reserved for a select few of the redeemed: all interested in the covenant are given a sanctifying knowledge of God. It is far more than a correct intellectual conception of God which was promised, namely, such a transforming revelation of Him that they will fear, love, and serve Him. It is an *obediental* knowledge of God which is here in view. It was the absence of that kind of knowledge in Israel of old that God complained of: "The Lord hath a controversy with the inhabitants of the land, because there is no truth, nor mercy, nor knowledge of God" (Hos. 4:1). The external method of teaching under the old economy was ineffectual, for the Spirit taught not the nation inwardly as He does the church.

"For I will be merciful to their unrighteousness, and their sins and their iniquities will I remember no more" (v. 12). This is the fourth promise, and embraces in its blessed arms the pardon of all their sins, the forgiveness of all their iniquities, and declares that these shall be so completely blotted out that their very remembrance, so to speak, shall be removed from the mind of God. Once more we would ask the reader to pay careful attention to the order of these promises, for it is almost universally disregarded, nay, contradicted in modern preaching. Three times over in this verse occurs the pronoun *their,* emphasizing the particularity of those persons whose sins alone are pardoned— namely, those who have been regenerated, reconciled, and given a sanctifying knowledge of God. God forgives none save those who are in covenant relation with Him.

Nothing could be plainer than what has been just pointed out, for the coherence of our passage is unmistakable. "I will be merciful to their unrighteousness": to whose unrighteousness? Why, to those with whom God makes this new covenant, namely, the members of the spiritual house of Israel (v. 10). And of what does this covenant consist? First, God declares, "I will put my laws into their minds and write them in their hearts," which is accomplished at their regeneration, and that lays a necessary foundation for what follows. Second, God affirms, "And I will be to them a God and they shall be to me a people," which denotes a mutual reconciliation, after a mutual alienation. Third, He promises, "All shall know me, from the least to the greatest," which signifies their sanctification, for it is such a knowledge that produces love, trust, submission. Finally, "For I will be merciful to their unrighteousness," and so forth, which at once disposes of the figment of a general atonement and universal forgiveness: as the mediator of the covenant (Heb. 8:6) Christ acts only for the covenantees.

"For I will be merciful to their unrighteousness, and their sins and iniquities will I remember no more." Once again we may perceive how greatly the new covenant excels the old. Under the Levitical economy there was forgiveness, but with limitations, and with a degree of obscurity resting upon it which testified to the defectiveness of the existing order of things. For certain sins no atonement was provided; though on sincere repentance, such sins were forgiven, as the case of David shows. At no point were the imperfections of the Mosaic economy more evident than in this vital matter of remission: as the Epistle of Hebrews reminds us: "But in those sacrifices there *is a remembrance* again made of sins every year" (10:3). Thus were the Jews impressively taught that they had to do with "the shadow" of good things to come, which could not make the comers thereunto perfect as pertaining to the conscience (Heb. 10:1). In blessed contrast therefrom, the forgiveness bestowed under the new covenant is free, full, perfect, and everlasting.

"For I will be merciful unto their unrighteousness." The word which is here rendered "merciful" is "propitious," emphasizing the fact that it is not absolute mercy without any satisfaction having been made to justice, but rather grace exercised on the ground of propitiation (Rom. 3:24, 25; 5:21). Christ died to render God propitious toward sinners (Heb. 2:17), and in and through Him alone is God merciful toward the sins of His people. So long as Christ is rejected, is the sinner under the curse. Therein the glory of the covenant shines forth, for the unsearchable wisdom of God is displayed and the perfect harmony of His attributes evidenced. No finite intelligence had ever found a solution to the problem: how can justice be inexorably enforced and yet mercy shown to the guilty? how can sinners be freely pardoned without the claims of righteousness being flouted? Christ is the solution, for He is "the surety" of the covenant (Heb. 7:22).

It is to be duly noted that no less than three terms are used in verse 12 to describe the fearful evils of which the sinner is guilty, thus emphasizing his obnoxiousness to the holy God, and magnifying the amazing grace which saves him. First, "unrighteousness": as God is the supreme Lord and governor of all, as He is our benefactor and rewarder, and as all His laws are just and good, the first notion of righteousness in us is the rendering to God that which is His due, namely, universal obedience to all His commands; hence, unrighteousness signifies a wrong done unto God. Second, "sin" is a missing of the mark, an erring from that end at which it is ever our duty to aim, namely, the glory of God. Third, "iniquity" has the force of lawlessness, a setting up of my will against that of the Almighty's, a determination to please myself and go my own way. How marvelous, then, is the propitious favor of God toward those who are guilty of such multiplied enormities. How great and how grand the contrast between the covenants: under the Sinaitic, a regime of justice was supreme; under the Christian economy, grace reigns through righteousness.

Such, then, are the particulars of the remarkable prophecy made through Jeremiah, anticipating—in fact, giving a grand description of—the gospel. They disclose beyond the possibility of mistake, the spiritual character of this covenant. The Messianic covenant, unlike the Sinaitic, effectually accomplished the eternal salvation of all who are interested in it. The blessings conferred upon them, as here enumerated, are the "things which accompany salvation" (Heb. 6:9), yea, they are the constituent elements of salvation itself. It therefore has respect to the antitypical Israel, the spiritual seed, and to them alone. The mere possession of external privileges, however valuable they may be in themselves, and the correct observance of religious worship, however consistently maintained, avails nothing in proof of being within the bounds of this covenant. Nothing can afford sure evidence that this covenant has been made *with us*, save a living faith uniting the soul to Christ and producing conformity to Him in one's life.

What has been last said ought never to be overlooked, for it is one main feature distinguishing this covenant from the Sinaitic. The new covenant actually does for those who are in it what the old one failed to do for the Jewish people. To them God gave a revelation, but it came to them in letter only; to the New Testament saints His revelation comes in power also (I Cor. 4:20; I Thess. 1:5). To them God gave the law as written upon tables of stone; to the New Testament saints God also gives the law, but writes it upon their hearts. Consequently, they chafed at the law, whereas we (after the inward man) delight in it (Rom. 7:22). Hence, too, they walked not in God's statutes, but continually transgressed them; whereas of His New Testament people it is written, "Ye have obeyed from the heart that form of doctrine which was delivered you" (Rom. 6:17). That which makes all the difference is that the Holy Spirit is given to indwell and energize the latter, which He was not in those who were in the Sinaitic covenant as such—we say "as such," for there was ever a godly remnant who were indwelt by the Spirit on the ground of the everlasting covenant.

Again, we may observe that this covenant is a display of rich and unmerited grace: such are all its arrangements and provisions. The very circumstances under which the Christian covenant was formally introduced furnishes clear proof of this: succeeding, as it did, an economy set aside on account of its unprofitableness—an economy inherently weak for spiritual ends, and perverted by the people who enjoyed its privileges. The abuse of the Sinaitic covenant deserved not higher favors, but merited summary judgment; yet it was among the Jews that God's Son tabernacled and performed His works of mercy. The application of the blessings of the Messianic covenant does, in every instance, also bear witness: to those blessings no man can lay claim. If conferred at all, they come as free gifts of undeserved grace. Its blessings are the bestowment of sovereign goodness. They who are brought within the covenant are the objects of God's electing love. To grace alone they owe all they become, the service they are enabled to perform, and all the blessedness they shall enjoy in heaven hereafter.

The stability and perpetuity of the new covenant are plainly involved in the statement made by Jeremiah (31:31-35). The very nature of its blessings is a proof of this. They effectually secured the great end which God has in view in His dealings with men, namely, the formation of a holy people for His everlasting praise. This end once attained, there is no room for any improvement. But that could not be said of the Sinaitic covenant: as it regarded this result it failed, and that almost continuously throughout the long history of the Jews. But so far from being unexpected, that failure was distinctly foreseen. From the first the Levitical economy partook of the nature of a preparation for something better. Its perceptible unprofitableness for those higher ends should have taught the people that it could not have been intended for permanency. Ultimately, they were plainly informed (Jer. 31) that their economy was to be superseded by another covenant, the blessings of which, in their very nature, securing what the existing arrangement had never attained unto. Here, too, its surpassing excellency appears.

VI

"Jesus the mediator of the new covenant" (Heb. 12:24). From the contents or blessings of the covenant we turn now to consider the measures and means which were to give effect unto their actual communication. First and foremost among these is the *Mediator*—a word denoting one who goes between two parties, to arrange any matters of importance in which they may have a common interest, or to settle any differences with a view to their permanent reconciliation.

It is in the latter sense the term is used in such connections as the present. What the precise work of the Mediator is, what He does to make his intervention efficient, depends of course on the relation of the parties toward each other and the matters of disagreement which have separated them. Now the character of that covenant of which Christ is the mediator enables us to form a definite conception of the nature and extent of His mediation.

The Messianic covenant is a dispensation of free promises of grace and mercy to guilty and condemned sinners. Should it be asked, Wherein lay the need for a mediator in connection with such gracious promises? Might they not have been given and fulfilled without requiring the intervention of a middle party? It would be sufficient answer to say that this question relates to the realm of fact and not of supposition. It is not at all a matter of what God might or might not, could or could not do, but what He *has* done; it has pleased Him to appoint a mediator. It has seemed most meet unto God, out of a regard to what is due unto Himself, to determine that His blessings shall be dispensed under certain definite conditions; and therefore it is for us to humbly acquiesce and gratefully accept what is graciously offered us, on the terms on which that offer is made. Nevertheless, it has pleased God to intimate sufficiently as to demonstrate unto us His matchless wisdom in such a constitution of things as the mediatorship of Christ discloses.

First, *sin is an evil* so offensive and malignant, and attended with consequences so sweeping and disastrous, as to necessitate (under the regime divinely appointed) a separation between God and those who commit it—a separation which can only be removed by means which shall leave the character and government of God uncompromised, and shall effectually stay the ravages of so fearful a plague. To represent the Most High as simply a loving Father to His creatures is not only extremely partial, but altogether an erroneous view of His relations to us. His love is indeed the originating impulse of all the blessings of the covenant. But God is also a moral Governor, a righteous King, whose character is reflected in the government which He exercises; and therefore does He manifest His holy hatred of sin and justly punishes it. Hence it is that when He seeks the return of sinners unto Himself it is by a system of mediation which vindicates His perfections and magnifies His law.

Second, *sinners themselves need* a mediator. They are enemies: not such as those who have indeed wandered from God, but are still influenced by some lingering affection for Him and would be glad to return if they only knew how; they are sinners not through inadvertence, but transgressors of settled purpose and from the heart. The holiness of God, just in proportion as they obtain glimpses of it, is hated by them. They choose the evil and loathe the good: they love darkness rather than light. They do not like to retain the knowledge of God in their minds, but do all they can to dismiss Him from their thoughts. It is neither carelessness nor involuntary ignorance which occasions this feeling, but positive hostility: the carnal mind is enmity against God. When confronted with the truth and made to feel they are under the divine condemnation, they regard God as their worst enemy, committed to their punishment, and are conscious of feelings of aversion, which nothing can allay but such views of God as mediation unfolds.

Nor is this all. We require someone to undertake for us who shall not only have power to bring us to a state of subjection and obedience, but to take care of our interests: to tend us and bear with us under our manifold infirmities. Our very consciousness testifies to the need of this. Our helplessness is painfully felt from the moment we are awakened to perceive the reality of our awful condition. And even though provision has been made for our access to God, and we are freely invited to avail ourselves of the same, yet so awe-inspiring are the views we must have of the divine character that we instinctively shrink from His ineffable purity. We are unmistakably aware that even in our sincerest approach to the thrice holy God we have need of someone to intervene between us: some "Daysman" (as Job expressed it) who can lay His hand upon us both.

Third, *Christ Himself* is thereby greatly glorified. This is the supreme end in the divine administration, for He is the Alpha and the Omega in all the counsels of God. It is entirely useless to speculate as to what might have been the particular status of Christ or what office He had filled, if sin had never defiled the universe. Evil *has* entered, entered by the permission of God, and that for His own wise reasons. That the entrance of sin into our world has provided opportunity for God to display His incomparable wisdom, and that it has been overruled to the magnifying of His dear Son, needs no labored effort of ours to show. The perfect love of Christ to the Father, evidenced by His voluntary self-abasement and obedience unto death, shines forth in meridian splendor. The grand reward He has received for His stupendous undertaking, and the revenue of praise which He receives from those on whose behalf He suffered, affords full compensation. On His head are "many crowns" (Rev. 19:12)—in virtue of His mediatorial office.

No formal mention of mediation was contained in the earliest covenants, though by implication they involved the idea of it. The covenants made during the infancy of our race were but partial disclosures of the scheme of mercy, bringing to light particular features of God's gracious purposes, adapted to the times when they were respectively given. Yet the germ of the truth respecting mediation was in both the Noahic and Abrahamic covenants, for the sacrifices which accompanied them bespoke a special intervention as the appointed means of ratifying the promises they contained. The promise (to Abraham) of a Seed in whom all the nations of the earth should be blessed, and (to David) of a righteous King under whose government the people of God should dwell in safety, only needed that expansion of meaning which was subsequently given, to realize all that the most effective mediation comprehends.

In the Sinaitic covenant, though, this grand truth came out much more distinctly. When on the mount God drew near to the people and spake to them out of the thick cloud, they said to Moses, "Behold, the Lord our God hath showed us his glory and his greatness, and we have heard his voice out of the midst of the fire: we have seen this day that God doth talk with man, and he liveth. Now therefore why should we die? For this great fire will consume us; if we hear the voice of the Lord our God any more, then shall we die. For who is there of all flesh, that hath heard the voice of the living God, speaking out of the midst of the fire, as we have, and lived? Go *thou* near, and hear all that the Lord our God shall say; and speak thou unto us all that the Lord our God shall speak unto *thee;* and we will hear and do it" (Deut. 5:24-27). Thus, at the request of the people, Moses became their mediator: an arrangement which the Lord approved of as wise and beneficial (v. 28).

It is quite apparent that the visible manifestation of God amidst the fire of Sinai and the awful utterances which struck upon their ears, were the things which influenced the great majority of the people in preferring their request: they were too destitute of spiritual apprehension to be capable of looking beyond what met their physical senses. Yet who can doubt that there were some, at least, of the people, sufficiently enlightened to feel most painfully their unfitness for any direct intercourse with God, and to whom the intervention of a mediator was a matter of felt necessity in order for them to feel confident in their worship. To elicit that very feeling on the part of the godly remnant was one end of the divine manifestation at Horeb, for the divine statement in reply to their request involved the assurance that they were right in entertaining this conviction, and accordingly God promised to raise up a prophet from amongst them like unto Moses, through whom all future intercourse with God should be conducted (Deut. 18:15-18).

It is apparent, then, that the appointment of a mediator is indispensable to the existence of any spiritual intercourse between a holy God and sinful men. The true reason for this springs from the nature of sin, viewed in connection with the relation which the Most High sustains to our guilty race. Accurate conceptions of what that relation involves, and of what sin is in itself and in its effects, will go far to determine the character of the Mediator's work as made known in Scripture, on the complete accomplishment of which the success of His mediation depends. Mistakes on these points vitiate our entire views of the gospel. The terms on which divine intercourse with sinners is possible is a matter of vital importance. That awful breach could not be healed by anything done by the offenders: the righteousness of God's character and government must by vindicated and the law honored before grace is conferred and true fellowship with God established. To effect this was the object of the work committed to Christ.

When Scripture refers to Christ as *the mediator* that term is comprehensive of the entire work of mediation in all its departments, which, as the spiritual deliverer of His people, He voluntarily undertook. We may dwell upon the different offices He sustains; we may delineate and illustrate the character and results of His actings in those offices separately; but His mediation embraces them all. Mediation is not something additional to what He does in the several capacities in which He is held forth in Scripture, but rather is it a term which, in the fullness of its meaning, includes them all; His prophetical, priestly, and regal offices are all essential to His mediation. Thus, in giving a brief exposition of His mediation, all that is necessary to our present design is to present a mere outline of the particulars. We cannot continue indefinitely this already lengthy study, so must now content ourselves with a succinct statement, which will afford a comprehensive view of the true state of the case.

First, Christ, as mediator, is the supreme *prophet*. Although in one aspect, His priestly work is the foundation of all His other dealings as mediator, yet since it is with His prophetical office that we first come into contact, we begin here. As prophet, Christ is the great revealer of the character and will of God. In His earliest instruction—the Sermon on the Mount—He explained and vindicated the revelation previously given, but which through the errors of blind guides had been perverted. In addition, He furnished in His own mission the supreme manifestation of God's love and grace. He revealed, too, the true nature of that salvation which fallen men needed, the character of that change which the Holy Spirit must effect in them, the certainty of a future life of bliss or woe according to present character, and the solemnities of that judgment with which the present order of things shall close. To His apostles He assigned the duty, under His own superintendence, of amplifying what He had in substance taught.

Christ, too, is the source of all inward illumination, whereby the truth is, in any case, practically apprehended and savingly believed. "No man knoweth . . . who the Father is, but the Son, and he to whom the Son will reveal him" (Luke 10:22) is His own statement. A clear and Scriptural knowledge of the truth is obtained only by divine teaching. Nor does this arise from any deficiency in the truth itself; the hindrance lies in the mind and heart of the sinner. There is a moral blindness, an aversion to holy truth, which no means—be they perfectly adapted to the object in view—can ever remove. The fallen sinner is so utterly depraved, so opposed to the divine requirements, that he has neither will nor desire to apprehend what is holy; and none but the Spirit of Christ can effect a cure. It is the province of Christ, as the great prophet of the church, to heal this diseased state. He enables the mind to understand and the heart to receive the truth.

Second, Christ, as mediator, is the great *high priest,* an office which involved the making of expiation and intercession. To these two particulars the Levitical dispensation bore a continuous and ample testimony: the numerous sacrifices, and the annual intervention of the high priest under the law were types—dim figures of what was to be realized in Him who was to come. The true meaning of those sacrifices may be gathered from the distinct explanations which accompanied them. They were substitutionary satisfactions for the soul that sinned, for it is "the blood that maketh an atonement for the soul." They were designed to teach the people the idea of the necessity for expiation for sin; and the intercession for them before God, founded on these sacrifices, completed the truth intended to be taught: they clearly intimated the arrangement by which alone their sins could be remitted, and the blessings which they needed obtained. And Christ, by His life and death, provided the substance or reality.

The views of the priestly work of Christ supplied by the types under the old economy, receive full confirmation in the testimony of the apostles. In their teaching there is no uncertain sound on this subject. As samples we cite the following: "A merciful and faithful high priest in things pertaining to God, to make propitiation for the sins of the people"; "But this man, because he continueth ever, hath an unchangeable priesthood. Wherefore he is able also to save them to the uttermost that come unto God by him, seeing he ever liveth to make intercession for them" (Heb. 2:17; 7:24, 25; cf. Rev. 1:5, 6). As the personally sinless One, Christ was (legally) made sin for His people, that they might be made the righteousness of God in Him.

Such is the very essence of the gospel; and they who deny it, place themselves outside the pale of divine mercy.

Third, Christ, as mediator, is *the King* of Zion. Under the Davidic covenant not only was this prefigured in the sovereignty conferred upon the man after God's own heart, but definite promises were given of the raising up of a righteous King, under whose government truth and peace should abound; and it is in Christ that they receive their perfect fulfillment. The New Testament represents His exaltation and the authority with which He is now invested as the designed recompense of the work which He accomplished (see Eph. 1:19-23; Phil. 2:8-11).

It was part of the divine arrangement that the administration of the economy of grace should be committed to Him by whose sufferings and death the foundation has been laid for a true intercourse between God and sinful men. The supreme object for conferring the regal dignity upon the Messiah was His own vindication and glory, but the subordinate design was that He should give practical effect to the divine purpose in the actual saving of all God's elect. The very nature of that purpose serves to determine the character and extent of the work committed to Him. That purpose respects the spiritual deliverance of God's people, scattered throughout the world, and therefore is it a work effected against every conceivable opposition. The rule of the Messiah is supreme and universal, for nothing short of that is adequate to the occasion. "Who is gone into heaven, and is on the right hand of God: angels and authorities and powers being made subject unto him" (I Peter 3:22). It is by the discharge of these three offices Christ effectually performs His work of mediation.

VII

First and foremost among the means ordained by God for the actual communication of the blessings of the covenant was the appointing of His Son to the mediatorial office, involving of course His becoming man. The covenant itself is a dispensation of free promises of grace to guilty and condemned sinners; the measures to give effect unto these promises are the *terms* on which the divine intercourse with sinners is alone possible; and the *means* are that by which true fellowship with God is established and maintained. As we have said, first among these measures and means was the ordination of Christ to the mediatorial office; and to equip Him for the discharge thereof during the days of His humiliation, He was anointed with the Holy Spirit (Luke 4:18; Acts 10:38). Thus was He furnished for all the exigencies of the stupendous undertaking upon which He entered, an undertaking that is executed by the exercise of His prophetic, priestly, and royal functions.

By the successful conclusion of His earthly mission and work, Christ laid a sure foundation for the recovery of God's fallen people and for their true fellowship with Him; yet more was still needed for the actualizing of the divine purpose of grace. As it is through Christ all its blessings are conveyed, so it is by Him the covenant is administered. Consequently, upon His exaltation to the right hand of God, He received a further and higher anointing, obtaining the promise of the Father in the gift of the Spirit, to be by Him dispensed to His church at His will (see Acts 2:33; Heb. 1:9; Rev. 3:1). Thus is He effectually equipped to secure the salvation of all His people. He has been exalted to be "a Prince and a Saviour, for to give repentance to Israel, and forgiveness of sins" (Acts 5:31). He is endowed with "all power in heaven and in earth" (Matt. 28:18). He "must reign till he hath put all enemies under his feet" (I Cor. 15:25). God has assured Him that "he shall see of the travail of his soul, and shall be satisfied" (Isa. 53:11).

The administration of the covenant in the actual application of its blessings, and in securing, beyond the possibility of the slightest failure, its ordained results, is an essential part of the mediatorial work of Christ. Therefore was he exalted to the right hand of the Majesty on high, to exercise sovereign power. His cross was but the prelude to His crown. The latter was not only the appointed and appropriate reward of the former, but having begun the work of salvation by His death, to Him was reserved the honor of completing it by His reigning power. "God raised him from the dead and set him at his own right hand . . . and hath put all things under his feet, and gave him to be the head over all things to the church which is his body" (Eph. 1:19). The salvation of the church, and the unlimited power and authority with which the Redeemer is now entrusted, are indispensable to its successful attainment.

The administration of the covenant by the Mediator as bearing on the salvation of sinners is a subject of vast importance. Christ now reigns, and nothing is more consoling and stabilizing than a deep conviction of this fact. His rule is not an imaginary one, but a reality; His reign is not figurative, but personal. He is now on the throne, and is exercising the power and authority committed to Him as the Messiah, in the complex constitution of His person, for the accomplishment of His people's salvation. But not only is this now denied by those who imagine that Christ's personal reign is as yet entirely future, it is most feebly grasped by many of those who profess to believe that the Savior is already on the mediatorial throne. It is one thing to admit it in words, and another to act thereon and enjoy the living power of it. It is the holy privilege of the Christian to have personal dealings with One who is invested with supreme sovereignty, and yet at the same time ever has his best interests at heart.

From the period of His ascension, the royal supremacy of Christ was distinctly recognized and frankly owned by all the apostles. They steadfastly believed in Him as their King and their God—ever accessible, ever near to them. They sought His direction in duty, and under His authority they acted. They relied upon His grace for the performance of their work, and to Him they ascribed their success. The assurance of His presence was a vital consideration with them: it strengthened their faith, energized their service, sustained them in their afflictions, and gave them victory over their enemies. Of this, their writings afford abundant evidence. It is impossible to peruse them attentively without perceiving that a living, ever-present Savior, invested with mediatorial power and glory, was their life and strength and joy. And with this, all healthy Christian experience, ever since their day, thoroughly coincides.

The government of Christ is administered by a wisely adapted system of means, appointed and directed by Himself. Chief among these means, in the matter of salvation, are His *Word* and His *Spirit,* the former containing all that it is necessary for us to know for our spiritual deliverance. It reveals the character of the Lord God, the nature of the relation He sustains to us, the things He requires of us, and the principles on which He will deliver us. It depicts what we are as fallen creatures, what sin is, and what are its wages. It unfolds the divine method of salvation through the sacrifice and mediation of the Son, His all-sufficiency for the work assigned Him, the way in which we become interested in its blessings, and the character of that obedience which, as the subjects of His grace, we must render to Him.

As a means, the Word is perfect for its purpose: it is fully and admirably fitted to produce the most practical effect on all who are brought to understand it. But Scripture declares, and innumerable facts echo its testimony, that this body of truth meets with such resistance from sinful men that no mere means can ever remove: that plain as are its statements, and satisfactory and conclusive its evidence, sinners naturally have not eyes to see nor hearts to receive. Fallen men are so utterly depraved, there is such an aversion in their hearts to all that is holy, that had they been left to themselves, revelation with all its merciful disclosures must have been given in vain. It is here that the work of the Spirit comes in: a gracious provision of Christ's to meet man's otherwise hopeless malady. By His power, the Spirit of Christ dispels the darkness of the understanding and subdues the enmity of the heart. This He does by regenerating us, which imparts a capacity for receiving and loving the truth.

When a sinner, after a career of heedless insensibility to the claims of God, is awakened to a consciousness of his guilt and danger, brought under deep and painful conviction, and after exercise of heart more or less protracted, is led to accept the mercy of the gospel and to find peace in Christ, it is in every instance a work of divine grace, the fruit of the Spirit's operation. True, every conviction is not the proof of a saving work, for some proceed from natural conscience or are aroused by some special providence: it is the result and not the degree of suffering attending them, which is the only sure criterion of their saving nature. Those convictions alone are gracious which truly humble the sinner, leading to the renunciation of all self-righteous dependence, inducing him to justify God in his condemnation and take the blame of his sins upon himself, and leave him a conscious suppliant for undeserved mercy. This is a state of heart which the Spirit of God alone can produce.

The actual reception of Christ in order that salvation may be a conscious possession and enjoyment is by faith, and that faith is obviously the consequence of the spiritual and radical change which has passed on the heart. We say "obvious," for an unhumbled and impenitent heart cannot savingly believe (Matt. 21:32), any more than one who is yet a rebel can surrender to the Lordship of Christ and take His yoke upon him. There can be no communion between light and darkness, no fellowship between Christ and Belial. While the heart remains hard and unbroken the Word obtains no entrance therein, as our Lord's parable of the sower makes unmistakably plain. The faith which saves is one that receives Christ as He is presented in the Word, namely, as one who abhors self-righteousness, hates sin, yet is full of compassion to those who are sick of sin and long to be healed by Him. Of such faith the Holy Spirit is the author in every instance.

In His administration of the covenant, then, Christ fulfils its promises by means of the ministry of the Word, under the agency of the Spirit. God's people are effectually called by His grace: by faith they accept His mercy and surrender to His will. The effectual call concerns their salvation, for it is a call to His kingdom and glory, this being its specific design. From the moment that spiritual principles and gracious affections exist in the heart, in however feeble a form, salvation commences; and we may rest fully assured that everyone in whom this good work is begun by the Spirit will continue and persevere in the course on which they have entered, until their salvation is completed and present grace passes into future glory. Between the first incipient manifestation of grace in the heart and finished redemption in the everlasting blessedness of heaven, there is an intimate, and by divine appointment, a necessary and sure connection. The very nature of the covenant insures this, for its blessings are entirely spiritual, providing for permanent relations with God.

Between the condition of Adam in a state of innocence and re-newed and believing saints, there is a vast difference. The former stood in his own righteousness, and there was no guarantee against his defection. He did fall, even when placed in the most favorable circum-stance, from continued obedience. If, then, believers now, with in-dwelling sin and all the infirmities which still cleave to them, amidst the manifold forms of temptation surrounding them—things which Adam in his purity never knew—have no higher security than he had, what could prevent their inevitable apostasy and destruction? But the effects of divine grace and the faithfulness of the Redeemer are pledged for their safety. He who pitied them when they were dead in tres-passes and sins, and brought them to know and love Himself, will never leave nor forsake them. The grace which first blessed them will continue to bless them unto the end. To render their salvation certain is the immediate purpose of the Mediator's government.

"The gifts and calling of God are without repentance" (Rom. 11:29). Of this the covenant itself supplies an express assurance, not only by its general statements, from which an inference to this effect might be fairly drawn, but in distinct terms. In one remarkable passage we find it thus stated: "They shall be my people, and I will be their God. And I will give them one heart, and one way; that they may fear me forever, for the good of them and of their children after them. And I will make an everlasting covenant with them, that I will not turn away from them to do them good; but I will put my fear in their hearts, that they shall not depart from me" (Jer. 32:38-40). The covenant does not provide a pardon for sinners, and then leave them in their sins. It is no licenser of ungodliness, or shelterer of the libertine. There is nothing in it which to the least degree encourages those embraced by it to sin that grace may abound.

The "fear" which God puts into the hearts of renewed souls is the divine antidote against indwelling sin, for as Proverbs 8:13 tells us, "The fear of the Lord is to hate evil"; and as we again read, "By the fear of the Lord men depart from evil" (Prov. 16:6). Therefore, until the sinner has by grace been brought to hate evil and depart from it, he is a stranger to the covenants of promise. Mark well, dear reader,

God does not promise to place His doctrine in our heads—many have that, and nothing more—but His *fear* in our *hearts*. A merely intellectual knowledge of doctrine puffs up with pride and presumption; but His fear in the heart humbles and produces a godly walk. "I will not turn away from them to do them good." True, says the Arminian; but they may turn from Him to do evil. Not wholly, constantly, and finally so, as we are here positively assured: "I will put my fear in their hearts that *they shall not depart* from me."

Thus far we have dwelt exclusively on the divine side of this aspect of our subject: the measures God has taken and the means He has appointed for fulfilling His purpose of grace in the covenant. Now we must turn to the human side, and consider what God requires from us before the blessings of the covenant can be bestowed upon us. Alas that in the few pulpits where the divine side is clearly enunciated, most of them are silent on the human, or vehemently assert there is no human side to it. It is another example of the woeful lack of balance which now obtains so widely in Christendom. Those to whom we are alluding are very, very fond of quoting, "He *hath* made with me an everlasting covenant, ordered in all things, and sure" (II Sam. 23:5), but one never, never hears them cite, still less expound, "Incline your ear, and come unto me; hear, and your soul shall live: and I *will make* an everlasting covenant with you, even the sure mercies of David" (Isa. 55:3).

In the passage last quoted we learn just who are the characters with whom God proposes to make this covenant, and the terms with which they must comply if He is to do so. First, it is with those who had hitherto closed their ears against Him, refusing to heed His requirements, and steeling themselves against His warnings and admonitions. To "incline your ear" signifies cease your rebellious attitude, submit yourselves to My righteous demands. Second, it is with those who are separated and alienated, at a guilty distance from Him. "Come unto me" means throw down the weapons of your warfare, and cast yourselves on My mercy. Third, it is with those who are destitute of spiritual life, as the "hear and your souls shall live" clearly enough denotes. It is *human responsibility* which is here being enforced. Comply with these terms, says God, and I will make this covenant with you.

This enforcing of our responsibility is most meet for the honor of God; and as the honor of His Father lies nearer to the heart of Christ than anything else, He will not dispense the blessings of His grace except in that way which is most becoming to God's perfections. There is a perfect consonance between the impetation of God's favor and the application of it. As the justice of God deemed it meet that

His wrath should be appeased and His law vindicated by the satisfaction made by His Son, so His wisdom determined that the sinner must be converted before pardon is bestowed upon him (Acts 3:19). We must be on our guard here, as everywhere, against extolling one of God's perfections above another. True, the covenant is entirely of grace—pure, free, sovereign grace—nevertheless, here too, grace reigns through righteousness, and not at the expense of it.

God will not disgrace His grace by entering into covenant with those who are impenitent and openly defy Him. It is not that the sinner must do something to earn the grand blessings of the covenant. No, no, he contributes not a mite toward the procuring of them. That price—and infinitely costly it was was fully paid by Christ Himself. But though God requires naught from us in the way of purchasing or meriting these blessings, He does in the matter of our actual receiving of them. "The honour of God would fall to the ground if we should be pardoned without submission, without confession of past sin, or resolution of future obedience; for till then we neither know our true misery, nor are we willing to come out of it; for they that securely continue in their sins, they despise both the curse of the Law and the grace of the Gospel" (T. Manton).

VIII

The assertion that there is a human side to our becoming the recipients of God's spiritual blessings, that there are certain terms which He requires us to first comply with, should occasion no difficulty. For as we have pointed out so frequently in this study, a covenant is a *mutual* compact, the second party agreeing to do or bestow certain things in return for what has been done or agreed upon by the first party to it. Before the sinner can enter into the actual benefits of Christ's atonement, he must consent to return to the duty of the law and live in obedience to God; for He never pardons any while they are in their rebellion and live under the full dominion of sin. This is clear from many passages: see, for example, Isaiah 1:16-18; 55:7; Acts 3:19. Therefore, till there be a genuine repentance (which is not only a sorrow for past offenses, but also a sincere purpose to live henceforth according to the will of God) we have no interest in the grace of the new covenant.

First, we are required to *enter into* solemn covenant with God, yielding ourselves unreservedly up to Him (II Cor. 8:5), henceforth to live for His glory: "Gather my saints together unto me: those that have made a covenant with me by sacrifice" (Ps. 50:5). Second, we are required to *keep* this solemn covenant, to live in a course of universal holiness: "All the paths of the Lord are mercy and truth unto such as keep his covenant and his testimonies" (Ps. 25:10). Only those who endure unto the end shall be saved, and for that there must be a diligent practicing of God's precepts and a constant taking to heart of His warnings and admonitions. "Perseverance in their course is not promoted by a blind confidence and easy security: but by watchfulness, by self-jealousy, by a salutary fear of coming short of the promised rest, prompting them to earnest effort and habitual self-denial. Perseverance does not suppose the certainty of salvation however careless a Christian may be, but implies a steady continuance in holiness and conformity to the will of Christ in order to that end" (John Kelly, to whom we are indebted for much in these articles).

"Though there are no conditions properly so called of the *whole grace* of the covenant, yet there are conditions *in* the covenant, taking that term in a large sense, for that which by the order of Divine constitution precedeth some other things, and hath an influence to their existence. For God requireth many things of them whom He actually takes into covenant, and makes partakers of the promises and benefits of it. Of this nature is that whole obedience which is prescribed unto us in the Gospel, in our walking before God in uprightness; and there being an order in the things that belong hereunto, some acts, duties and parts of our gracious obedience, being appointed to be means of the further additional supplies of the grace and mercies of the covenant, they may be called *conditions* required of us in the covenant, as well as duties prescribed unto us" (John Owen).

It will be evident from this last quotation that we are not advocating any strange doctrine when we insist that the terms of the covenant must be met if its privileges are to be enjoyed. None was clearer and more definite than Owen in his magnifying of the free grace of God; yet none saw more clearly than he did that God treats with men throughout as moral agents. (We can readily repeat the same teaching from others of the Puritans.) Let it be pointed out, that the *first* blessing of the covenant—regeneration or God's putting His laws in our hearts—depends on no condition on our part: that is purely a sovereign and gratuitous act on the part of God. But to a full or *complete* interest in all the promises of the covenant, faith on our part (with which evangelical repentance is inseparable) is required. Here, too, we insist that if on the one hand there can be no justification without believing, yet on the other hand that very faith is given to us and wrought in us.

In further corroboration of the point we are now laboring is the usage of the term "earnest" in the New Testament. In both II Corinthians 1:22 and 5:5 we read of "the earnest of the Spirit," while in Ephesians 1:13, 14 we are told that He is "the earnest of our inheritance." Now an earnest is a token payment or installment of what has been agreed upon between two or more parties, being a guaranty of the full and final discharge. This figurative expression is used because the right which the believer has to eternal life and glory is by compact or covenant. On the one side, the sinner agrees to the terms stipulated (the forsaking of sin and his serving of the Lord), and yields himself to God by repentance and faith. On the other side, God binds Himself to give the believer forgiveness of sins and an inheritance among the sanctified; and the gift of the Spirit clinches the matter. When we consent to the terms of the gospel, God engages Himself to bestow the inestimable blessings purchased for us by Christ.

Under the new covenant God requires the same perfect obedience from the Christian as He did from unfallen Adam. "Although God in them (His commands) requireth universal holiness of us, yet He doth not do it in that strict and rigorous way as by the Law (i.e. as given to Adam), so as that if we fail in any thing either as to the matter or manner of its performance, and in the substance of it or as to the degrees of its perfection, that thereon both that and all we do besides should be rejected. But He doth it with a *contemperation of grace* and mercy, so as that if there be a universal sincerity in respect unto all His commands, He both pardoneth many sins and accepts of what we do, though it come short of legal perfection; and both on the account of the mediation of Christ. Yet this hindereth not but that the command of the Gospel doth still require *universal holiness* of us, and a perfection therein, which we are to do our utmost endeavour to comply withal, though we have a relief provided in sincerity on the one hand, and mercy on the other. For the commands of the Gospel do still declare what God approves and what He doth condemn, which is no less than all holiness on the one hand, and all sin on the other; as exactly and extensively as under the Law. For this the very nature of God requireth, and the Gospel is not the ministry of sin, so as to give an allowance unto the least, although in it pardon be provided for a multitude of sins by Jesus Christ.

"The obligation on us unto holiness is equal as unto what it was under the Law, though a relief be provided where unavoidably we come short of it. There is, therefore, nothing more certain, than that there is no relaxation given us as unto any duty of holiness by the Gospel, nor any indulgence unto the least sin. But yet upon the supposition of the acceptance of sincerity, and a perfection of parts instead of degrees, with the mercy provided for our failings and sins; there is an argument to be taken from the command of it unto an indispensable necessity of holiness, including in it the highest encouragement to endeavour after it. For, together with the command, there is also grace administered enabling us unto that obedience which God will accept. Nothing, therefore, can avoid or evacuate the power of this command and argument from it, but a stubborn contempt of God arising from the love of sin" (J. Owen).

A threefold contrast may be pointed out in connection with the obedience required by God under the Adamic and under the Messianic covenants. First, the *design* of it is entirely different. Under the covenant of works man was obliged to render obedience to the law in order for his justification; but not so under the covenant of grace, for there the believing sinner is justified on the ground of Christ's obedience being imputed to him, and the obedience of the Christian afterwards is necessary only that God might be honored thereby as an expression of his gratitude.

Second, the *enablement to* it, for under the new covenant God works in us both to will and to do of His good pleasure. Under the covenant of works man was left to his own natural and created strength. Under the one, God gave the bare command; under the other, He furnished His grace and Spirit so that we are empowered unto that sincere and evangelical obedience which He accepts of us. When God bids us come to Him, He doth likewise draw us to Him.

Third, in the *acceptance* of it. Under the covenant of works no provision was made for any failure, for it had neither sacrifice nor mediator; consequently, the only obedience which God would accept under it was a perfect and perpetual one. While God requires the same flawless obedience under the new covenant, yet provision has been made for failure, and if our efforts be genuine, God accepts an imperfect obedience from us because its defects are fully compensated for by the infinite merits of Christ which are reckoned to the believer's account. This sincere obedience (called by many writers "new obedience" and by others "evangelical obedience") is required from us as the means whereby we show our subjection to God, our dependence upon Him, our thankfulness unto Him, and as the only way of converse and communion with Him.

We must now consider *the time when* this covenant came into operation. This cannot be restricted to any one moment absolutely, as though all that is included in God's making of it did consist in any single act. If we revert for a moment to the original promise it will be found that God said, "Not according to the covenant that I made with their fathers, in the day that I took them by the hand to bring them out of the land of Egypt" (Jer. 31:32). Now that was not a literal day of twenty-four hours, but a season into which much was crowded: many things happened between Israel's Exodus from the house of bondage and their actual encamping before Sinai, things which were preparatory to the making and solemn establishment of the old covenant. So was it also in connection with the making and establishing of the new covenant: it was gradually made and established by sundry acts both preparatory and confirmatory. In his able discussion of this point, Owen mentioned six degrees: we here condense his remarks, adding a few observations of our own.

The first entrance into the making of the new covenant was made by the mission of John the Baptist, who was sent to prepare the way of the Messiah, and therefore is his mission called "the beginning of the gospel" (Mark 1:1, 2). Until his appearing, the Jews were bound absolutely and universally by the Sinaitic covenant, without alteration or addition in any ordinance of worship. But his ministry was designed to prepare them, and cause them to look unto the accomplishment of God's promise to make a new covenant. He therefore called the people off from resting in and trusting upon the privileges of the old covenant, preaching unto them the doctrine of repentance and instituting a new ordinance of worship—baptism—whereby they might be initiated into a new condition and relationship with God; pointing them to the predicted Lamb. This was the beginning of the fulfillment of Jeremiah 31:31-33; compare to Luke 16:16.

Second, the incarnation and personal ministry of the Lord Jesus Christ Himself was an eminent advance and degree thereof. True, the dispensation of the old covenant yet continued, for He Himself, as made of a woman, was made under the law (Gal. 4:4), yielded obedience to it, observing all its precepts and institutions. Nevertheless, His appearing in flesh laid an axe to the root of that whole dispensation. Hence, upon His birth the substance of the new covenant was proclaimed from heaven as that which was on the eve of taking place (Luke 2:13, 14). But it was made more evident later on by His public ministry, the whole doctrine whereof was preparatory unto the immediate introduction of this covenant. The proofs He gave of His messiahship, the fulfillment He provided of the prophecies concerning Him, were so many signs that He was the appointed mediator of that covenant.

Third, the way for the introduction of this covenant being thus prepared, it was solemnly enacted and confirmed in and by His death, for therein He offered that sacrifice to God by which it was established, and hereby the promise properly became a "testament" (Heb. 9:14-16). There the apostle shows how the shedding of Christ's blood answered to those sacrifices whose blood was sprinkled on the people and the book of the law in confirmation of the first covenant. The cross, then, was the center whence all the promises of grace did meet, and from whence they derive all their efficacy. Henceforth the old covenant, and its administration, having received their full accomplishment, no longer had any binding force (Eph. 2:14-16; Col. 2:14,15) and only abode by the patience of God, to be taken away in His own good time and manner.

Fourth, this new covenant had the complement of its making and establishment in the resurrection of Christ. God did not make the first covenant simply that it should continue for a season, die of itself, and be arbitrarily removed. No, the Levitical economy had a special end to be accomplished, and nothing in it could be removed until God's design was realized. That design was twofold: the perfect fulfilling of that righteousness which the law enjoined, and the undergoing of its curse. The one was accomplished in the perfect obedience of Christ, the surety of the covenant, in the stead of those with whom the covenant was made; the other was endured by Him in His sufferings; and His resurrection was the public proof that He was discharged from the claims of the law. The old covenant then expired, and the worship pertaining to it was continued for a few years longer only by the forbearance of God toward the Jews.

Fifth, the first formal promulgation of the new covenant, as made and ratified, was on the day of Pentecost, seven weeks after the resurrection of Christ. Remarkably did this answer to the promulgation of the law on Mount Sinai, for that too occurred the same space of time after the deliverance of the people of God out of Egypt. From the day of Pentecost onward, the ordinances of worship and all the institutions of the new covenant became obligatory unto all believers. Then was the whole church absolved from any duty with respect to the old covenant and its worship, although it was not manifest as yet in their consciences. When Peter said to those of his hearers who were pricked in the heart that "the promise is unto you and to your children," he was announcing the new covenant unto members of the house of *Judah,* and his "and to them that are afar off" (compare Dan. 9:7) extended it to the dispersion of *Israel;* and when he added "save yourselves from this untoward generation" (Acts 2:39, 40) he intimated the old covenant had waxed old and was about to vanish away. Sixth, this was confirmed in Acts 15:23-29.

It only remains for us to say a few words on the relation between the original and final covenants. It is important that we should distinguish clearly between the everlasting covenant which God made before the foundation of the world, and the Christian covenant which

He has instituted in the last days of the world's history. First, the one was made in a past eternity; the other is made in time. Second, the one was made with Christ alone; the other is made with all His people. Third, the one is without any conditions so far as we are concerned; the other prescribes certain terms which we must meet. Fourth, under the one Christ inherits; under the other Christians are heirs: in other words, the inheritance Christ purchased by His fulfilling the terms of the everlasting covenant is now administered by Him in the form of a "testament."

Should a reader ask, Does my getting to heaven depend upon the everlasting covenant or the new one? The answer is upon *both*. First upon what Christ did for me in executing the terms of the former; second, upon my compliance with the conditions of the latter. Many are very confused at this very point. They who repudiate man's responsibility will not allow that there are any "ifs" or "buts," restricting their attention to God's "wills" and "shalls"; but this is not dealing honestly with the Word. Instead of confining ourselves to favorite passages, we must impartially compare Scripture with Scripture, and over against God's "I will" of Hebrews 8:10-12 must be placed the "But Christ as a Son over his own house: whose house are we *if* we hold fast the confidence and the rejoicing of the hope firm unto the end . . . for we are made partakers of Christ, *if* we hold the beginning of our confidence steadfast unto the end" of Hebrews 3:6, 14! Does this render such a vital matter uncertain, and place my eternal interests in jeopardy? By no means: if I have turned "from transgression" God has made an everlasting covenant with me and has given to me the same Spirit which abode—without measure—on the Mediator (Isa. 59:20, 21). Nevertheless, I can have Scriptural assurance of this only so long as I tread the path of obedience.

PART EIGHT

The Covenant Allegory

Those of our readers who are particularly interested in the divine covenants would be disappointed if we closed our lengthy comments thereon and ignored the last eleven verses of Galatians 4, and therefore we feel it necessary to devote a chapter to their consideration. That this passage is far from being free of difficulties appears from the diverse expositions of the commentators, for scarcely any two of them agree even in substance. Nor will the limited space now at our disposal allow us to enter into as full an elucidation as could be wished, nor permit the pausing now and again to furnish collateral proofs for what is advanced, as would be our desire. Brevity has its advantages, but it does not always make for clarity. We must, however, content ourselves now with a comparatively terse running comment on this passage, and that, according to the limited light which we have therefrom.

Galatians 4:21-31 is in several respects very similar to the contents of II Corinthians 3. In each case the apostle is opposing himself to the errors which had been sedulously propagated amongst his converts by Judaizers. In each case he shows that the fundamental issue between them concerned the covenants, for any teacher who is confused thereon is certain to go astray in all his preaching. In each case the apostle appeals to well-known incidents in the Old Testament Scripture, and with the wisdom given him from above proceeds to bring out the deep spiritual meaning thereof. In each case he establishes conclusively the immeasurable superiority of Christianity over Judaism, and thus completely undermined the very foundations of his adversaries' position. Though of peculiar importance to those unto whom the apostle wrote immediately, yet this passage contains not a little of great value for us today.

"Tell me, ye that desire to be under the law, do ye not hear the law?" (Gal. 4:21). Here the apostle addresses himself to those who had been lending a ready ear to their spiritual enemies. By his "ye that desire to be under the law" was signified those who hankered after subjection to Judaism. His "do ye not hear the law?" means, Are you willing to listen unto what is recorded in the first book of the Pentateuch and have pointed out to you the dispensational significance of the same? Paul's design was to show those who were so anxious to be circumcised and submit themselves to the whole Mosaic system, that, so far from such a course being honorable and beneficial, it would be fraught with danger and disgrace. To yield unto those who sought to seduce them spiritually would inevitably result in "bondage" (see 4:9) and not "liberty" (5:1). To prevent this, he begs them to listen to what God had said.

"For it is written, that Abraham had two sons, the one by a bondmaid, the other by a free woman. But he who was born of the bondwoman was born after the flesh; but he of the free woman was by promise. Which things are an allegory" (vv. 22-24). Very remarkable indeed is this, for we are here divinely informed that not merely did the Mosaic rites possess a typical significance, but the lives of the patriarchs themselves had a figurative meaning. Not only so, but their affairs were so controlled by providence that they were shaped to shadow forth coming events of vast magnitude. Paul was here moved by the Spirit to inform us that the domestic occurrences in Abraham's household were a parable in action, which parable he had interpreted for us. Thus we are granted an insight to passages in Genesis which no human wisdom could possibly have penetrated.

The transactions in the family of Abraham were divinely ordered to presage important dispensational epochs. The domestic affairs of the patriarch's household were invested with a prophetic significance. The historical incidents recorded in Genesis 16 and 21 possessed a typical meaning, contained beneath their surface spiritual truths of profound importance. The apostle here reminds his readers of the circumstances recorded of the two wives of Abraham, and of their respective offspring, and declares that the mothers adumbrated the two covenants, and their sons, the respective tendencies and results of those covenants. In other words, Sarah and Hagar are to be viewed as the representatives of the two covenants, and the sons which they bore as representatives of the kind of worshipers which those covenants were fitted to produce.

"For it is written, that Abraham had two sons, the one by a bondmaid the other by a freewoman." The apostle's design was to wean those Galatians who were Judaistically inclined from their strange infatuation for an obsolete and servile system, by unfolding to them its true nature. This he does by referring them to an emblematic representation of the two economies. Abraham had a number of other

sons besides Ishmael and Isaac, but it is to them alone—the circumstances of their birth, subsequent conduct, history, and fate—that
Paul's discussion exclusively relates.

In her unbelief and impatience (unwilling to wait for God to make
good His word in His own time and way) Sarah gave her maid to
Abraham in order that he might not be wholly without posterity.
Though this caused confusion and brought trouble upon all concerned, yet it was ordained by God to presage great dispensational
distinctions, nor did it in any wise thwart the accomplishment of His
eternal purpose. "Abraham had two sons": Ishmael, the son of an
Egyptian, a bondslave; Isaac the son of Sarah, a free woman, of the
same rank as her husband. As we have already said, these two mothers
prefigured the two covenants, and their children the worshipers which
those covenants tended to produce.

"But he who was of the bondwoman was born after the flesh; but
he of the free woman was by promise" (v. 23). Great as was the
disparity between the two mothers, greater still was the difference
between the way in which their respective sons were born. Ishmael
was born in the ordinary course of generation, for "after the flesh"
signifies to the carnal counsel which Sarah gave to Abraham, and by
the mere strength of nature. In connection with the birth of Ishmael
there was not any special promise given, nor any extraordinary divine
interposition. Vastly different was it in the case of Isaac, for he was
the child of promise and born in direct consequence of the miracle-
working power of God, and was under the benefit of that promise as
long as he lived. What is here specially emphasized by the apostle is
that the son of the slave was in *an inferior condition* from the very
beginning.

"Which things are an allegory" (v. 24). An allegory is a parabolic
method of conveying instruction, spiritual truths being set forth under
material figures. Allegories are in words what hieroglyphics are in
printing, both of which abound among the Orientals—Bunyan's *Pil-
grim's Progress* is the best-sustained allegory in the English language.
"For these [feminine] are the two covenants" (v. 24). Here the
apostle proceeds to give us the occult meaning of the historical facts
alluded to in the preceding verse. He affirms that the domestic
incidents in the family of Abraham constituted a divinely ordained
illustration of the basic principles in regard to the condition of
spiritual slaves and of spiritual freemen, and are to be regarded as
adumbrating the *bondage* which subjection to the law of Moses
produced and the *liberty* which submission to the gospel secures.

"These are the two covenants." This cannot of course be understood literally, for it was neither intelligible nor true that Sarah and

Hagar were actually two covenants in their own persons. The words *is* and *are* frequently have the force of *represent*. When Christ affirmed of the sacramental bread "This is my body," He meant, this bread emblemizes My body. When we read of the cliff smitten by Moses in the wilderness (out of which gushed the stream of living water) "that rock was Christ" (I Cor. 10:4), it obviously signifies, that rock prefigured Christ. So too when we are told "the seven stars are the angels of the seven churches and the seven candlesticks which thou sawest are the seven churches" (Rev. 1:20), we are to understand that the one symbolized the other.

"These are the two covenants." There has been much difference of opinion as to exactly which covenants are intended. Some insist that the reference is to the everlasting covenant of grace and the Adamic or covenant of works; others argue it is the Abrahamic or covenant of promise and the Sinaitic; while others conclude it is the Sinaitic and the Christian or that which is made with the people of God in the gospel. Really, it is more a matter of terms than anything else, for whatever nomenclature we adopt it comes to much the same thing. "The one from mount Sinai, which gendereth to bondage, which is Hagar" (v. 24): by which is meant, that order of things under which the nation of Israel was placed at Sinai, appointed for the purpose of keeping them a separate people, and which because of its legalistic nature was fitly foreshadowed by the bondslave.

"The one [covenant] from mount Sinai, which gendereth to bondage" or produces those of a servile spirit, for it made slaves of all who sought justification and salvation by their own doings. It is to be carefully borne in mind that the relation entered into between God and Israel at Sinai was entirely a *natural* one, being made with the nation as such; and consequently all their descendants, upon their being circumcised, automatically became subjects of it without any spiritual change being wrought in them. "So far as this covenant gave birth to any children, those were not true children of God, free, spiritual, with hearts of filial confidence and devoted love; but miserable bondmen, selfish, carnal, full of mistrust and fear. Of these children of the Sinaitic covenant we are furnished with the most perfect exemplar in the Scribes and Pharisees of our Lord's time" (P. Fairbairn).

"For this Agar is mount Sinai in Arabia" (v. 25). Here again "is" signifies "represents": Hagar prophetically anticipated and prefigured Mount Sinai—not the literal mount, but that covenant which Jehovah there entered into with the nation of Israel. Nor is this mode of expression by any means unusual in Scripture: when representing Samaria and Jerusalem by two women the prophet said, "Samaria is

Aholah and Jerusalem Aholibah" (Ezek. 23:4). "And answereth to Jerusalem which now is" (v. 25). "Answereth to" signifies "corresponds with," or as the margin gives it, "is in the same rank with": the origin, status, and condition of Hagar supplied an exact analogy to the state of Jerusalem in the apostle's time. Jerusalem, which was the metropolis of Palestine and the headquarters of its religion, stands for Judaism.

"And is in bondage with her children" (v. 25). Judaism was subject to an endless round of ceremonial institutions, which the apostles themselves declared to be a yoke "which neither our fathers nor we were able to bear" (Acts 15:10). Those under it enjoyed none of that spiritual liberty which the gospel bestows upon those who submit to its terms. That large part of the nation which had no interest in the covenant of promise made with Abraham (whereof faith was an indispensable prerequisite for entering into the good of it), was indeed outwardly a part of Abraham's family and members of the visible church (as Hagar was a member of his family); yet (like Ishmael) they were born in servitude, and all their outward obedience was of a slavish character, and their privileges (as his) but carnal and temporal.

"But Jerusalem which is above is free, which is the mother of us all" (v. 26). Here Paul shows what was prefigured by Sarah. Three things are said in describing the covenant and constitution of which she was the appropriate emblem, each of which must be duly noted in the framing of our definition.

1. "Jerusalem which is above." This word "above" (*ano*) is generally employed of location, and would thus signify the heavenly Jerusalem (Heb. 12:22) in contrast from the earthly. But here it is placed in antithesis from "which now is" (v. 25) and would thus mean the prior and primitive Jerusalem, of which Melchizedek was king (Heb. 7:2) and to whose order of priesthood Christ's pertains. Or the "above" may have the force of excellency or supremacy, as in "*high* calling" (Phil. 3:14). Combining the three: Sarah shadowed forth the entire election of grace, all true believers from the beginning to the end of time.

2. Which "is free": such was the status and state of Sarah in contrast from that of Hagar, the bondslave. Suitably did Sarah set forth that spiritual liberty which is to be found in Christ, for He redeems all His people from the bondage of sin and death. Believing Gentiles are freed from the curse of the moral law, and believing Jews are freed from the dominion of the ceremonial law as well.

3. "Which is the mother of us all." The reference is not to the church either visible or invisible, for she cannot be the parent of herself; rather is it the everlasting covenant of grace which is in view,

in which were included all true believers. Thus the differences between the systems represented by Hagar and Sarah are: the one was earthly, carnal, slavish, temporary; the other, heavenly, spiritual, free, eternal.

"For it is written, Rejoice, thou barren that barest not; break forth and cry, thou that travailest not: for the desolate hath many more children than she which hath a husband" (v. 27). This was obviously brought in by Paul to confirm the interpretation he had made of the covenant allegory. It is a quotation from the predictions of Isaiah. Four things call for our consideration: (1) the needs-be for this comforting promise which God then gave; (2) the precise place in Isaiah's prophecy from which this quotation is taken; (3) the particular manner in which it is here introduced; (4) its striking pertinency to the apostle's purpose.

The *needs-be* for this reassuring word given by the Lord to His believing yet sorrowing people in the days of Isaiah is not difficult to perceive, if we bear in mind the exact terms of the promise originally given to the patriarch and his wife, and then consider the state of Israel under Judaism. The grand promise to Abraham was that he should be "a father of many nations" (Gen. 17:4) and that Sarah should be "a mother of nations" (Gen. 17:16). But at Sinai Sarah's natural children were placed under a covenant which erected a middle wall of partition, shutting them off from all other nations. How rigorous the restrictions of the covenant were and the exclusiveness it produced, appear plainly in the unwillingness of Peter (till supernaturally authorized by God) to enter the house of Cornelius (Acts 10:28).

The Sinaitic covenant consisted largely in "meats and drinks and carnal ordinances"; yet was it imposed only "till the time of reformation" (Heb. 9:10). It was well adapted to Israel after the flesh, for it encouraged them to obedience by the promise of temporal prosperity and restrained by fear of temporal judgments. Amid the great mass of the unregenerate Jews there was always a remnant according to the election of grace, whose heart God had touched (I Sam. 10:26), in whose heart was His law (Isa. 51:7). But the nation as a whole had become thoroughly corrupt by the time of Isaiah, being deaf to the voice of Jehovah and fast ripening for judgment (1:2-6). The godly portion had diminished to "a very small remnant" (1:9), and the outlook was fearfully dark. It was to strengthen the faith of the spiritual and comfort their hearts that Isaiah was raised up.

The quotation here made by Paul was from Isaiah 54:1, and its very *location* intimated clearly that it looked forward to gospel times; for coming immediately after that graphic description of the Redeemer's sufferings in the previous chapter, it at once suggests that we are then given a picture of those new covenant conditions which followed His death. This is ever God's way: in the darkest night He causes the stars of hope to shed forth their welcome light, bidding His people to look beyond the gloomy present to the brighter future. God had not forgotten His promise to the patriarch; and though many centuries had intervened, the coming of His Son would make good the ancient oracles, for all the divine promises are established in Christ (II Cor. 1:19, 20).

Let us next note the *manner* in which Paul introduces Isaiah's prediction into his discussion: *"For it is written."* It is clear that the apostle cites the prophet to establish what he had affirmed regarding the allegorical significance of the circumstances of Abraham's household. This at once fixes for us the elucidation of the prophecy. Paul had pointed out that Abraham had sons by two diverse wives, that those sons represented the different type of worshipers which the two covenants produced, that Sarah (as representing the Abrahamic covenant), which he here likened unto "Jerusalem which is above," is "the mother of us all." In turn, Isaiah refers to two women, views them allegorically, apostrophizing the one as "barren" and contrasting her from one "who had a husband," assuring the former of a far more numerous progeny.

How *pertinent* Isaiah's prediction was to the apostle's argument is evident. His design was to turn away the hearts of the Galatians from Judaism, and to accomplish this he demonstrates that that system had been superseded by something far more blessed and spiritually productive. "For it is written, Rejoice, thou barren." Whom was the prophet there addressing? Immediately, the godly remnant in Israel, the children of faith, those who had their standing in and derived their blessing from the Abrahamic covenant. Isaiah addressed them in the terms of the allegory. Just as the historical Sarah was childless for many years after she became the wife of Abraham, so the mystical Sarah (Abrahamic covenant) had for long centuries shown no sign whatever of coming to fruition. But as the literal Sarah ultimately became a mother, so the mystical one should bear a numerous seed.

Marvelous indeed are the ways of God, and remarkably is His decree wrought out through His providences. That parable in action in the household of Abraham contemplated that which took thousands of years to unfold. First, was the marriage between Abraham and Sarah, which symbolized the covenant union between God and His people. Second, for many years Sarah remained barren, foreshadowing that lengthy period during which God's purpose in that covenant was suspended. Third, Hagar, the bondslave, took Sarah's place in the family of Abraham, typifying his natural descendants being placed under the Sinaitic covenant. Fourth, Hagar did not permanently supplant Sarah, adumbrating the fact that Judaism was of but temporary duration. Fifth, ultimately Sarah came into her own and was divinely enabled to bear a supernatural seed—emblem of the spiritual children of God under the new covenant.

"Rejoice, thou barren that bearest not." The Abrahamic covenant is here represented as a wife who (like Sarah) had long remained childless. Comparatively few real children had been raised up to God among the Jews from Moses onward. True, the nation was in outward covenant with Him, and thus was (like Hagar in the type) "she who hath a husband"; but all the fruit they bore was like unto Ishmael— that which was merely natural, the product of the flesh. But the death of Christ was to alter all this: though the Jews would reject Him, there should be a great accession to the spiritual family of Abraham from among the Gentiles, so that there would be a far greater number of saints under the new covenant than had pertained under the old.

"Now we, brethren, as Isaac was, are the children of promise" (v. 28). Here the apostle begins his application of the allegory. As Sarah prefigured the covenant of grace, so Isaac represented the true children of God. Paul was here addressing himself to his spiritual brethren, and therefore the "we" includes all who are born from above— believing Gentiles as well as Jews. "We," the children of the new covenant, represented in the allegory by Isaac. Our standing and state is essentially different from Ishmael's, for he (like the great mass of those under the Sinaitic covenant) belong to the ordinary course of mere nature; whereas genuine Christians are "the children of promise"—of that made to Abraham, which, in turn, made manifest what God had "promised before the world began" (Titus 1:2). The relation into which believers are brought with God originates in a miracle of grace which was the subject of divine promise.

"But as then he that was born after the flesh persecuted him that was born after the Spirit, even so it is now" (v. 29). Here the apostle brings in a further detail supplied by the allegory which was germane to his subject. He refers to the opposition made against Isaac by the son of Hagar, recorded in Genesis 21:9. This received its counterpart in the attitude of the Judaizers toward Christians. They who still adhered to the old covenant were hostile to those who enjoyed the freedom of the new. Probably one reason why the apostle mentioned this particular was in order to meet an objection: How can we be the "children of promise" (God's high favorites) seeing we are so bitterly hated and opposed by the Jews? The answer is, No marvel, for thus it was from the beginning: the carnal have ever persecuted the spiritual.

"Nevertheless what saith the Scripture? Cast out the bondwoman and her son: for the son of the bondwoman shall not be heir with the son of the free woman" (v. 30). Here is the final point in the allegory (taken from Gen. 21:10, 12) and which incontestably clinched the apostle's argument that Israel after the flesh are finally set aside by God. Hagar represented the Sinaitic covenant and Ishmael its carnal worshipers, and their being cast out of Abraham's household prophetically signified God's setting aside of Judaism and the fact that the natural descendants of Abraham had no place among his spiritual children and could not share their heritage (cf. John 8:34, 35). The two cannot unite: pure Christianity necessarily excludes Judaism. In its wider application (for today): none who seek salvation by law-keeping shall enter heaven.

"So then, brethren, we are not children of the bondwoman, but of the free" (v. 31). Here the plain and inescapable conclusion is drawn: since Christians are the children of promise, they and not carnal Jews are the true heirs of Abraham. Since the new covenant is superior to the old and believers in Christ are freed from all debasing servitude, it obviously follows they must conduct themselves as the Lord's freemen. The time had now arrived when to cling to Judaism was fatal. The controversy turned on the question of who are the real heirs of Abraham—see 3:7, 16, 29. In chapter 4 the apostle exposes the empty pretensions of those who could claim only fleshly descent from the patriarch. We are the children of Abraham, said the Judaizers. Abraham had two sons, replies Paul—the one of free, the other of servile birth: to which line do you belong? whose spirit have you received?

To sum up. Paul's design was to deliver the Galatians from the Judaizers. He showed that by submitting to Judaism they would forfeit the blessings of Christianity. This he accomplished by opening up the profound significance of the covenant allegory, which presented three principal contrasts: birth by nature as opposed to grace; a state of bondage as opposed to liberty; a status of temporary tenure as opposed to permanent possession. Just as Hagar was rightfully the handmaid of Sarah but was wrongfully accorded the position of Abraham's wife, so the Sinaitic covenant was designed to supplement the Abrahamic but was perverted by the Jews when they sought from it salvation and fruitfulness.